CURIOSITIES OF F

SOME UNUSUAL IDEAS ON FLYING

FROM FLAPPING WINGS TO THE JET AGE

ARTHUR W. J. G. ORD-HUME

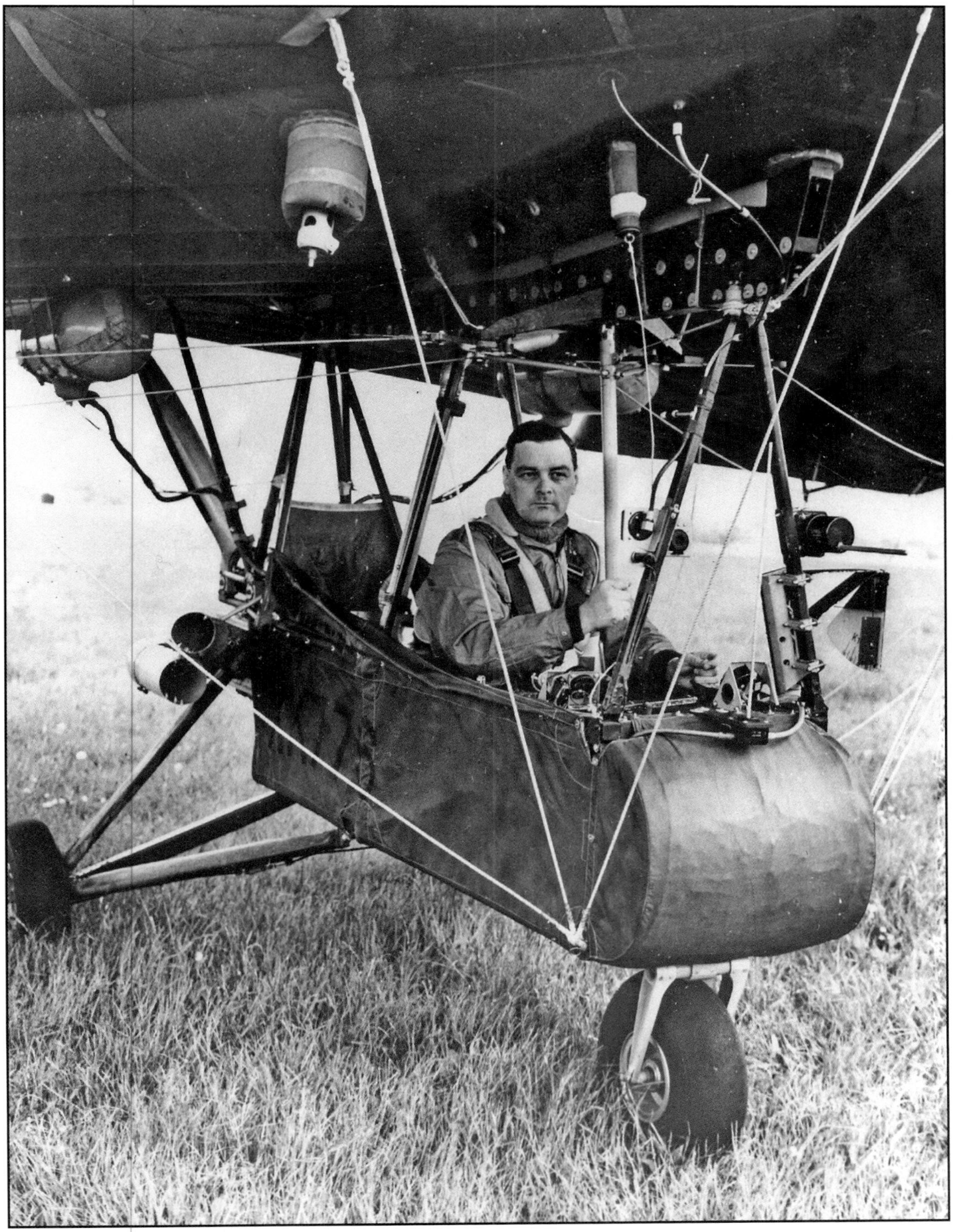

First Published in the United Kingdom, 2012
Stenlake Publishing Limited
54-58 Mill Square, Catrine, KA5 6RD
01290 551122
www.stenlake.co.uk

ISBN 9781840335705

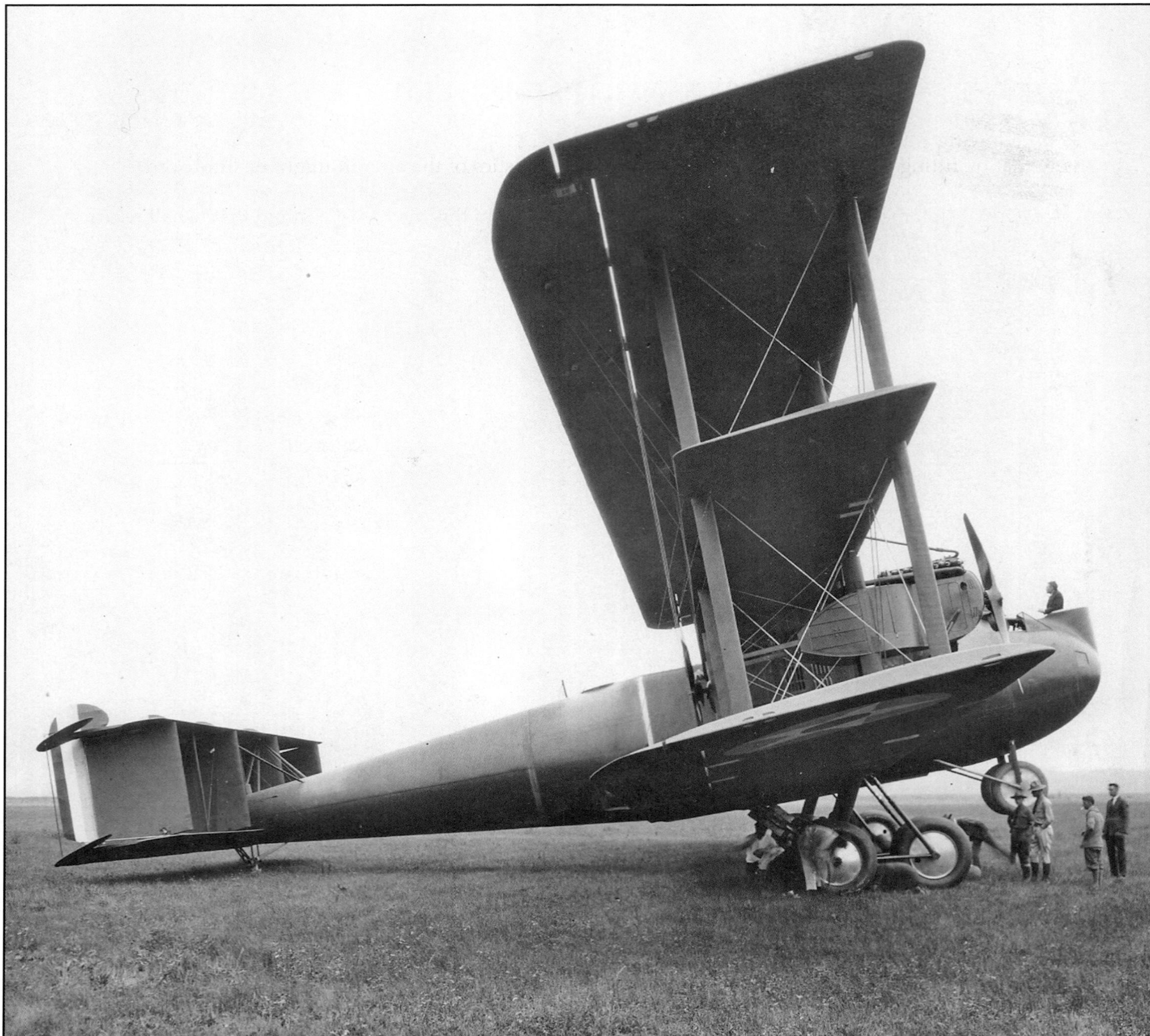

The art of matching a design specification to the results of air tests on the real aeroplane is a long-established challenge to designers. The former is the product of optimism tempered by an urge to be commercial and get the order. The latter is the sheepish admission that there might, in reality, just be a very slight disparity. Pilots hold their employer's reputations in their hands but company loyalty cannot mask a failure. America's wonderful long-range Barling Bomber, detailed on pages 22 and 23 was to have a 'cruising radius' of 1,300 miles at more than 100 mph. This turned out to be optimistic: flat-out it went at 96 mph. Worse, the maximum range was just 170 miles. But it did have a monocoque plywood fuselage and six engines. And it cost the US taxpayer $1.25m in 1923 money.

INTRODUCTION

Flight is a mature science now. Aircraft designers have at their disposal vast powers of calculation in the form of computers, wind-tunnels and advanced aerodynamics. In the century and a half since heavier than air flight first became a 'done deal' at the hands of Yorkshireman Sir George Cayley, aeroplanes have become less and less experimental and chances of failure reduced to those enjoyed by bookmakers facing an odds-on outsider in the Derby.

Don't forget that it was long after Blériot had successfully flown the Channel in his monoplane before designers around the world settled on the best shape for the aeroplane. As late as the First World War, some people weren't quite sure whether it was better to have the tail at the front (so to speak) or the wing at the back. In allowing this indecision to be perpetuated for so long they missed out on an important trick, namely that by fitting the tail at the front, the flight characteristics of the aircraft might be improved.

Just in case that statement sounds a bit too worrying so early on in this book, rest assured that I shall return to it at the appropriate time and demonstrate that the tail is often better at the front as in the pre-war Focke-Wulf Ente or some of the modern, mainly foreign-designed, kitplanes such as the Rutan Long Eze, the American Aircraft Falcon XP, Craig Catto Goldwing and the Rutan Quickie among others.

But going back to that point of design, today's budding planemaker has at his disposal copious banks of data, computer programming power and laboratory test facilities that he can interrogate long before anybody actually starts cutting wood or metal. Clever flight simulators actually let the test pilot 'fly' the aeroplane before it even exists! All this virtually guarantees that the end product will be a sound flyer and any test flight problems that manifest themselves will be restricted to those that pose little threat to life or limb. Indeed, the maiden flight is something of an anticlimax these days, test pilots being excused a sense of ennui.

It was once very different. As recently as the last quarter of the 20th century, the test pilot was the touchstone by which a design was judged successful or not. And many a good test pilot was lost during the refining process that took aviation from the realms of guesswork into an established and proven form that could be verified and ultimately predicted mathematically.

Up to that time, aircraft design was based on two principal processes – trial and experiment was the first, and experience was the second. Experts had the well-known epithet 'if it looks right then it will fly right' tattooed on their left buttocks. This, though, didn't stop horrifying accidents caused (sometimes even created) by the alleged 'development' of aeronautics. Each design pushed the frontiers fractionally further and if that could be conquered without death and mayhem, then that was Progress spelled with a capital 'P'.

Aeroplane design was a solid profession which, from personal experience, was not understood by accountants and bank managers, shareholders and investors and, with the notable exception of 'Blossom' Miles, most women. The designer was a man of mystery and genius who justified (and often expected) the encomium of his fellow workers. All that didn't alter the simple fact that, despite the science of the time, it was still a 'suck-it-and-see' task.

Designing an aeroplane called for skills that were verging on the arcane. It created myth and legend and in so doing legitimised the veil of secrecy with which many designers would shroud their latest projects until the jubilation (or confrontation) that followed the first attempt at flight.

Aeroplane designers, then, were not the men you met in the pub or on the golf course. Doubtless they were all thin, earnest middle-aged men with spectacles and a water-cooled slide-rule. With shapeless tweed jacket having leather patches sewn on the elbows, the designer was usually imagined as possessing a hesitant grasp of life outside the drawing office. He most likely couldn't drive a car and had soup-stains on his tie. Shopping was something he didn't understand unless it was for an obscure 'single malt' and a favourite tobacco. He probably enjoyed the company of dogs but not necessarily people.

But there was also another sort who was quite different. The amateur engineer and artist (a dangerous mix if ever there was one!) had no real grasp of either aerodynamics or engineering but nevertheless possessed unshakeable confidence that everybody else was wrong and that he alone had stumbled upon a Holy Grail of Aeronautics and the true secret of something others had missed. Like the perpetual-motionists of old, he knew how things ought to fly – and it was certainly not the way these professional designer-chappies were trying!

The designs for aircraft devised by these self-taught and usually deluded dabsters were inevitably fascinating concoctions even if only as demonstrations of how fundamental principles can be overlooked if you metaphorically plant a vase of pretty flowers in front.

Occasionally the inventor elected to be his own tester and inevitably paid the ultimate price for over-confidence or too many flowers. One case in point was Richard Taylor's experimental aircraft of 1936. Taylor was an educated man who, like others of his time, had some thoughts about wings and their structures. Wings were too complicated, he believed, and he knew of ways to simplify them by creating a sort of sparless geodetic construction using wire. To prove his concept, Taylor had no lift-struts for his special and clever wing. With a friend on the other side, he 'proved' the strength of his structure to his own satisfaction by gently raising the entire aircraft off the ground by the wingtips. For this test, the cockpit was empty, of course...

On January 7th 1937, he made his first flight in G-AEPX at Hamsey Green Aerodrome in Surrey. The aircraft got airborne but seconds later the wings folded upwards and the designer-builder died in the wreck of his handiwork.

For years Edward Lanier in California experimented with hollowed-out wing sections. He was on to something and his curious Vacuplane flew tolerably well. His father was the inventor of the ice cream cone, and the young Lanier discovered at an early age that a cone, if dropped, always landed on its side. It was a Eureka moment for him: he had hit upon the Secret of Making a Wing Fly! Without bothering to try to analyse just why this happened, he went on to make a series of ice cream cone inspired aircraft. Their moderate success was probably more due to his accidental use of a better airfoil section than to the lessons of the vanilla whip.

A man with an idea is often a dangerous animal. Sometimes, like Burnelli and his 'flying wing' airliners, he makes a passable fist of it but cannot interest manufacturers in producing it or convince airlines that they need it. Others, like the Dutch-born Alexander Herbert Holle, get pretty close to solving the problem they've set themselves, only to find that the answer is too complex and that the problem can be solved with a more readily acceptable solution by following a wholly-different path. Holle's Varioplane really was clever and, judging by his detailed patent drawings, could have won an award for extremely complex over-engineering. It flew successfully and was even taken up by Blackburn but all these endeavours were eventually overcome by the economics of reason and practicality.

Again, some aircraft with outrageous design concept at their root are the work of pure artists who spice up what might otherwise be a rather dull science (to some) to something exciting in the way certain of those who follow art recognise beauty, if not exactly artistry, in a pile of bricks. In the 1930s an American invited the local newspaper to photograph his dream machine – a wooden frame fitted with paddle-wheels and an engine. When 'scaled up' (he said) it would do 500 miles an hour!

The story of curious ideas about flight started when I was trying to categorise the large number of photographs of improbable flying machines in my collection. The idea of sharing them with you was the end result of this exercise.

I have tried to avoid the creation of a 'negative' approach to my task for we can all learn something even from failure. Some years ago somebody put together a collection of aeroplanes heralded as being of the 'World's Worst Aircraft', yet the author failed to draw attention to one fundamental point, namely that throughout history no designer ever set out to design a bad aircraft. Some were overtaken by external events, others fell victim to events of their own making, but all were nevertheless honest attempts at solving the mystery of flight, for mystery it still is to many.

Howard Hughes, eccentric film-maker and notable American pilot, built his gigantic wooden flying boat. Despite its being as impracticable as one could imagine, he still succeeded in flying it, so, along with Jane Russell's bra (which he also famously constructed), it was his personal achievement. Britain's Planet Satellite was an honest attempt to improve upon a successful American idea. Because that idea was not really understood, its early endeavours at flight proved so dangerous that the authorities put down their corporate feet and banned further attempts.

Another expensive failure, also British, was the Tawney Owl of 1960 which actually did fly, but only high enough to cross the hedge and far enough to reach its crash site in the next field. The reason was the rather basic one that a cut-out in the trailing edge of the wing creates a loss of lift almost double the area that has been cut away. It was a fact that youthful glider-designer C H Lowe-Wylde had discovered when he fitted engines to his gliders back in the early 1930s.

The enormous all-wood Woking-designed Tarrant Tabor, designed by Farnborough engineer Walter Henry Barling, was tall and had many wings and engines of copious horsepower, including ones on the very top-most wing. During early taxi trials, the erstwhile pilot unfortunately opened the throttles of the uppermost engines. So high above the ground were these powerful motors that their thrust promptly stood the aircraft on its nose which was immediately compressed killing the two pilots. Small wonder, then, that on the subsequent Handley Page four-engined biplane airliners the throttles were ingeniously sequenced so that even if you banged all four open at once, the lower engines always accelerated before those on the top wing. Many previous scribes have written scathingly about the Tarrant Tabor, some even forgetting Woking's great aeronautical heritage established by Martin & Handasyde (the famed Martinsyde company). The truth is that the Tabor was a great leap of faith. Cleverly designed and possessed of cutting-edge construction, the Tabor was in the same bracket as the much later Brabazon and Princess: it had the wrong engines, the designer's intended choice not being available.

The Tabor's problems began when it was forced through official intransigence to change from a biplane into an unwieldy triplane just because instead of four big engines it was intended for, it would now need to accommodate half a dozen smaller ones. Its premature and fatal demise was not aided by some Farnborough engineer's calculation that to get the centre of gravity right it needed one thousand pounds weight of lead in the nose. The justification for this change, apparently made without recourse to Tarrant himself or Walter Barling the designer, was never investigated. It cannot have done other than assist in the ultimate disaster.

Young Barling, only 19 years old when this happened, then went to America where he put the lessons learned into the almost equally huge Wittemann-Lewis XNBL-1 'Barling Bomber' built at Ohio and assembled at New York's Teterboro Airport in 1920. Commonly described as 'a copy of the Tabor', it was anything but. A triplane, it had upper and lower wings of equal span and chord, and a shorter-span, narrower-chord middle wing which mounted all six of its engines. No doubt scared at the tip-over risk, young Barling arranged a novel undercarriage totalling ten wheels which included double nosewheels. Sadly, this Tarrant 'soundalike' only had a range of 170 miles which hardly qualified it for the requirement of 'long-range' bomber. Although it managed to fly reasonably well, it was not reckoned to be an economic proposition.

Most of the failures so far described were caused by technical or aerodynamic shortcomings. Others are more basic and many of these centre on unconventional forms of flight. First among these unconventional ones has to be man-powered flight. That it established itself as a challenge taken on and won (remember a human-powered aeroplane actually crossed the Channel in 1979) was the joyous conclusion to literally centuries of experiments. Some of those undertaken in the past hundred years are worth including here. Most will have forgotten that the first successful man-powered flight took place in Italy in 1937 and that the Hall of Fame should remember Emilio Casco for his prowess. As we have oft seen before, though, memories tend to be selective and the majority of us remember only that which we want to!

The eccentric engine designer Granville Bradshaw (of ABC Scorpion and Wasp fame) was an advocate of the flapping-wing'd approach while Cecil H Latimer-Needham conducted a life-long study of birds to see how best to replicate their behaviour. A clutch of designers evolved a variety of approaches to fitting Man with wings, some were based on bicycles; others with pedal-powered helicopter rotors, all (but the Italian Enea Bossi) under-estimated the power needed for flight compared with the continuous power available from the muscles of an athlete.

If manpowered flight became an achieved challenge by the end of the last century, other visionaries saw the possibilities of flight by other means.

Although the term 'flying saucer' was unknown before 1950, circular-winged aircraft were certainly anything but unknown. The first was the British-designed Lee Richards Annular Biplane of 1913, the culmination of a series of ring-shaped aircraft wings that he successfully flew. In America, Cloyd Lawrence Snyder, described as a foot-doctor, took out a patent for an ultra low aspect-ratio-winged aircraft in 1926 and it was subsequently built in 1932 by Arup of South Bend, Indiana. The first of a series of flying wing aircraft that were actually of parabolic form, these flew outstandingly well and were used as flying advertisement-hoardings without incident for some years.

After this so-called Dirigiplane of Snyder and Arup came a raft of other curious circular and near-circular aircraft including the Vought Skimmer, Chance-Vought XF5V and many others. There were also several quite circular-winged aircraft. Following the Second World War, however, the round aeroplane became synonymous with the mysterious 'flying saucer' phenomenon and alleged alien intervention (remember that ordinary people, too, are fallible) and, instead of being a charming diversion, round aircraft became something of an obsession especially with our American friends. Which is where Avro Canada came in with its Avrocar.

There is much mystery surrounding Avro Canada's Avrocar. It was an attempt to build a working flying saucer and it flew after a fashion. News spread quickly that round flying things were being tested in Toronto. The US Government is said to have been so interested that it 'acquired' the whole project and prohibited Avro from doing any further work on it. Several other flying-saucer-like aircraft (best to call them 'aerodynes' – a technical term for things you and I don't quite understand) have been designed and built, some of which have flown.

Jet packs, flying platforms and magic carpets have all been experimented with. All were probably equally dangerous although Igor Bensen's Flying Carpet placed the pilot in the centre of a frame with an engine and horizontal rotor at each corner which must have served to focus the mind of the poor guy in the middle. While immensely attractive to the adventurous, the concept of the jet-pack is somewhat diminished by the fact that in the event of a power failure or similar, the machine cannot glide but must revert to a gravity-attracted heavy weight with pilot attached. Half a century ago, the US went through an odd phase of encouraging single-seat utility helicopters. Hmm! No wonder they were dubbed 'Army Bensens' after the D-I-Y gyroplanes devised by Igor Bensen.

Flying wings are merely another extension of the variety of ways in which a heavier-than-air machine may soar through the air. From Dunne's tailless biplane glider of the early 20th century to the Granger Brothers' Archaeopteryx, tailless aircraft have come and gone at regular intervals. Handley Page's Manx (built by the designer of the Dart Kitten ultralight) and the raft of General Aircraft gliders that presaged Armstrong-Whitworth's tailless jet wing, questioned the need for tailplanes, indeed fuselages – going some way to confirming that aircraft components have evolved by convention rather than necessity. The flying wing's characteristically restricted centre of gravity range and consequent need for careful loading was no deterrent to the numerous designers who followed those pioneers from the eccentric René Arnoux to others such as Geoffrey T R Hill, the brothers Horten, Alexander Lippisch, Kostyantin Kalinin and John Knudson Northrop

By the 1990s, very advanced teams of engineers, scientists and visionaries were working (mostly, one should point out, at America's NASA headquarters) to devise solar-powered aircraft which could stay aloft for indefinite periods thanks to fuel cells charged during the sunlight hours. These experiments resulted in a number of remarkable pilotless (and, incidentally, tailless) machines that were tried and tested.

Talking of pilotless aircraft (but not of surveillance drones and military spy planes) one man deserves a special place in my Curiosities of Flight Hall of Fame – 77-year-old retired engineer Maynard Luther Hill (1926-2011). Since childhood he had nurtured the idea of flying a model plane across the Atlantic Ocean. On August 11th 2003, his 'Spirit of Butts Farm' landed on Marrin Beach, County Galway, 38 hours and 23 minutes after leaving Cape Spear, Newfoundland. The 6-foot span model weighed less than 11 lbs and was powered by a 10cc four-stroke engine which used rather less than a gallon of fuel. Designated TAM (Trans-Atlantic Model) 5, its four predecessors had been lost at sea. The 1,882-mile flight was controlled using lap-top computers and satellite communications by a team of American, Canadian and Irish enthusiasts. Top marks for succeeding!

Wild ideas have occasionally come up trumps and worked a treat. The jet engine was one of the early ones but best-known of all is the Hawker Harrier which, after a series of very public development problems (it fell off the back of a truck it was attempting to land on at a Paris Air Show), turned out to be the best British invention for some while. Now, like all good British inventions, it has, of course, been scrapped.

This book, then, is a personal collection of aeronautical curiosities, most of which have long been forgotten. In each case I shall try to explain the shortcomings of the design and suggest why it was neither successful nor wise. I must warn you that some of your own favourite non-flyers may not be here and other aircraft that earned a poor record from their pilots (and critics) might also be found missing. This is because it's my collection and not yours! I have selected the ones I want to use to illustrate my point that ideas and mistakes are both eternal and often perpetuated without justification. The causes behind mistakes and failures are never remembered which means that they are doomed to be repeated in a progression that is not linear but cyclic. And besides, you have your own reasons for branding an aircraft as unsuccessful which are probably different from mine.

There is also a more mundane reason. Most of the aircraft that others have branded as failures simply do not justify that classification. But if some of the expected aircraft are not included in my clutch of curiosities, then be prepared to find some that are unexpected. In each case, however, I shall attempt to provide a valid justification for inclusion.

One old adage springs to my mind as apposite. I once worked in the drawing office of a well-known aircraft company where, upon the wall, there hung a notice reading: 'Once a project starts to go wrong, all attempts at improvement will only make it progressively worse!' Experience suggests that this notice ought to have had a wider circulation...

This little book sets out to illustrate some of the curious ideas that people have had regarding flight and some of the duties expected of aircraft. Not all were unsuccessful at flying but most of the less practical ones have happily been overtaken by that chariot known as 'progress'. The successful ones have shown that being a visionary isn't always a bad thing.

Many of these strides into the unknown are, by their nature, hidden from our view and thus do not make the headlines. Who would have thought of replacing rivets in metal aircraft with glue – but that's just what Norman de Bruyne pioneered with his Redux bonding, famously used on the de Havilland Comet jet airliner.

My categories have to include airships and manpowered flight. There's some helicopters and gliders and experimental types. While any analysis of curiosities of flight could quite easily stray no further than military jet fighters (and American ones in particular), I discounted that approach on the grounds that it was too obvious a path to pursue. After all, space shuttles, stealth planes and rocket 'ships' are fodder for the kids, not for discerning types like you and me!

Flying cars and wondrous ways of crossing the Atlantic, on the other hand, are a different slice of the cake. Of course there's a few military odd-balls included even if only to show funny thinking in high places, and there's the odd bit of 'high-tech' in the form of those solar-powered aeroplanes and so on.

The 210-odd pictures in this book have been loosely grouped into sections but like all things you attempt to order, you can never get the ideal sequence chronologically at the same time as selected by technical progress or event. Expect, then, to find airliners and homebuilts, pedal-power and turbojets rather mixed up. Anyway, it's more fun that way!

I find it curious that most who are enthusiastic about aircraft have much less interest in engines. This is a shame for the world of aircraft power units is a fun-filled palace of varieties. Let me provide a typical example that's sufficiently recent to show how even great minds can get carried away. In the 1950s, intelligent people were revising the ideas of the physicist Hermann von Helmholtz who, back in 1873, devised what became known as the 'square-cube' relation. Never mind what it means (simplified, it asserts that Force cubed equals Weight squared) but its modern interpreters got into a real flap over it!

The most novel deduction came from one of the finest brains in the land – Dr Alan Arnold Griffith of Rolls-Royce – who asserted (I suspect hypothetically) that if you perfectly scaled down a jet engine to, say, half its size in dimensions, the ratio of thrust to weight would automatically improve. The extension of this was that a cluster of small, individual engines would be lighter than an original single engine of the same power and, conversely, a lot of small engines totalling the weight of one big one would give more power than the single motor. The Air League of the British Empire actually proposed a transatlantic express airliner carrying 44 passengers and capable of flying at 1,500 knots (1,612 mph) powered by 70 engines.

So attractive was the reasoning behind this impossible monster plane that the 'square-cube' rule assumed the status of a 'law of physics' and its disciples quite forgot that in scaling things ever smaller there is quickly reached the point where the notion breaks down. This is the point where the properties of materials defeat the scale-effect. Toy-makers had long known that a true scale model of something like a car would be so impossibly fragile that you could not pick it up without crushing the bodywork.

The 'square-cube' rule remains a byway of engineering that, while fringing on the strange mathematical world of fractals, belongs in the compartment marked 'theory'. The practice, though, was quite different which is why the enthusiastic proposals for dozens of engines powering an airliner never came to pass. However, the man in America who fitted ten Clinton go-cart engines along the leading edge of his Piper Cub's wings defeated the square-cube rule on grounds that only demanded commonsense and no maths.

All the chosen material within these covers – and some of it may be a surprise to my more sensitive readers – has been selected with the sole purpose of emphasizing that there are more people with no knowledge of what they are doing than one might expect. At the same time, there are many more people who should know what they are about but who suffer basic technical blockages than you might think! A clever aircraft design is an achievement: if it fails to find a market, though, it becomes a waste of resources and a candidate for my book of curiosities. However, that does not make it a 'bad' aircraft, merely an unlucky one. Cunliffe-Owen's Concordia is just one example of this argument.

It's a broad mix, but one that has been selected with infinite care to inform and, I hope, amuse. I think that is the very least one should do before being too critical!

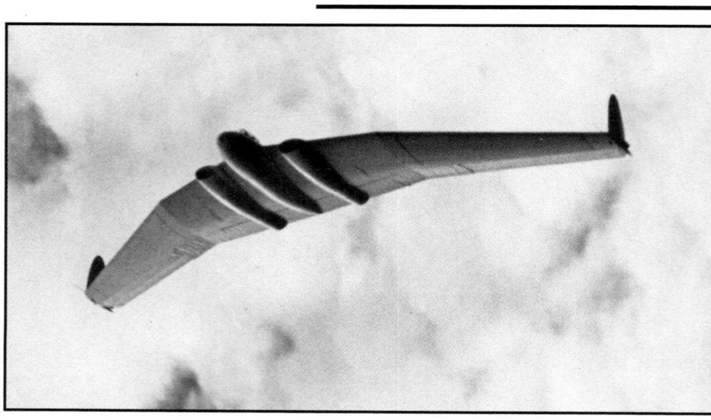

An old adage asserts 'less is more'. True or false, there's an element of truth in it when it comes to tailless aircraft. One might imagine that doing away with most of the fuselage and the whole tail would be a good way of cost-cutting. Not so! Every single tailless aircraft ever built right back to the dawn of aviation has far and away exceeded the cost of making a conventional aeroplane. Here is Armstrong-Whitworth's AW.52, TS363, pictured at the Farnborough Air Show on September 11th, 1948, ten days after its maiden flight. Power was from two Rolls-Royce Nene jets. Wingspan was 90 feet and maximum speed 500 mph. Historically it was the first aircraft from which an emergency exit was made using a Martin-Baker ejector seat. But that was another story.

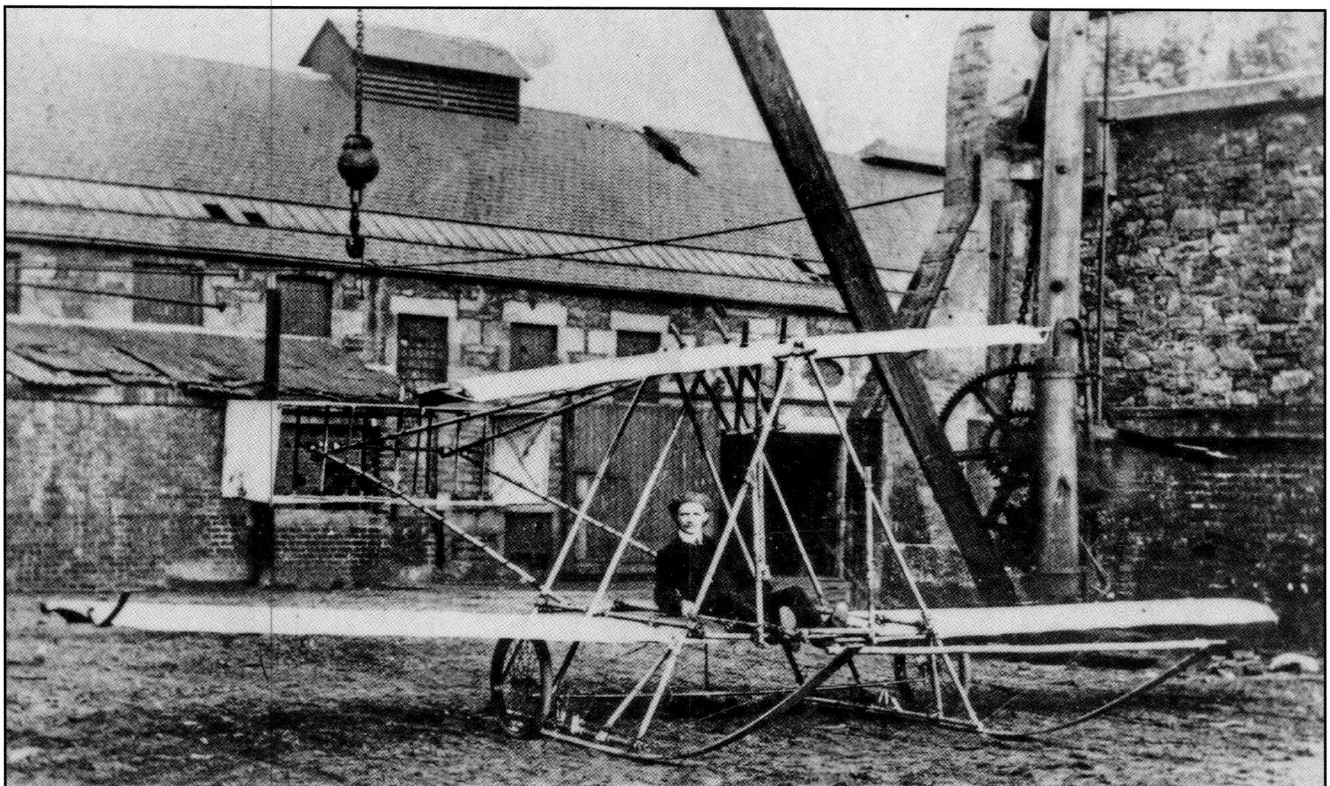

Preston A Watson lived and worked in Dundee where he hoped to become one of Scotland's aviation pioneers. In 1903 he had built a Wright-type glider to which he later fitted a small French motor. Although his family later claimed that it had flown (which would have earned him the credit for being one of the first Britons to fly), this is both unproven and, sadly, unlikely. Between 1908 and 1909, he built a second machine known as the Biplane No.1. It was made of steel tube and bamboo and incorporated a then-novel rocking-wing system to provide roll and yaw control. This idea would be tried again in the 1930s in the Grice Biplane. It was powered by a twin-cylinder horizontally-opposed Dutheil et Chalmers engine, possibly the same as used in the earlier machine. Pictured here in a rather industrial setting, it did not fly and was later rebuilt as a glider used by the Dundee Aero Club in 1911. Watson persevered building two more machines on the same principle. These did, apparently, fly, but the pivoted wing was of dubious merit. The outbreak of the First World War put an end to Watson's experiments and, having joined the RNAS, he was killed in 1915.

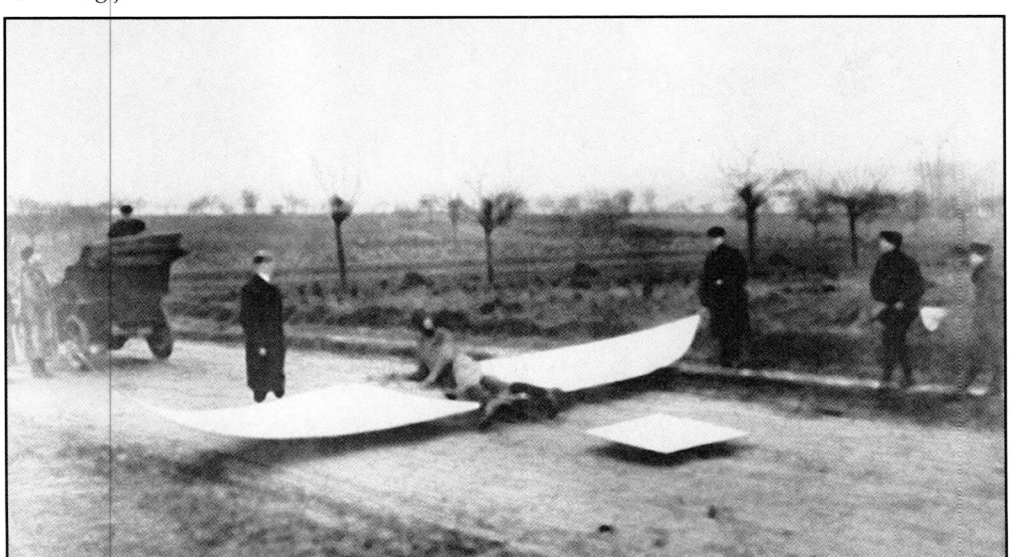

In 1907 the French engineer and inventor Édouard Bélin discovered a way of transmitting pictures by telephone. Although the fax machine was many years away, he thought of it first. And the following year his son built this glider mounted on two high-axled bicycle wheels. No visible means of control can be detected. The scheme appears to have involved the car and a rope. The significance of the bystander holding the two flags is as uncertain as what happened next. As his name does not appear in the Roll of Honour one may safely assume that terra firma failed to release the lad and his failed flyer.

Opposite: The pioneer British aviator Horatio Claude Barber (1875-1964) designed one of the earliest and most successful canard aircraft that ever flew. His Valkyrie was robust, easy-to-fly and was eventually made in four 'sizes' – single-seat trainer powered by a 30 hp Green capable of 45 mph; a model powered by one 60-80 hp Green to carry pilot and passenger (or two light passengers) at 40-50 miles an hour as a trainer; a single-seat military monoplane powered by a 40-50 hp Green and flying at 45 miles an hour; Passenger-carrying model powered by 50 hp Gnome engine and capable of between 50 and 55 mph. Barber founded his Aeronautical Syndicate Ltd at Larkhill in June 1909 and a year later moved into sheds at Hendon where he built twelve machines and ran a school teaching, among others, several Army officers. It was said that pilots trained on the Valkyrie quickly and safely: others said, darkly, that they needed retraining to fly a conventional aircraft safely (which was quite possible). At that time government intransigence ensured that Britain had no military training scheme and so when, in July 1911, 36-year-old Barber (described as being of independent means and having spent £10,000 on his development work) gave four aircraft to the Government, Stanley Spooner (editor of *Flight*) waxed lyrical. 'Nothing but contempt can be felt by Britishers... in connection with the grant of funds... for placing our Army and Navy upon equal footings with aerial weapons of offence with other nations... It is to men like Mr Barber who help forward the British industry by designing and constructing entirely British machines...' and so on. Barber, remember, was based on Claude Grahame-White's airfield. And Claude, four years his junior, would soon embark on his 'Wake Up Britain' campaign. Barber sold up his business in April 1912. In this picture, the pilot's seat is directly above the wheels, the control-column fitted between the top longerons, the rudder bar being visible in front of that.

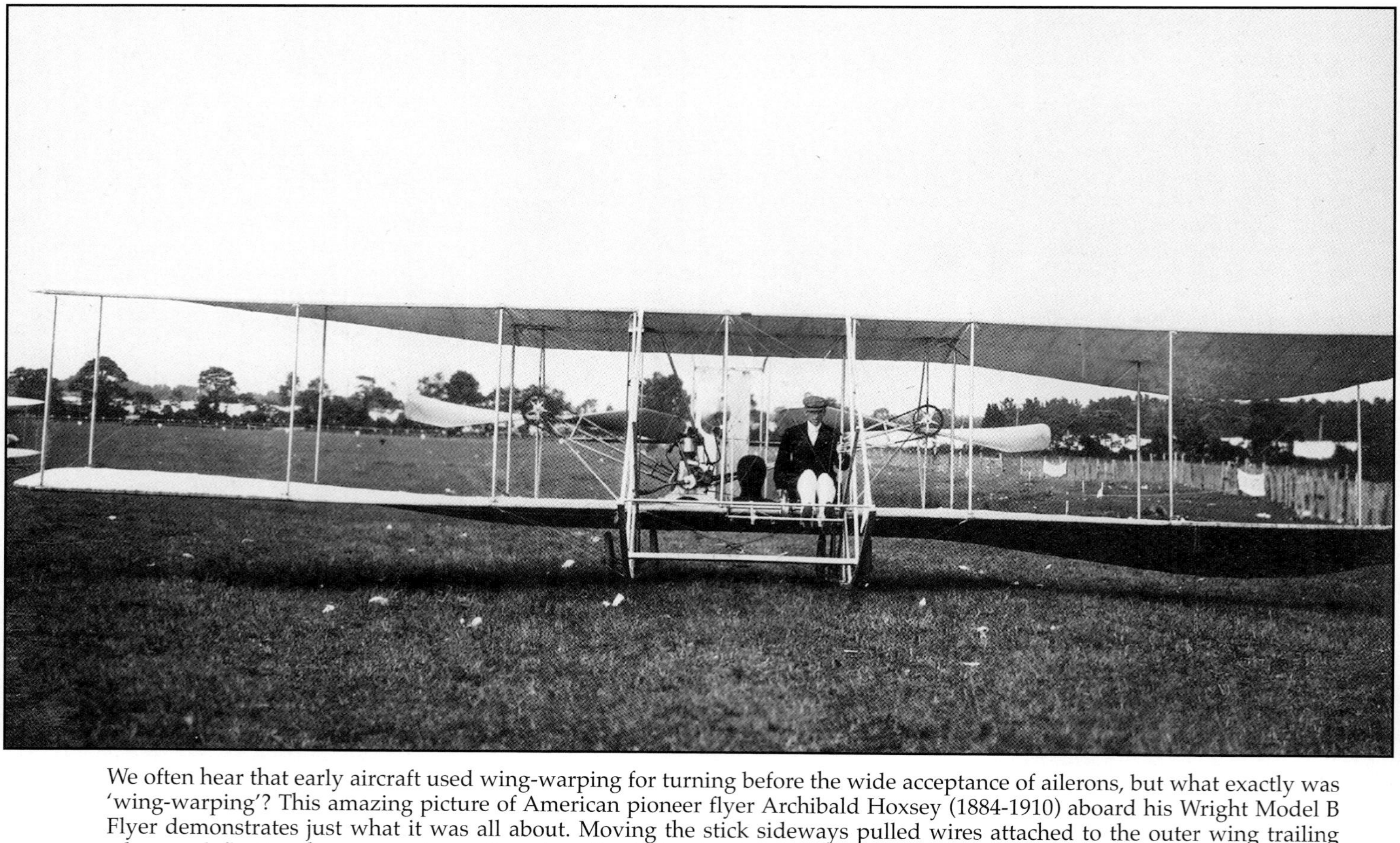

We often hear that early aircraft used wing-warping for turning before the wide acceptance of ailerons, but what exactly was 'wing-warping'? This amazing picture of American pioneer flyer Archibald Hoxsey (1884-1910) aboard his Wright Model B Flyer demonstrates just what it was all about. Moving the stick sideways pulled wires attached to the outer wing trailing edges so deflecting them up or down, the wing effectively pivoting on its chord at the front spar. The only bracing was in the plane of this spar, allowing the wing trailing edges to be flexed in this manner. Poor Hoxsey was to lose his life in this aircraft very soon after this picture was taken. Theodore Roosevelt, US President, made his first flight with Hoxsey – the first president to get airborne – and then, on December 30th, 1910, he set a new world altitude record of 11,474 feet. The next day at the Los Angeles aviation meeting he set off to beat his own record but something went horribly wrong and he was seen by many thousands of horrified spectators to spin from 7,000 feet before hitting the ground.

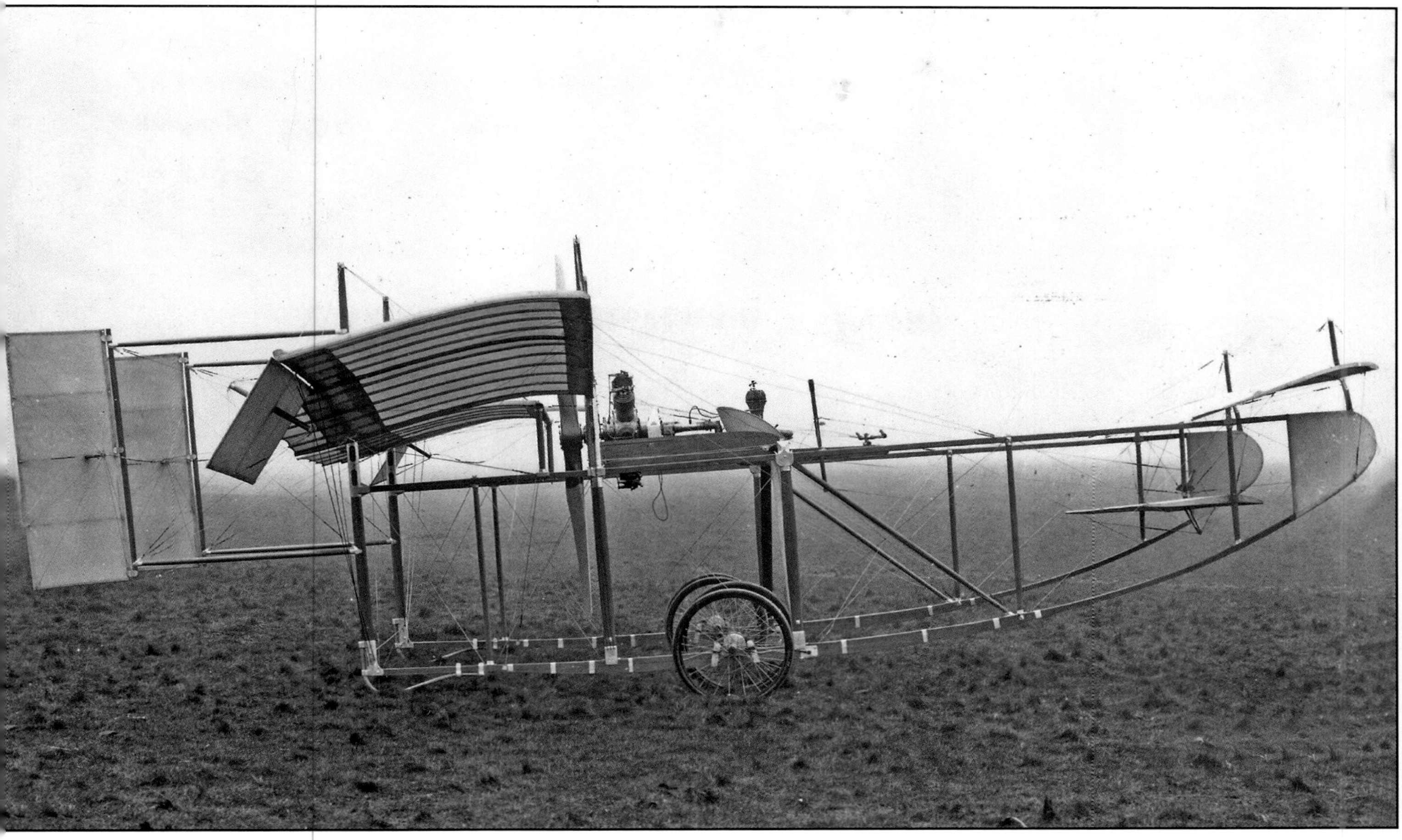

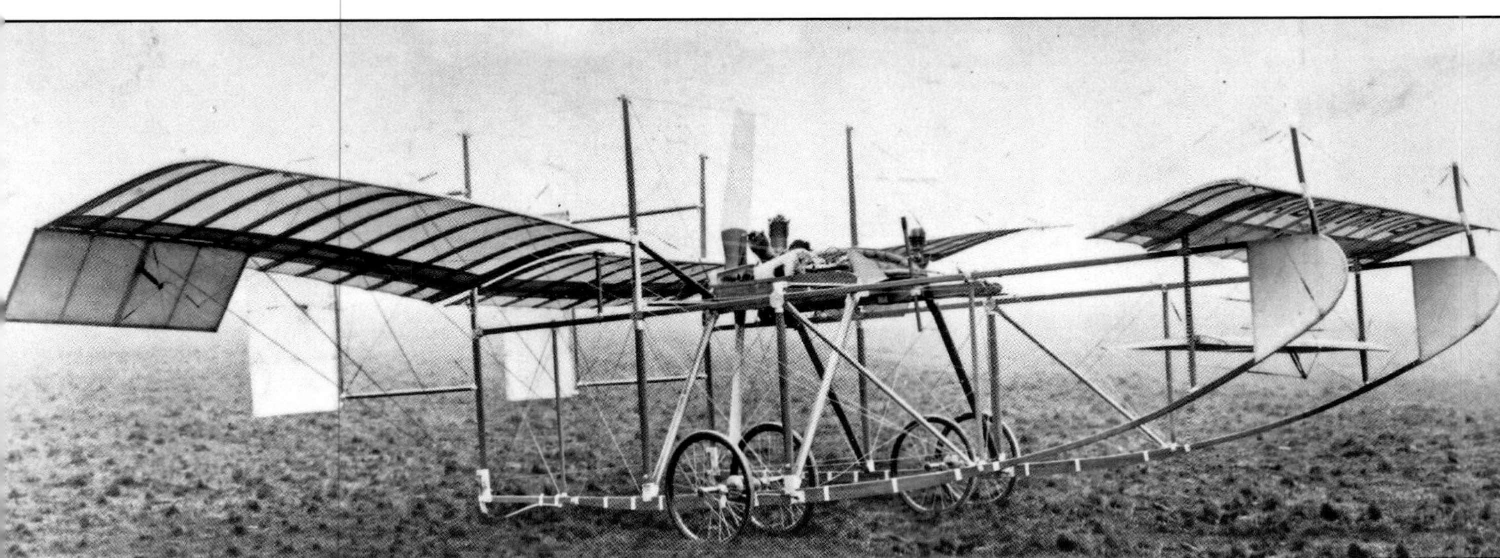

In this view of one of Horatio Barber's Valkyrie, the geometry of the tail-first structure can be appreciated. Rather like a monoplane version of the Bristol Boxkite, Barber built and flew his first model on Salisbury Plain. It was described as 'The first, and almost the only, successful 'tail-first' monoplane' (Jane's *All the World's Aircraft*, 1910). This model, powered by a 50 hp Gnome rotary engine, made many long distance flights in 1910 and 1911, a notable trip being from Hendon to Brighton and back while carrying a passenger. The pilot sat in front of the engine on a flat and almost backless seat. Horatio Barber, who earned the first ever degree in aeronautics, later made history by carrying the first air freight: he transported a box of Osram light bulbs in a Valkyrie from Shoreham to Hove on July 4th, 1911.

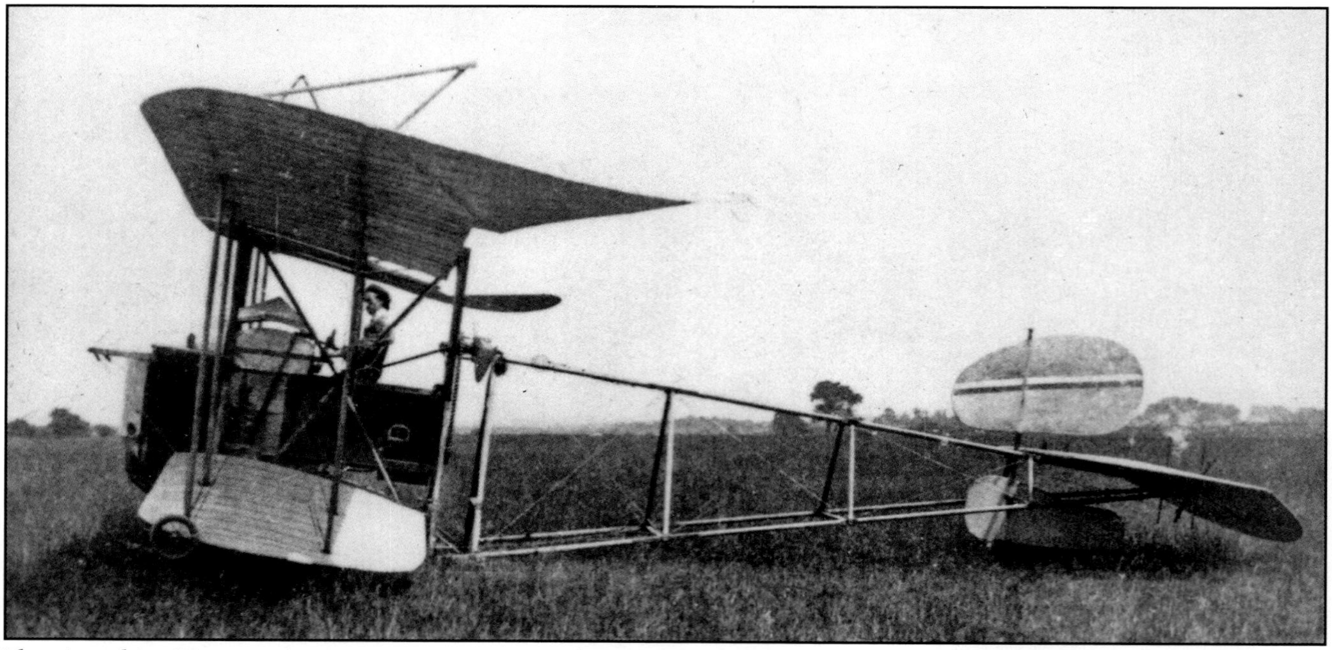

There's nothing like a good mystery and a foreigner who suddenly disappears as war breaks out is clearly suspect! But Walter B Megone of Hawkinge in Kent was a questor for flight and, between 1912 and 1914, he built at least two curious biplanes with the assistance of a friend, Victor Hunt, and others. Both were two-seat pusher biplanes. The rear fuselage was a triangular truss, the top member being attached to a bearing in the propeller hub. The engine was a Green variously described as being of 35 hp or 65 hp and mounted low down in the nose, driving the 10 feet diameter propeller through a clutch-connected layshaft and chain drive. The propeller hub was hollow so that the control cables to the tail could pass through and along the top rear fuselage tubular steel member. This picture shows the second version of the biplane with long-span lower wing. Note the little wheels on the wing-tips to cater for the numerous occasions when touchdown involved one or the other wing-tips. Megone and his test pilot, Hunt, experienced many trials and tribulations (i.e. crashes) but experiments continued up to the outbreak of war in August 1914. Megone then vanished leaving his aircraft locked in its shed. Nothing was ever heard from him or about him, but the rumours abounded! The same chunterings surrounded the popular Gustav Hamel, who disappeared over the Channel that May: he was also thought to be a Kaiser collaborator.

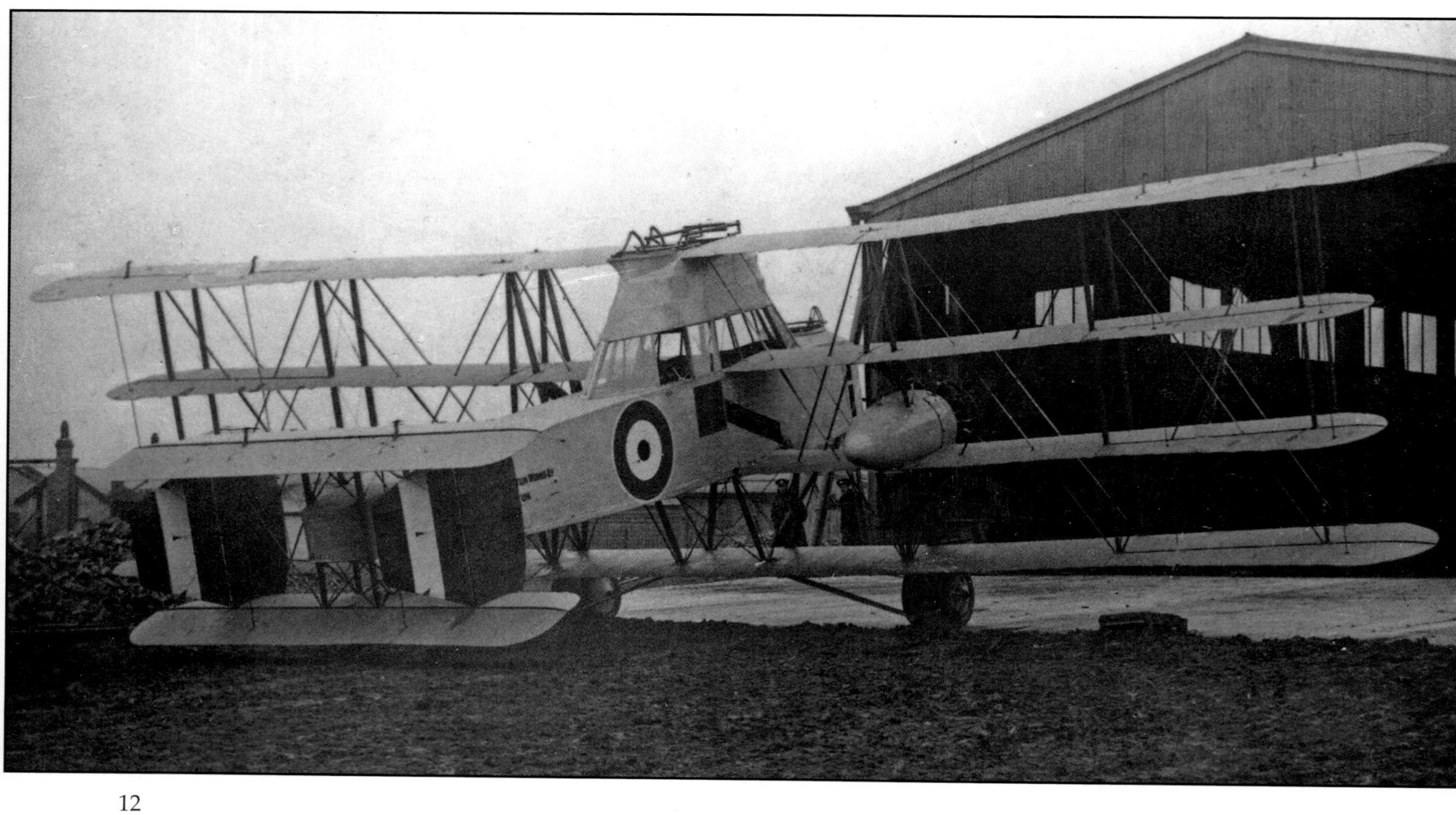

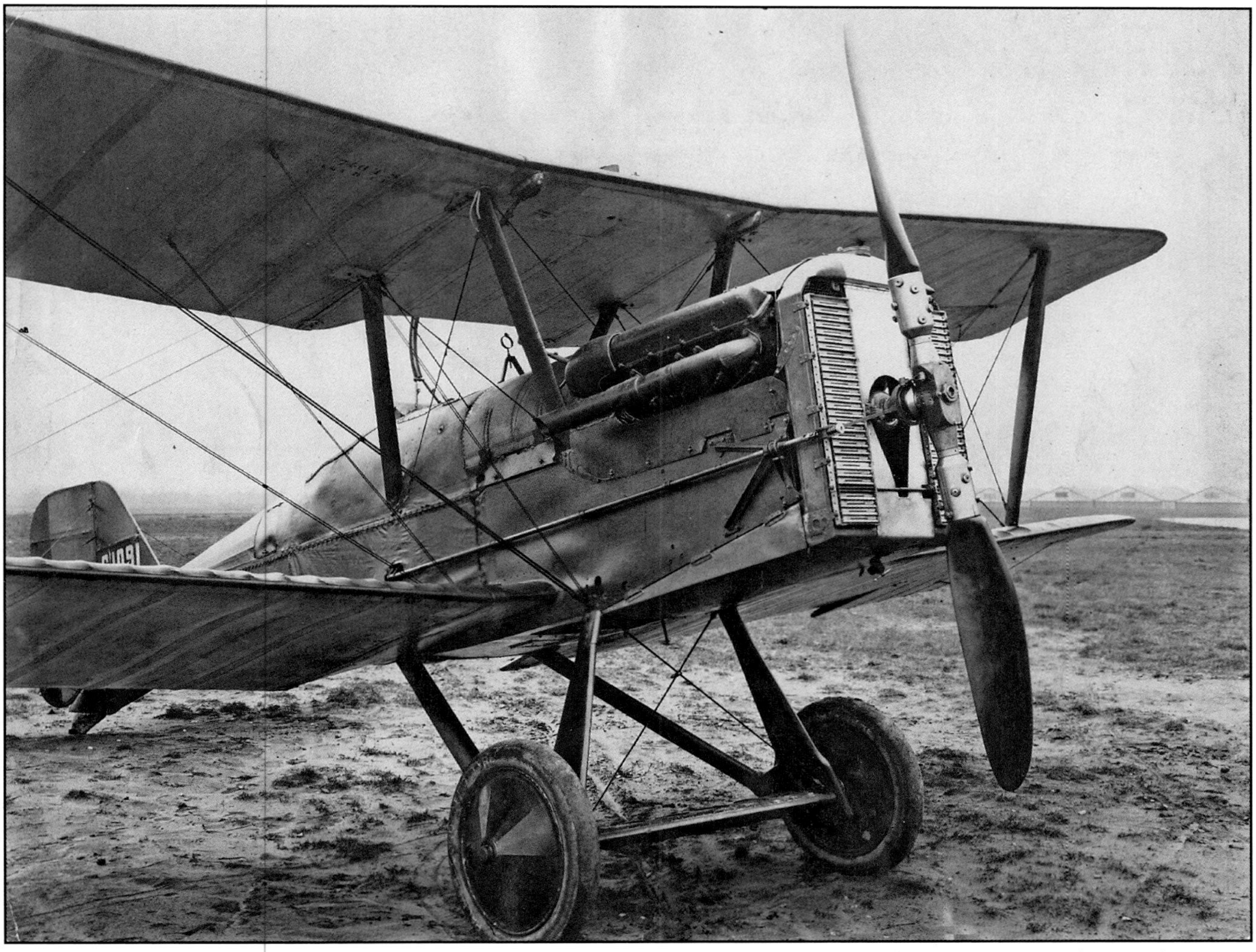

Variable-pitch propellers have a curious history since first they were proposed by the French aeronautist Joseph Eustache Croce-Spinelli (1843-1875) in 1871. Croce-Spinelli never got to make his V-P prop for he lost his life through asphyxiation when he ascended to 29,000ft in a helium balloon without oxygen. In 1876 Alphonsé Pénaud specified a variable (or adjustable) pitch airscrew in his 1876 patent, and in 1910 airships had a form of changeable-pitch airscrew to enable them to manoeuvre and use reverse thrust. The engineering was still in its early stages though and it was found that considerable forces were needed to overcome the extreme friction loads in moving a fast-spinning propeller blade about its hub. The Royal Aircraft Factory at Farnborough began work on this problem at the end of 1916 and by the early part of 1917 had a trial installation ready for air-test in SE.5A, C1091. This rare photograph shows the system used. A shaft extends forwards from the cockpit along the outside of the fuselage and located with a thrust bearing in a rigidly-braced bracket attached to the front of the engine bearers. This bracket is prevented from moving under extreme load with a heavy 'V' brace. In front of this, a universal joint connects to a pinion which rotates inside a worm-drive on the outer end of a pivoted arm, the other end of which forms a yoke encircling the crankshaft immediately behind the propeller. Each propeller blade has a long spigot located in sockets within a solid machined hub. A short connecting rod with a roller at its extremity rides the surface of the face of the yoke. When the pilot turns a worm-drive wheel in his cockpit, the shaft rotates, the worm wheel at its end pushing or pulling the yoke lever behind the propeller hub. The propeller-blade link rollers push or pull their connecting shafts to twist the propeller blades. Because the yoke can really only push, it is probable that the blades incorporated a spring return. The whole system appears prone to rapid wear and tear and cannot have been reliable. It was, however, a recorded early air-test. The date of the picture is April 20th 1920.

Opposite: Quadruplanes are rare these days – and those days, too. The sole Supermarine Type 29 Nighthawk was the first design of Noel Pemberton-Billing's Supermarine Works after its re-naming in 1917. The Nighthawk was an attempt to make a machine capable of hunting and engaging Zeppelins and to this end it had extensive crew accommodation for between three and five people and fuel to give it from 9 to 18 hours' endurance on its two 125 hp 9-cylinder Anzani radial engines. In the nose was mounted a searchlight while on the top wing central gun turret was a 1-lb Davis cannon. The main fuselage nose (level with the third wing) had a pair of .303 Lewis guns. The wingspan was 60 feet, length 37 feet and height 17 feet 8 inches. One prototype was built with the serial number 1388 and first flown in February 1917 by the well-known test pilot Clifford B Prodger. With a 60 mile an hour cruise speed and an appalling rate of climb (it took an hour to get to 10,000 feet), the Nighthawk was scrapped: a second aircraft, allocated 1389, was cancelled. Even so, had any self-respecting Zeppelin pilot caught sight of this great chariot of the skies staggering towards him he could be forgiven for fleeing for home!

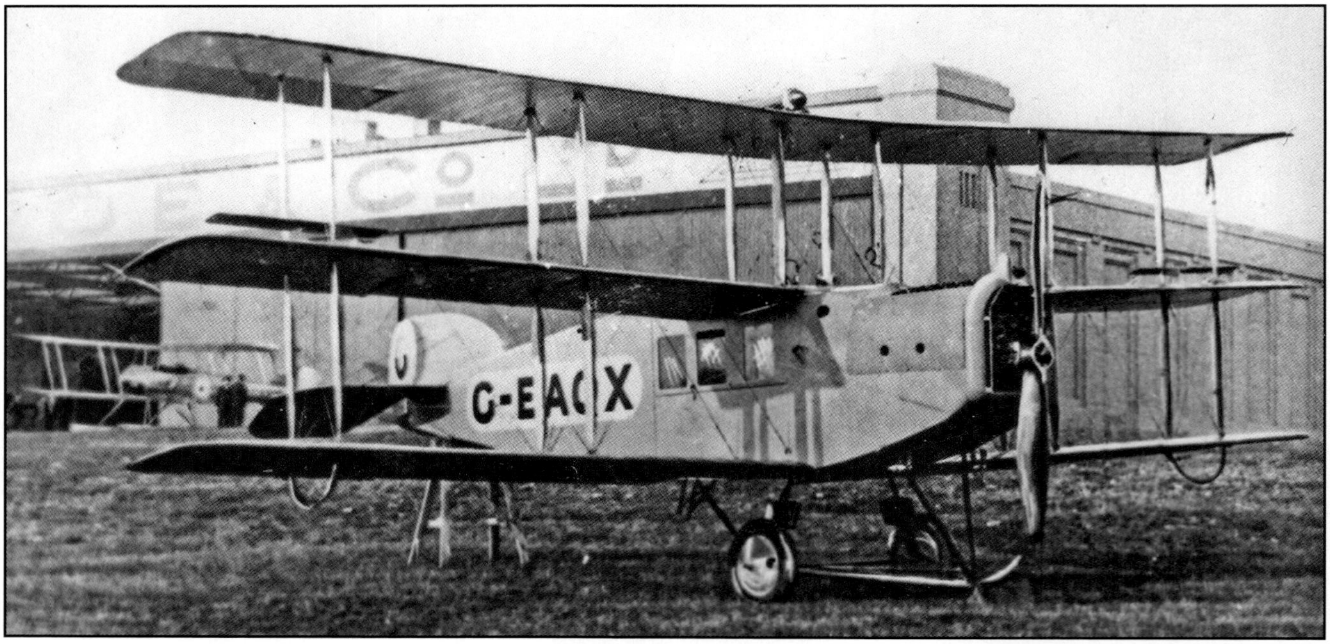

In February 1920 A V Roe decided to introduce a commercial triplane with an enclosed passenger cabin for four passengers. It was built of surplus Avro 504K parts, particularly wings and struts, tail and undercarriage. The engine was the 160 hp water-cooled Beardmore. With seats removed, the cabin offered 113 cubic feet of freight space. A second example, with a 240 hp Puma engine, was entered for the Air Ministry's Small Commercial Aeroplane competition of 1920 and was pitted against the Austin Kestrel, Beardmore WB.X, Bristol Seely Puma, Sopwith Wallaby and Westland Limousine Mk.III. The last-mentioned won the £7,500 prize. The prototype 547, G-EAQX seen here, was offered to Instone Air Line and others but after testing was rejected. That November the newly-formed Queensland and Northern Territories Aerial Services Ltd bought it for £2,798 to use on a leg of its projected Melbourne-Darwin route. Sadly the machine, now registered G-AUCR, did not live up to expectations and its delicate undercarriage collapsed on landing. Rebuilt, it was entered for the Aerial Derby staged at Sydney in 1922 where it came second at 69.5 mph. Even so, the 547 was disappointing: QANTAS used it for joy-riding for a while but resolved never again to do business with A V Roe & Co.

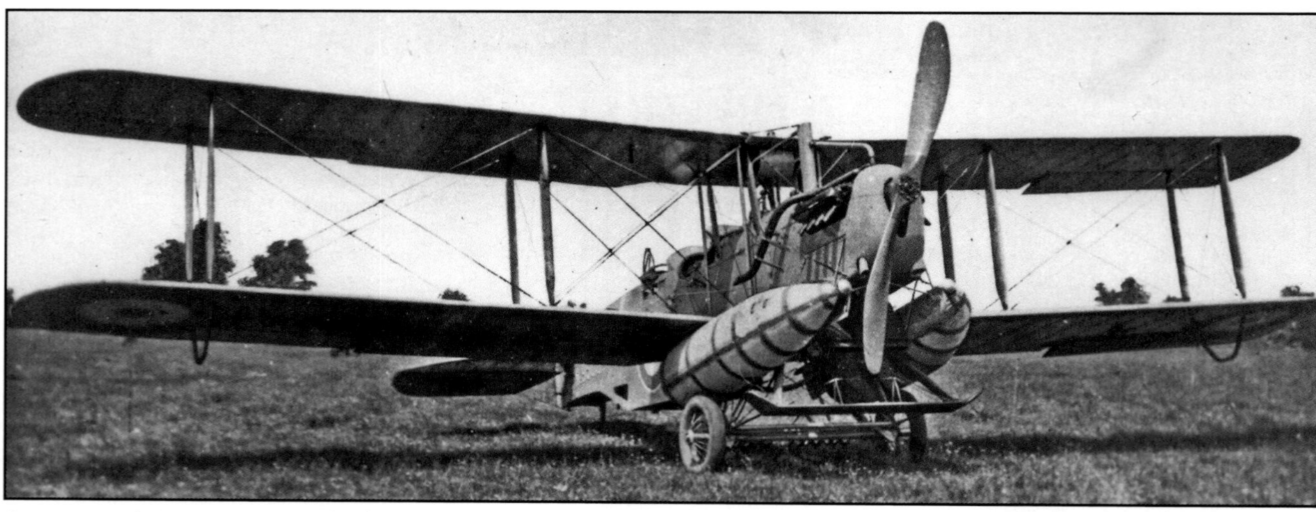

Some aircraft do not warrant the hubris of their creators, the shame of their builders or the reputed infallability of those in high places who specify them. One aircraft in this unfortunate class was the Westland Walrus. Westland didn't 'design' it and therefore didn't want to build it, its specifiers didn't really know what they wanted – and the design was empowered to use up a surplus of DH.9A wings and engines. The Navy wanted reconnaissance aircraft and to save time and money reckoned that up-dating old RAF machines would be the way forward. Armstrong Whitworth had been briefed to fit as many bits of DH.9A as they could to create a hybrid called the Tadpole. Various circumstances led to Westland being invited to 'improve' the design for aircraft carrier operation calling for sets of jaws to grab the longitudinally-stretched deck arrester wires. The whole undercarriage had to be jettisonable for a water landing and the aircraft had to be able to float. There were plenty of other changes not the least was the substitution of the old 400 hp Liberty engine with the Napier Lion II of 450 hp. With the addition of flotation bags either side of the nose, the new aircraft, called the Walrus, looked supremely ugly. There were many problems in flying the thing but it did not prevent an order for 36 machines being issued. The three-seater housed its crew in three separate cockpits and the aircraft few at only 124 mph. The Walrus stayed in service until replacement by Blackburn Blackburns and Avro Bisons in 1925. The picture is of prototype N9500 first flown by Stuart Keep in February or March, 1921.

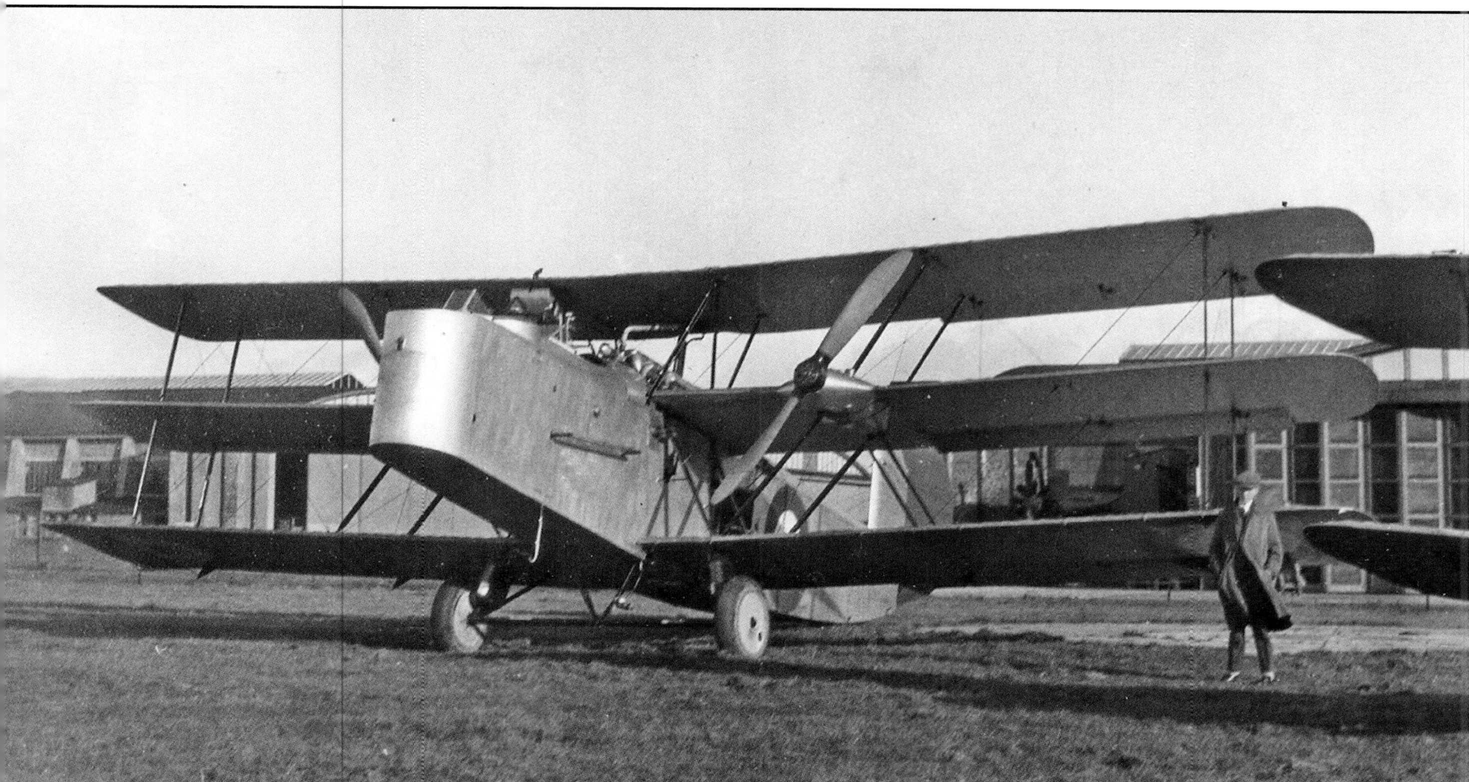

Visitors to the 1924 Hendon Air Pageant were confronted by this curious aircraft pictured at Yate. Designed by Harold Bolas (who died in 1936 aged 63), the Parnall Possum triplane was built as a medium-range postal and military transport to Specification 9 and 11/20. Novel was the fact that despite two very large and slow-turning propellers, it was a hark-back to the Wright Brothers and only had one engine. The 450 hp Napier Lion 12-cylinder 'broad-arrow' water-cooled engine was mounted in the middle-wing centre-section of the fuselage where bevel gearing and shafting ran out through the wing to a secondary gear-box that drove one of the two 9 feet 6 inch diameter propellers. These were of coarse pitch and so observers on the ground heard the fairly normal growl of a Napier Lion running at about 1,700 rpm to the accompaniment of the gearbox whines and the thwack of a slow-speed pair of wooden airscrews; their leisurely rotation could clearly be seen from the ground.

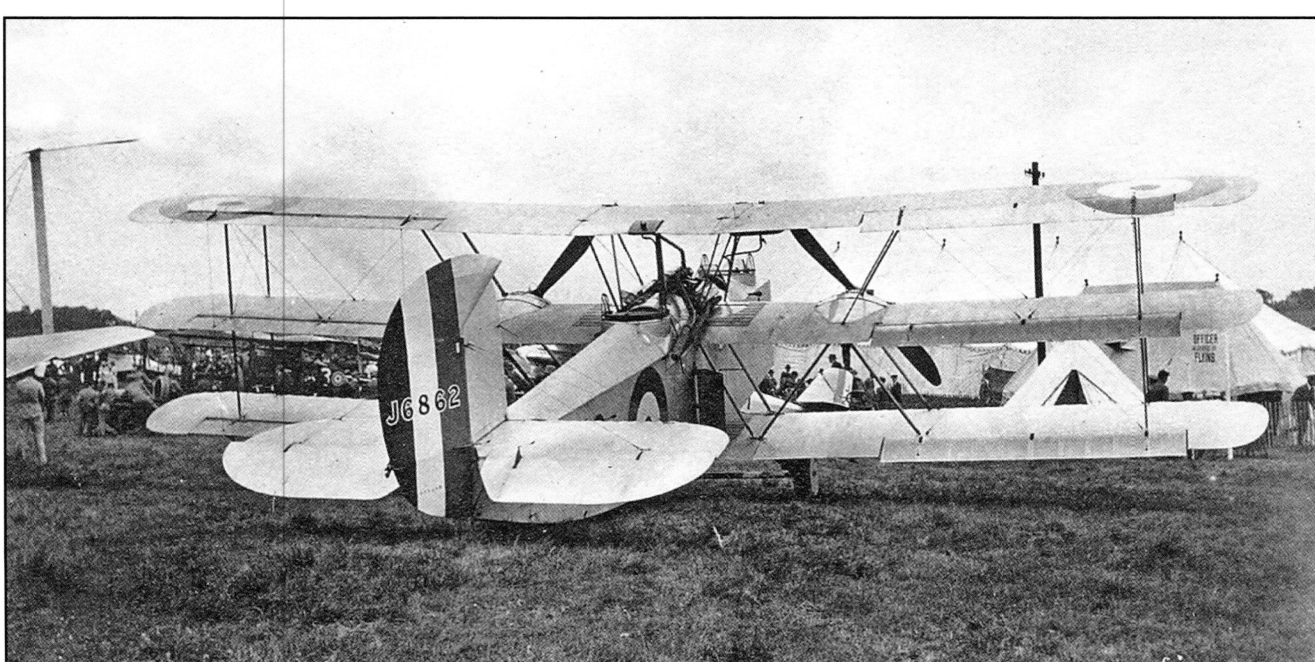

Built between 1923 and 1925, Parnall made just two machines, the second starring at the following year's Hendon show. J6862, pictured here, was the prototype. Both aeroplanes were retired to Martlesham Heath where they flew occasionally for some while but eventually they disappeared, fate unknown.

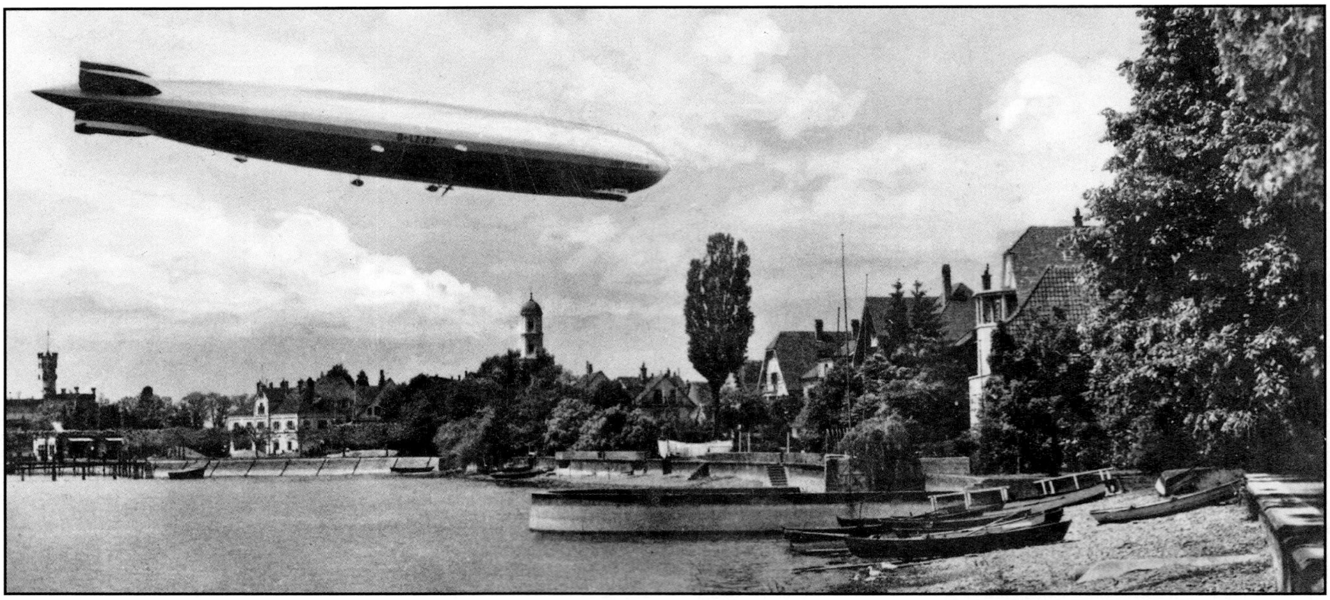

Airships have long inspired awe in the minds of people upon catching sight of these monsters of the air. Pre-dating heavier-than-air aircraft, they already had a long history by the time Count Ferdinand von Zeppelin (1838-1917) saw his peaceful dream machines used as weapons of war in the 1914-18 conflict. They were certainly impressive and by the 1920s brought a standard of comfort, spaciousness and reliability to long-distance travel quite unrivalled by anything else that flew. Here is possibly the greatest of them all, the Graf Zeppelin (D-LZ127) proceeding serenely through the skies over Langenargen on Lake Constance (Bodensee) south east of its birthplace and base at Friedrichshafen. It is pictured in 1928 soon after its maiden flight on September 18th. With a crew of 40, the Graf Zeppelin, under the command of its talented and illustrious captain, Dr Hugo Eckener (1862-1954), could carry a payload of 15,000 kg over a distance of 10,000 km non-stop. It maintained the first regular transatlantic passenger service conveying 20 passengers in luxurious surroundings. It undertook some amazing long distance flights including a round-the-world flight in 1929. From stem to stern it was 776 feet long, 100 feet in diameter and, with five 550 hp Maybach engines, cruised comfortably at 80 mph.

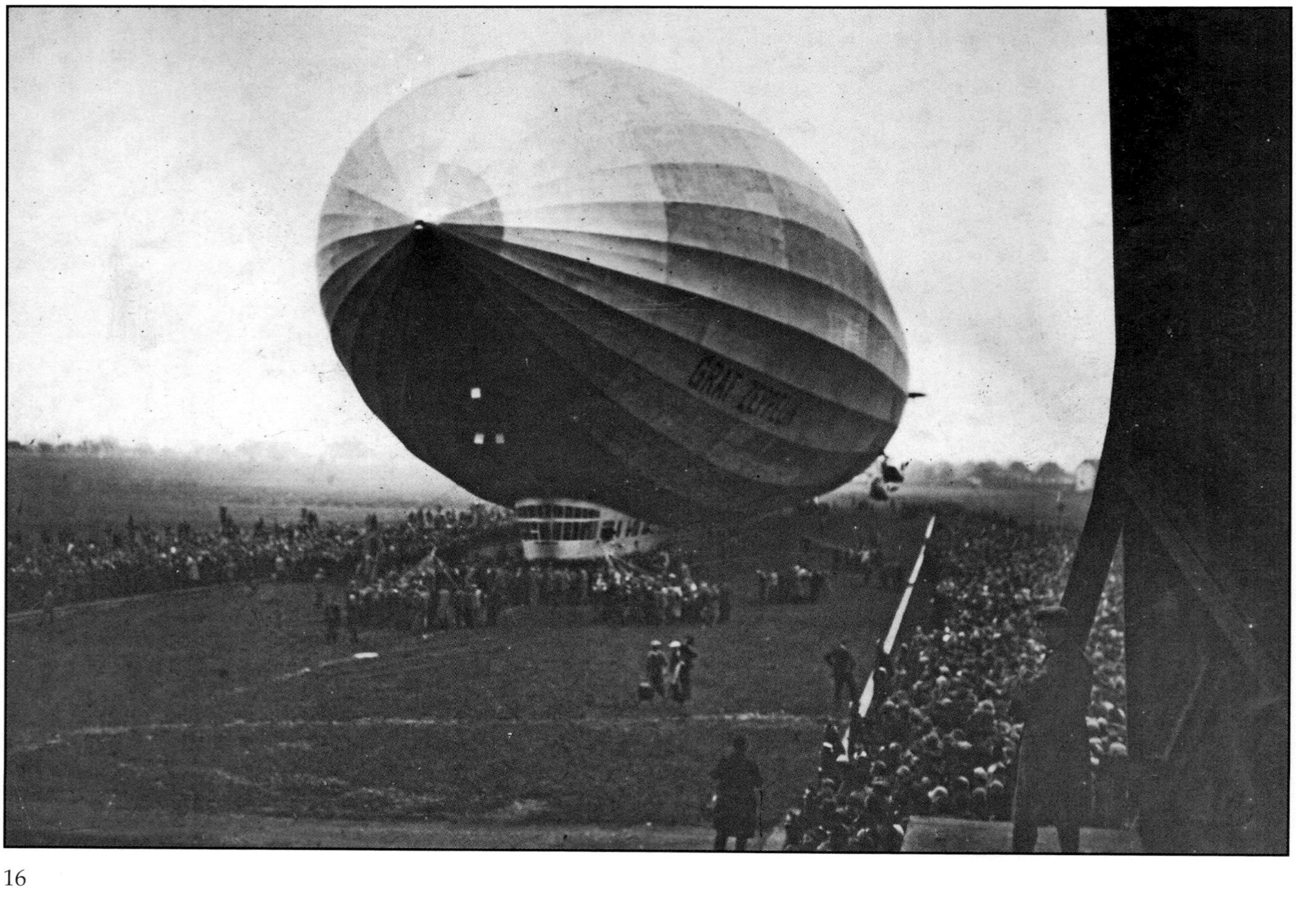

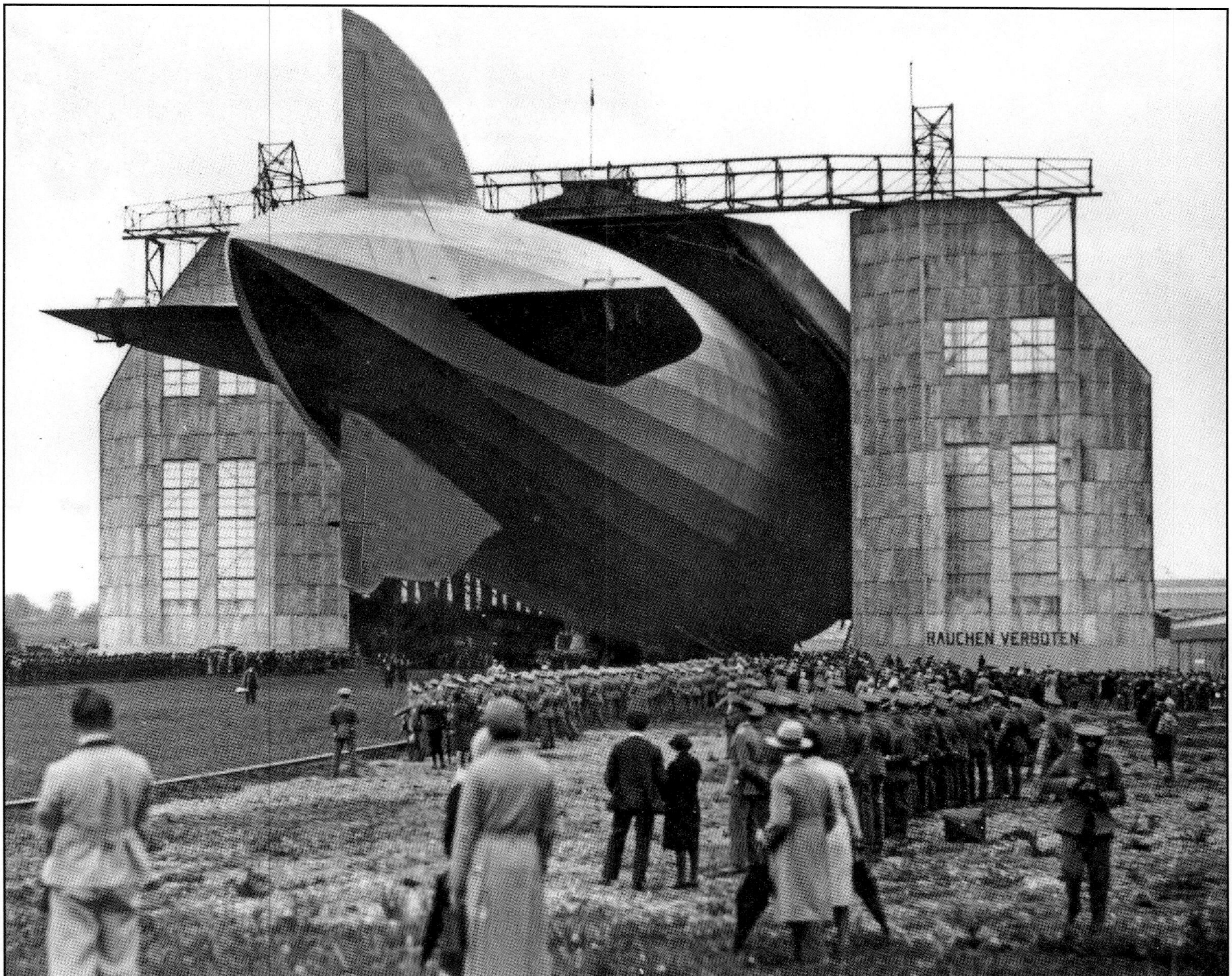

An impression of the enormous size of these Zeppelins can be gained from this news photograph which also gives some idea of the extreme difficulty and complexity of handling such giants on the ground. With the huge doors of its Friedrichshafen hangar opened, a vast team of handlers was needed to move it in or out, an unexpected gust of wind risking disaster. Filled with highly inflammable hydrogen gas, the sign on the right hand door ('No Smoking') marked a vital safety measure. A plea to America to supply non-burning but expensive helium gas was rejected on political grounds. Germany's giant hydrogen-filled airships sailed on, the inevitable disaster becoming ever closer. A censor has carefully painted out the swastikas on the upper and lower fins of this picture.

Opposite: Pictured in December 1928 at Friedrichschaffen, the bulk of the Graf Zeppelin is manoeuvred back to its hangar by an army of men pulling on ropes. The size of the gondola is notable in this view. One pair of engines can be seen hanging from the lower right side of the airship in this view which is taken from just inside the left hand door mid-way platform.

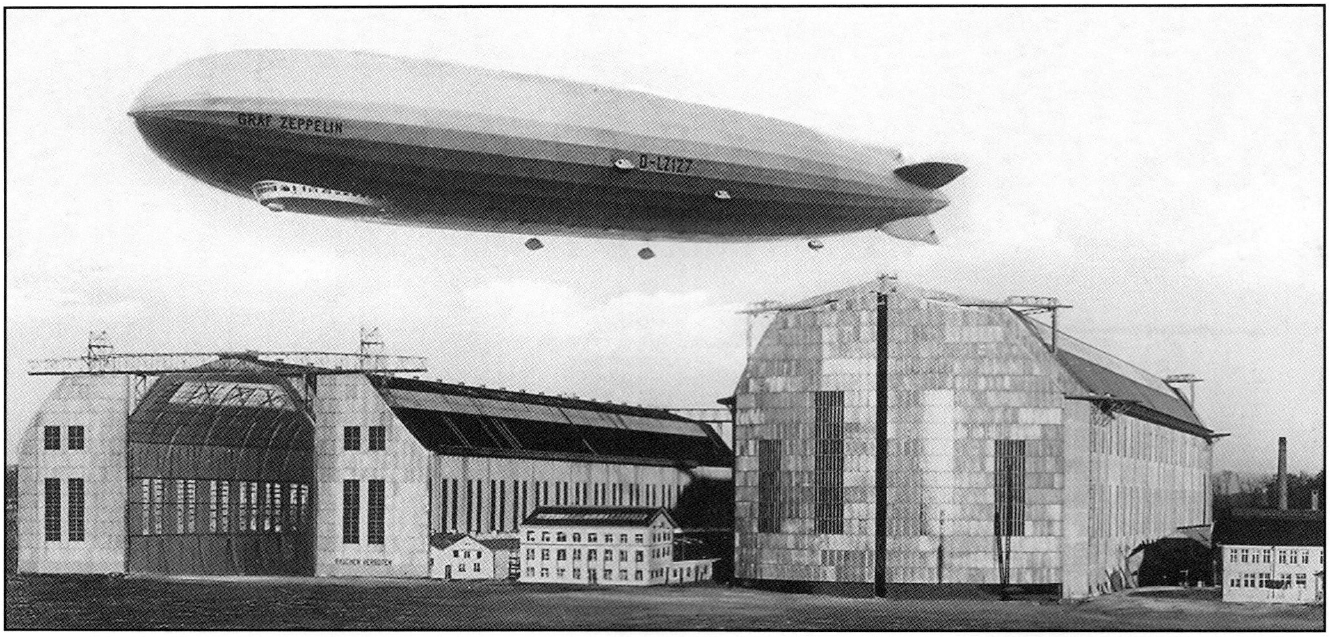

Germany's Graf Zeppelin was a milestone achievement in long-distance passenger transport. And yet it is almost impossible to overstate the enormity of the logistics involved in airship operation. Besides being susceptible to even minor variations in wind speed and direction, getting the things into the air and then safely back into their sheds was a gargantuan operation demanding huge manpower resources. Even so, from its first transatlantic flight in October 1928 (it flew the 6,168 miles from Friedrichshafen to Lakehurst, New Jersey, in 111 hours), the 776 feet long monster gave nine years of almost uninterrupted service. Here it is supposed to be seen in flight over its shed close to Lake Constance but the image, published as a German postcard, is a fake, an unassociated picture of the airship being superimposed on an otherwise fine shot of the sheds. The perpetrator of this sin did not realise that the viewing angle he arranged represented the airship in a 20 degree starboard bank: look at the angle of the vertical fins!

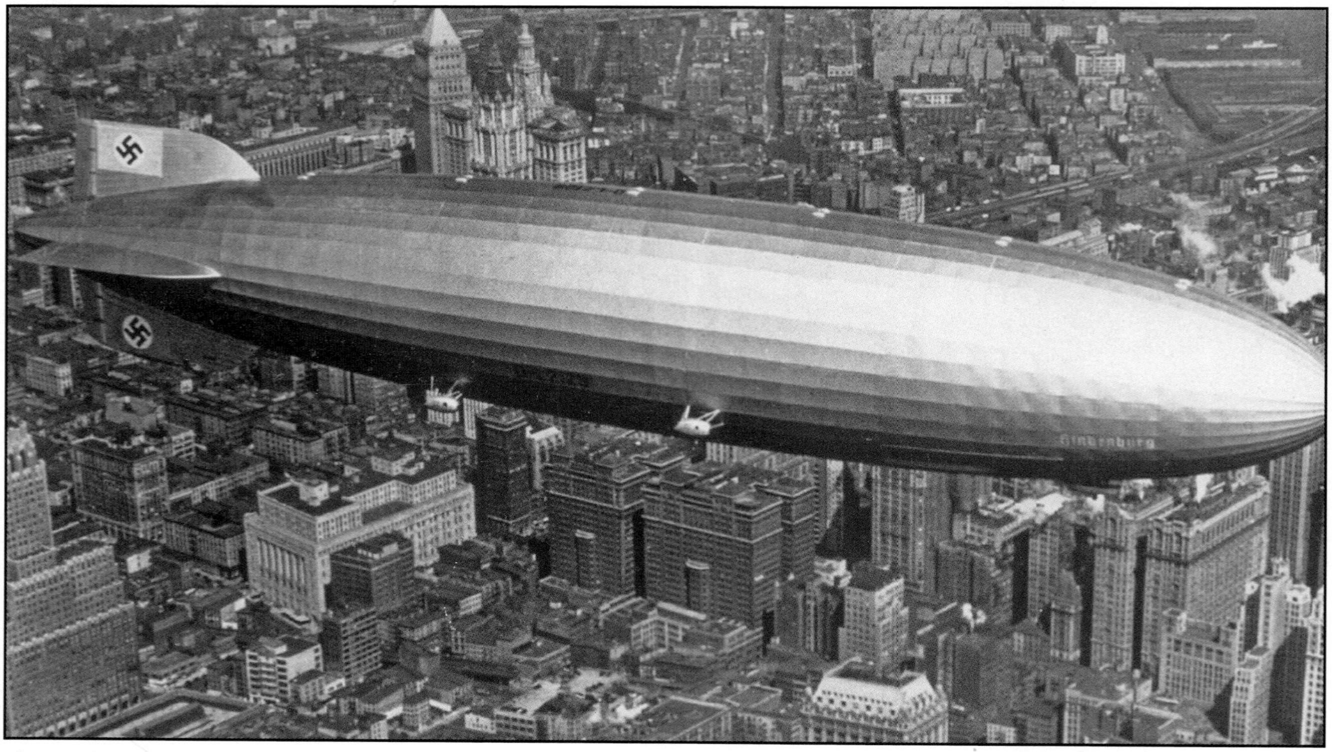

The Graf Zeppelin was succeeded by the even larger Hindenburg. Construction by Luftschiffbau Zeppelin had begun in 1931 and it was not until March 4th, 1936, that LZ129 made its maiden flight carrying a total of 87 people. It had been designed specifically for helium-filling in the hope that the American embargo on the gas might relent. It wasn't to be and Hindenburg, with its crew of between 40 and 60 serving between 50 and 72 passengers, operated the North Atlantic route in style. Powered by four 1,200 hp Daimler-Benz diesel motors, the Hindenburg was 803 feet long and 135 feet 1 inch in diameter and cruised at a sedate 85 miles an hour. The volume of gas that it carried was 7,062,000 cubic feet. Here it is pictured in flight over New York in 1936.

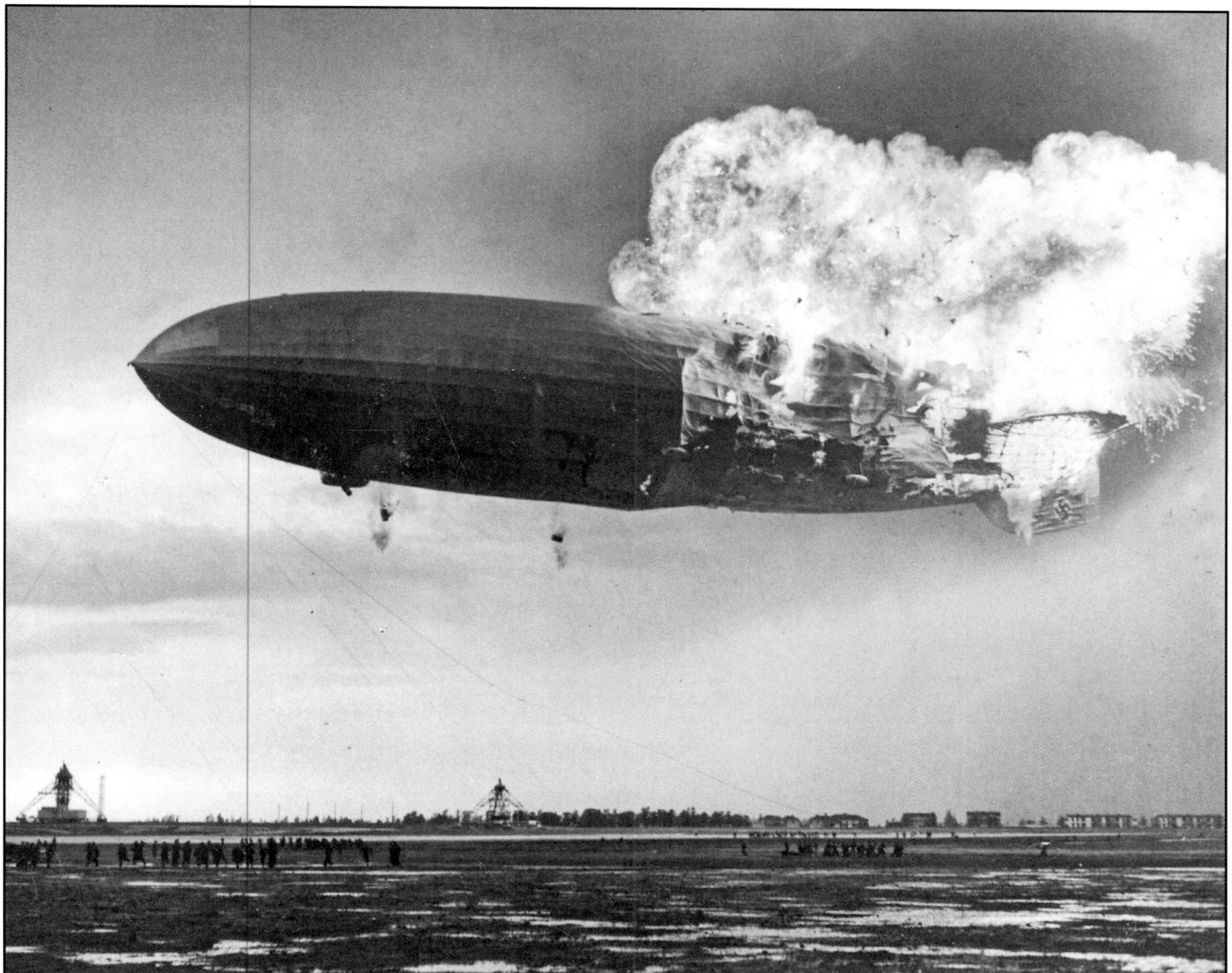

Britain's own airship era had ended with the R.101 disaster on October 5th, 1930 with the death of 48 souls at Beauvais in France. Germany proceeded alone with airships until Thursday, May 6th, 1937, when the great Hindenburg, LZ129, launched just one year and two days earlier, unexpectedly erupted into a storm of fire in the air as it prepared to moor at Lakehurst in New Jersey.

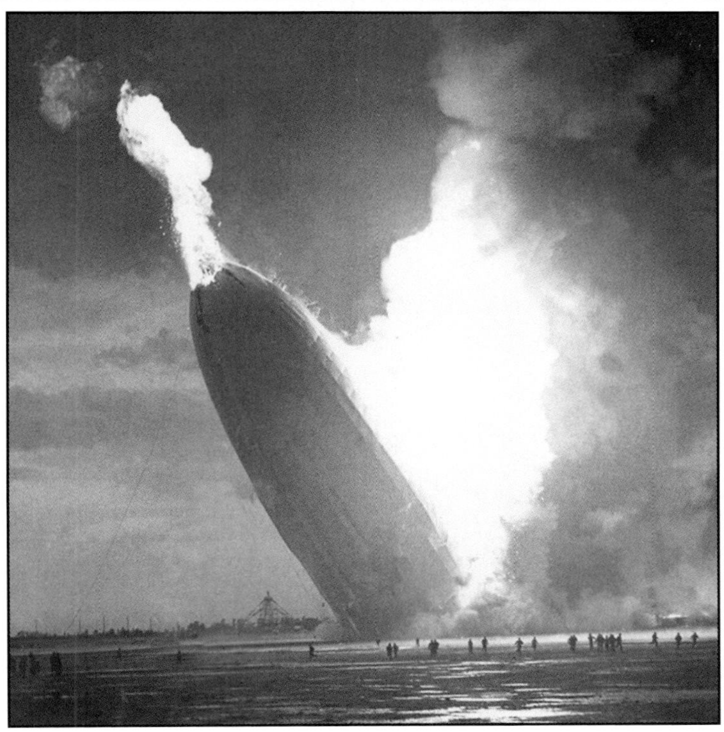

The event that ended the days of the hydrogen-filled airship at Lakehurst, New Jersey, only lasted some 30 seconds. From a stable height of 300 feet, the rear of the Hindenburg burst into flames as it prepared for mooring. As the tail quickly settled, a gush of burning gas bursts through the nose. It took less than half a minute for the great airship to be destroyed although the diesel fuel for its five engines continued to burn on the ground for several hours. There were only 36 passengers on board but there was a full complement of 61 crew. On that day 35 died plus one unfortunate member of the ground crew. It brought to an end Germany's great airship era and, on June 18th, 1937, the Graf Zeppelin was retired to be melted down for scrap during March 1940. Unwieldy and ultimately dangerous, hydrogen-filled airships slipped silently into history.

The Russian-born Igor Sikorski established an early reputation as a maker of enormous aircraft. During the opening years of the First World War, Sikorski's vast biplanes with their fuselage-top pedestrian walkways created wonder and a degree of admiration. So when, in 1916, a certain J Chessborough H Mackenzie-Kennedy advised the War Office that he had worked as Sikorski's assistant in Russia and would now like to build some Really Big Bombers for the British war effort, he was given both the benefit of any doubt and a degree of largesse. The outcome was the Kennedy Giant, a four-engined biplane with the designation 'No.3'. The reaction of our own big-bomber-builder, Frederick Handley Page, is unrecorded but if anybody could see through the sham that would unfold it would have

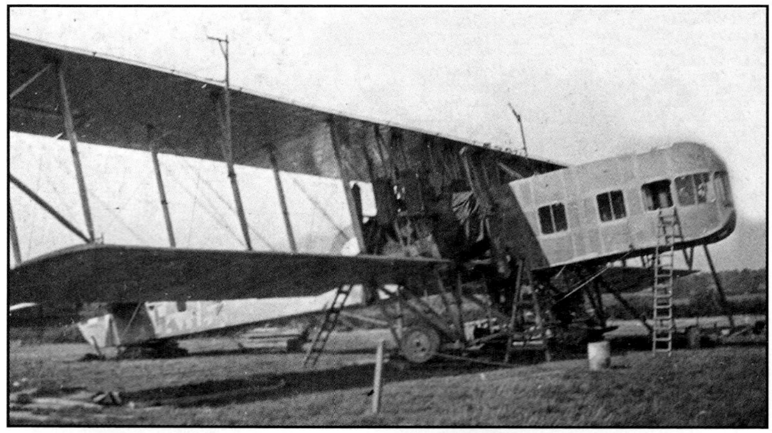

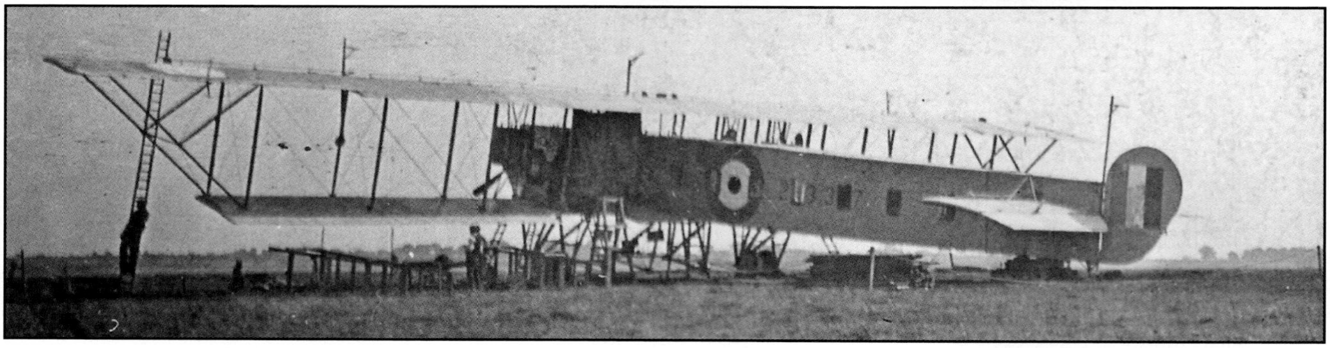

been he. The Giant was built at Hayes by The Gramophone Co Ltd (later to become EMI) and Fairey Aviation Ltd, two virtually adjacent sites. Because no hangar was large enough to accommodate it, erection took place in the open in a convenient corner of Northolt Aerodrome. The wingspan was 142 feet or half as much again as a Boeing 737-300 and the empty weight was 19,000 lbs. Early on it became obvious that the centre of gravity was in the wrong place, so the nose was extended bringing total length to 80 feet. Another change was made to the rudder, extending it above the fuselage top line, as seen here. Allocated the military serial 2337, the problem now was engines. The three rough snapshots seen here are rare survivors, the first showing the aircraft after that tail was enlarged but before the nose was lengthened: the assemblers have stored all their trestles and ladders under the lower wings. The designer wanted the latest and most powerful aircraft motors: the Air Ministry allocated him four 200 hp Salmson radials – puny power by any standards. With these the aircraft could barely drag itself forward. The second picture shows the engines installed while the third shows the installation of airspeed and drift calibration prior to flight. Various test pilots were asked to make that maiden flight: all discovered they had other pressing commitments. Finally Frank T Courtney was persuaded and in November 1917, a strong wind and frost-hardened ground suggested the moment was nigh. Clearly underpowered and with the Centre of Gravity still too far aft, a convenient bump in the ground tossed the lumbering Giant into the air for several yards. Courtney had had enough and closed the throttles, The Giant had, technically, flown. Returned to its parking patch, it stayed as a monument to folly for some years until weather and souvenir-gatherers reduced it to a rotten hulk which was burned on site about 1924. Courtney, one might suggest, had slain the Giant.

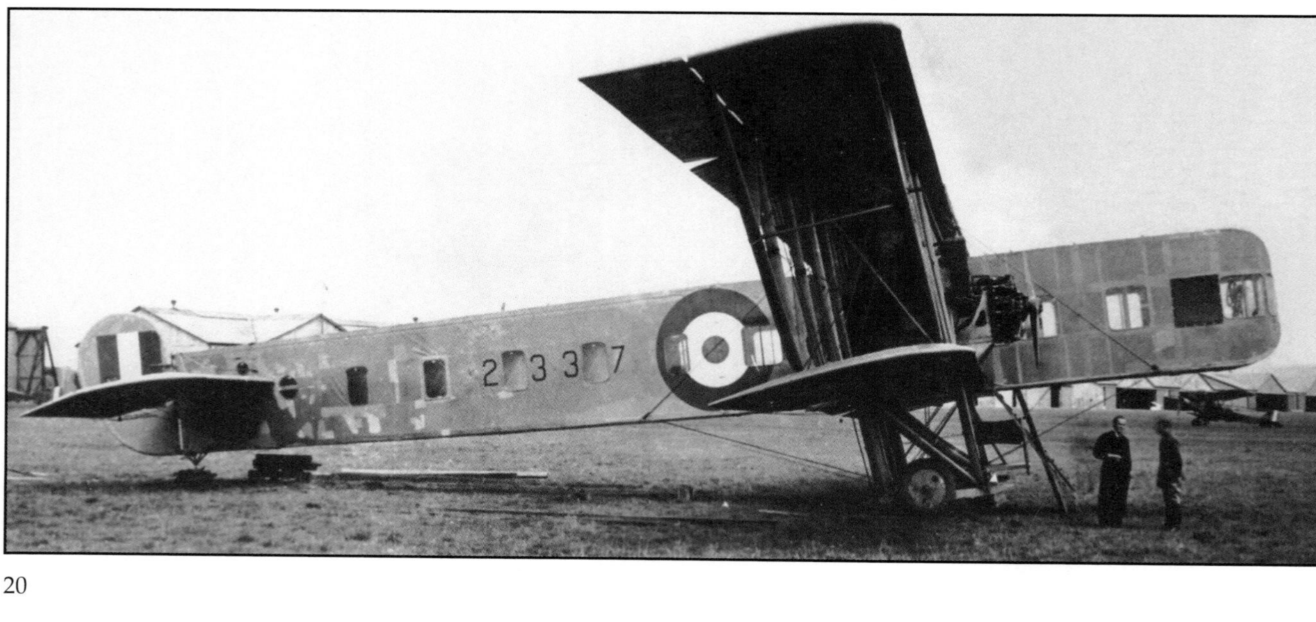

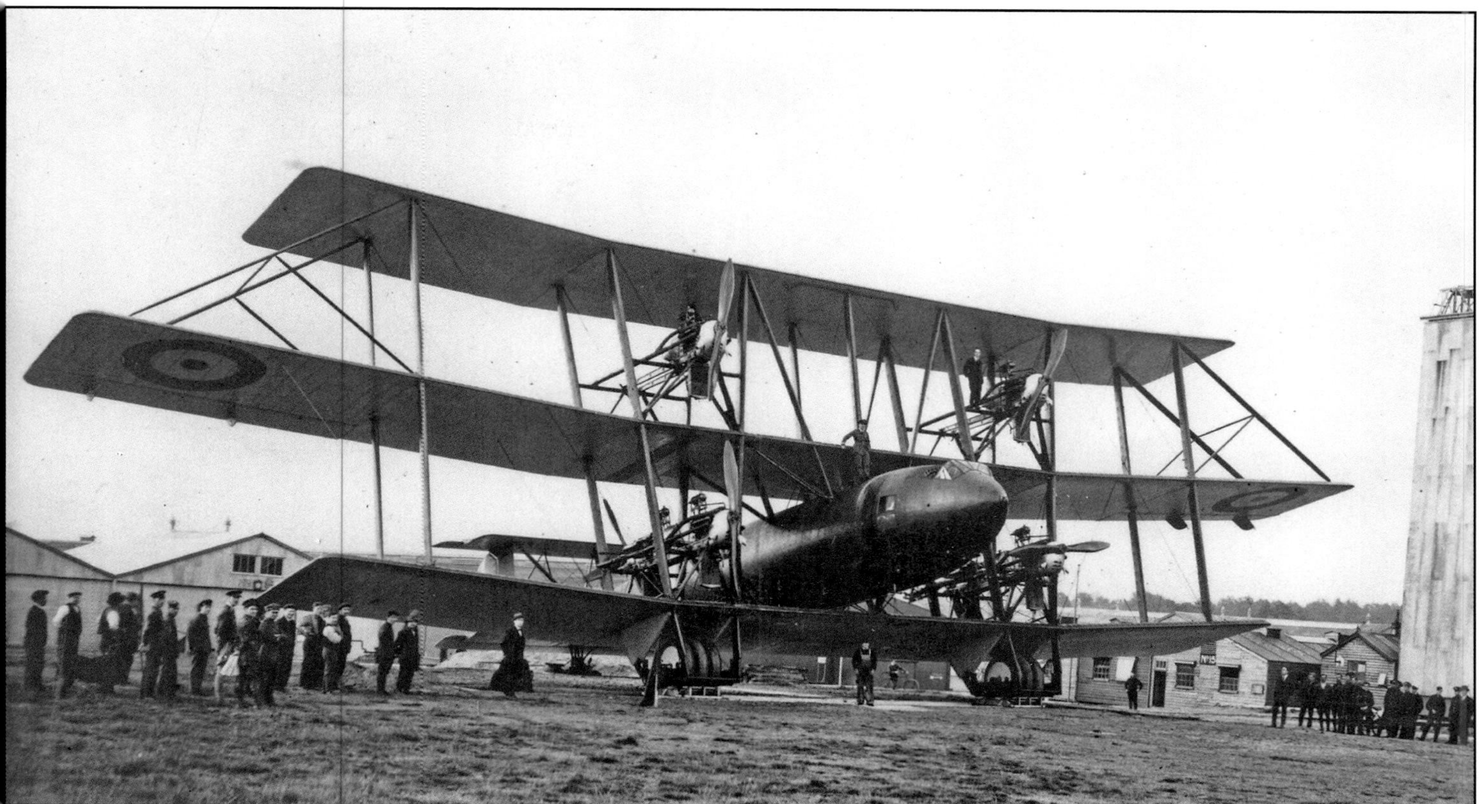

Resident in Byfleet, Surrey, Walter George Tarrant (1875-1942) was a master builder of quality houses. During the First World War he became interested in the conservation of material used in aircraft construction and patented a system of strut construction that used timber offcuts. Like Woking's great aircraft manufacturer Martinsyde, Tarrant championed the war effort and having met up with a young American-born designer, Walter Henry Barling (1890-1955) who was at the Royal Aircraft Factory, Farnborough, set about building a heavy long-distance bomber capable of attacking the Kaiser's heartland. The outcome was what, for its time, was the world's largest aircraft. Called the Tarrant Tabor and bearing the serial number F1765, completion of the aircraft took until the early summer of 1919. Intended as a four-engined sesquiplane having a 130 feet span top wing, it proved impossible to obtain the intended four Siddeley Tiger engines, each of 600 hp. Forced to use six Napier Lion engines each of 450 hp, a third wing was built to create a triplane. Four engines were arranged in back to back pairs (tractor-pusher) in the lower wing gap, and two tractors in the upper gap. With a central wingspan of a little over 130 feet, the height of the top wing above ground was 37 feet 3 inches. All-up weight was 45,000 lbs of which 9,000 lbs was available for passengers and cargo and 10,000 lbs for fuel. Tarrant had already recognised the civil potential of his aircraft and showed how range could be varied according to the number of people carried. Taken to Farnborough for assembly, on May 26th, 1919, Tabor was prepared for its first flight. Somebody from the RAE thought the Centre of Gravity was wrong and put 1,000 lb of lead in the nose without telling Tarrant or his team. Test pilot was to be Captain Frederick George 'Dusty' Dunn, AFC, with Captain Percy Townley-Rawlings, DSC, as co-pilot.

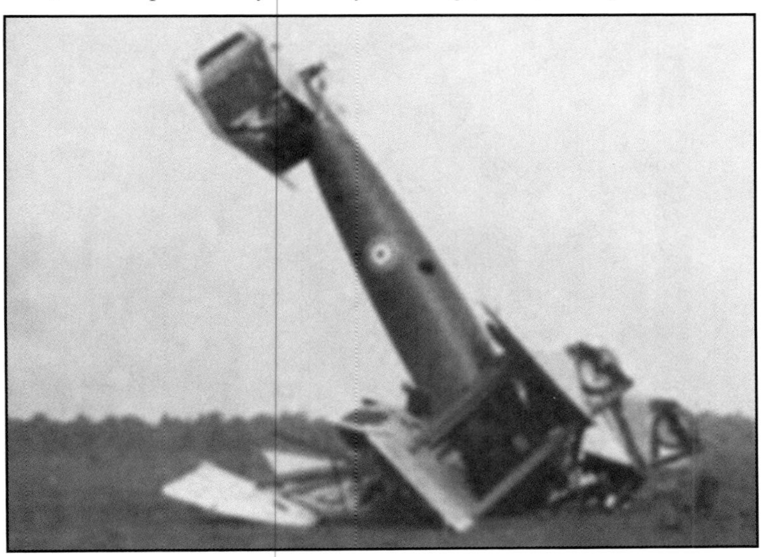

The Tabor was started up and began to taxi forward. To turn, the crew opened up the two top engines – and the aircraft immediately tipped up on its nose, crushing the cockpits. Pilot Townley-Rawlings was killed instantly, his companion Dunn died in hospital later that day. Tarrant's involvement with aircraft ceased henceforth. This rather poor snapshot of the Tarrant Tabor standing on the leading edge of its middle wing, fuselage nose crushed, marks the sad end not just of a project spoiled by officialdom but of two talented pilots.

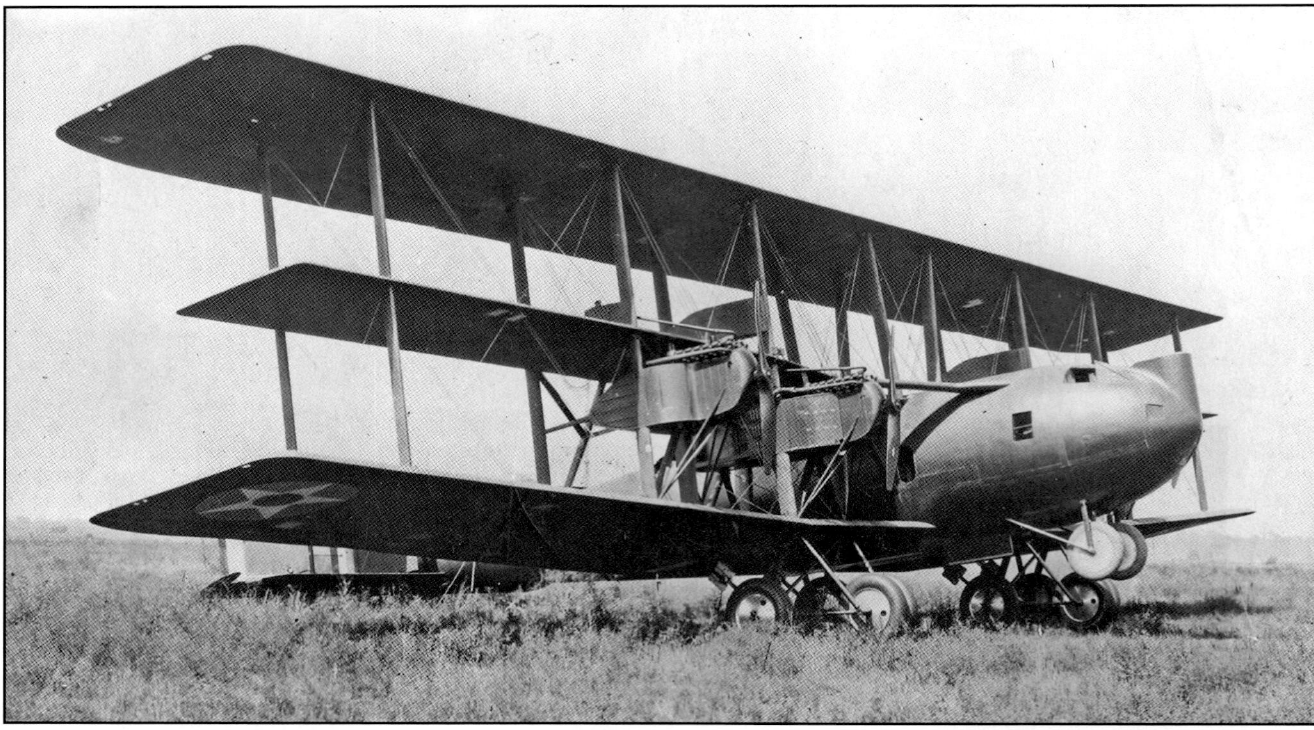

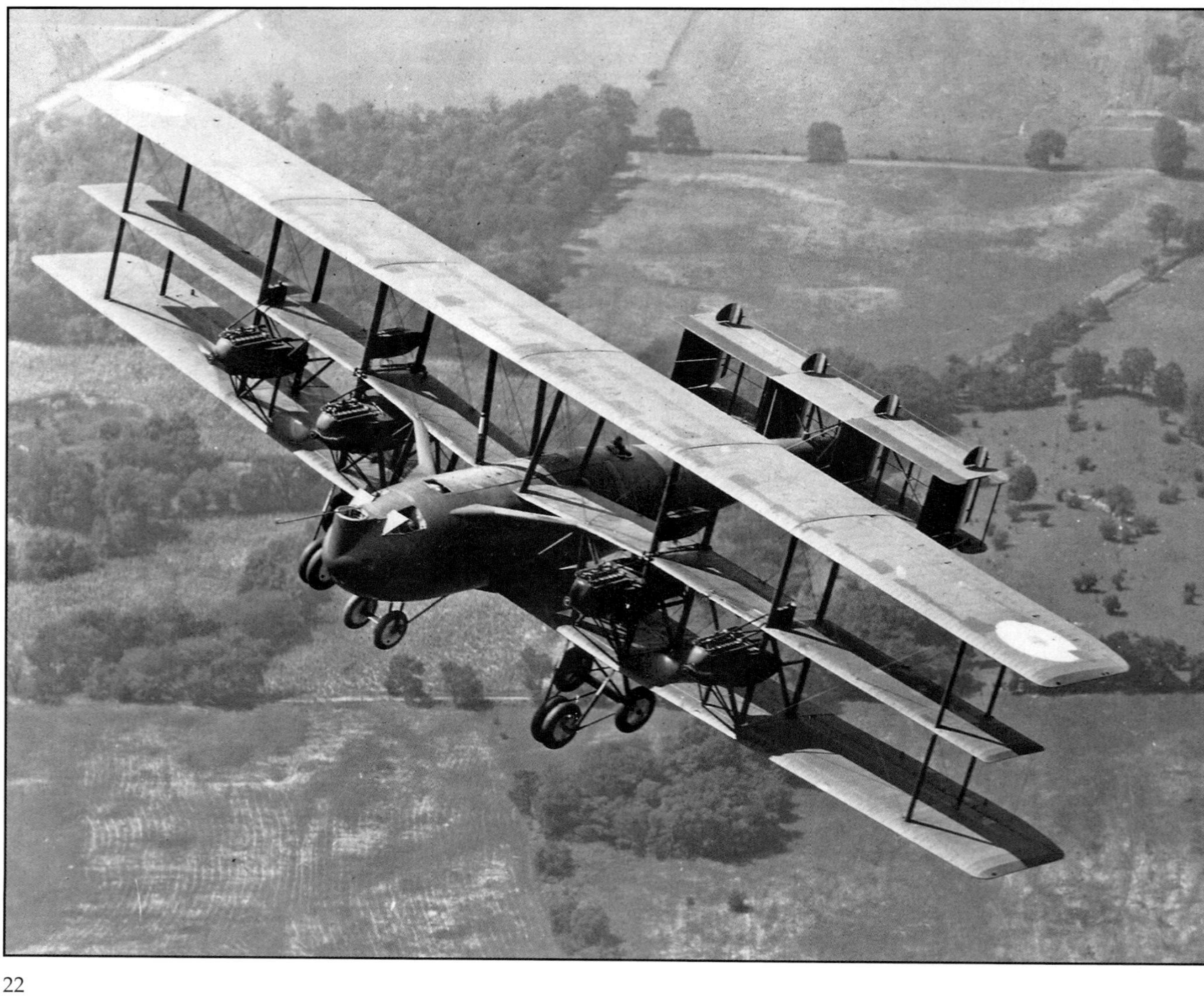

Opposite upper: After the fiasco of the Tarrant Tabor, victim of official incompetence and the sort of thinking that gave the less-respected Kennedy Biplane its fatuous piddle-powered engines, Walter Barling had had enough of both the Air Ministry and Farnborough and, sensing better opportunities abroad, went back to America where he joined the Wittemann-Lewis Aircraft Company, Inc, a business founded around 1920 by the son of a German émigré, Charles Rudolph Wittemann, and industrialist Samuel P Lewis. The mandate was to build a prototype experimental long-range heavy night bomber for the US Army Air Service. Called the Wittemann-Lewis XNBL-1 but popularly known as the Barling Bomber, it was the biggest aircraft in the world. Barling learned from the enforced mistakes made at Woking and Farnborough and designed the aircraft from the start as a triplane, the six engines mounted in four nacelles on the centre wing which would be of narrower chord than the upper and lower ones and, curiously, gull-shaped at the centre-section. Despite the planning, the Barling was destined to become America's 'white elephant'. Powered by six 420 hp Liberty L-12A engines, the 120 feet span triplane was 65 feet long and 27 feet high. The all-up weight was 42,560 lbs. On August 22nd, 1923, the giant made its first flight at Wilbur Wright Field, Dayton, Ohio. In command was Harold R Harris with co-pilot M S Fairchild. Flight engineer was Douglas Culver and Barling went along as passenger. The 28-minute flight revealed some depressing conclusions. The enormous aerodynamic drag of the all-silver-painted airframe with its 10-wheel undercarriage gave a top speed of just 96 mph. Worse, though, was the range – just 170 miles. The aircraft had cost $525,000 to build plus $700,000 for the hangar in which to keep it.

Opposite lower: How disappointed must the US authorities have been with the Barling Bomber. The press and popular magazines of the time had trumpeted its anticipated performance promoting it as having a 'cruising radius of 1,300 miles at over 100 mph' and adding that it was the world's largest and heaviest aircraft. It did have some novel features, one of which was that the incidence of the vast quadruple-finned biplane tail could be adjusted in flight from the cockpit. In its bombing configuration it was to have had its normal crew of two (pilot and co-pilot) increased to eight men. Its main public showing was at the St Louis Air Meet of 1923. It made brief news on September 18th, 1924. During a demonstration flight at Dayton, pilot Harris spotted a loose engine component that was gradually moving forward into the propeller. In the best tradition, engineer Culver climbed out onto the middle wing went to the recalcitrant engine and made a repair – all at 3,000 feet at 90 mph! But Barling's Big One was not fit for purpose, was quietly dismantled by 1928 and the parts dispersed before anybody could query the huge expense involved. And makers Wittemann-Lewis were ruined by the project, declared bankrupt in 1924.

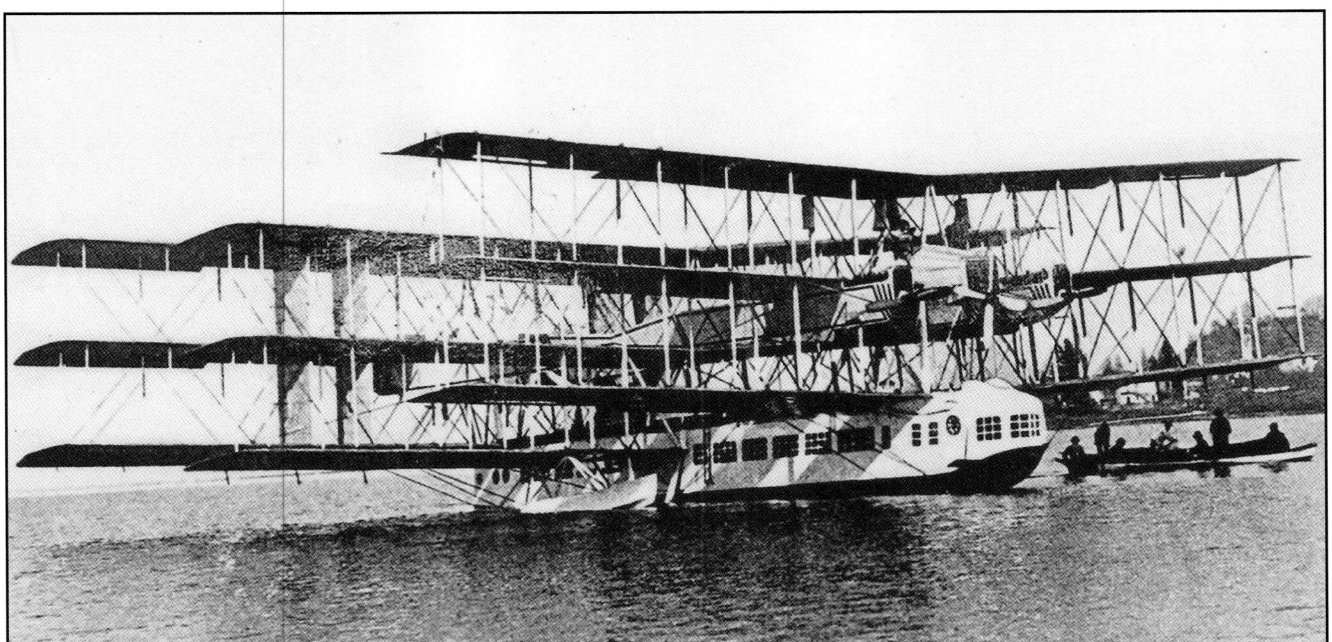

It is a well-established aerodynamic fact that wing-tips produce vortices in the air which reduce the efficiency of a straight wing by up to eight percent. The narrower the wing the less the effect and sweeping the wing back is even better. Today, the vortices are virtually eliminated by turning up the wing-tips as on the European Airbus. Biplanes in the past had to make the best of a bad job by combating what was called 'the biplane effect' where wings can interfere with each other. Mind you, short multiple wings make for extreme manoeuvrability as in the Sopwith and Fokker triplanes, but you wouldn't really want to go above three wings. Armstrong Whitworth did once make a quadruplane, but only once. So the question has to be whatever came over the talented Italian designer Gianni Caproni (1886-1957) when he created an eighteen-winged monster flying boat in 1921. It was intended as a 100-passenger long-range airliner to fly 100 passengers between Italy and America. With its three sets of triplane wings spanning 98 feet 5 inches, the Caproni Ca.6o Noviplane was 77 feet long, stood 30 feet high and weighed 55,000 lbs. Power was provided by eight 400 hp Liberty L-12 water-cooled V-12 engines which were estimated to give the aircraft a maximum speed of 100 mph. On March 4th, 1921, the Noviplano taxied out onto Lake Maggiore and began its take-off run. As the huge aircraft became airborne witnesses saw that there was no rigidity in the structure and that its wings were twisting relative to the fuselage. At a height of 60 feet it broke in two just ahead of the middle set of wings and crashed into the lake, fortunately without loss of life. The wreck was recovered and over the following year rebuilding was undertaken. Then there came a mysterious fire which completely destroyed the craft. *Un beneficio inaspettata*?

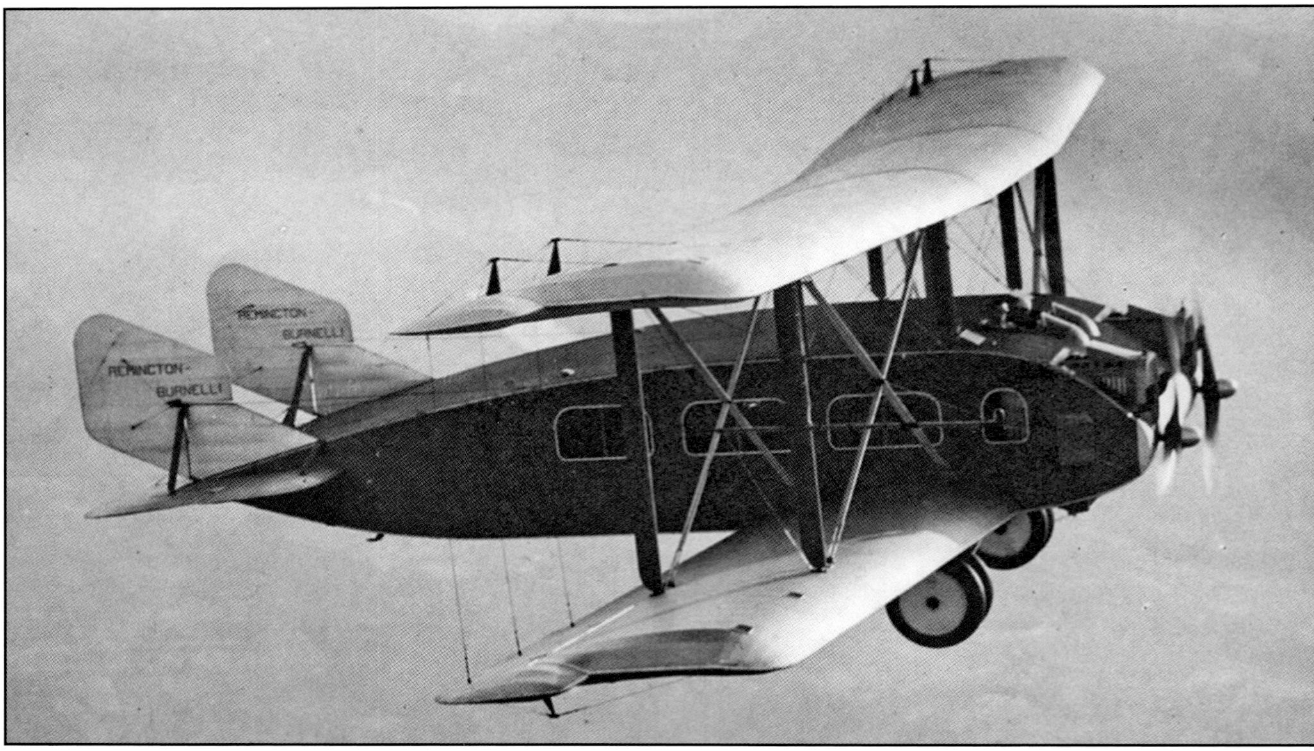

Some inventors have a dream that appears to offer untold benefits. The problem is that even if the dream works, there's always the chance that nobody else wants to share it. That, sadly, was the fate which befell Burnelli's 'lifting fuselage' airliner. Texas-born Vincent Justus Burnelli (1895-1964) spent his entire life trying to get people interested in what he called his flying-wing aircraft. The fuselage was a deep airfoil section having an engine at each front corner and a spacious cabin behind. Conventional outer wings and a tail carried on booms completed the ensemble. His first aircraft, pictured here, was called the Remington Burnelli RB-1 of 1920 and had a span of 74 feet and a length of 41 feet 2 inches. The cabin interior was 14 feet wide with seating for 30 passengers. Power came from two 400 hp Liberty XII engines side by side in the nose, pilot and co-pilot in side-by-side cockpits on top. Construction was undertaken by The Airliner Engineering Corporation of Amityville, Long Island.

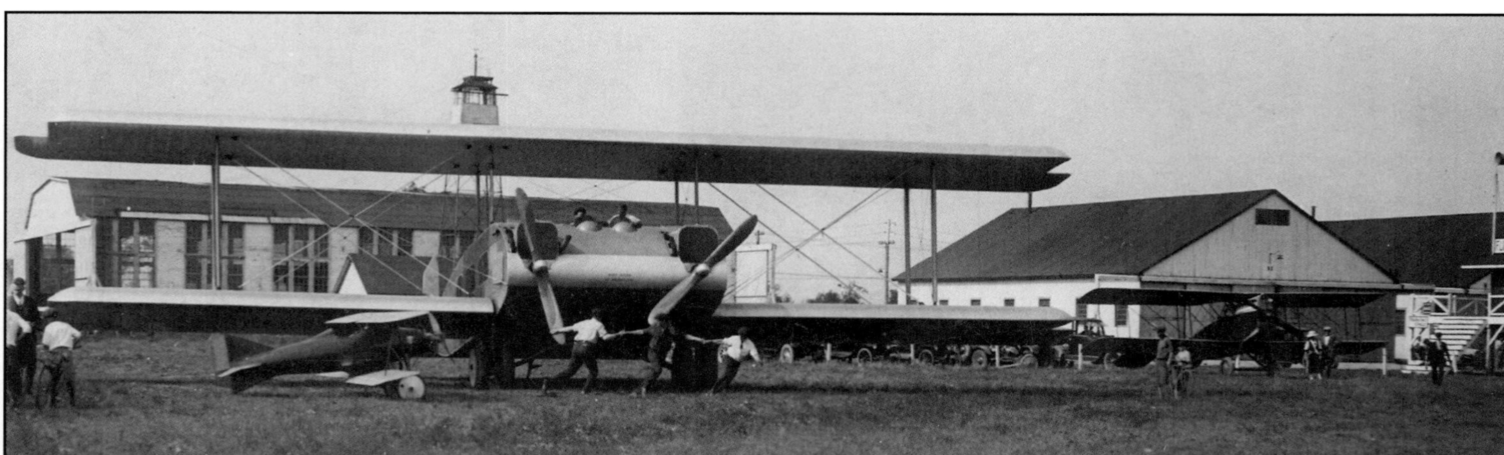

In this picture of the RB-1 standing with other aircraft, three men have joined hands to pull over the propeller of the starboard engine. The designer had patents on everything to do with his lifting-body principle and these, like Orville Wright, he guarded closely. It was said he avoided any opportunity to share his work with others, even shunning membership of the Aviation Manufacturers' Association. This, sadly, ensured he remained outside the mainstream US aviation industry and, some believe, led to government attitudes that ultimately killed off his brainchild. During a heavy storm off Staten Island in 1923, the RB-1 was destroyed by immersion in salt water. Its successor, the RB-2, was immediately distinguishable by having single mainwheels and a pair of 550 hp Galloway Atlantic engines. Improved control surfaces gave the new model a span of 80 feet and a passenger cabin 18 feet by 14 feet, the whole fuselage being alclad-covered instead of the RB-1's fabric covering. From this Burnelli made the CB-16, an executive monoplane airliner made for P W Chapman, chairman of US Lines. This all-metal machine was a true ground-breaker. It was the first multi-engined US aircraft capable of single-engined performance at its design gross weight and was also the first American twin to have a retractable undercarriage. It cost £230,000 but stalled on take-off in 1929 and crashed without injury.

Another aspect of the 1924 Remington-Burnelli revealing the slight sweep-back to the wings and the corrugated metal fuselage sides. The spacious windows of the passenger cabin are as large as those on a motor-coach and, of course, could be slid open by the occupants if required. It is also a sign of the times that even with so large an aircraft, nobody had yet thought of the benefits of providing a tailwheel. The thinking of the time was that a skid would help slow the aircraft down when landing, a valid excuse at a time when wheel-brakes for aircraft had not yet been adopted.

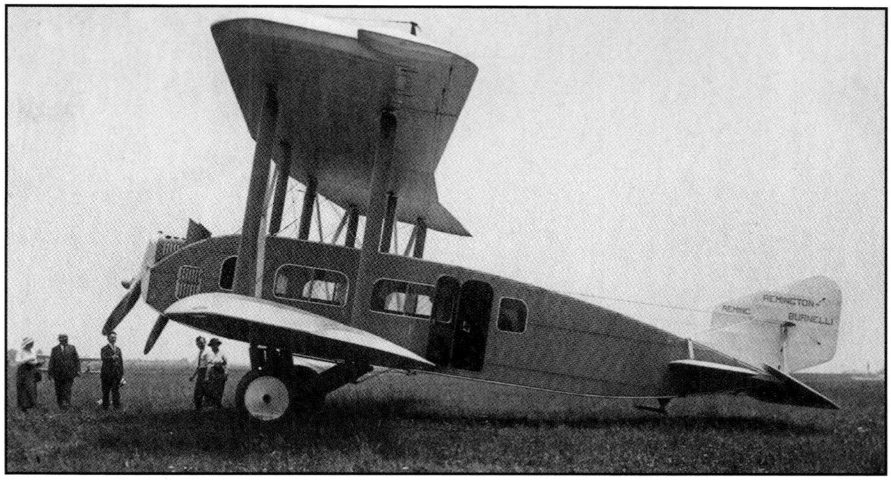

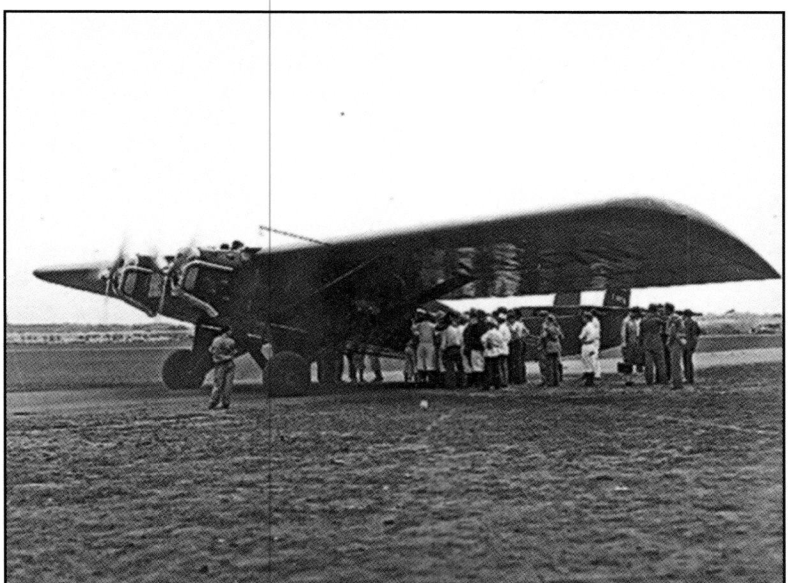

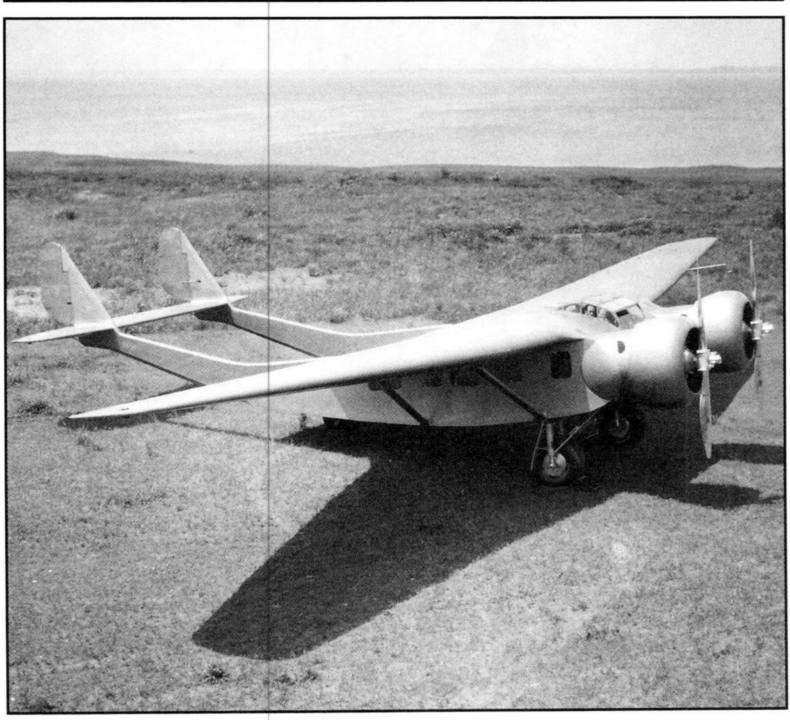

Burnelli had numerous business partners and backers: none seem to have stayed too long. One that did was the pioneer airline pilot and industrialist, Illinois-born Inglis Moore Uppercu (1877-1944). When Burnelli Aircraft Ltd of Keyport, New Jersey, produced a series of elegant transports aimed at the smaller airlines that needed quick-change freight capacity, the designation 'UB' revealed the two men's business relationship. Sequential numbering appears not to have been a company strongpoint: the first picture here shows the 16-passenger Burnelli UB-20, X397N, of 1930. It was the first US aircraft with stressed-skin covering and was powered by a pair of 750 hp Packard engines. It made history when it took part in a publicity stunt with the Sun Oil Company. A Ford car was fixed under the fuselage and then flown to great height whereupon a mechanic climbed down through a hole in the aircraft floor into the car and started the engine to prove something about the sponsor's oil. The second picture shows the UB.14 of a decade later before it was painted. First flown in 1940 as a 14-18-passenger, it was powered by two 340 hp Pratt & Whitney Wasp radials. The 71-foot span all-metal aircraft, X14740, flew extremely well and attracted the attention of Southampton-based British manufacturer Cunliffe-Owen which modified the design and built G-AFMB as the British Burnelli OA-1 15-seater powered by a pair of 710 hp Bristol Perseus XIVC radials. Meanwhile on January 13th 1935 the prototype UB-14 took off with crossed ailerons after maintenance, cartwheeled into the ground at an estimated 130 mph and was totally destroyed without rupturing fuel tanks or injuring the crew. A new model, called the UB-14A, was now built. Slightly smaller than its predecessor, X15320 had two 680/750 hp supercharged Hornet engines. Vincent Burnelli survived America's Great Depression, impressed a lot of people, but never sold an aeroplane. He would continue to promote his dream right up to his time of death. Charlatan or genius? Undoubtedly the latter as time has confirmed. His idea of a wide aerodynamic body re-emerged recently in the Sorrell SN-7 Hiperbipe homebuilt.

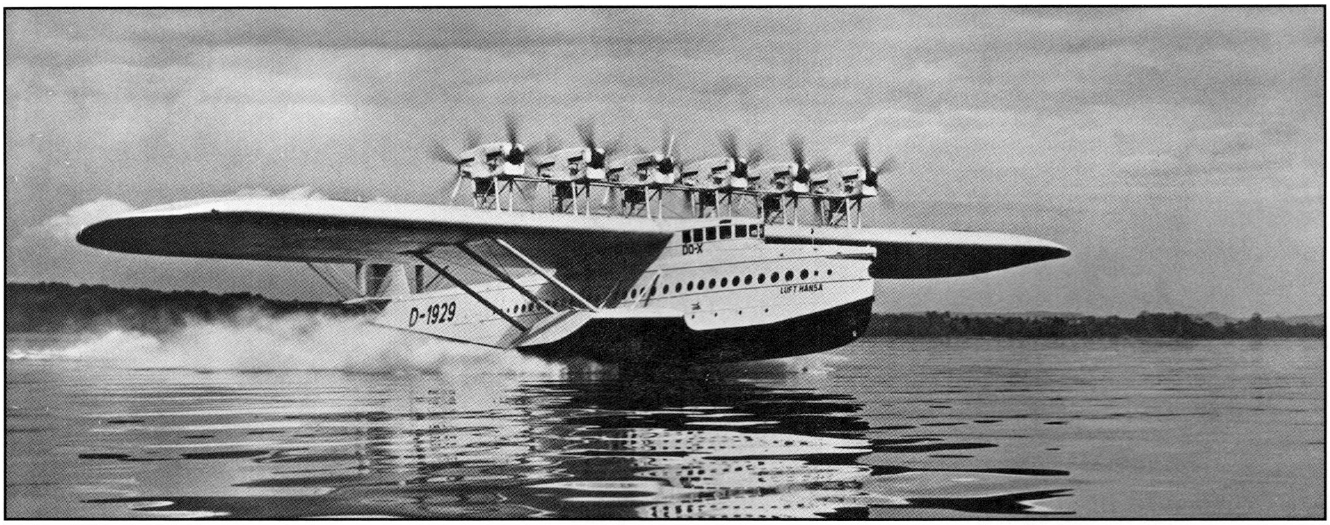

With the clarity of hindsight, the high-drag wrong-winged 12-engined Dornier Do.X flying boat was never going to succeed. But at the time design work on the great passenger transport began – 1925 – everything seemed possible, especially to designer Claude Honoré Desiré Dornier (1884-1949). After four years in the making, his massive transatlantic hopeful was ready for trials. With a crew that varied between 10 and 14 and, depending on fuel load, between 66 and 100 passengers, it was the largest and most powerful flying boat in the world. At 46 tons it was also the heaviest. Power came from a dozen Bristol Jupiter radial engines, each developing 435/580 hp, six as tractors and six as pushers in wing-top nacelles. The Dornier Do.X had a huge hull and a vast high-drag wing of 157 feet 5 inches span and 30 feet chord. This gave a wing area of 4,844 square feet and, crucially, an aspect ratio of just 5.25. The first flight was on the 12th of July, 1929. Tests showed that it could only reach 1,500 feet maximum ceiling. Changing the engines to the 640 hp Curtiss Conquerer 12-cylinder inlines allowed the maximum operating ceiling to soar to 1,650 feet! The tests were impeded by a number of minor mishaps and technical problems: a demonstration visit to Southampton was a day late. Then came the ultimate test – a flight from Friedrichshafen to New York. It was a fiasco! The mechanical hold-ups and mishaps *en route* took it beyond a joke. The elapsed time for the flight was nine months! Three Do.X aircraft were built, none was a success. But everybody remembers Dornier's 'Howard Hughes' moment!

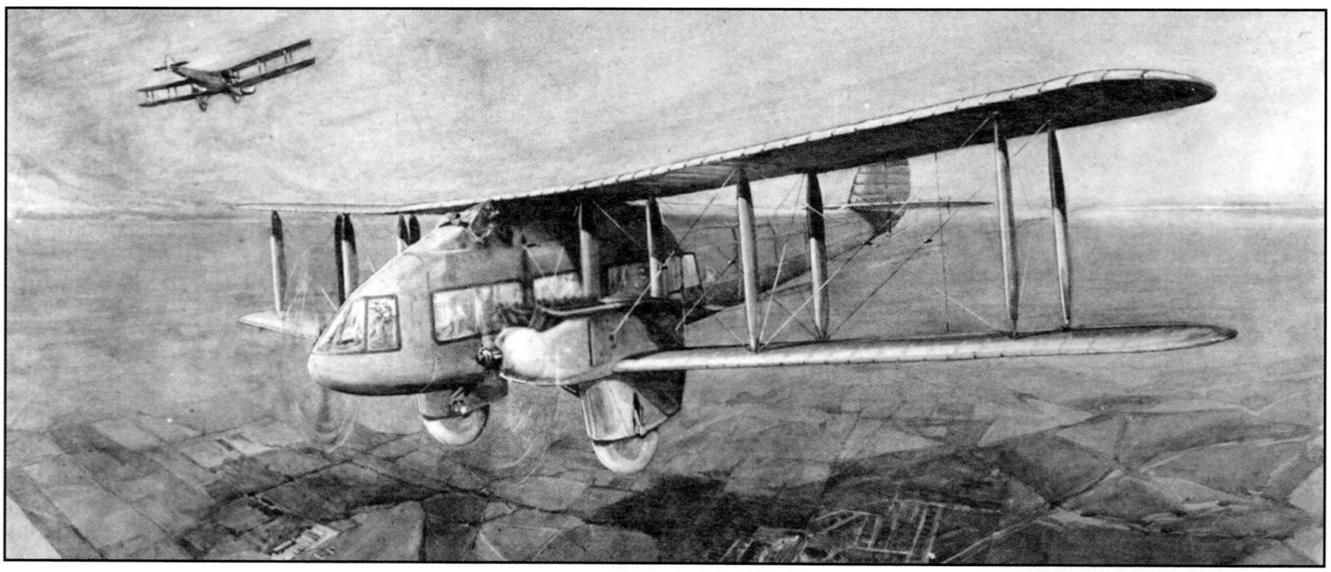

An ancient Arabic proverb says that 'with one eye on the past you can clearly see the future, but with no sight of the past, the future is a blur'. This has a relevance to this artist's sketch produced in 1922. Newspaper magnate George Holt Thomas (1869-1929) was the man who saw a future in aviation long before anybody else in Britain. His bold decision to form The Aeroplane Supply Company in 1911 led to the creation of The Aircraft Manufacturing Company in June 1912, a business that became universally known as 'Airco'. With Geoffrey de Havilland as designer, this in turn 'morphed' into The De Havilland Aircraft Company Limited at Stag Lane Aerodrome. Holt Thomas (who meanwhile had opened the airline Air Transport & Travel Ltd, founded in October 1916) saw that the end of the First World War created a vacuum in aircraft demands. Nobody wanted new designs and, after rejection of numerous ideas, he sold Airco to Birmingham Small Arms Ltd (BSA) in 1919. Geoffrey de Havilland, seeing no interest in aviation at BSA, founded his eponymous company on September 25th 1920 with partial backing from Holt Thomas. It was a long struggle to make ends meet and, as before, projects came and went. In 1922 de Havilland schemed out a comfortable twin-engined cabin biplane airliner having a trousered undercarriage. It was annotated 'Airco 17', a curious title seeing as how Airco was long-disbanded. It was merely a project and one never built. When, in 1932, Edward Hillman wanted an economy airliner, the DH.84 emerged with more than passing resemblance to the project of a decade earlier. And the DH.89 was even more like this old sketch from the early days of struggle at Stag Lane.

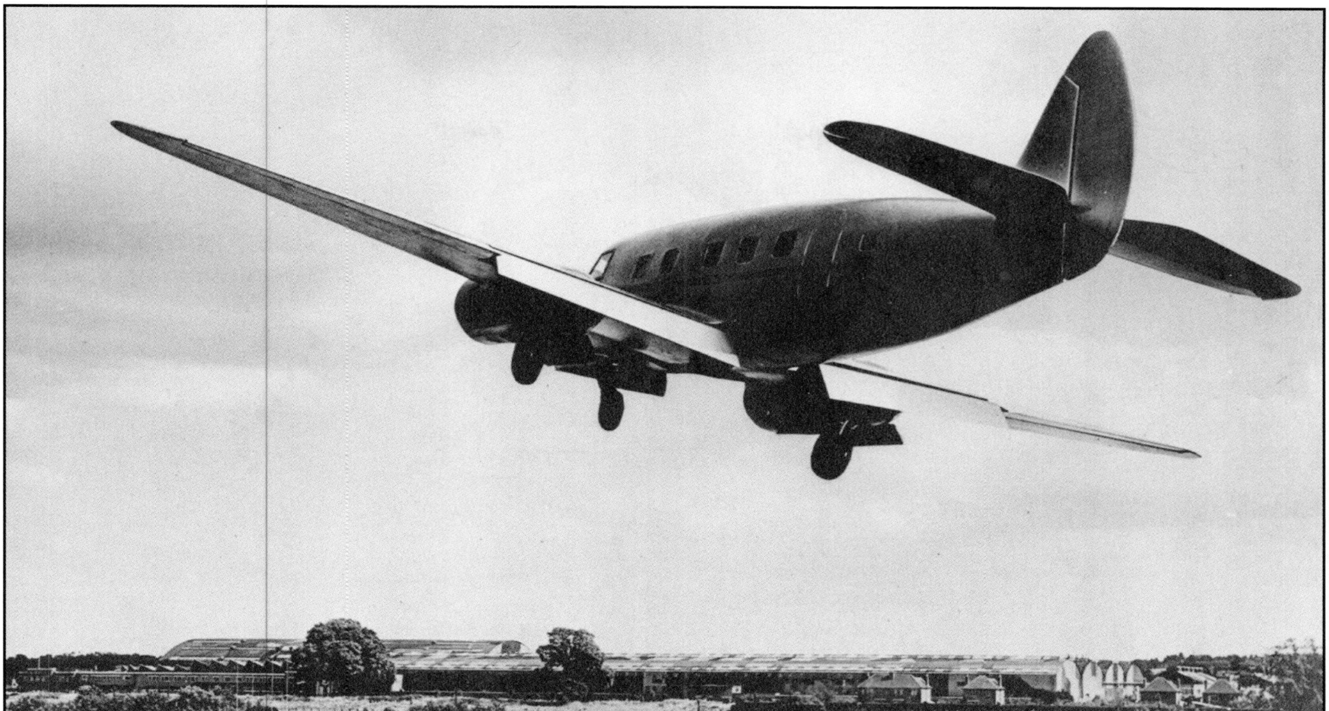

William Garrow-Fisher was 40 years old when he designed the Concordia airliner for Cunliffe-Owen Aircraft Ltd of Southampton. He had been chief technician of the ill-fated Scottish Aircraft & Engineering Company formed before the war to create a Clydeside aviation industry and produce, among others, the Kay Gyroplane. Sir Hugo Cunliffe-Owen (who died aged 77 in 1947) had built the British Burnelli OA-1 in 1938 for which American ace stunt flyer Clyde Pangborn (1895-1958) had been employed as test pilot: he would become the company's post-war test pilot. As it was, test pilot Aubrey Corbin made the prototype's first flight on May 19th, 1947. The Concordia with its two 550 hp Alvis Leonides radial engines was a medium-range 10-seat airliner competing in a market overrun with cheap Government surplus Dragon Rapides (Dominies), Douglas Dakotas, Avro Ansons and bigger Yorks and Lancastrians – all proven types. It was not an auspicious time for our aviation industry, the spectacular thing being its corporate inability to identify market trends and needs. The managing director was Marcus James Henry Bruce (1890-1956). There was nothing wrong with the Concordia, two of which were built, but it was the wrong aeroplane for its time.

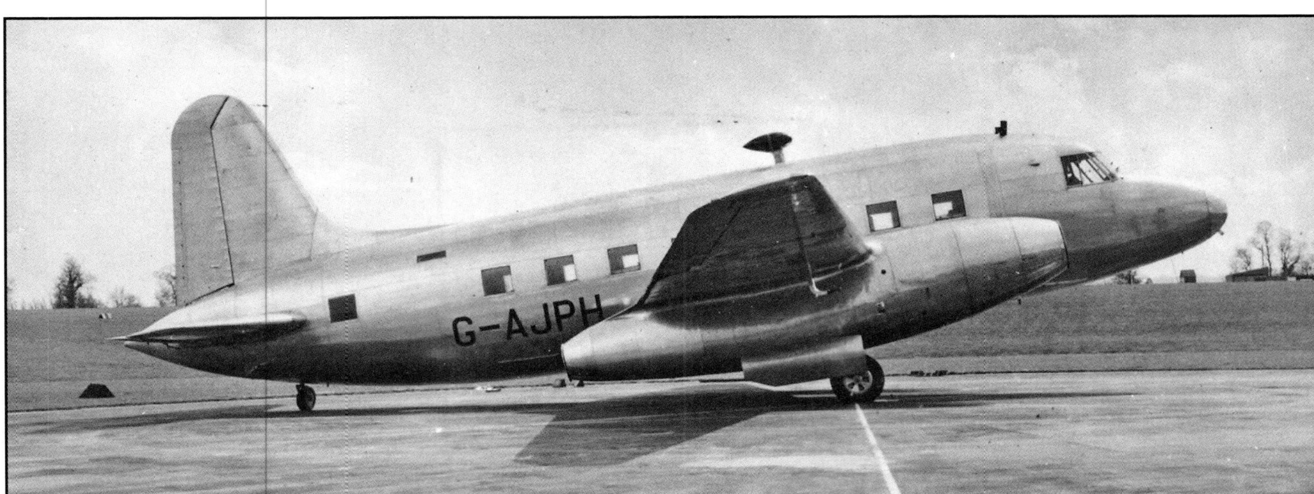

The first post-war British airliner to enter service, the Vickers Viking was also the first ever to be built in large quantity. It was also the last aircraft to be designed by Vickers' veteran designer, Reginald 'Rex' Kirshaw Pierson (1891-1948). The prototype was flown by J 'Mutt' Summers on June 22nd, 1945, at Wisley. By the time production ceased at the end of 1947, more than 160 had been delivered. The 107th airframe was built to a Ministry of Supply order as a test-bed for the Rolls-Royce Nene turbojet. Claimed to be the first British pure-jet transport, G-AJPH also bore the serial number VX856 and made its maiden flight at Wisley in the hands of Summers on April 6th 1948. With seating capacity for 24 passengers, the Nene Viking set up a new record, flying from Heathrow to Villacoublay in 34 minutes 7 seconds to mark the 39th anniversary of Blériot's Channel crossing on July 25th, 1948. Later reinstated as a standard Mk.1B, it was used by Eagle Airways for trooping until being scrapped at Blackbushe in September 1962.

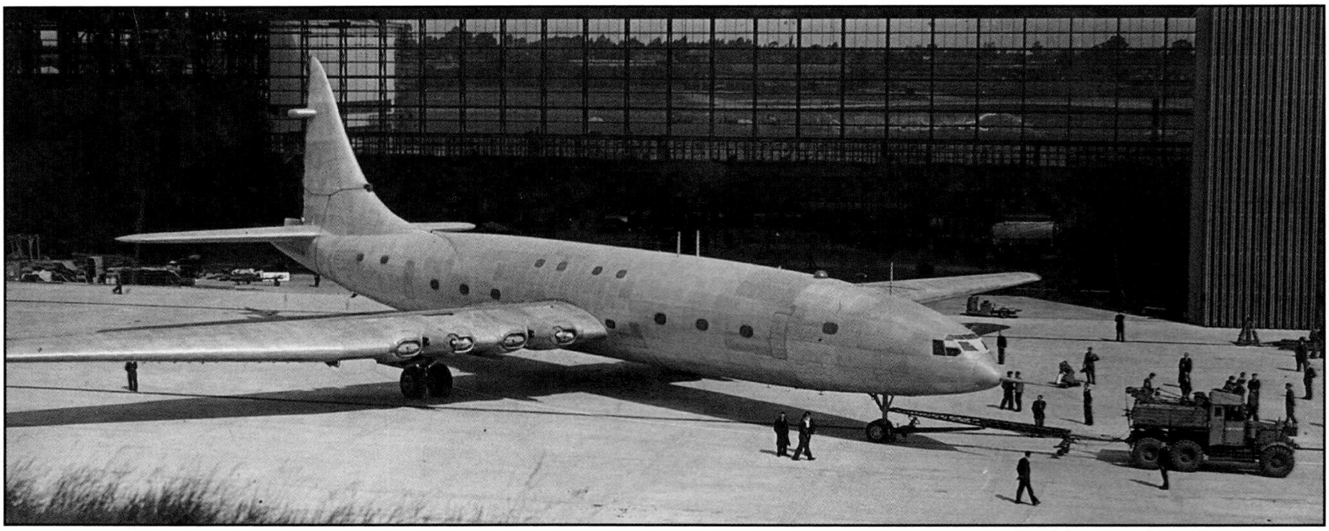

Mention of the TSR-2 and the Bristol Brabazon tends to remind many of the unenlightened days of Duncan Sandys when he was Minister of Supply. While the TSR-2 was a political pawn, the Brabazon was in a wholly different class. The Brabazon Committee had specified the requirements for post-war civil airliners as early as 1943 so the first problem was that Bristol's Type 167 was the product of a mixture of pre-war thinking, post-war postulating and civil transport needs honed in HP.42 biplanes and Short S.25 flying boats. Designed by Leslie G Frise and A E Russell, the machine was big in every respect. For a start, the 25 feet diameter fuselage was larger than most present-day Boeing airliners so as to accommodate berths, lounge, dining room and even a cinema for the spacious patronage of the total complement of just 100 passengers. Not for these the rigours of the 'economy seat'! Here, on August 18th, 1948, it is rolled out, sans tail surfaces and engines, to undergo fuel-flow trials. Behind is the huge hangar that had to be built to house it while the 8,000 feet long runway ploughed straight through the village of Charlton the residents of which had, expensively, to be 'relocated'. Brabazon was 177 feet long and stood 50 feet high. With a maximum take-off weight of 290,000 lbs, it was to have an initial rate of climb of just 750 feet/minute and cruise at 25,000 feet of 300 mph.

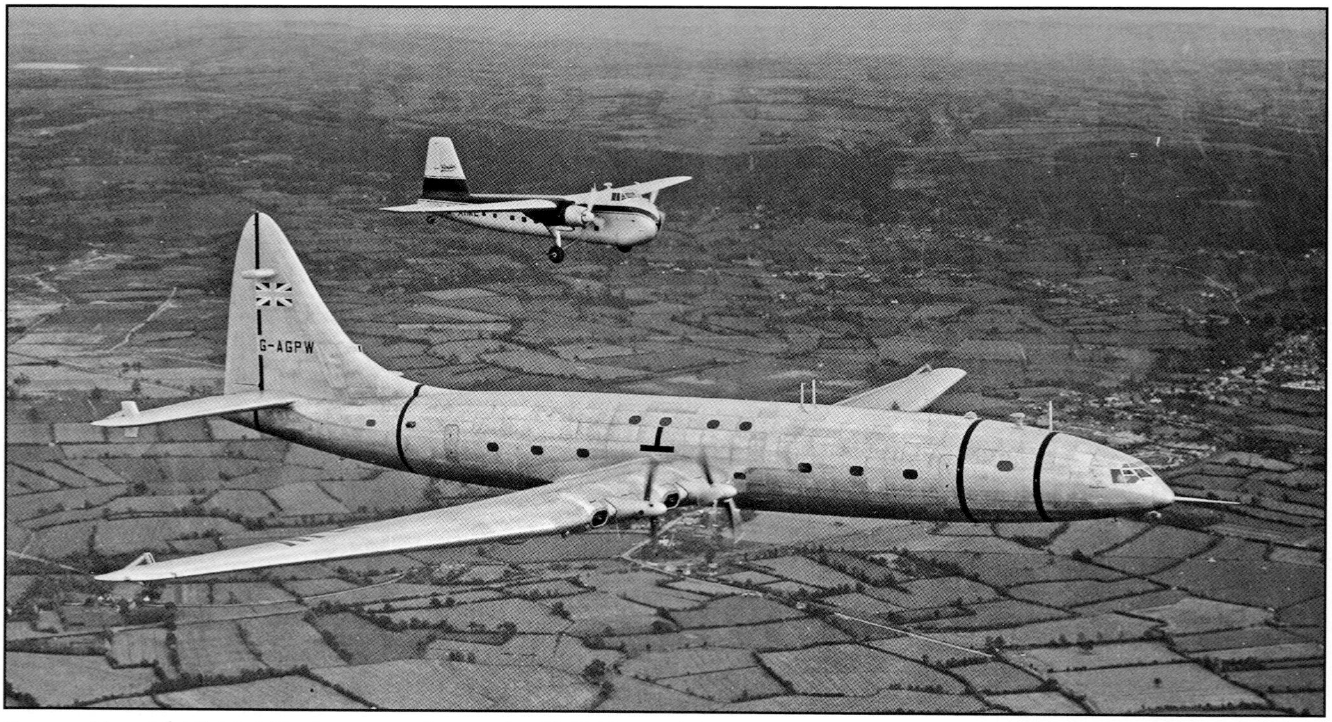

Powered by eight Bristol Centaurus engines each of 2,500 hp and driving four pairs of contra-rotating airscrews, the Brabazon was hampered by being not just obsolescent but obsolete by the time of its first flight. As G-AGPW and commanded by test pilot Arthur John 'Bill' Pegg (1906-1978), the 230 feet span monster lumbered into the air on September 4th, 1949. It pioneered a number of new technologies and manufacturing process, not the least of which was the extensive use of power-assisted controls. The problem was that it was too large and carried too few passengers too slowly to be economical. On July 17th, 1953, Sandys announced in the Commons that, having spent well in excess of £3.4m on it, it would be axed forthwith. After 164 flights totalling 382 flying hours, G-AGPW was cut up for scrap by R J Coley & Co of Hounslow. A second example, G-AIML (which was to have been the Mk.II with Proteus turboprops), was also cut up when only half-completed.

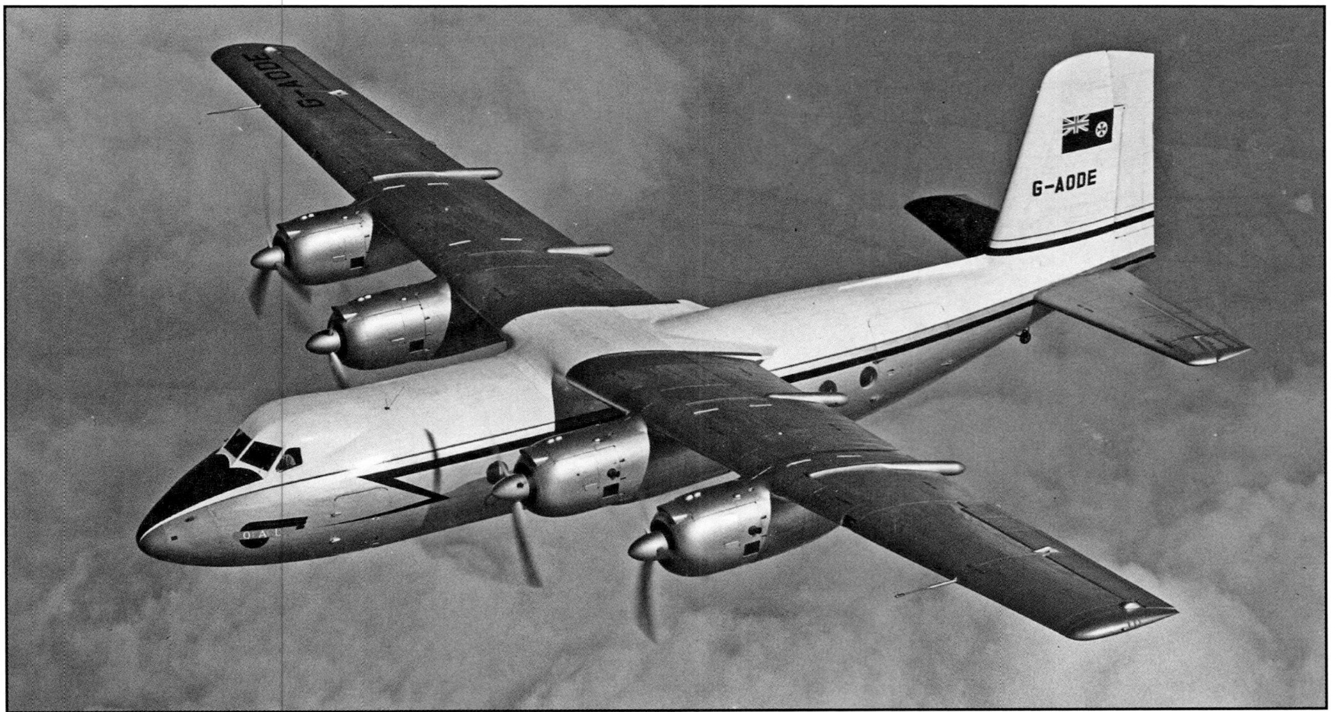

The original Handley Page Herald is a curiosity if only because it was ill-conceived. Edwin W J Gray was in charge of design at the Reading office – the former Miles Aircraft which HP acquired in 1947. It was here that he designed the HPR.7 as a four-engined passenger transport powered by four Alvis Leonides Major radials. The debate started almost immediately because these engines were only known as helicopter engines and they had not been used in a fixed-wing machine before. In due course, G-AODE the prototype was first-flown at Radlett on August 25th, 1955, and the following month shown at Farnborough. A production batch of 25 aircraft was laid down but despite demonstration flights, the Herald was not attracting customers. Speaking confidentially to a small group at the Royal Aero Club, I avowed that the Herald would remain a white elephant until re-engined with a pair of the turbo-prop engines then making a name for themselves in the new Vickers Viscount. By a coincidence, within a year G-AODE had been withdrawn to emerge in March 1958 with two Rolls-Royce Dart 527 turbo-props! G-AODE now garnered the long-awaited orders and became a reasonable success with 52 machines being built.

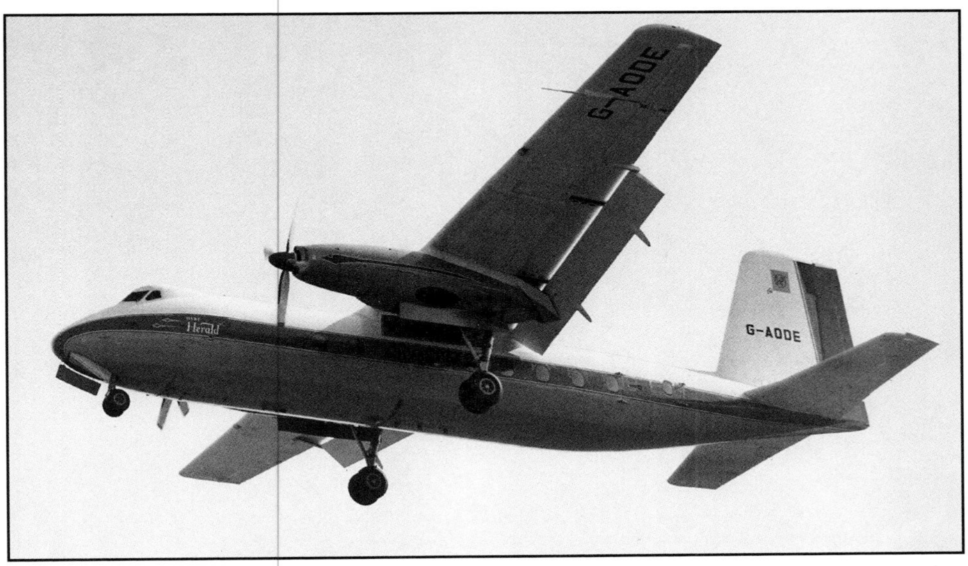

A projected 25-strong production batch of Leonides-powered HPR.4 Heralds was cancelled as it became obvious even to the most staunch supporter of piston power that the rival Dart-engined Vickers Viscount was not only an outstanding success but that it pointed the way to the future. G-AODE was grounded and modified to take a pair of 2,105 ehp Dart 527 turboprops. Like all major revamps, there's always the inbuilt resistance to the real solution – scrap what you've got and start again. The Herald mods resulted in a bit of a hotch-potch aeroplane, albeit a successful one. The new engines had to be mounted some 30 inches outboard of the original inboard piston engines which themselves were part of the undercarriage fairings. By leaving the wheels where they were, the new engine position resulted in a curiously joggled head-on view. The aerodynamics were upset as well, the tailplane requiring an inverted leading-edge slot. The fuselage was 20 inches longer and the huge fin and rudder required a large dorsal fin on top of the rear fuselage. But the Dart Herald was a success and over fifty were built. First flown in this configuration on March 11th, 1958, this picture shows G-AODE before the dorsal fin was fitted. The venerable prototype, however, came to a sticky end when test pilot Hedley George Hazelden (1915-2001) experienced engine failure and in-flight fire. An amazing forced-landing in a field at Milford near Godalming in Surrey on August 30th, 1958. 'Hazel' and his crew escaped but the venerable 'ODE was burned out. They had been *en route* to the Farnborough SBAC Show.

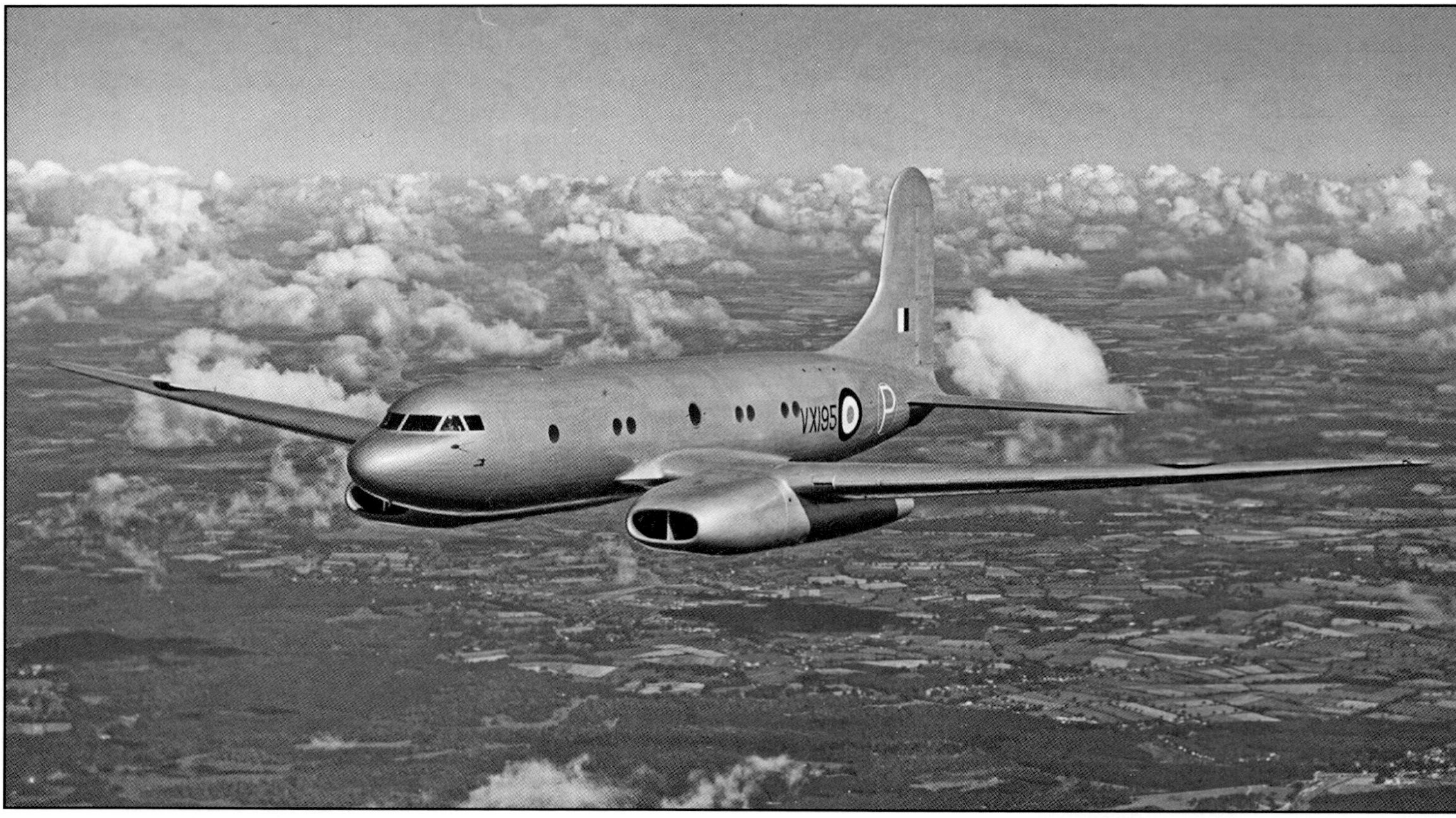

Most people believe that the Comet was the world's first four-jet airliner but it was preceded by almost a year by Avro's Tudor Mk.8. This made its maiden flight at Woodford, Cheshire, on September 6th, 1948 in the hands of Avro chief test pilot Joseph Harold 'Jimmy' Orrell. The aircraft was actually the second prototype Tudor Mk.1, VX195, rebuilt to Mk.4 standard and then fitted with four Rolls-Royce Nene engines. This gave it a cruising speed at 25,000 feet of 350 mph. The Comet, by comparison, first flew on July 27th, 1949. In fairness, this was the first aircraft designed solely as a jet while the Tudor 8 was a case of 'new wine in old bottles'. As for the Comet, that was the first-ever pure jet airliner assembled using Redux bonding where metal is glued to metal with a special resin.

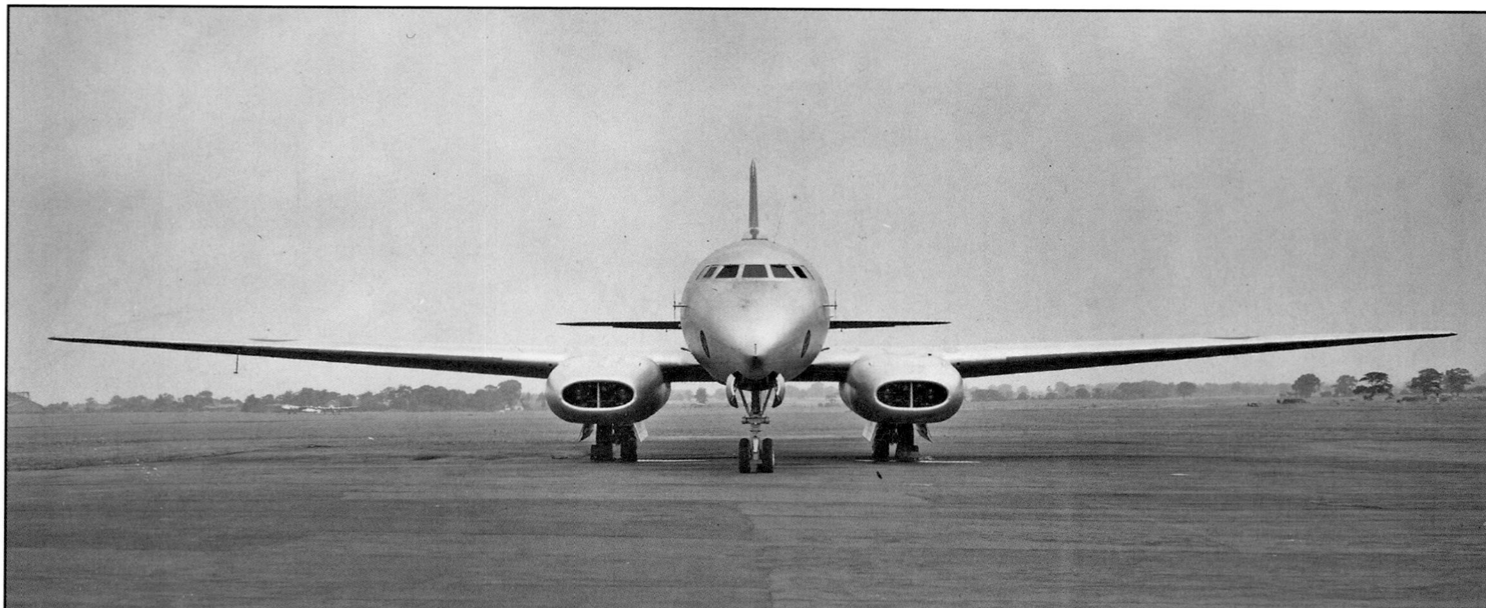

The Avro Tudor 8 trials spurred a final development of the airframe called the Avro 706 Ashton. The main difference was that a tricycle undercarriage was fitted to keep the jet pipes from blasting any runway dirt which could be deflected into the tailplane. Power came from four paired Rolls-Royce Nene jet engines. First flown on September 1st, 1950, WB450 was demonstrated at that month's Farnborough Air Show.

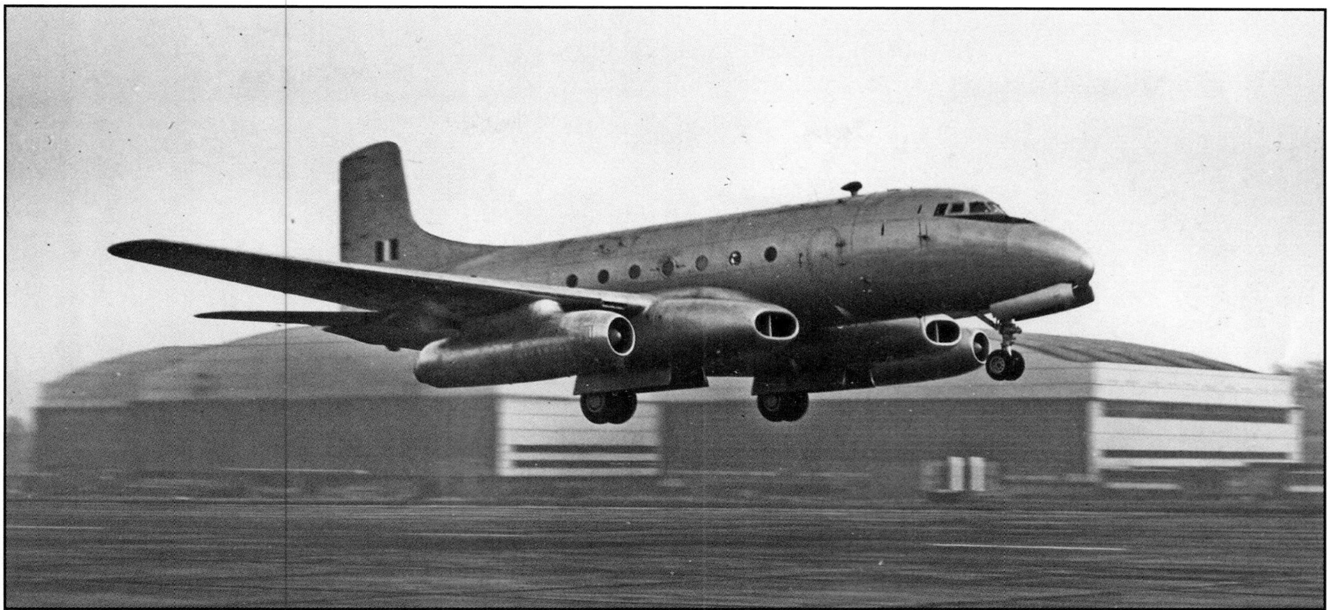

Several variants of the Ashton were built including this, the six-engined Ashton Mk.3. Originally with just four engines like the Mk.1, it was first flown on December 18th, 1951 but in 1955 went to the Bristol Engine Co as a test-bed for advanced makes of re-heat Bristol Olympus turbojets. These were mounted in under-wing nacelles outboard of the main Nene engines.

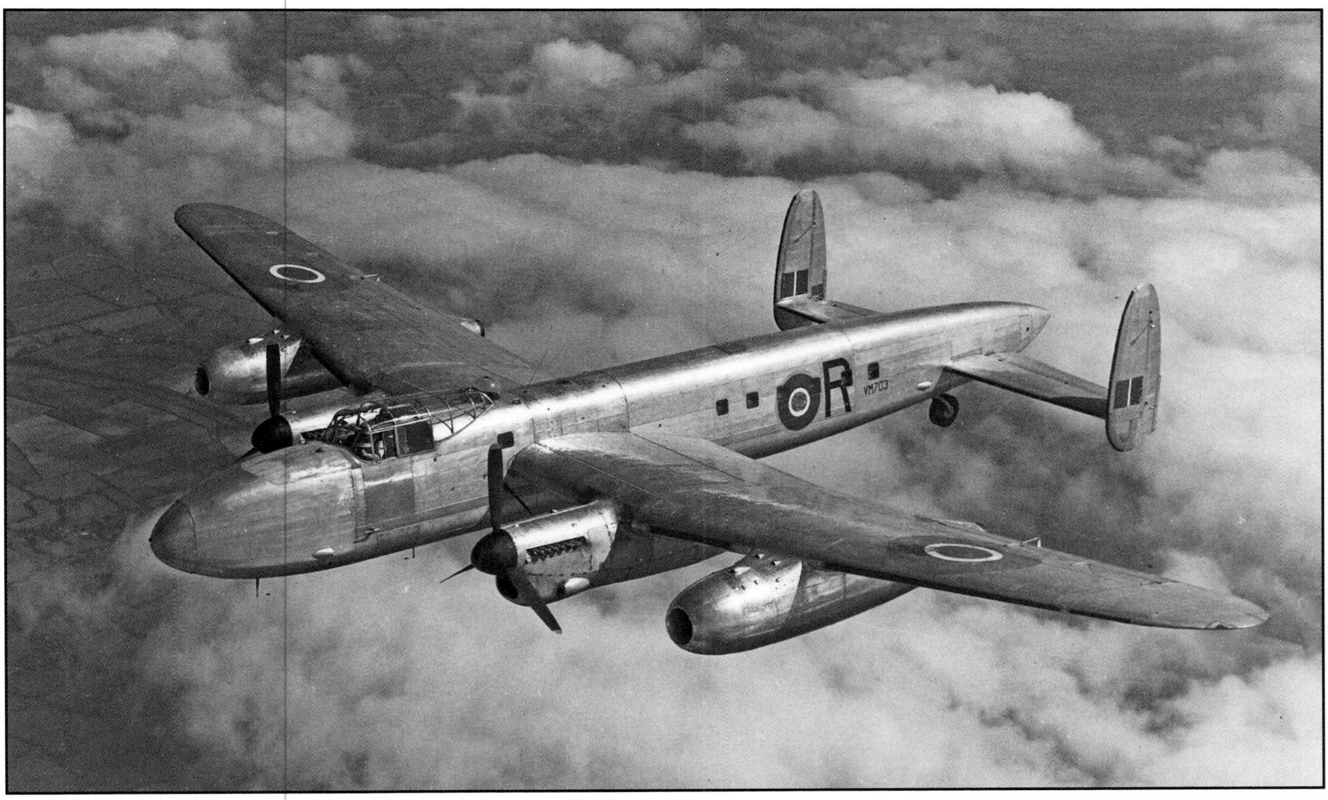

The Avro Lancastrian transport was a civilian conversion of the Lancaster bomber and a large number entered service with the re-establishing of airline and transport operations in 1945. This was the time when increasingly large gas turbine engines were being developed and these had to be air-tested. The Lancastrian was a 'safe' choice for conversion and a surplus Mk.1 aircraft was modified by Rolls-Royce at Hucknall. The first installation was in VH742 with a pair of 5,000 lb static thrust Nene 1 turbojets replacing the outer engines. The second conversion, seen here, used a Lancastrian C. Mk.2 to take a pair of de Havilland Ghost engines. The conversion was undertaken at Hatfield to drawings provided by Rolls-Royce. Because of the larger Ghost nacelles, there had to be a reduction in both aileron and flap area. This was first flown on July 24th, 1947, by John Cunningham and C D Beaumont of the DH Engine Division. There were numerous Lancastrian conversions like this including one with Armstrong Siddeley Sapphire engines. Always the showpiece at SBAC exhibitions, the propellers were feathered for a 'pure jet' flypast.

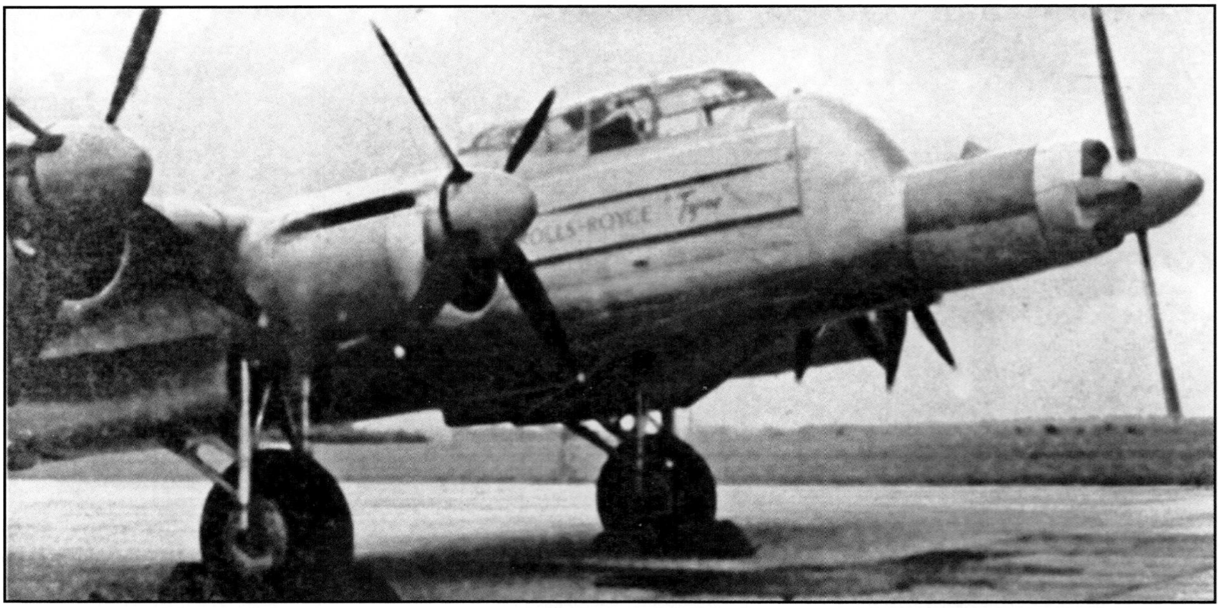

Long before board games encouraged an awareness of trivia and ages before 'pub quizzes', old flyers (and some young spotters) used to play a game which went something like this. 'How many engines has a Dakota?' (answer three); 'How many engines has a Junkers Ju/52?' (answer one, two or three). 'How many engines has a Piper Cub?' (answers eight or, for a better score, ten). 'How many engines has a Lancaster?' (answers three, four, five or, if you feel really mean, six). Yes, these were games aimed at those who were up to speed on the latest conversions and flying test-beds both at home and in America's sometimes eccentric 'Experimental' category. Here's one of those long-forgotten subjects – the five-engined Avro Lincoln B.2, G-37-1. Formerly four-engined RF530, this became the Rolls-Royce Tyne flying test-bed.

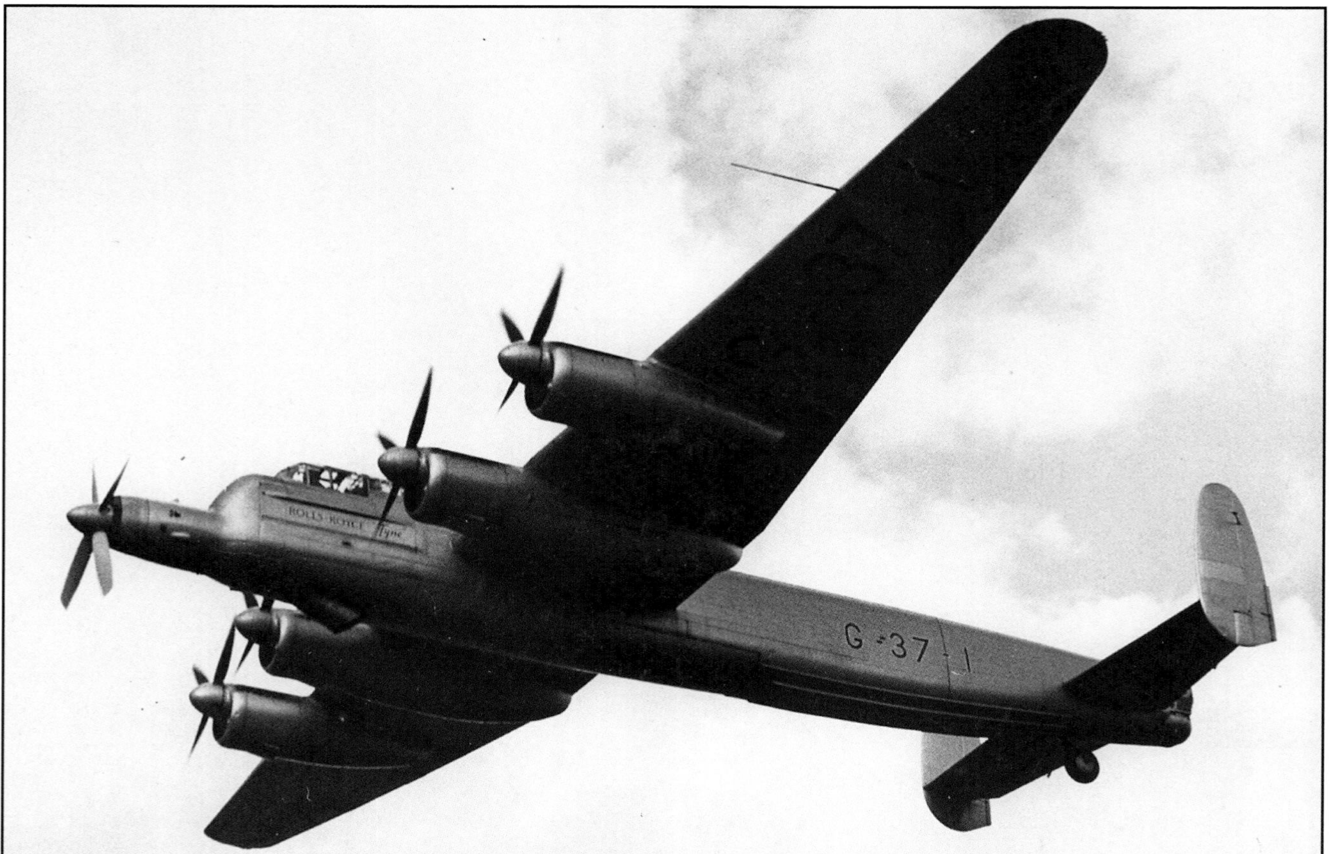

As part of the Vickers Vanguard development, Rolls-Royce had to air-test its new 4,500 hp Tyne engine, Avro Lincoln RF533 was selected and, after strengthening work at Hucknall, the turboprop engine was installed in the nose. Now marked as G-37-1, the five-engined bomber derivative embarked on trials that lead to the successful launch of the Viscount development at Weybridge.

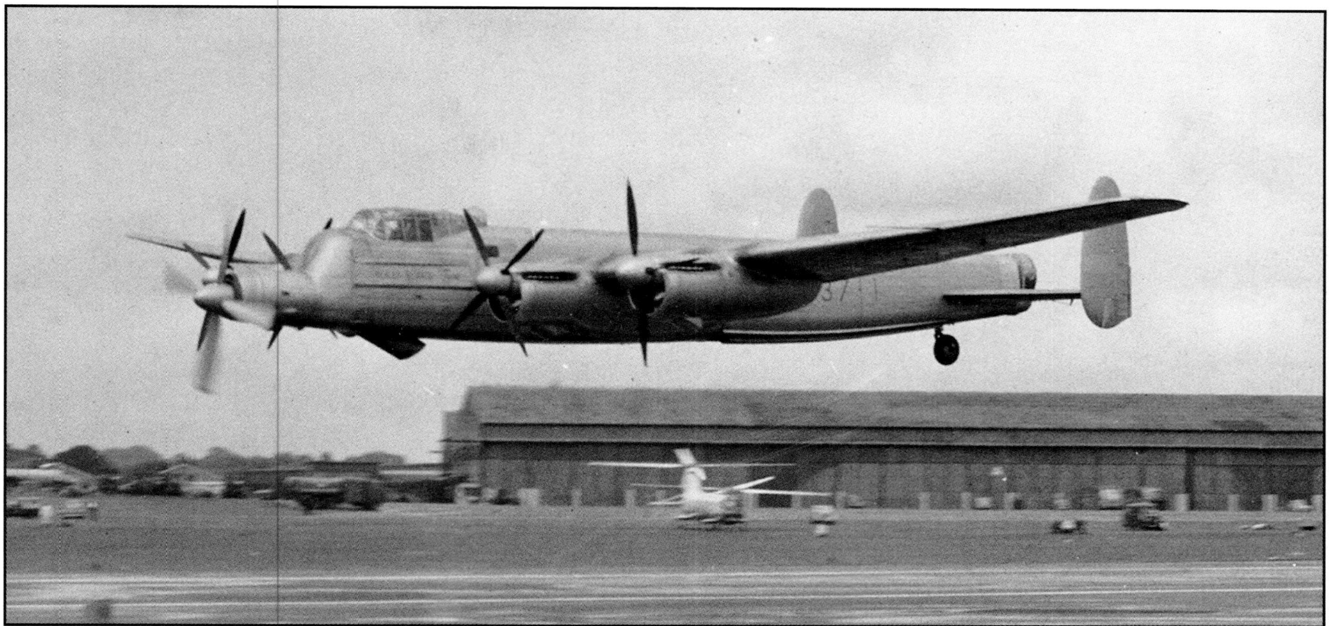

Invited to take part in the Society of British Aircraft Constructors' then annual show at Farnborough on September 9th, 1956, it was hard for the Rolls-Royce team not to put on a show with its Tyne test-bed. A full throttle fly-past was made with all four Merlins making their characteristically impressive sound and the Tyne quietly spinning at low revs. Then the Lincoln came round again and, to the horror of many a veteran RAF pilot, all four Merlins were not just throttled back, but stopped with airscrews feathered. Remember these were gentler days and jet engines were still 'the new kid on the block' for many. The apparently powerless Lincoln descended in a gentle swoop and in low fly-past position, the Tyne in the nose was opened up to full thrust. To the amazement of the watching crowds, the giant Lincoln soared upwards in a steep climb – still apparently with no visible power and all four props stationary. Here is the moment the turboprop in the nose was opened up to power.

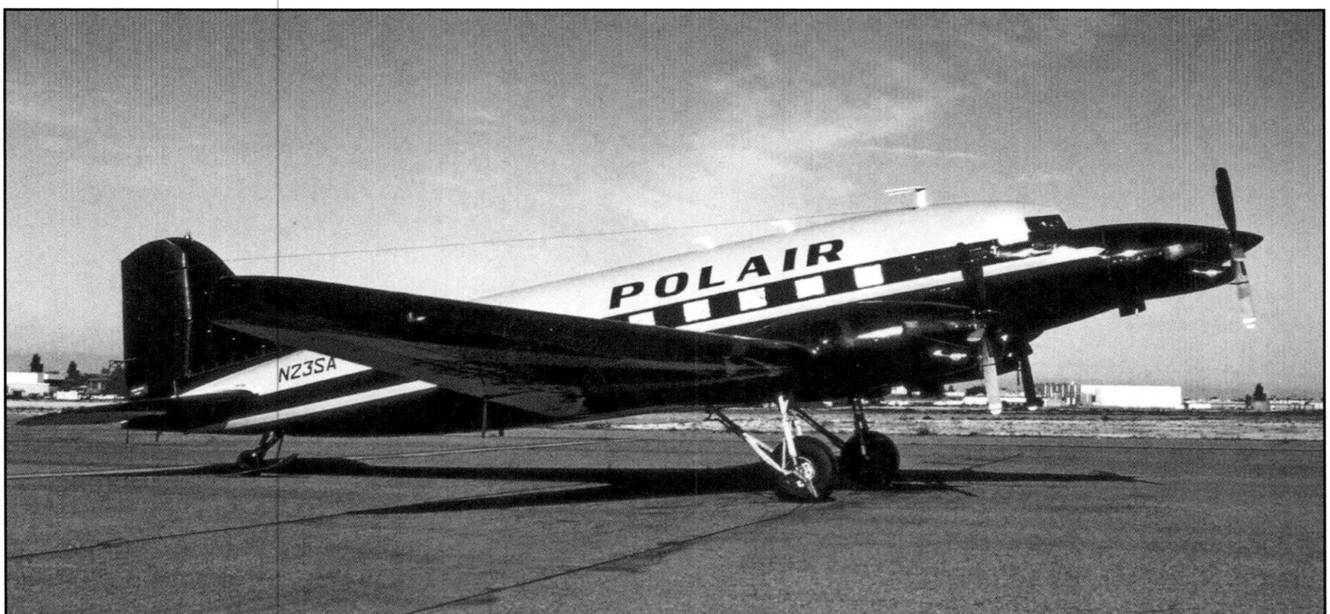

Back to those spotters' quizzes and how many engines has a DC-3! Jack Michael Conroy (1920-1979) was an amazing engineer who gave a new lease of life to many an old transport aircraft by fitting it with turbojets. Best known for his development of the Pregnant Guppy and the larger Very Pregnant Guppy airliner component transports, Conroy Aircraft Corp was formed in 1968 at Santa Barbara, California, and here a small number of DC-3 aircraft were converted by the installation of three Pratt & Whitney PT-6A turboprop engines fitted with five-blade Hartzell airscrews so creating the Conroy Tri Turbo Three (TT-3). The first made its maiden flight on November 2nd. 1977, and, as N23A, it attended the Farnborough Air Show in 1978 and the Paris Air Show the following year. Possessed of STOL capabilities, the aircraft could be flown safely on any one of its three motors with comfort and safety. Other DC-3 aircraft were fitted with Dart 510/512 engines removed from Viscount 812 aircraft owned by Continental Airlines. Further development was curtailed by the death of founder Jack Conroy and not helped by the simple fact that McDonald Douglas would not support the venture, preferring to sell new aircraft. By 1998 this particular aircraft was surplus and dismantled at Oshkosh, Wisconsin.

Since the earliest days of flying, the ultimate challenge was understood to be the Atlantic with its minimum distance of 1,800 miles of water. A Canadian-born inventor, Edward Robert Armstrong (1876-1955) thought he had the solution when he came up with the floating Seadrome. He was certainly onto something but it would be a long while and in a totally different field that his invention would become a world-beater. Initially his idea was to build a chain of his patented Armstrong Seadromes across the Atlantic. Spaced at 350 miles apart, each would be a floating steel platform of about 30,000 tons displacement supported some 70 feet above sea-level on hollow steel piers, each of which terminated in a ballast tank 100 feet below the water surface. The iron and steel structure would offer a 1,200 feet long runway having a width of 200 feet. To the sides would be extensions to locate hotel, restaurant, maintenance and operational buildings. Steel cables anchored the entire thing to the sea bed and rough seas passed harmlessly beneath the landing area.

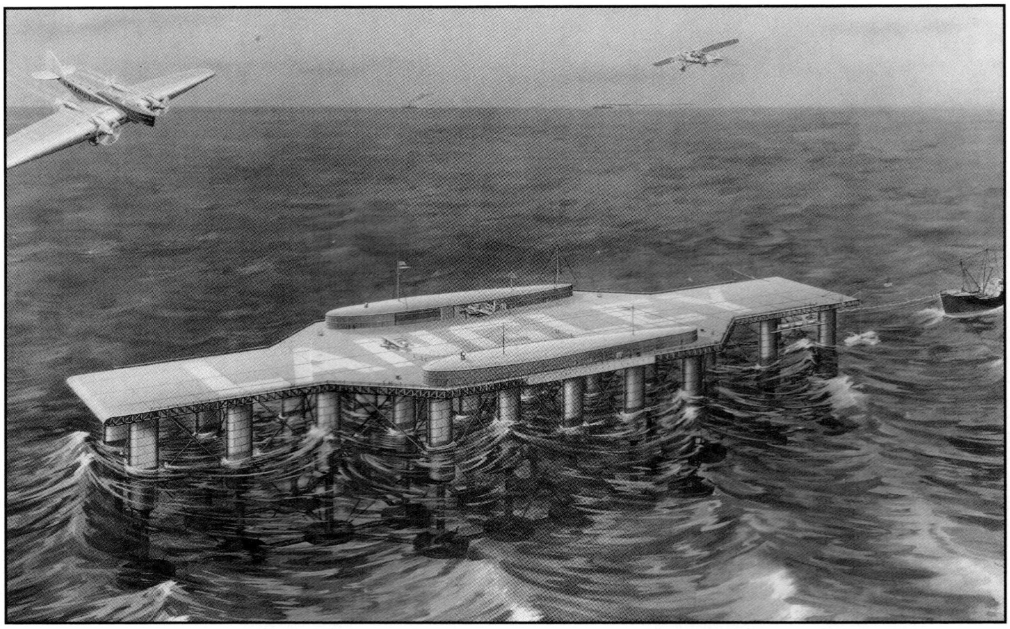

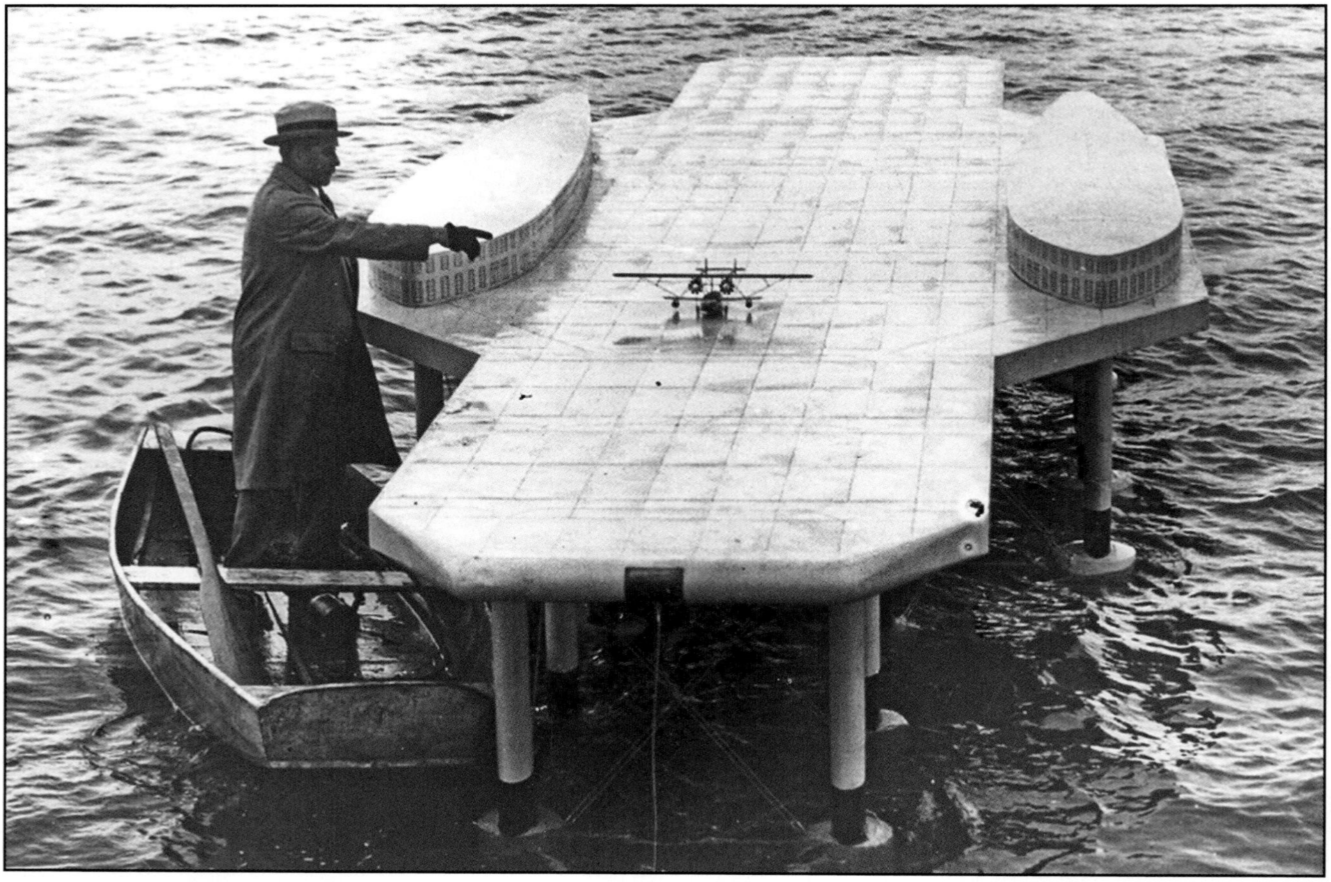

Promoted regularly from 1927 onwards, by October 1929, Armstrong summoned the Press to a New York pond where he demonstrated a 1/32nd size model of his Seadrome. The plan was now to bridge the Atlantic with eight of these erections each some 400 miles apart. Somehow he failed to foresee that his chain of Seadromes would be obsolete as soon as built if not sooner, for the progress in aviation was such that there was a real possibility of aircraft being able to fly the Atlantic non-stop within a decade or so. But a man with what he thinks is a good idea is never easy to reason with.

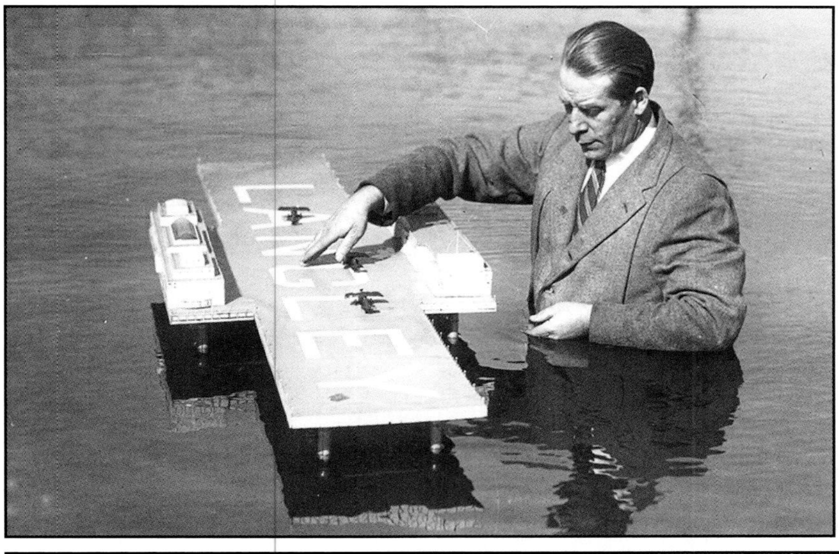

Armstrong was popular with the American press for his practical demonstrations where he would stand in a water tank in a smart three-piece business suit complete with silver watch and chain immersed up to his chest alongside a scale model of his Seadrome. The idea was killed off by the Depression which deprived him of the necessary investment capital. As the 1930s advanced, there was greater potential for long-range land aircraft. And intermediate stopping places were quite redundant. But Armstrong wasn't finished yet! He had one more or less final fling to come.

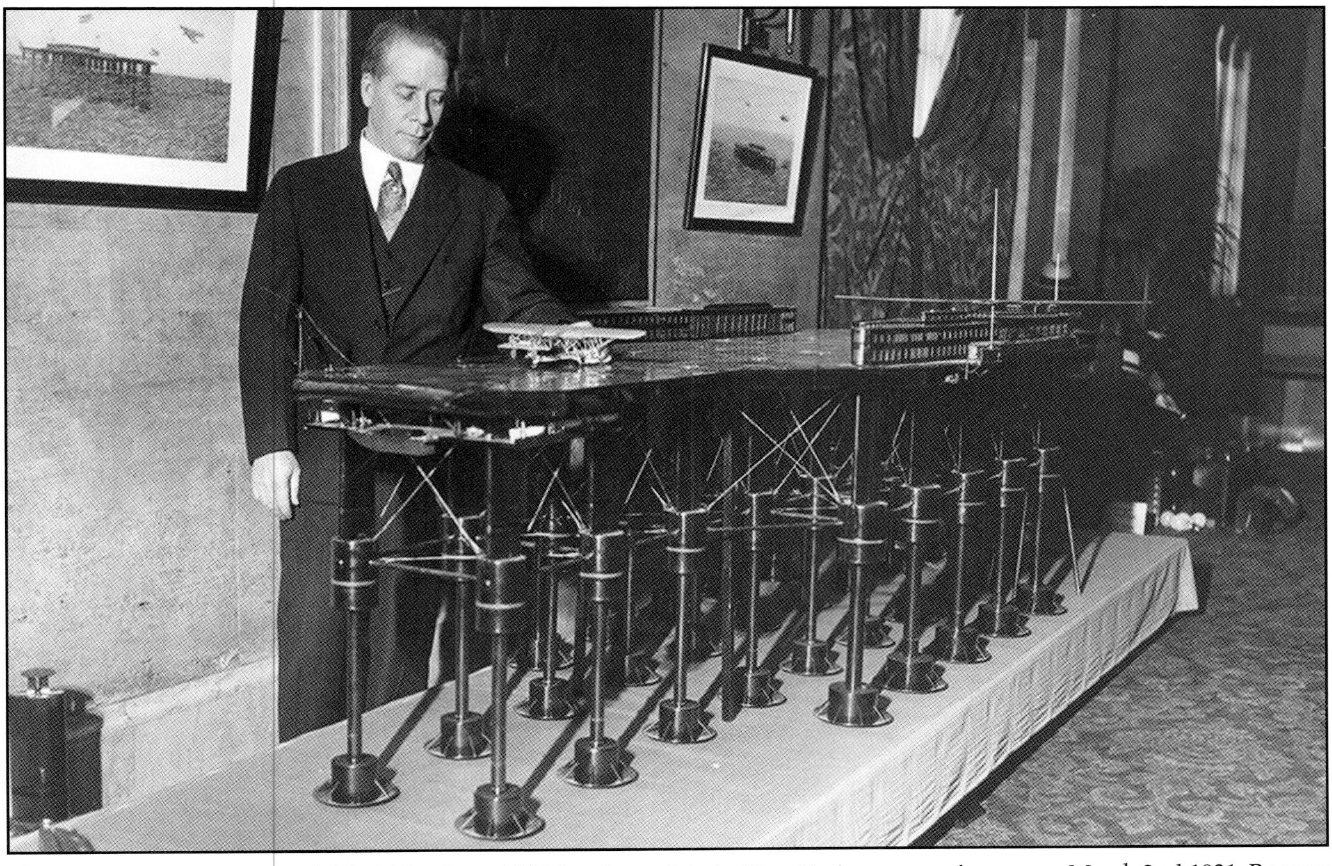

This is Armstrong posing with his 12 feet long $4,000 scale model at a New York press conference on March 2nd,1931. By now he was proposing not so much a chain of Seadromes to service transatlantic airliners as a solitary destination, a resort in its own right with dancing, fishing and drinking being the attractions he chose to promote. Remember that these were the days of Prohibition and somebody must have suggested that his idea would be a neat way around that infamous Eighteenth Amendment!. The Seadrome was to be named the Langley and constructed in the shallow water of the Delaware before being towed out to its anchorage in the North Atlantic. 'The two-hour flight to the station is expected to cost about $25 for the round trip', he told the press. In November 1933, *Time* magazine printed a carping resumé of events. 'A perennial gift to Sunday feature editors for the last five years has been the Armstrong Seadrome, vividly imaginative project for a chain of floating airports across the Atlantic. The perfect publicity subject, it offered serious readers masses of data on construction of huge platforms, stabilized high above the waves by means of weighted pillars, on problems of anchorage, navigation, operation, economics. For gumchewers there were exciting pictures of a seadrome at night, in mid-ocean position, with flags flying, floodlights blazing, beacons stabbing the dark sky, gorgeous express planes gliding down to safe landings. Even the windows of the drome's elegant hotel underlying the deck were pricked out with cozy lights.' This was all very well, but Armstrong had the last laugh, for his Seadrome became the inspiration behind today's semi-submersible off-shore oil rigs.

It has long been known that, during its Communist years, getting sensitive information out of a Russian was a little like trying to part a Scotsman from his best malt. And the old Soviet news agencies were paradigms of obfuscation. News pictures were invariably third or more generation copies of heavily retouched originals. On February 23rd 1963 this photograph 'did the rounds' from 'an Official Soviet Source'. The entire caption reads: 'High manoeuvrability, safe take-off and landing are guaranteed for this round-winged glider built by the Russians in 1962. Photo published in military newspaper *Red Star* reporting successful test and vertical take-off capability'. To get that sort of performance out of a round-winged aircraft is impressive: it is even more remarkable out of a glider! Don't ask! I don't know either!

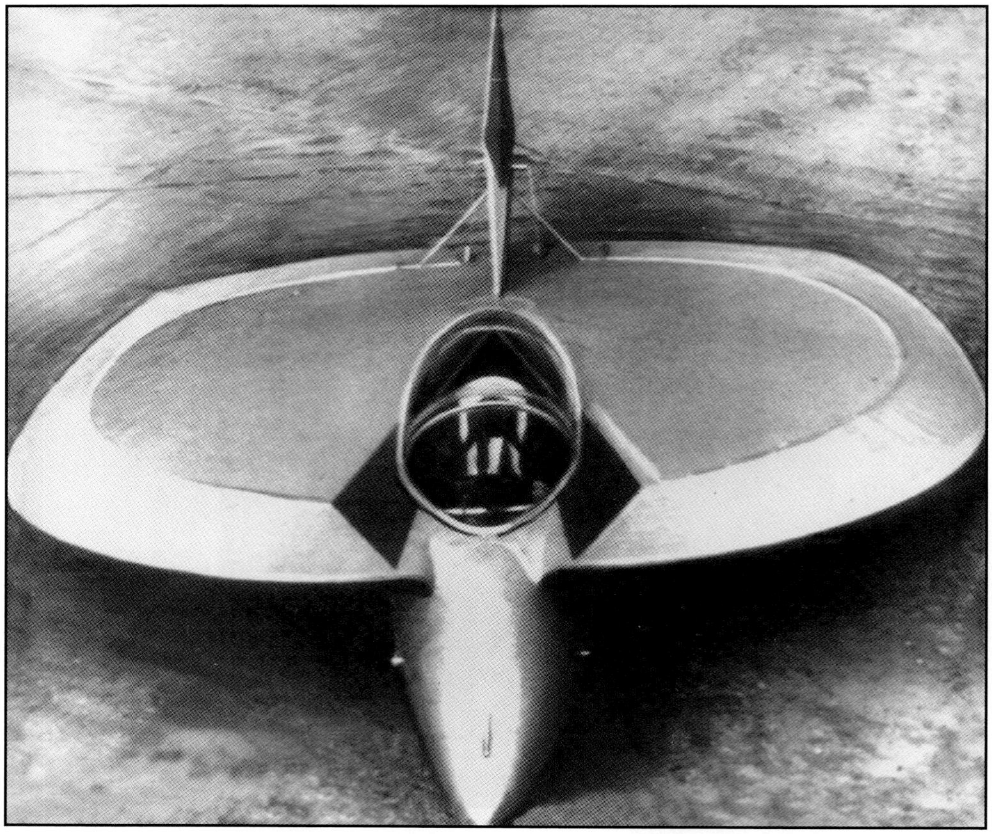

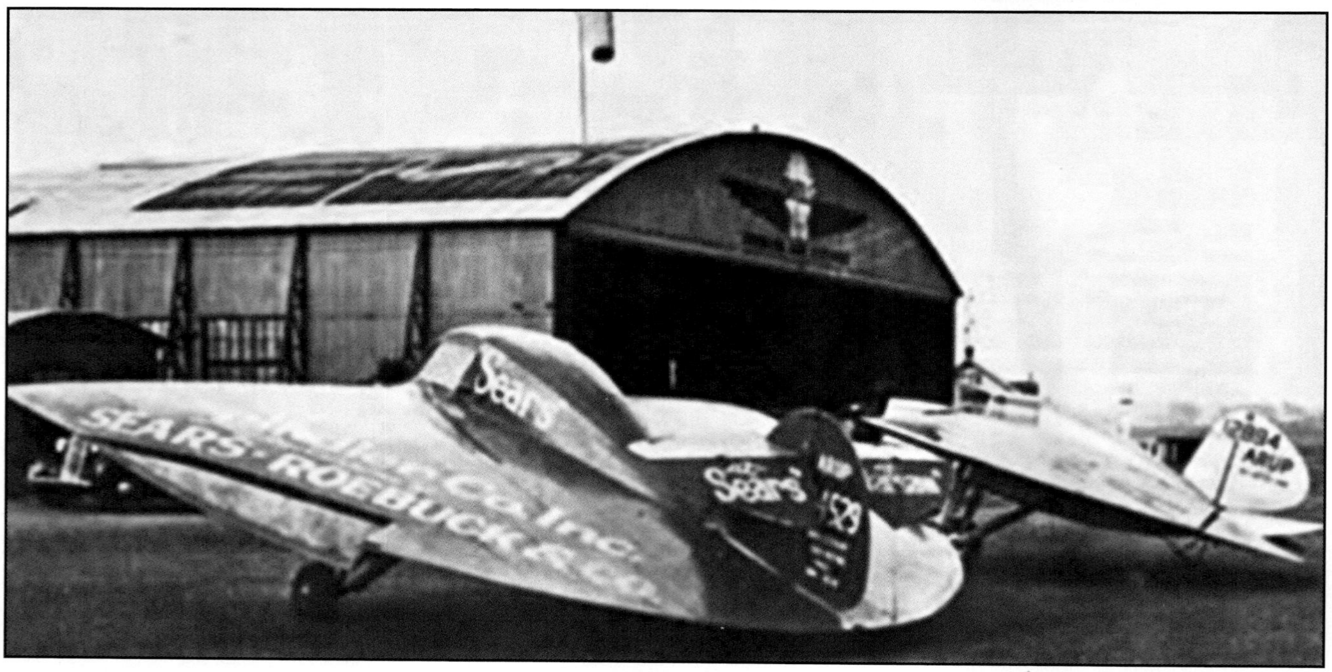

Historically we find that 'flying wings' came in all shapes and sizes, some (like Burnelli) with fuselage and tail, others (like the AW.52) a real wing and nothing else. But the term 'flying saucer' is of more recent origin. Among the first to experiment with a mainly circular wing was Arup. This was the brainwave of one Cloyd Snyder in 1926. With engineer Raoul Hoffman he built a series of parabolic-winged aircraft started with the Dirigiplane followed by the Monowing and finally led to the formation of the Arup Manufacturing Corporation in 1932. Here with engineer Raoul Hoffman and Glenn Doolittle as test pilot, he was able to refine his earlier experimental aircraft and create a small series of new machines under the name of Arup. This picture shows the S.4 with the S.2 behind. Note that both are covered with advertisements. Although ultimately found commercially wanting, the aircraft enjoyed a long and useful life thanks to their inherent stall-proof flight characteristics, lower take-off and landing speeds and greater lift. Designer Dr Snyder was hampered by insufficient working capital and a company that lacked good management.

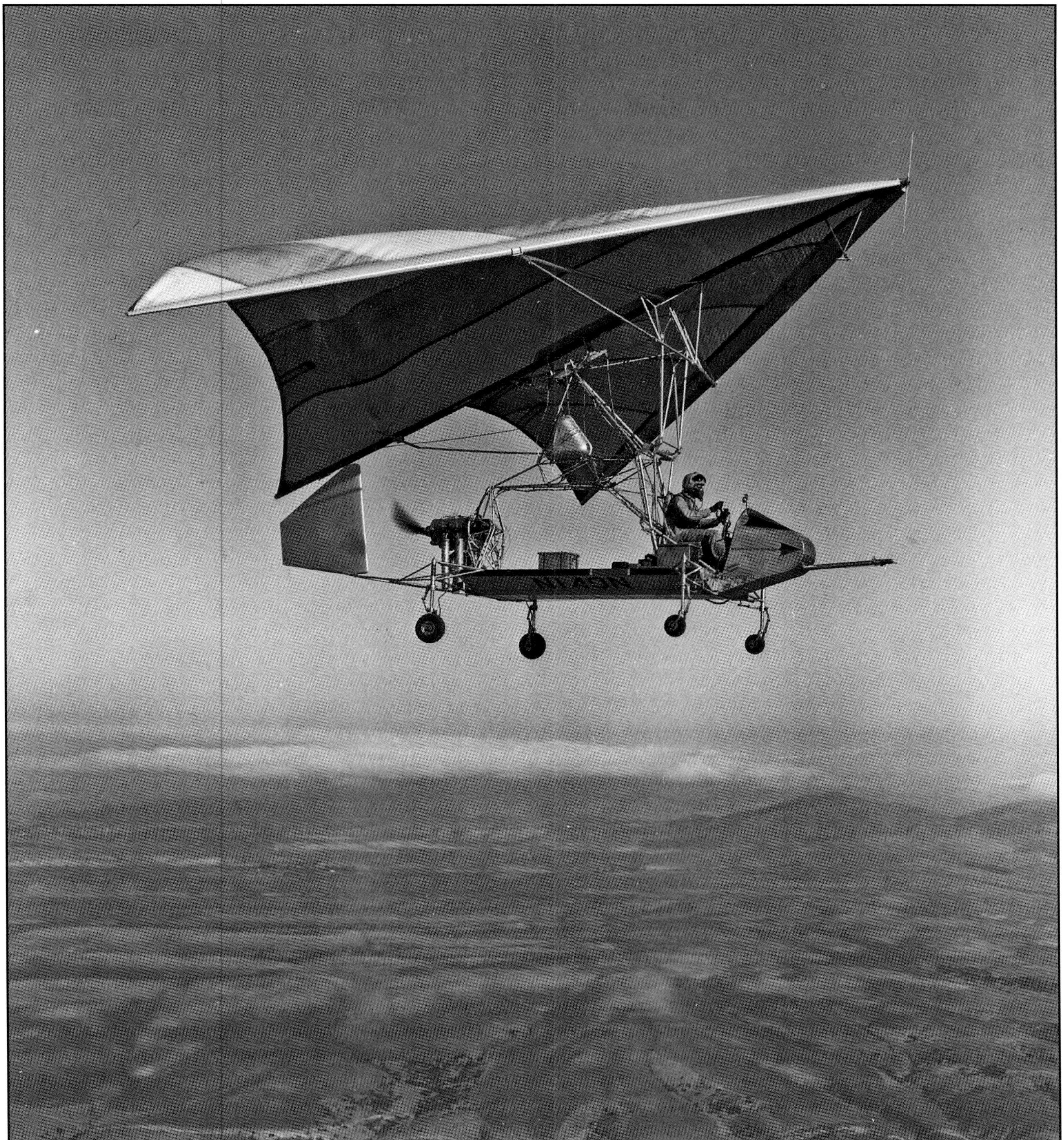

Experiments with flexible wings or 'sailwings' were undertaken by RAE Farnborough during the early part of the war as a cheap means of dropping equipment from the air. However, it fell to Francis Melvin Rogallo (1912-2009), a Californian engineer, and his wife to perfect the idea with his 1948 invention of what he called his 'self-inflating wing'. The principle became the foundation of the sport of hang-gliding – a very simple airfoil formed by an airproof membrane stretched over a pivotable 'A' frame. The Ryan Aeronautical Company of San Diego, California, took up the idea and built the Flex-Wing as a research vehicle for the US Army's Transportation Research Command. It made its first flight on May 23rd, 1961. This was followed by a slightly larger version, the XV-8 Fleep or Flexible Wing Aerial Utility Vehicle, better known as the Flying Jeep. A 210 hp Continental engine gave the 1,100 lb aircraft a speed of 60 mph and a take-off run (on a four-wheeled undercarriage) of less than 500 feet. Programme manager for Ryan was Cecil Craigo who reckoned the machine had a wide potential for ranchers and other civilian use. No military contracts were forthcoming and Ryan's other work prevented any further development. Only two of these small and very foldable aeroplanes were made. It is said that the number of separate undercarriage legs reflects the uncertainty of the designer about how his creation might land…

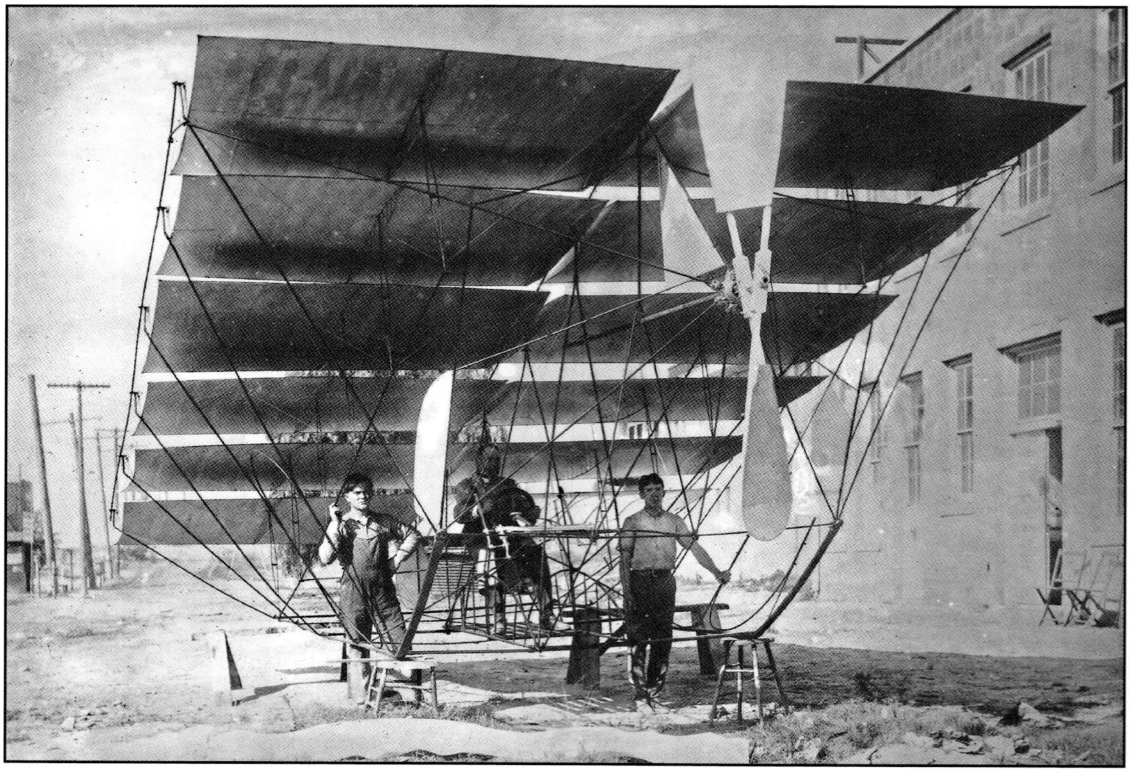

As we have already seen (and will continue to see throughout this little book), one of the hardest things to do is to part an inventor from his cherished idea. It is a task demanding dauntless courage and immense powers of persuasion. James Slough Zerbe, for example, believed that wings were best described as *multum in parvo*. His five-winged 'Multiplane' was shown at the Los Angeles International Air Show of 1910 but seems to have crashed rather thoroughly while still on the ground due to running into a pothole. 'Add more wings!' he cried – and so was born the six-winged model, the complex controls of which included wing-warping rather than ailerons in the hope, no doubt, of a need for controlling direction becoming a necessity. It seems that the necessity never arose. Mr. Zerbe disappeared soon afterwards but not before leaving behind a commendable compendium on aviation for boys and another on wireless, both of which entered many popular editions over the years.

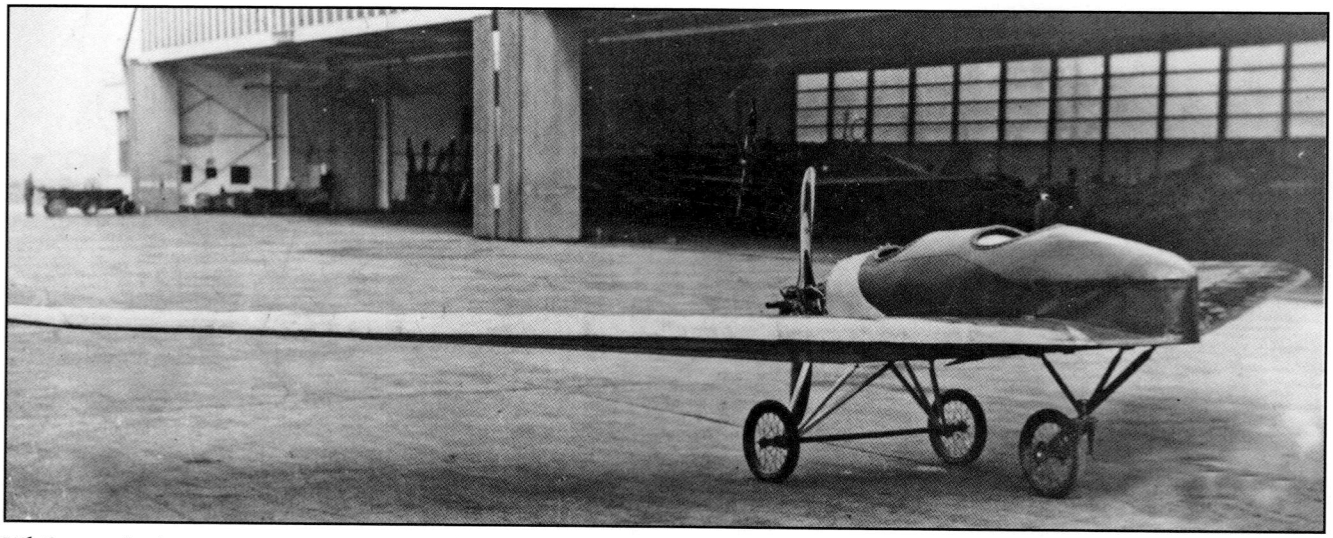

While one faction was growing wings with abandon, more venturesome inventors were economising by eliminating things such as fuselage and tail. One of the earliest in this field was the Swiss-born artist and engineer Alexander Soldenhoff (1882-1951) who, like so many pioneers, began making model aircraft in his youth. But his great achievement came with his now-forgotten tailless light aircraft. Here is his 32 hp Bristol Cherub-powered LF5 of 1929. With a wing-span of 32 feet 10 inches, a length of 16 feet 2 inches, and 188 square feet of wing area, this novel machine was flown by Anton Riediger in 1930 and demonstrated at Düsseldorf. Here it attracted the attention of Germany's inventive Gottlob Espenlaub, a contemporary of Alexander Lippisch who was another protagonist of tailless aircraft. Espenlaub endorsed Soldenhoff's dream of making 'the flying machine for everybody' – a sort of early Volksplane. It came close when he moved to Böblingen and met up with Hanns Klemm but in the end it came to nothing and tailless development shifted elsewhere.

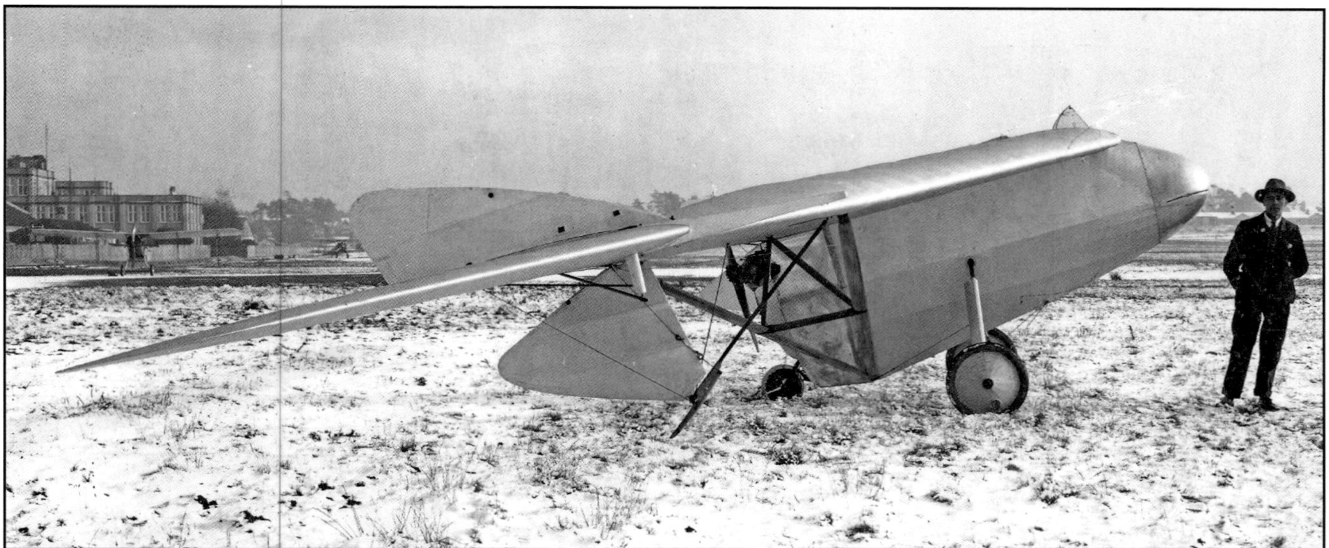

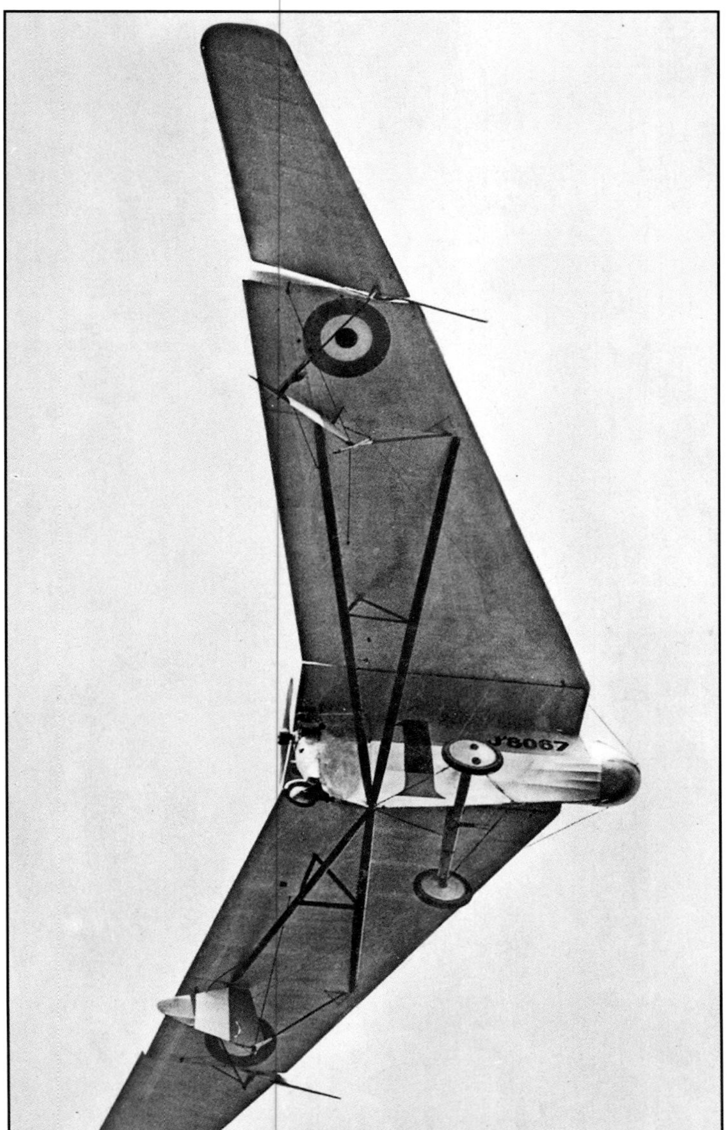

Geoffrey Terence Roland Hill (1895-1955) had been a First War pilot and then joined Handley Page as a test pilot although he was soon working on ways to reduce the loss of control at the stall. He considered tailless aircraft to have some considerable future since the control of the wing could be direct by the use of moving tips or elevons. He and his wife built a tailless glider which first flew on December 31st 1924 in the Sussex Downs. The previous year he had presented a report on tailless aircraft to the Aeronautical Research Council. Hill fitted a 32 hp Bristol Cherub engine to his glider and achieved encouraging results. The Air Ministry and the RAE now became interested and Westlands undertook to build a proper version of Hill's powered glider. It would be called the Westland Pterodactyl Mk. 1 and here we see Hill posing with it at a snowy Yeovil.

The Cherub-engined Pterodactyl Mk.1 appeared in 1925. Two pilots sat in separate cockpits placed side of side in the nose. By this time Hill and a pair of assistants were working within the Westland organisation. A star of the 1926 RAF Pageant at Hendon Aerodrome that July 3rd, it is seen here bearing the RAF serial J8067 and a large numeral '1' indicating its place in the New Types Park display.

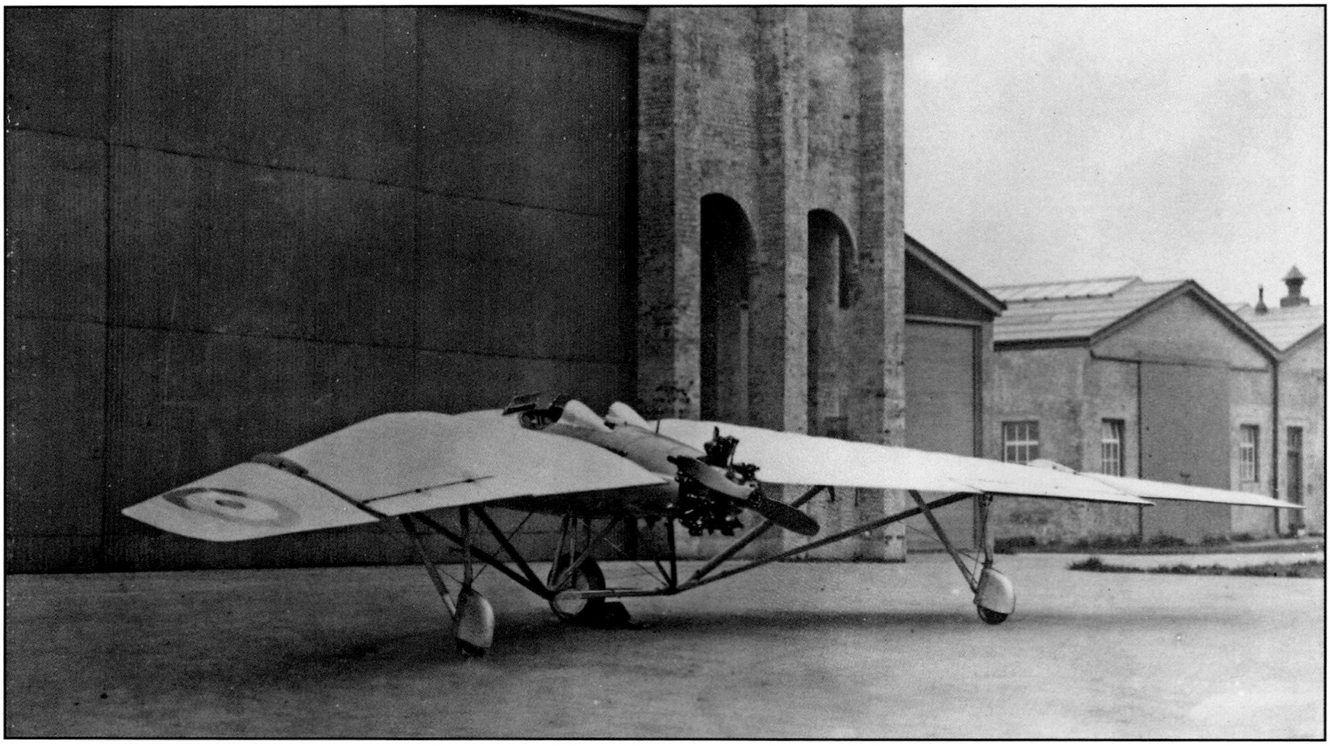

When the little Bristol Cherub engine of what was now the Mk.IA was replaced by a 70 hp Armstrong Siddeley Genet radial, the machine was styled the Mk.IB and allocated the RAF serial number J9251. This had a more robust single-wheel undercarriage and the outboard underwing balancing wheels were provided with spats. Wingspan was 45 feet 6 inches and length 17 feet. With the Genet the all-up weight was 1,280 lbs and the maximum speed 70 mph. This aircraft is preserved in South Kensington's Science Museum in London.

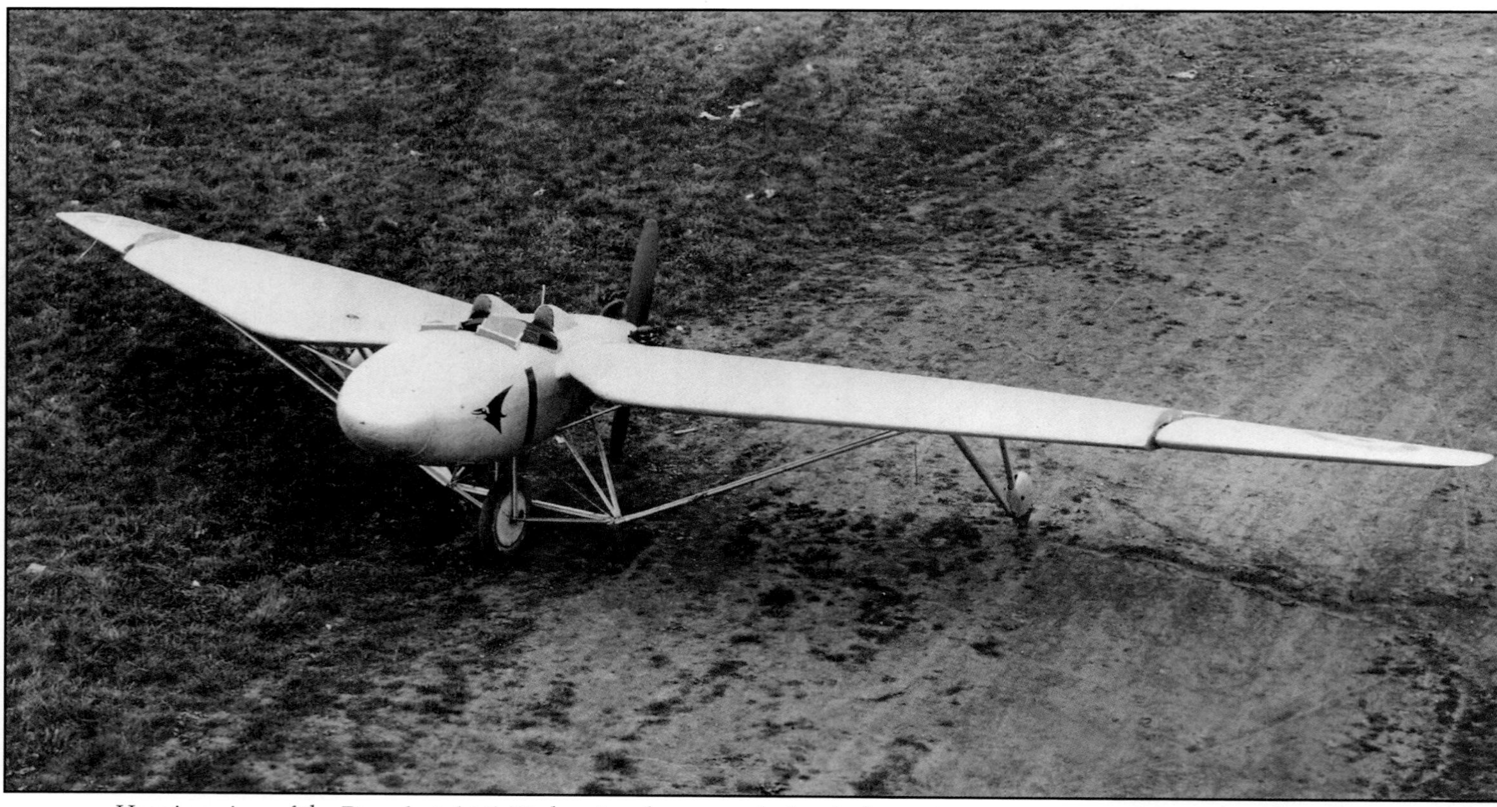

Here is a view of the Pterodactyl Mk.IB showing the two cockpits, the hinged tip controllers to the wings and the position of the outer balancing wheels. Overall the aircraft had a very small frontal area and, noticeably, no vertical fin or rudder surface, turning being under the influence of the movable tips to the wings.

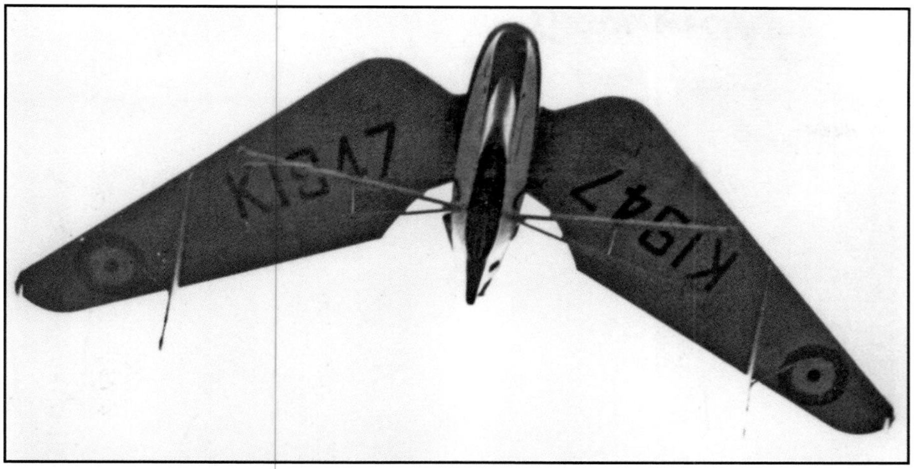

The three-seat cabin Pterodactyl Mk. IV was powered by a 120 hp de Havilland Gipsy III engine and featured a unique control system where the wings could be moved forwards and backwards to adjust the angle of sweepback through a 4.75-deg angle. This was controlled by a crank-handle in the cabin roof. A pair of landing wheels was arranged in tandem along the fuselage centre-line with balancing wheels outboard under the wings. Allocated the RAF serial K1947, this was seen on June 27th 1931 at the Hendon Air Pageant, again a feature of the 'New Types' park.

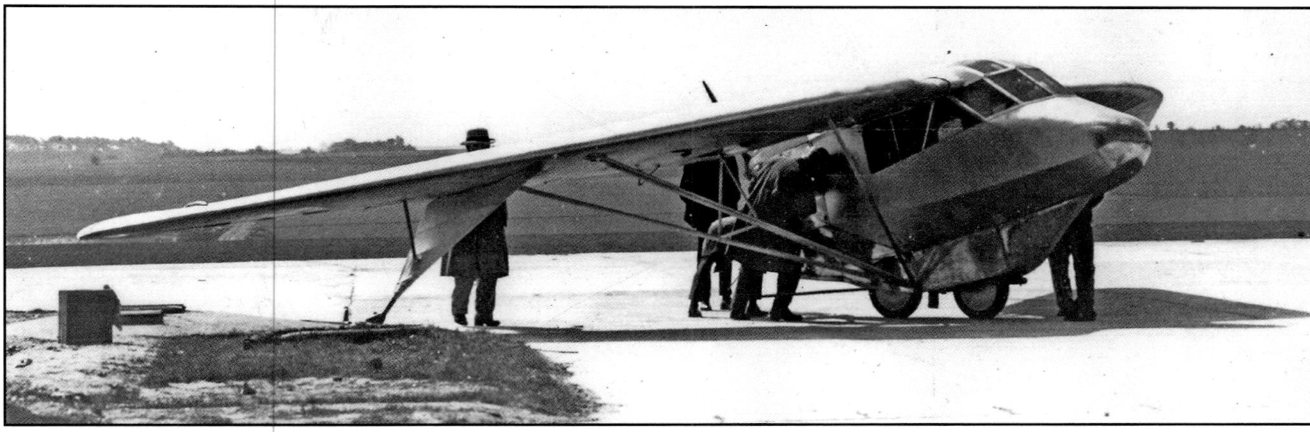

It is probably fair to say that Hill and the small team that he led within Westland were obsessed with the idea of tailless aircraft. The Air Ministry attitude, quoted by Derek James in his book on Westland Aircraft, was that the Pterodactyls were 'too much, too soon'. The variable-sweep system on the Mk.IV was of limited range but proved ample to adjust the centre of pressure to compensate for changes to the centre of gravity when the cabin held just a pilot or pilot and one or two passengers. In this picture the aircraft appears to have run into something hard which has dented the nose.

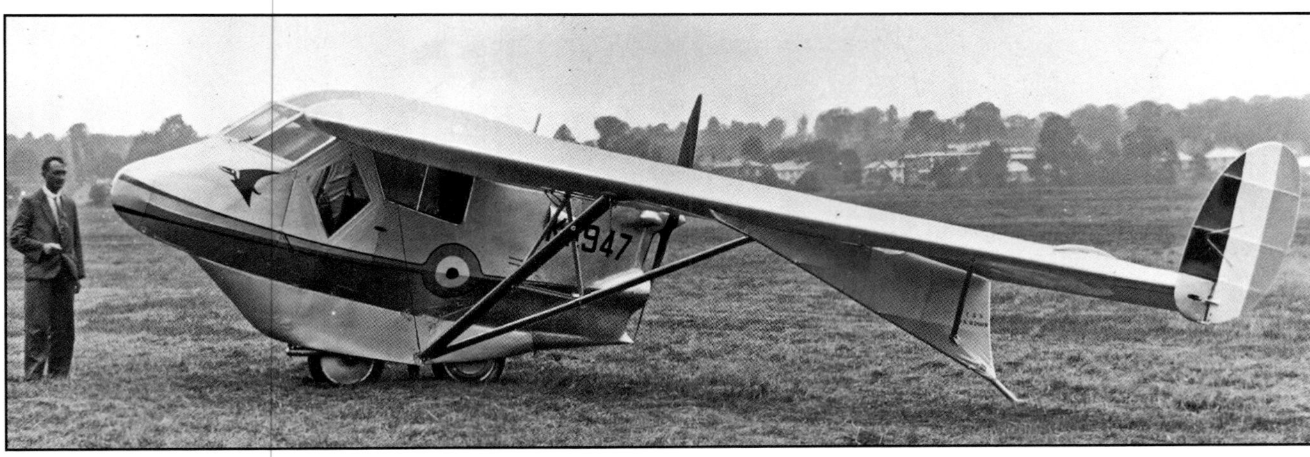

Subtle changes followed the first flight in June 1931 and its Hendon Air Pageant public debut on June 27th. By August, the heavy strut that extended upwards from the lower attachment point of the lift struts to the front spar at the root end had been replaced by a simple cable, it having been determined that the load here was always tensile and not as first believed both tension and compression under various conditions. Additionally small but effective wing-tip fins and rudders were fitted as seen here. The diamond window was a feature of the cabin door and did not appear on the opposite side. Once more Hill stands near the nose. When displayed at the following year's Hendon show, K1947 was rather crudely painted up to resemble a prehistoric bird with 'face' and teeth on the nose. Despite very good handling characteristics and a cabin capacity of three with space for luggage, overall performance with the Gipsy II engine was inferior when compared with other club and private-owner aircraft on the market. This, together with the depressed economic climate of Britain in the early 1930s, prompted Westland not to put the Mk.IV into production.

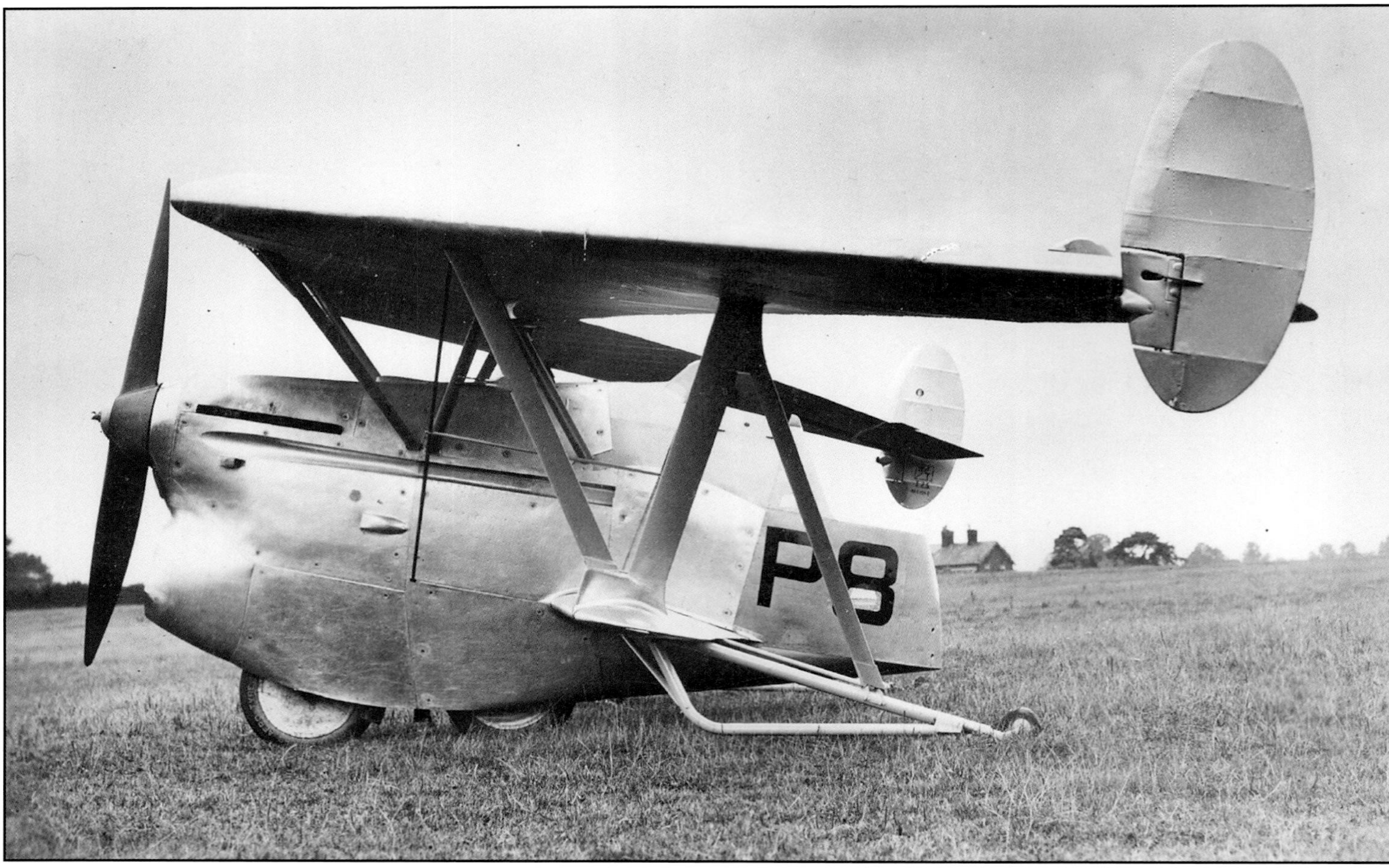

After the decision not to adopt the Mk.IV, Geoffrey Hill and his team embarked on a fresh Pterodactyl model which would be for a high-performance military version that could be armed. The attraction here was that a rear gunner would have a superior field of fire since the only things that interfered with his sight were the wingtips. Westland submitted proposals to the Air Ministry in 1931 and the Specification F.3/33 was written around these. It would be a two-seat tractor fighter having two fixed forward-firing Vickers machine-guns and one movable Lewis gun in the rear cockpit. The engine was a variant of the Rolls-Royce Kestrel, the 600 hp evaporatively-cooled PV.G which would become the Goshawk.

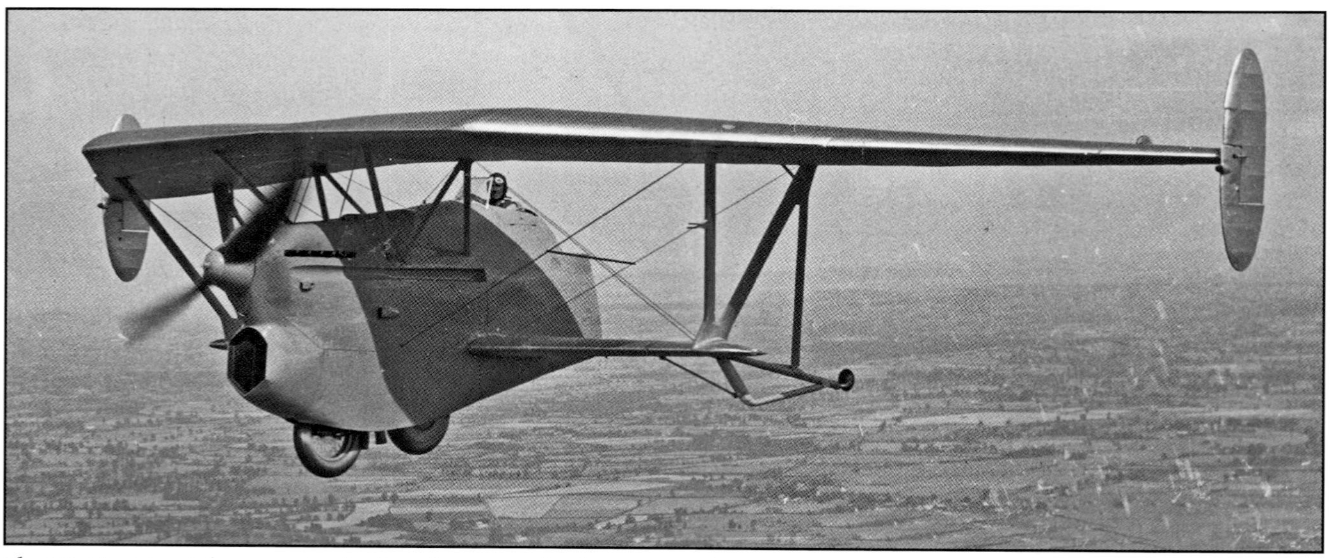

The Mk.V retained the now-standard tandem two-wheeled main undercarriage and balancing outriders only this time they were attached to what in effect was a lower wing of narrow chord which could be box-braced with Raf wires. The centre section had a straight leading edge to which the swept-back outer panels were attached. However, the trailing edge sweep-back commenced at the wing centre creating a comprehensive set of unknowns for the stress analyst. Bearing the Westland type number P8, the Mk.V went through numerous trials and tribulations before being taken by road to RAF Andover for its official first flight.

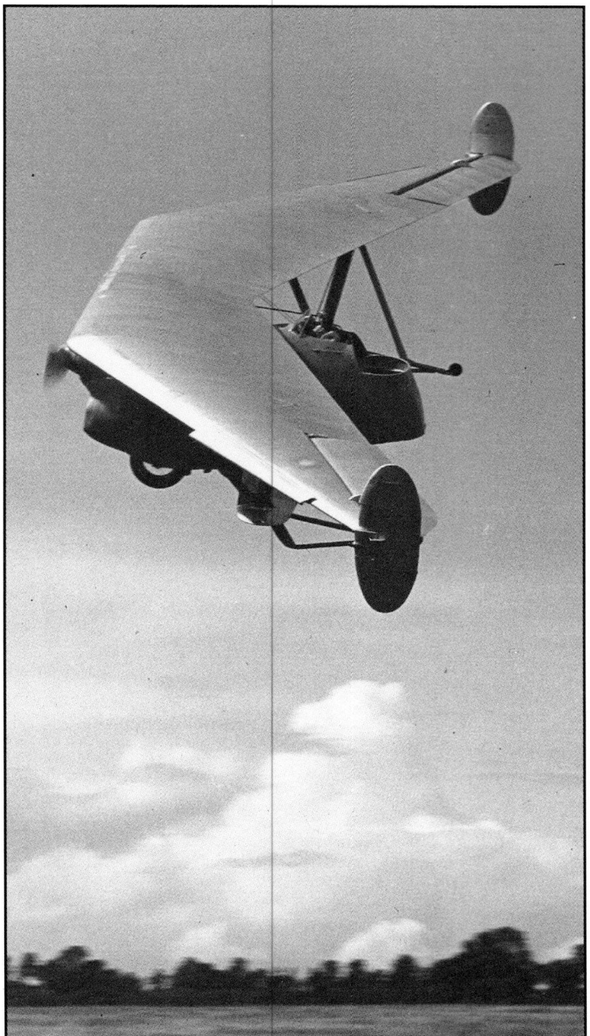

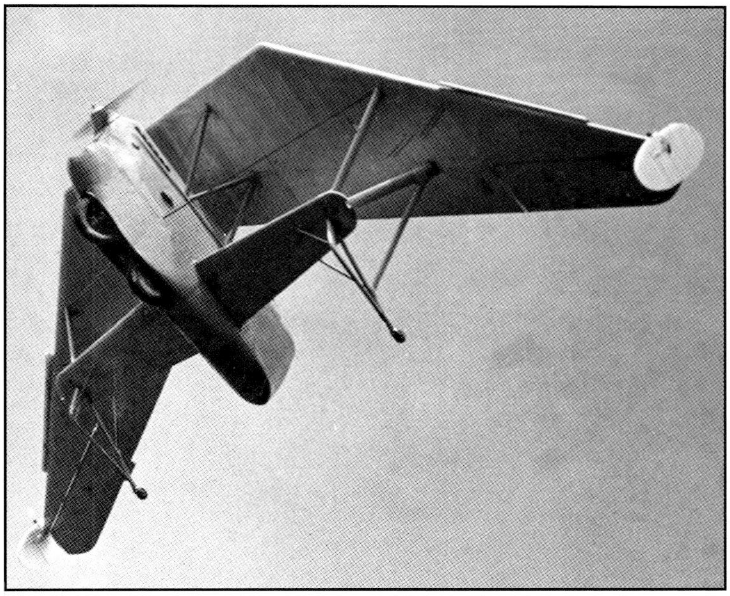

The Pterodactyl Mk.V was a curious shape but was remarkably docile in the air. Although the rear gun-turret was mocked up, a real one was never fitted and neither were the front or rear weaponry. This picture clearly shows the leading-edge slots.

Seen from above, the large controlling surfaces can be seen. These served as elevators and ailerons and hence the name 'elevons'. Originally it was hoped that they would also serve at aids to turning in the same way as a rudder, but after experiencing a number of large-radius skidding turns that appeared to bear little relationship to the degree of bank, Hill and his team conceded that rudders were needed. By mounting them at the wing-tips, their effectiveness was enhanced and so they could be quite small. Of course they were of no use for ground manoeuvring.

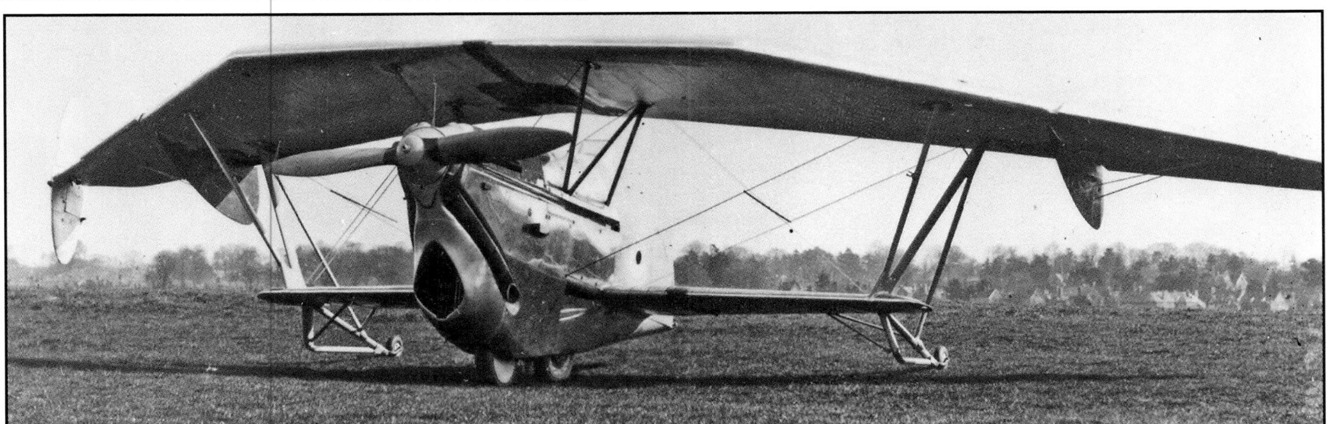

Very early on in the Mk.V's trials there were problems with engine overheating. To overcome this, a 615 hp Goshawk II was installed and the nose now adopted a pair of downward-recessed exhaust pipes. Small additional fins appeared underneath the wings outboard of the struts. Given the serial number K2770 early in 1935, the Mk.V continued its testing. Geoffrey Hill, spurned in his hopes to become Westland's technical director when Sir Ernest Petter appointed his son Edward to that post, resigned but agreed to see the Pterodactyl Mk.V through its tests. Edward Petter was not interested in the project and managed to abandon plans for further development which included the Pterodactyl Mk.VI Kestrel-engined pusher fighter and a four-engined tailless flying boat. Early in 1936 the Mk.V went by road to Farnborough for storage where it was broken up the following summer. An enterprising project was at an end. As for Hill, he went on to become Professor of Mechanical Engineering at University College, London, and during the war was greatly involved in barrage balloon development and protection systems and RAE Pawlett. In 1951 he was responsible, with Prof David Keith-Lucas (1911-1997), for the development of the 'aero-isoclinic' wing first used on the Short SB.1 glider and later on the Sherpa.

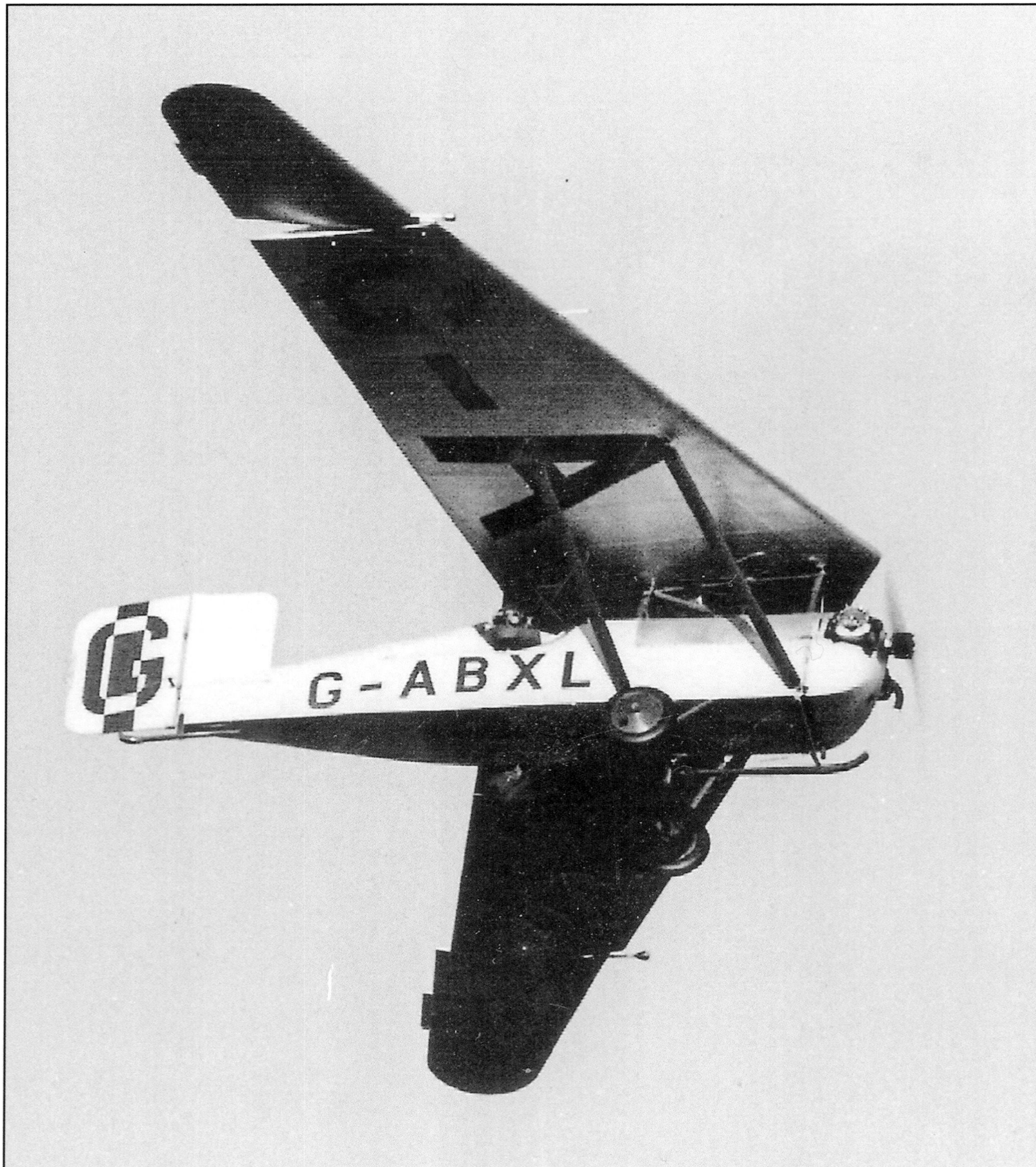

The two Granger brothers, Richard Francis Turney and Richard John Turney, were lace manufacturers in Nottingham who, created the Experimental Light Plane Club during the 1920s. They designed and built gliders but their crowning achievement was the Archaeopteryx, a single-seat tailless ultra-light powered by a 30 hp Bristol Cherub Mk.I horizontally-opposed flat twin. Design assistance came from Cecil Hugh Latimer-Needham who had also produced a tailless design, his Halton Meteor. The Granger machine had pivoted wing-tips which acted as combined elevons and ailerons after the style used by Klemm in Germany on the precursor of the Swallow. Completed in October, 1930, it gained its Certificate of Airworthiness and was displayed at the Royal Air Force Flying Club's display at Hatfield on June 15th, 1935. It proved to be a successful and eye-catching flyer but was soon consigned into storage. Happily it survived the years and was restored by The Shuttleworth Trust at Old Warden, where it flew again in the 1990s. The first truly tailless ultra-light, its rather idiosyncratic flying characteristics dictated that it did not herald a new trend, but it was a gallant attempt.

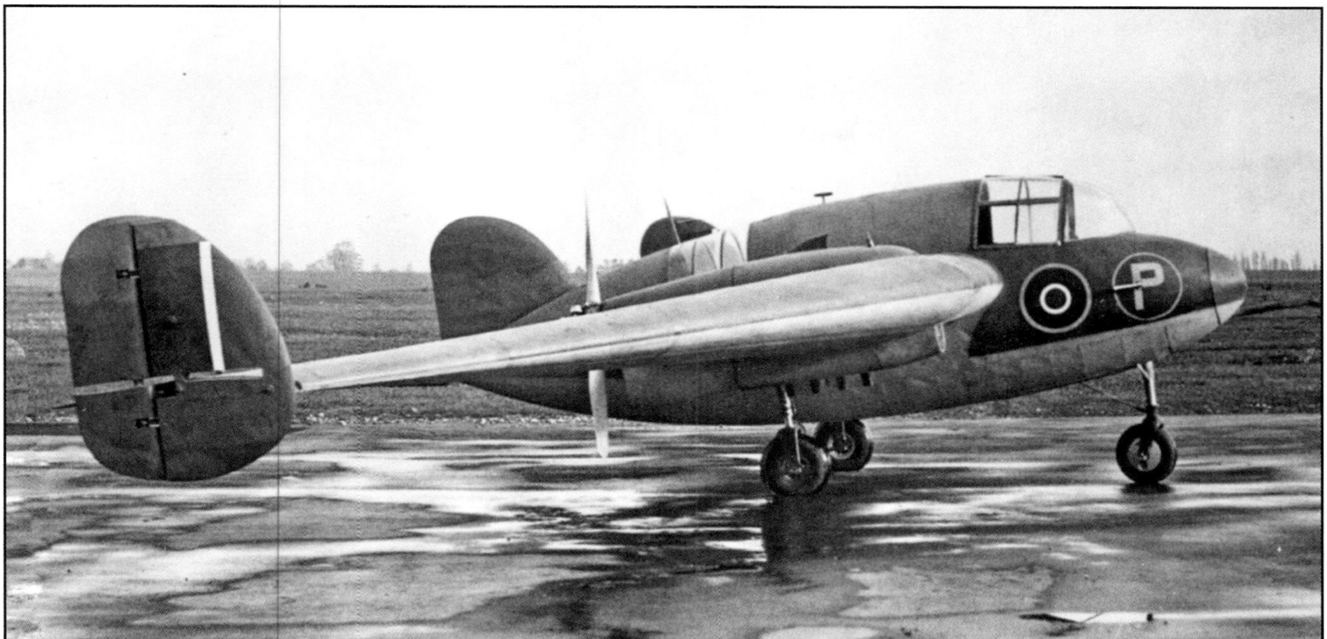

Westland's Pterodactyl tailless designs inspired Handley Page's aerodynamic research head Dr Gustav Victor Lachmann and experimental test pilot Major James Lucas Broome Hope Cordes to visit the Westland works at Yeovil on March 16th 1937. Westland's test pilot Harald Penrose and Bill Widgery gave all the help they could bearing in mind that the guru of tailless flight, Professor Geoffrey Hill, was 'no longer associated with the company'. There seemed, nevertheless, an opportunity to develop a small aircraft but 'HP' was adamant that Hampden and Halifax production must not be disrupted and that manufacture would have to be undertaken elsewhere, preferably by a small firm with low overheads. And so, in July 1938, Dart Aircraft Ltd, a two-man firm created by A R Weyl and B Zander to make sailplanes and the JAP-engined Dart Kitten ultra light agreed to build the prototype so long as all the duralumin metal fittings were supplied from Cricklewood. Grice & Young at Dunstable, another two-man outfit, made the steel parts. Not surprisingly, Dart entered a cash-flow situation with Weyl having to meet payments out of his own pocket. Dart was forced to beg a £200 subsidy from HP in order to get the machine finished by the end of 1938, some eighteen months behind HP's schedule. Lachmann had several important patents on the HP.75 Manx but under the Defence Regulation 18B, he was still technically a German citizen and so, like Weyl, was briefly interned as an alien.

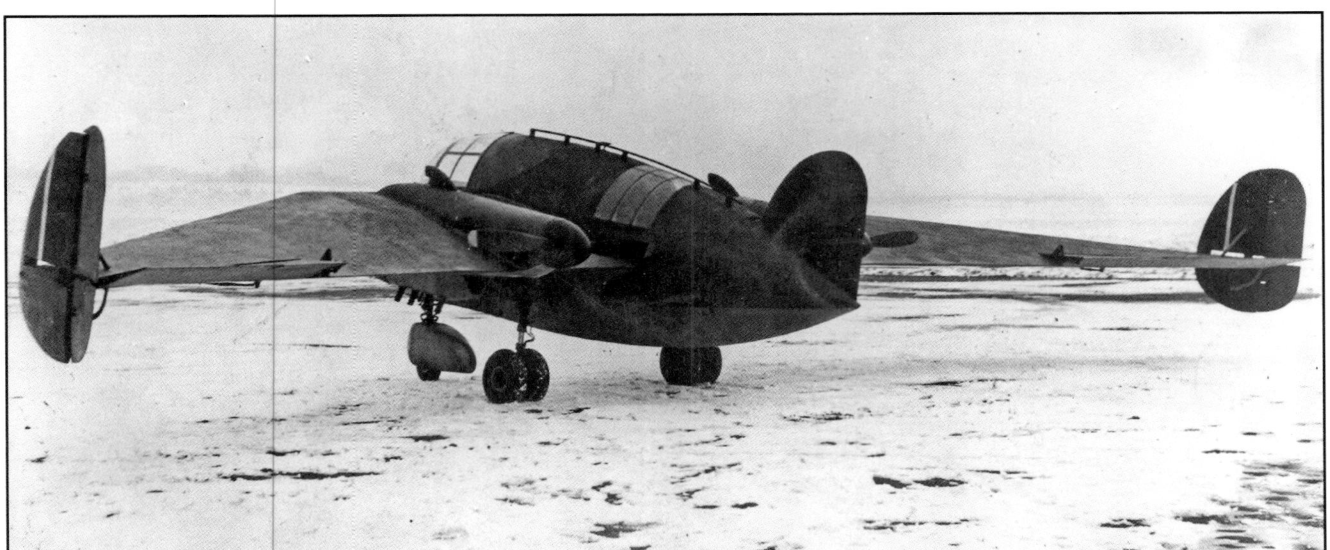

Handley Page's Manx is pictured here at Radlett in September 1942 being readied for its first taxi trials to be undertaken by John F Marsh who would make the first flight on June 25th the following year. This view shows the aircraft in its original form with 'wheel-barrow' nose wheel. The crew comprised pilot and observer and the machine was finished in standard day camouflage colours with yellow underside. Bearing the Class B registration H0222, the Manx was powered by two Gipsy Major II engines: in early tests an engineer stepped backwards into a spinning prop and was killed. The Manx had other problems but eventually flew sufficiently well to contribute to the HP.80 Victor bomber. It was still contributing data until 1946 when it was scrapped.

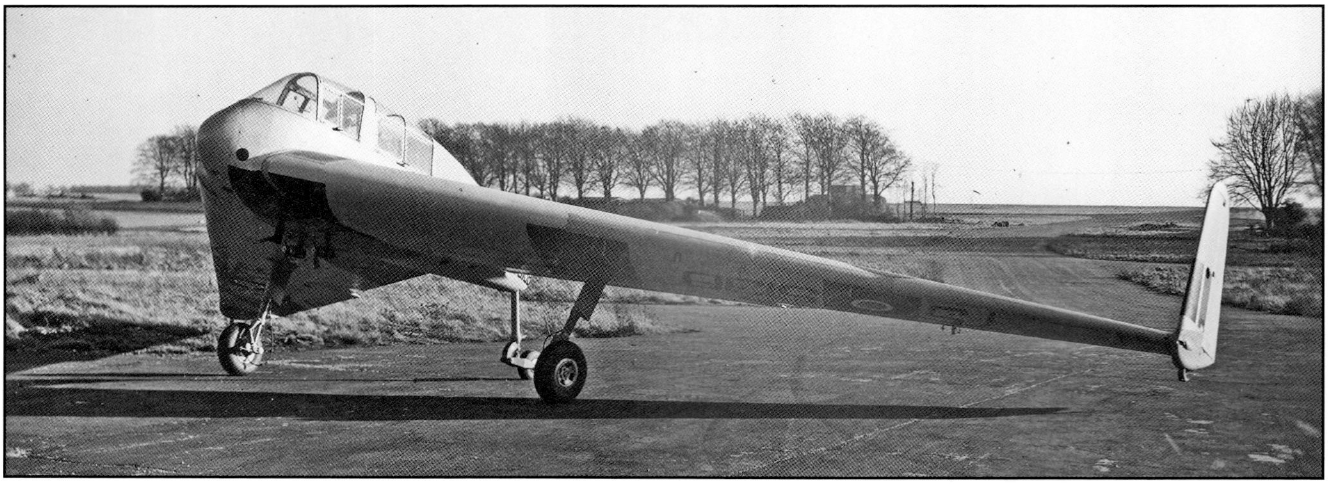

General Aircraft Ltd at Hanworth experimented with tailless gliders during the latter years of the war. The GAL.56 appeared in three versions to evaluate different angles of sweepback. The first aircraft, pictured here, was the Medium-V (TS507) having constant sweepback on both leading and trailing edges. Second was the Medium-U (TS510) which had a parallel-chord centre section, while third was the Medium-V (TS513) with increased sweepback. The machine seen here was the first to fly in November 1944.

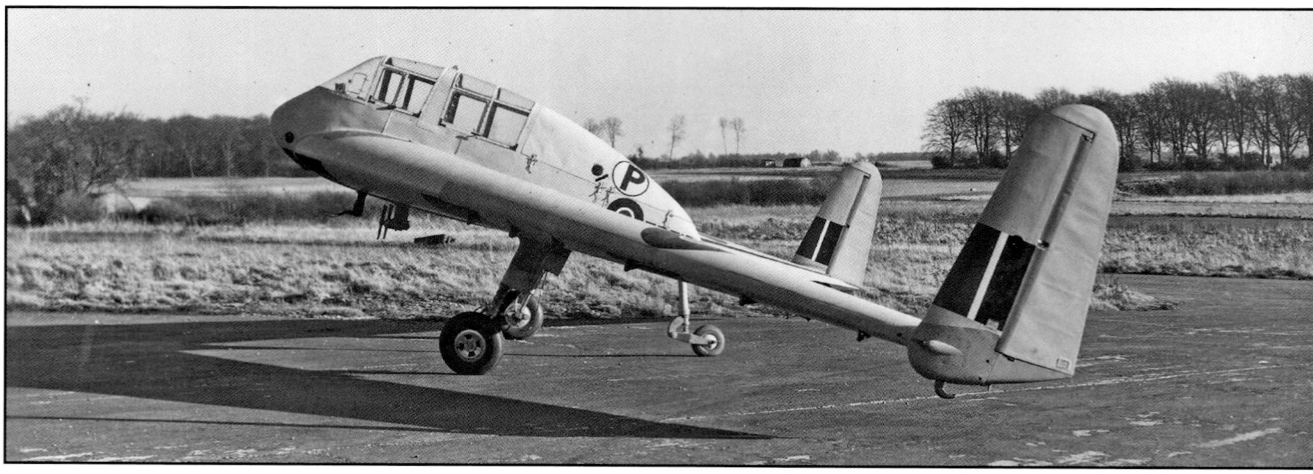

Viewed from any angle the General Aircraft Medium-V was a curious shape with its high nose and peculiar short-coupled 'reverse-tricycle' undercarriage. On the ground, pilots reported it was 'scarcely steerable' once the rear wheel had touched. Which may be why each of the wing-tip fins had a small skid attached to the lowest part. This picture was taken by the Ministry of Supply in January 1947.

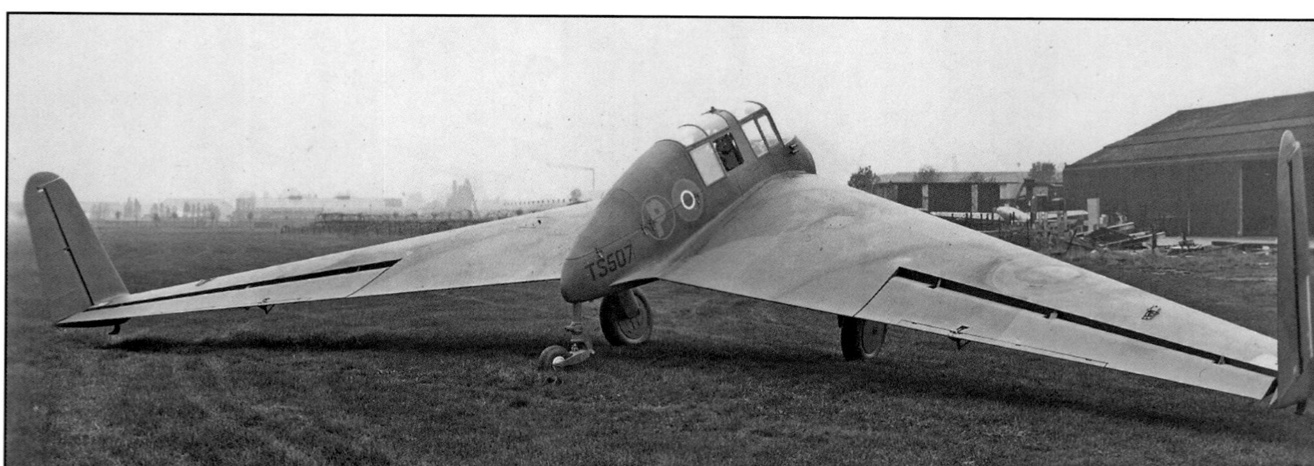

All three of the GAL.56 gliders were taxing to fly and demanded constant attention from the pilot. Each carried a crew of two and the nominal span was 42 feet 4 inches. This aircraft eventually claimed the life of one of the world's leading glider pilots, Robert Kronfeld (1904-1948) when he was unable to recover from a manoeuvre. This brought the experiments to a halt.

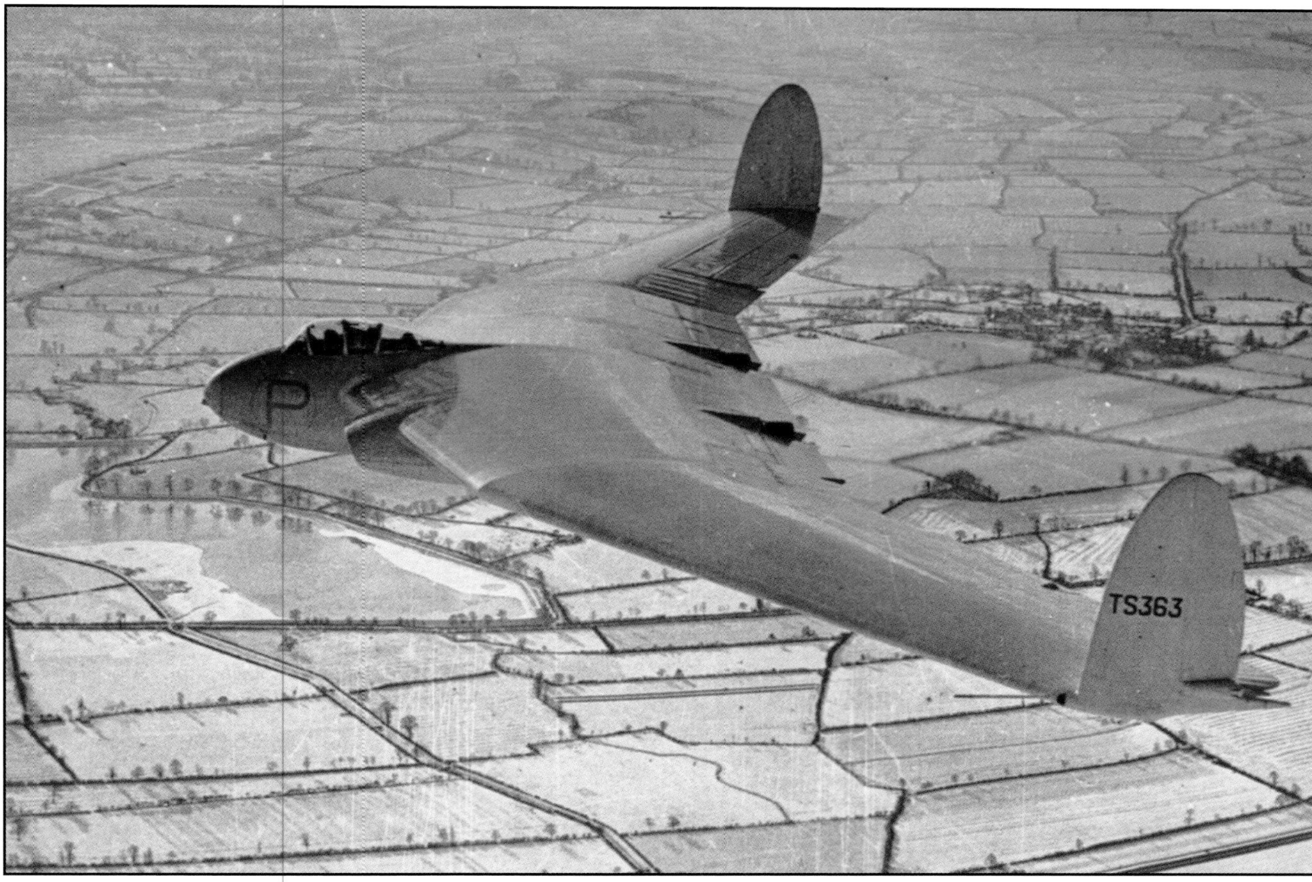

The 1939-45 war had re-kindled an interest in flying wings and, with the advances in the aerodynamics of laminar-flow, the opportunity was seen to produce a new generation of high-performance aircraft. Armstrong Whitworth began work on the wooden AW.52G (G meaning glider) in May 1942 and on March 2nd, 1945, test pilot Charles Turner-Hughes made the first flight at Coventry's Baginton Aerodrome towed off by a Whitley bomber. The next development was to fly a powered version. A pair of Rolls-Royce Nene turbojets was selected and the new all-metal AW.52 had a crew of two but only the pilot was provided with a Martin-Baker ejector seat. The engines not only provided thrust but also suction to provide boundary-layer control for the laminar-flow wing. Serialled TS 363, the prototype made its first flight at Boscombe Down on November 13th. 1947. Eighteen months later, test pilot John Oliver Lancaster experienced uncontrollable wing flutter and was forced to eject – the first man to use a Martin-Baker seat in an emergency.

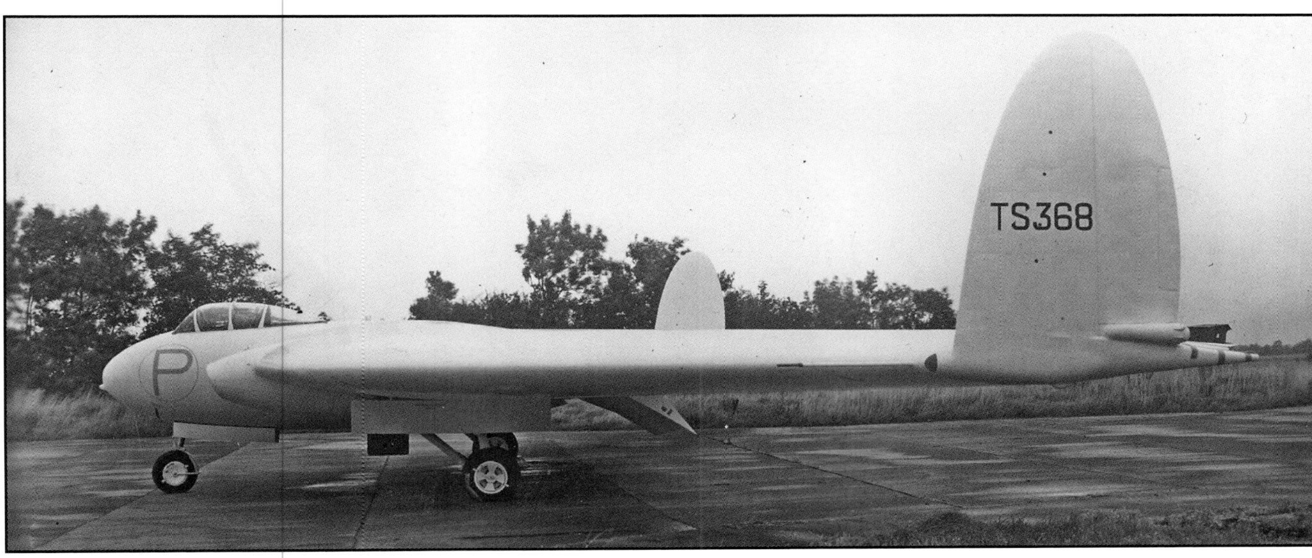

A second AW.52, TS368, was also built and flown. This had lower-powered Rolls-Royce Derwent engines and is seen here revealing details of the retractable nosewheel undercarriage and the large central flap. Overall, the results proved disappointing and the project was abandoned.

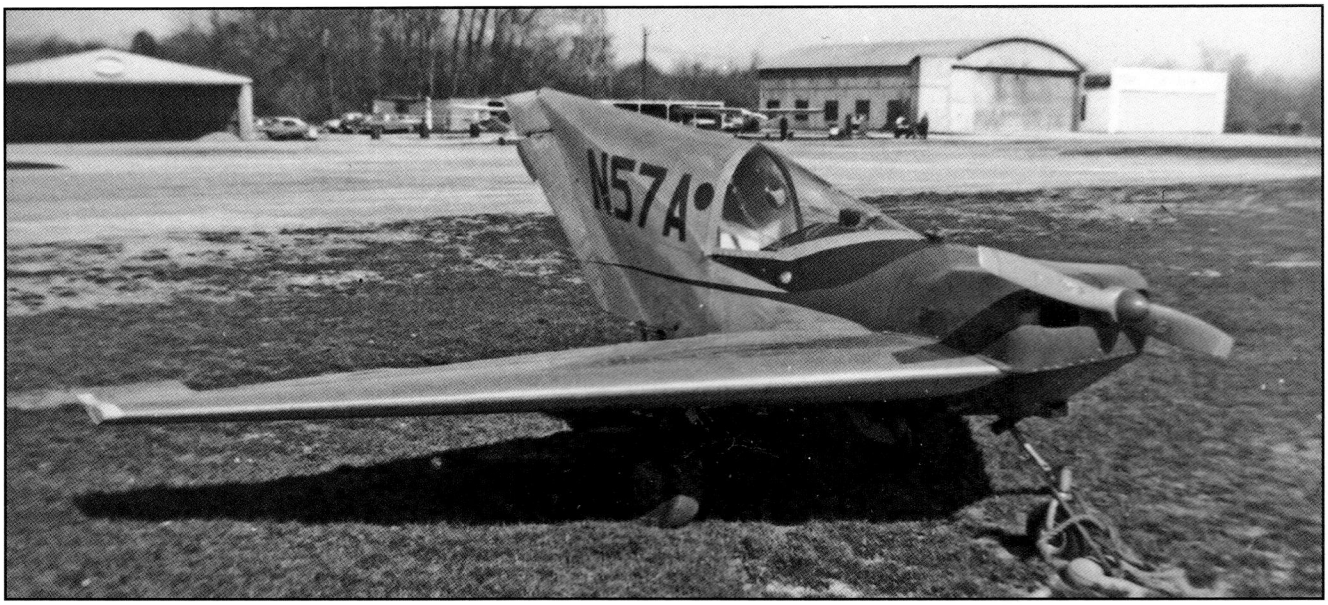

Marion 'Jim' Baker of Huron, Ohio, was a flight test mechanic at Wright-Patterson air force base and cherished the idea of building a very light delta-wing single-seat racing aircraft. Design of his MB-1 Delta Kitten began in 1952 under curious circumstances. He had acquired a crashed Cessna 140 and planned to use engine, propeller, some cowlings, the undercarriage and sundry other parts in his homebuilt. By 1957 he was able to begin construction and, with its 85 hp Continental C.85 engine, he was ready for first hop on July 25th 1960. With license number N57A, a wingspan of 18 feet and a length of 13 feet 3 inches, his striking Delta Kitten had cost just $2,000 to build. Maximum take-off weight was just 843 lbs and the wing had a leading edge sweep-back of 45 deg. In 1961 he won the Experimental Aircraft Association (EAA) Design Trophy. However stunning a design or brilliant the designer, an aircraft demands regular and careful maintenance. On July 29th, 1976, N57A crashed at Mansfield, Ohio, killing its pilot. The rivets securing the elevator operating bracket to the elevator had corroded and sheared off.

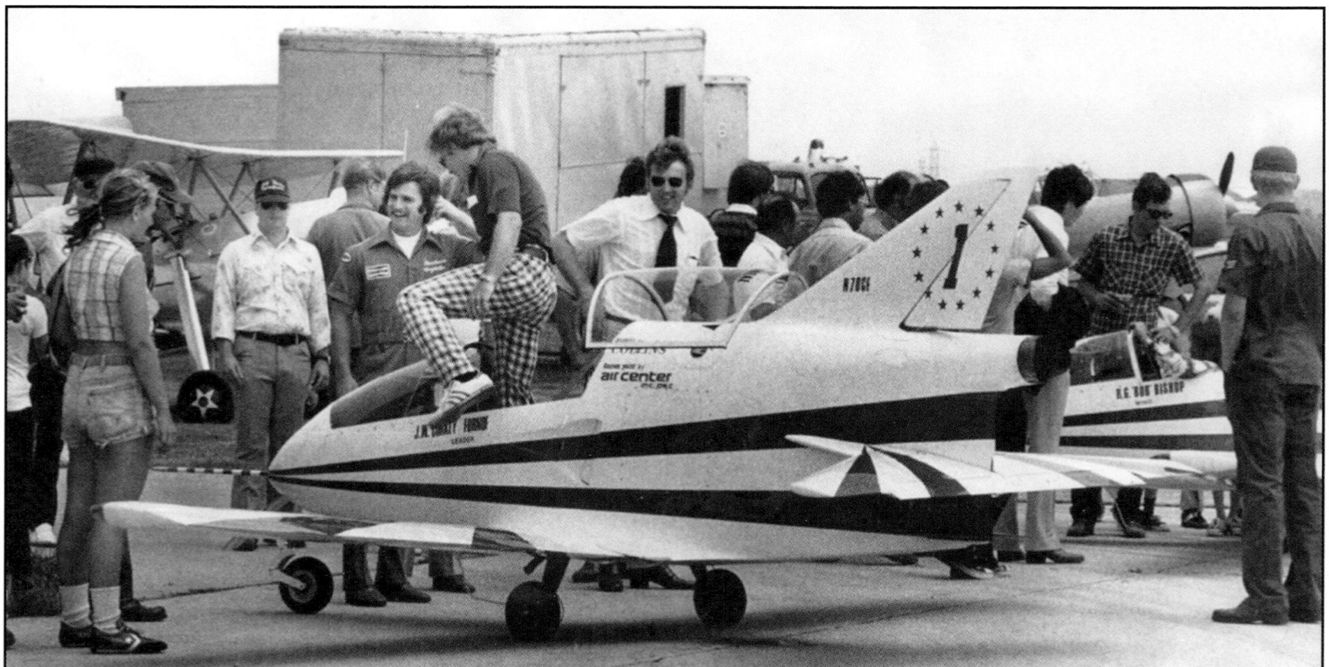

From earliest times, home-built aircraft have always played a part in aviation for the pioneers were all amateurs. But the closing decades of the 20th century saw an explosion in the design and innovation of amateur aviation. Sooner or later there would have to be a home-made jet plane and in the 1970s that came to pass with American Jim Bede's tiny jet, the Bede BD-5J. A version of Bede's successful piston-powered Micro of 1971, the BD-5J was powered by a 202 lb static-thrust Microturbo TRS 19 turbojet. With a length of 12 feet 4 inches and a span of 25 feet 7 inches, the maximum take-off weight was only 960 lbs. Maximum level flight speed was 276 mph and the stalling speed 76 mph. Here stunt flyer Corky Fornoff decamps from his jet at DuPage County Airport, West Chicago, on the occasion of the 17th annual air show in September 1976. Parked next to his aircraft is another BD-5J flown by Bob Bishop seen in the check shirt.

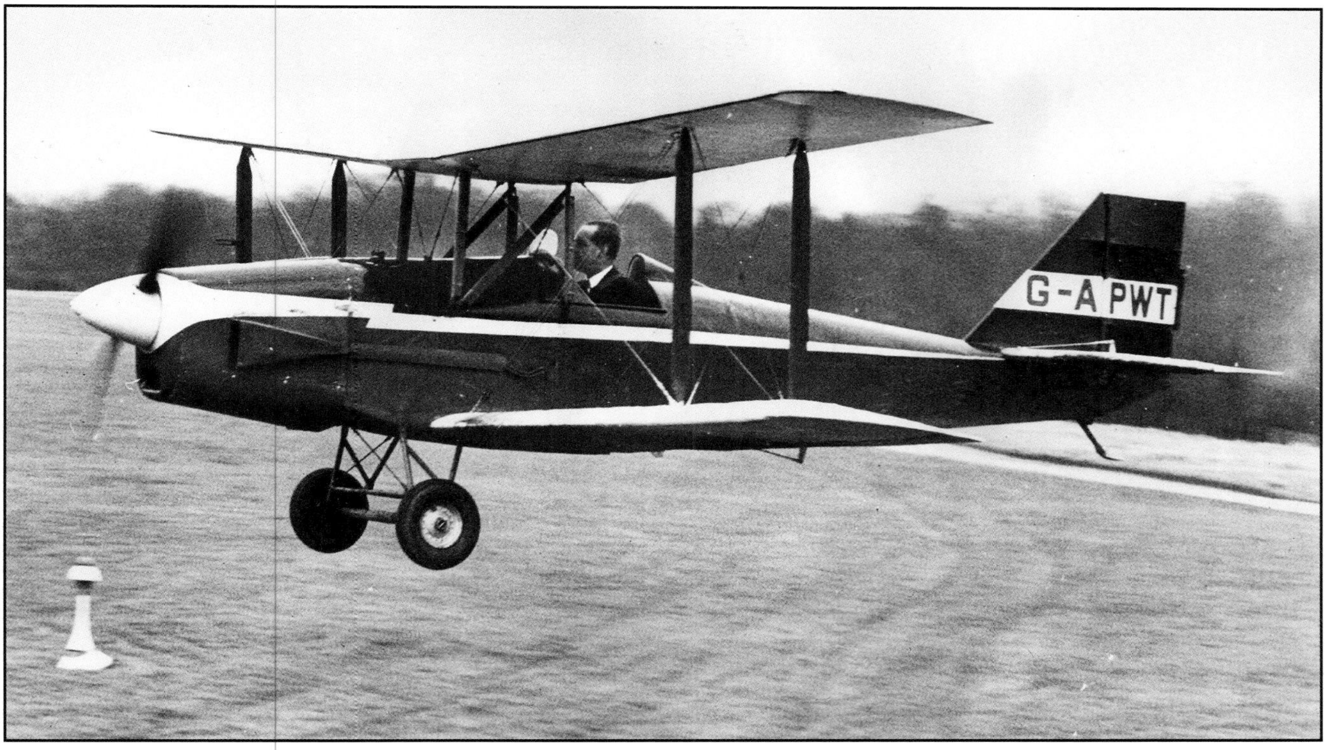

The world's smallest turbo-prop aircraft was this Currie Wot homebuilt after it had been fitted with a 60 hp Rover TP.60 gas turbine in 1961. The engine, together with 43 inch diameter variable-pitch propeller, was 43 inches in length and weighed 235 lbs complete with airscrew and all accessories. It could be fitted into any small aircraft without major change. The engines (there was also a 90 hp model) were designed by Rover with the idea of fitting them into cars at some future date. Of course, it never came to pass and the aircraft use of the gas turbine was quickly abandoned. In the Wot G-APWT, the engine proved itself to be smooth in operation and virtually vibration-free. What a lost opportunity! Here it is pictured on test at Birmingham's Elmdon Airport

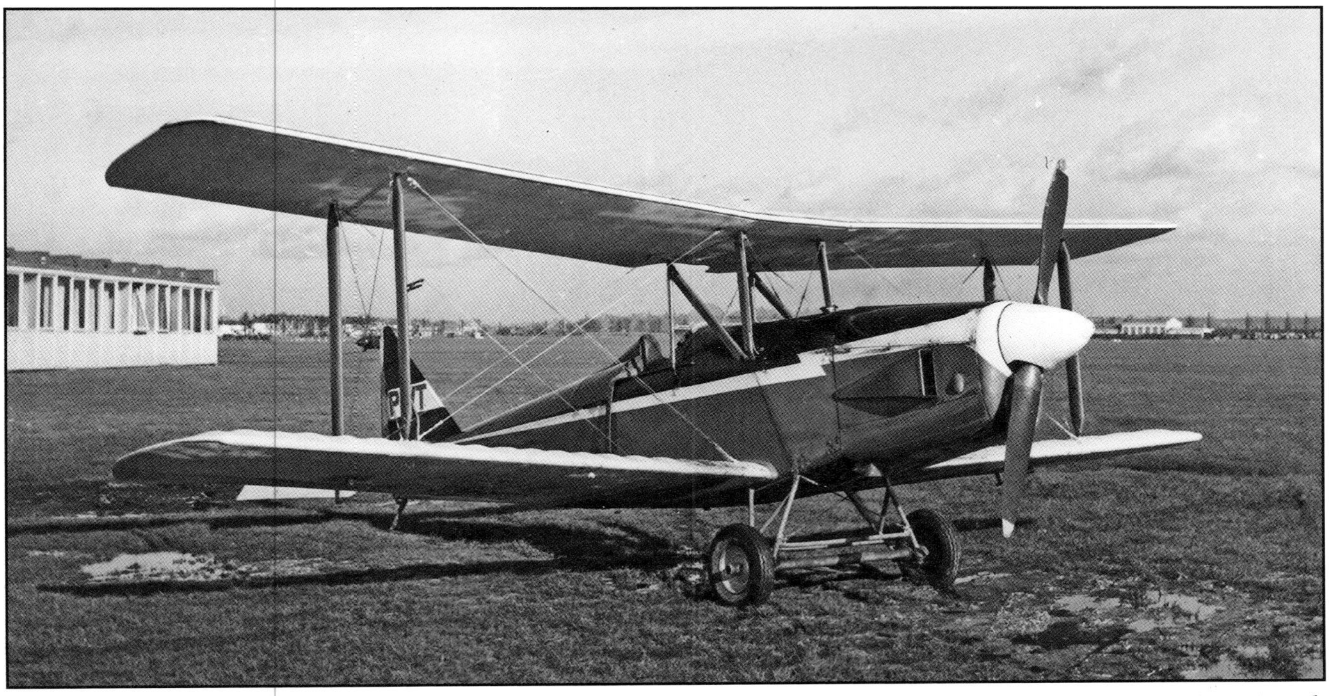

Originally designed by John Currie in 1938, the Currie Wot was a highly-successful post-war revival and may were built with a variety of engines. This one was built by Vivian Bellamy at Eastleigh and registered G-APWT in October 1959. Initially it flew with a 37 hp Aeronca-JAP flat twin, then a 62 hp Walter Mikron II in-line four-cylinder and, as seen here, the Rover gas turbine developed from a naval auxiliary power unit. It was flown in this form by Bellamy on January 26th 1960. Later it was refitted with the larger-still 70 hp Rover TP.60/1 but eventually reverted to the Mikron. Flown for a while on floats, G-APWT was thus probably the most versatile of single aircraft types in post-war Britain.

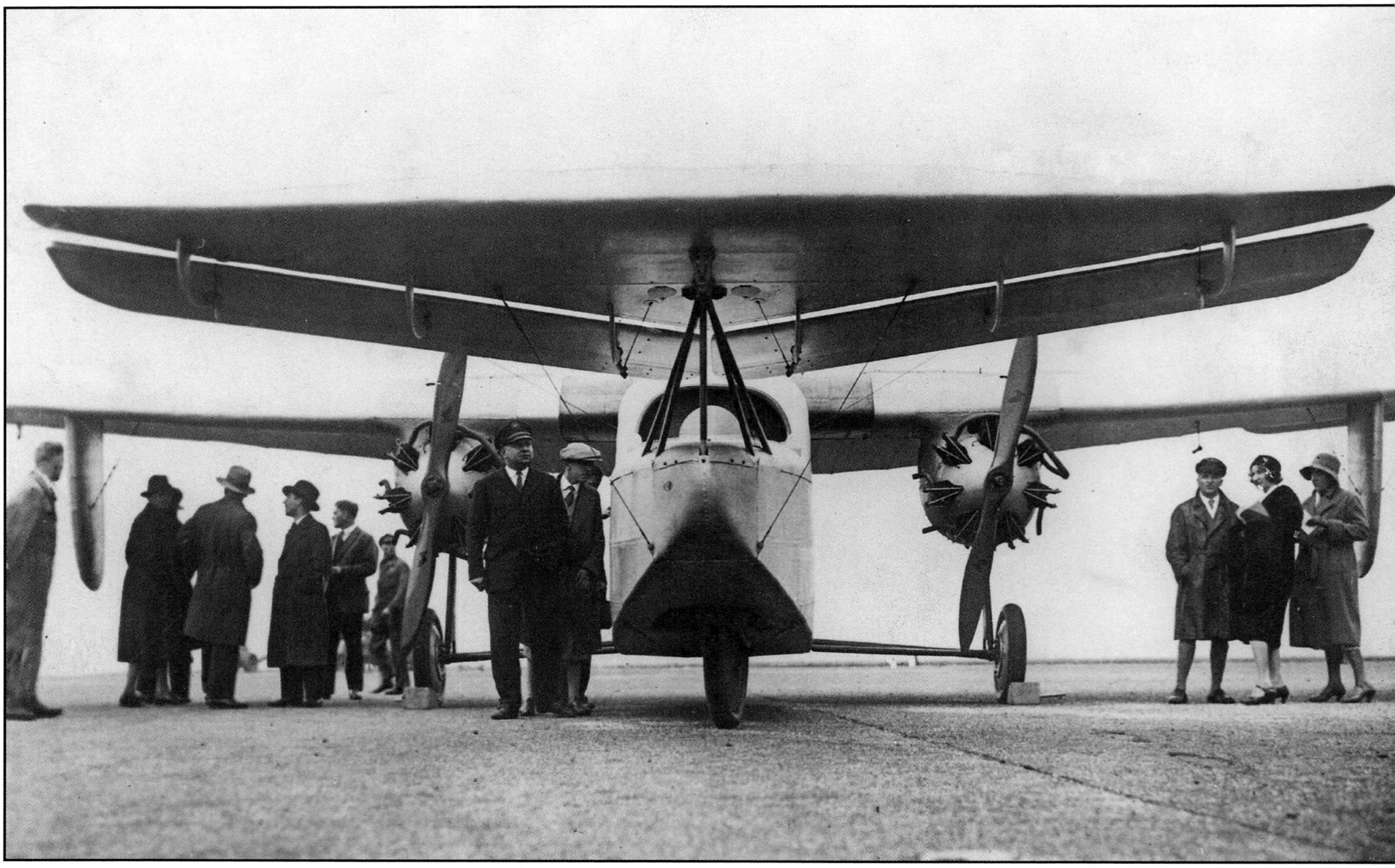

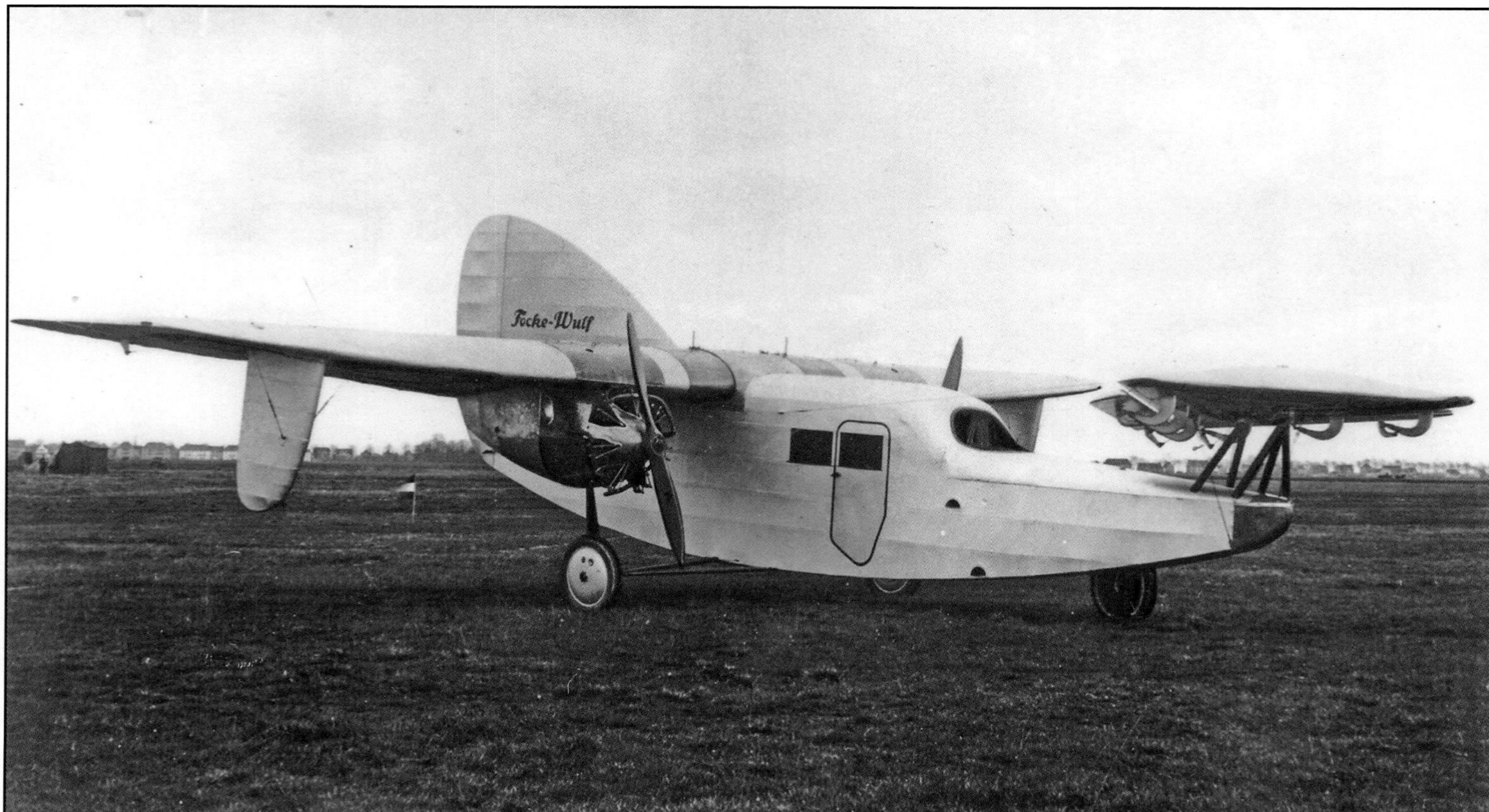
Focke-Wulf

Opposite upper: Tail-first aircraft have a theoretical aerodynamic advantage over the more accepted or conventional aircraft layout. This is that whereas in an 'ordinary' aircraft, pulling the stick back to climb means pushing the tail down first in order to raise the wing's angle of attack, having the elevator at the front keeps the aircraft at even height while immediately adjusting the angle of attack. This detail is instantly appreciated by those who fly crop-spraying aircraft. In 1927, Focke-Wulf introduced its Ente, an open-cockpit canard monoplane that flew tail-first. Powered by two 110 hp Siemens Sh.14 radial engines, the 32 feet 10 inch-span prototype first flew on September 2nd 1927. Here the unregistered aircraft is seen being admired at Tempelhof, Berlin, on its first public showing two weeks later. The second picture (*opposite lower*) reveals the two half-moon steps needed for the pilot to get into and out of the cockpit. The second machine would differ in having a small square cabin window just ahead of the passenger cabin door. Viewed as an aviation curiosity even then, the Ente displayed some unusual features, not the least of which was the fact that the two under-wing fins were slightly convergent so that, if extended, they would have met in front of the 'tail' at the nose. Also the front wing (the canard surface) could be rocked from side to side (as on Britain's curious Grice tandem-wing). All was not well, though, and having established its flying credentials, a broken control rod caused a crash on September 29th which killed company partner, test pilot Georg Wulf (1890-1927).

Opposite lower: A second Ente (which is German for 'duck') was built, this one would eventually bear the civil registration D-1960. It is pictured at roll-out and without markings. With a loaded weight of 3,638 lbs, it was rather disappointing that the cruising speed on a total of 220 hp was no more than 88 mph.

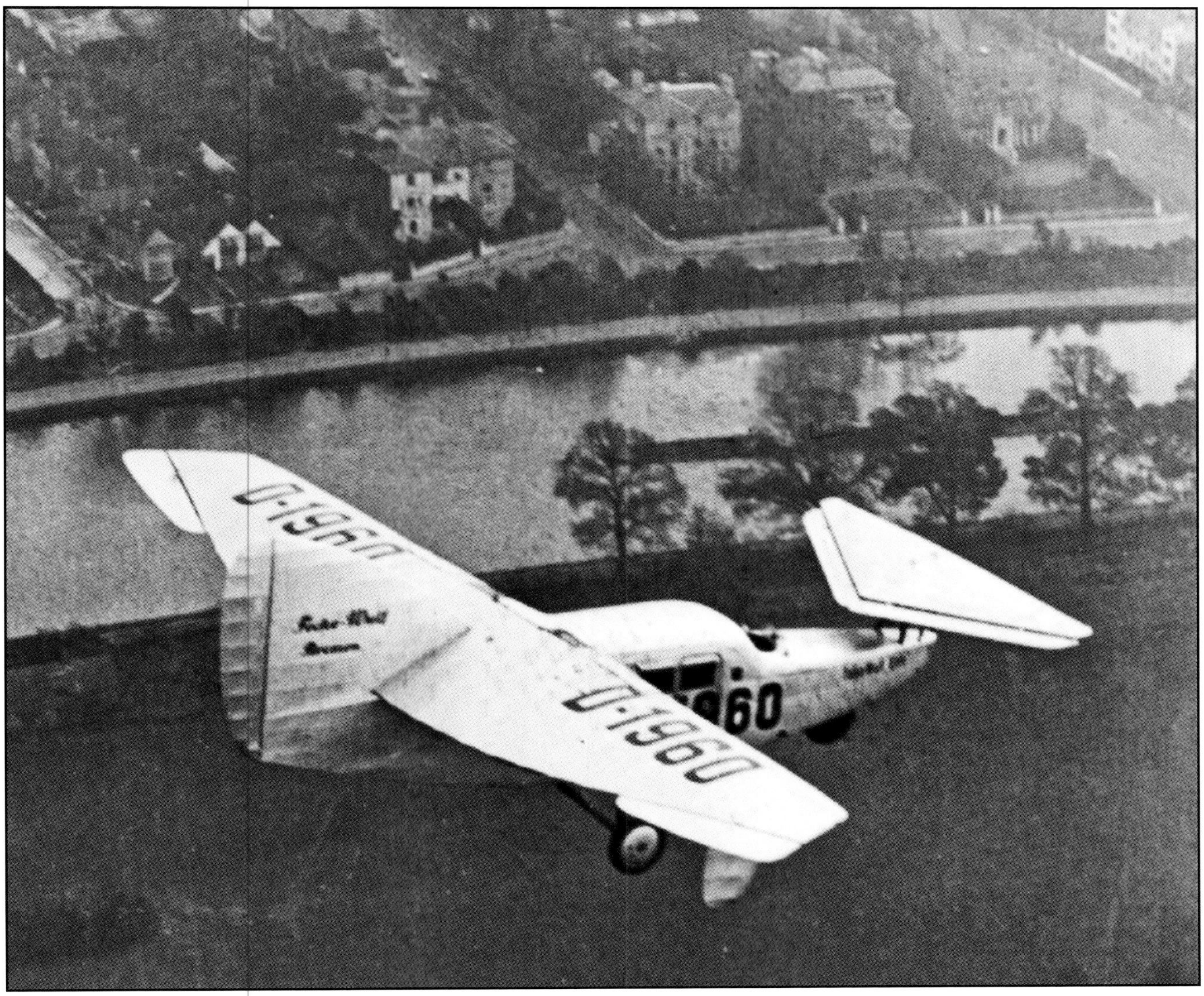

In the late autumn of 1931, the second example of this novel-shaped aeroplane embarked on a European tour which brought it to West London's Hanworth Air Park on November 7th. Flown by Focke-Wulf's chief pilot Cornelius Edzard (1898-1962), it undertook a number of demonstration flights, one being with the then well-known aviatrix, The Hon Mrs Victor Bruce. Differing slightly from the first example, the canard surface on this one was not see-sawable but was fixed. In this publicity photograph it is flying down the River Thames parallel to the A307 Portsmouth Road on the opposite river bank. The junction with Anglesea Road is in the centre of the picture. With pilot and three passengers, the Ente had certain attractions but was not particularly efficient aerodynamically nor, with a maximum speed of just 88 mph, did it measure up to other aircraft of similar power and size. The Ente faded in the face of what turned out to be the German air force re-armament programme.

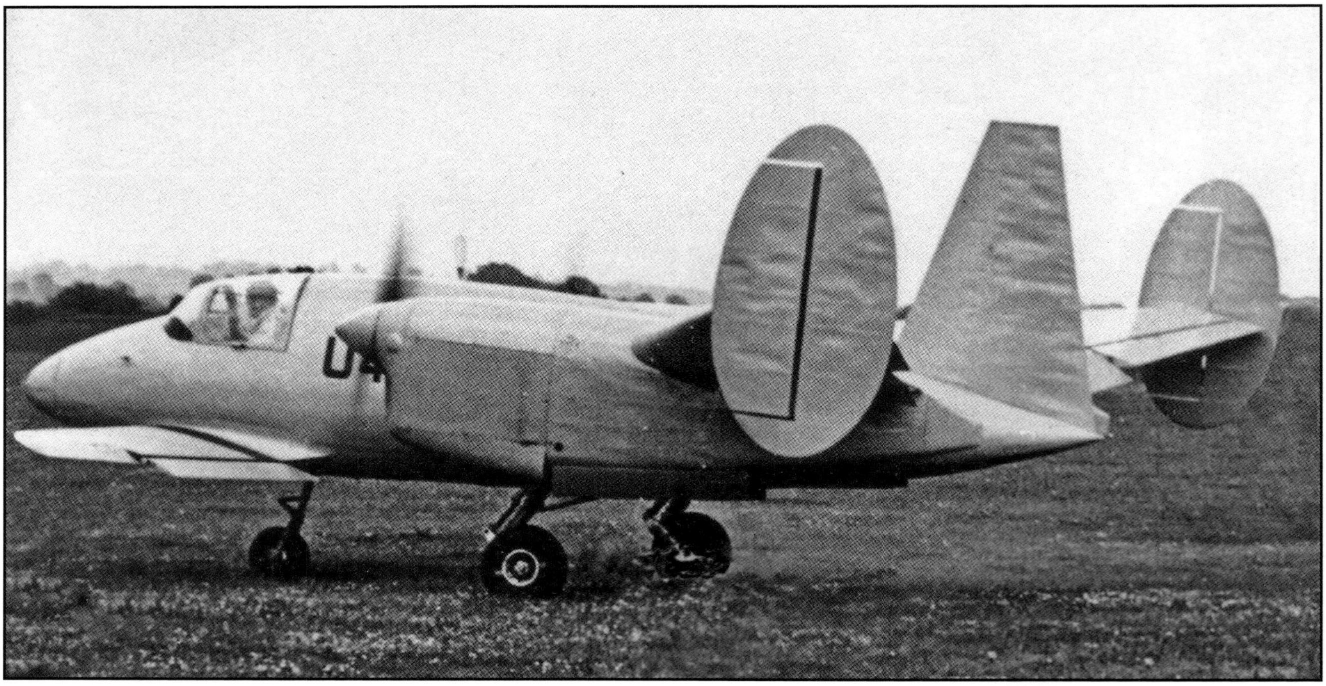

Another maker who flirted with the tail-first concept was Miles Aircraft Ltd. During 1942 the RAF had reported a need for a high-altitude high-speed bomber having a range of 1,500 miles. Miles came up with an attractive canard design under the designation M.39 Libellula. While this was not adopted, a small all-wood version called the M.39B was built and flown under the markings U0244, and powered by a pair of 140 hp Gipsy Major engines. Completed in the early summer of 1943, George Miles made the first flight on July 2nd. It proved astonishingly stable and easy to fly and, with its retractable tricycle undercarriage, it had a presentable performance. The front wing spanned 25 feet, the rear one 37 feet 6 inches, both wings being provided with trailing-edge flaps. Tare weight was just 2,405 lbs and the maximum all-up weight of 2,800 lbs. The initial rate of climb was 1,100 feet/minute, the top speed 164 mph and the stall came at 59 mph. After extensive trials following purchase of the sole example by the Ministry of Supply for the Royal Aircraft Establishment, in February 1945 it was returned to Miles at Woodley as U4.

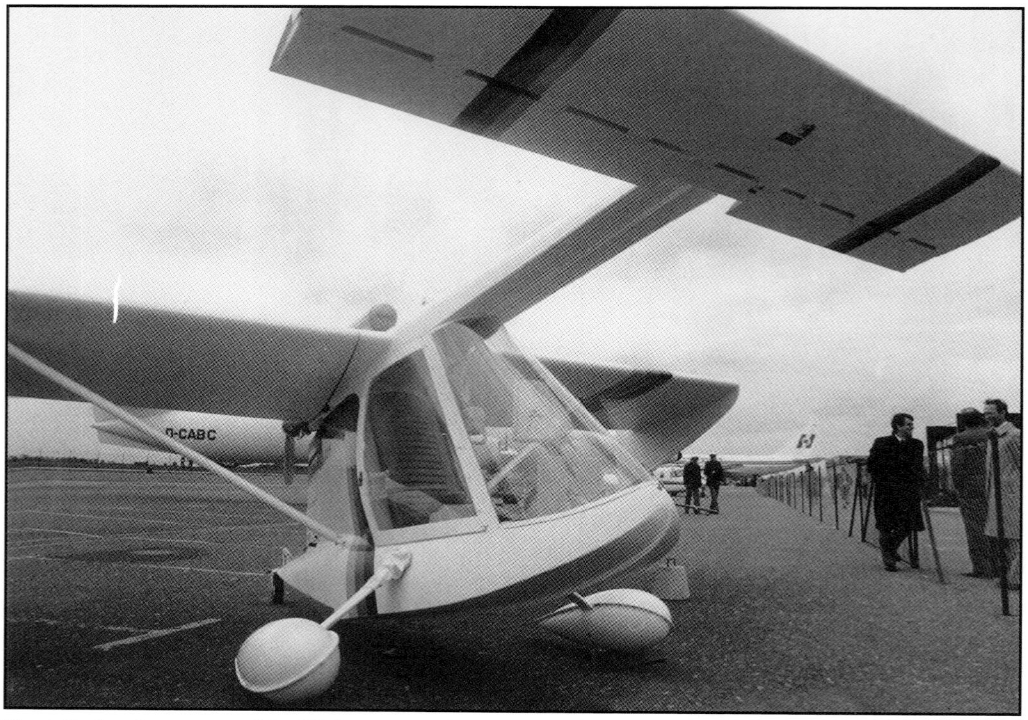

Founded by Pierre-George Latécoère (1883-1943) in 1917, his eponymous French company was renowned for its seaplanes. Today the company, run by Pierre-George, Jnr, is a contributor to Airbus Industries and also Boeing in America. But at the 1983 Paris Air Show the company revealed its Latécoère 225 side-by-side two-seat microlight. What was so unusual was that this 24 hp PUL 425-powered pusher was not only a canard but an amphibian. Designed by Nono Hersen, the 225 was of composite construction with swept-back main wings. The main wheels fold back and their fairings act as sponsons when operating from water. The tailwheel was steerable. With a span of 26 feet 4 inches and a length overall of 16 feet 3 inches, the 225 weighed just 280 lbs empty and after a 262 feet take-off run could fly at 75 mph. On water the unstick distance was 492 feet. The prototype, F-WZLM, made its first flight on July 18th, 1984 and this photograph, taken at Hanover's Internationale Luftfahrt-Austellung (Germany's international air show) staged in May 1984, was before the flight trials began.

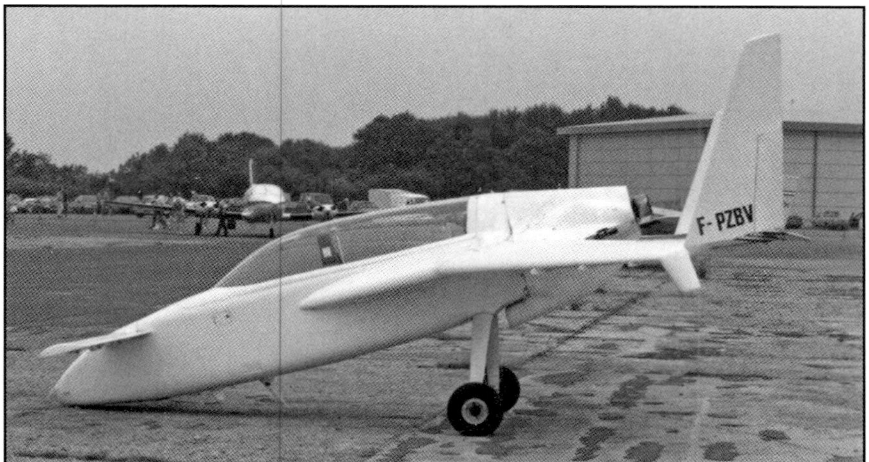

At first sight, the work of brothers Dick and Burt Rutan might earn the soubriquet of being 'pre-crashed' if only for the fact that the curious shape of this canard is enhanced by the practice of always retracting the nosewheel undercarriage when on the ground. The Vari Eze of 1975, seen here in this French-made example, is a homebuilt comprising composite materials. Expanded polystyrene foam, glass fibre and epoxy resin make up almost the entire airframe. Étienne Lance built F-PZBV at Blois in August 1990.

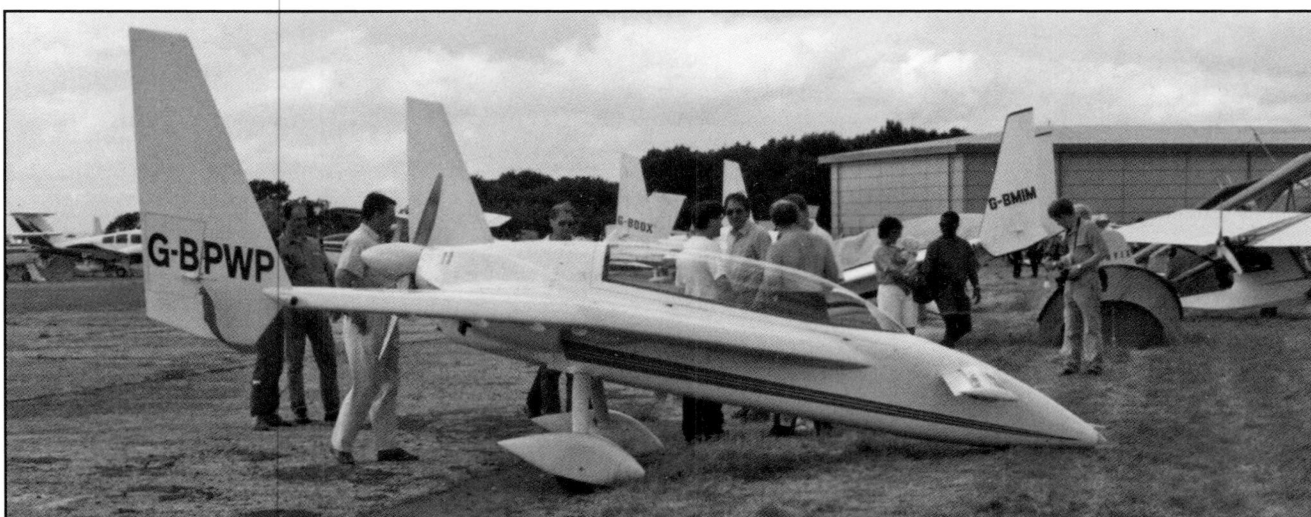

Larger but of the same format, the Rutan Long Ez shares the same nose-in-the-grass attitude when parked. The fixed mainwheels contrast with the manually-retractable nosewheel, the folding of which is said to eliminate the need for a parking brake, to raise the propeller of the pusher engine high enough for comfortable hand-swinging and to make it easier to enter the cockpit. Here we see two examples, first is G-BPWP built by Douglas A Field and powered by a 120 hp Continental engine, and second F-PDEB which made its first flight on April 3rd, 1985, at Poitiers. Unfortunately it was written off at Liamone (Corsica) on September 4th, 1993. Designer Burt Rutan (1943-) designed and built a number of decidedly strange-looking machines among them the 'proof-of-concept' Grizzly (joined tandem wings) and the Voyager created to fly round the world non-stop which it did in 1997.

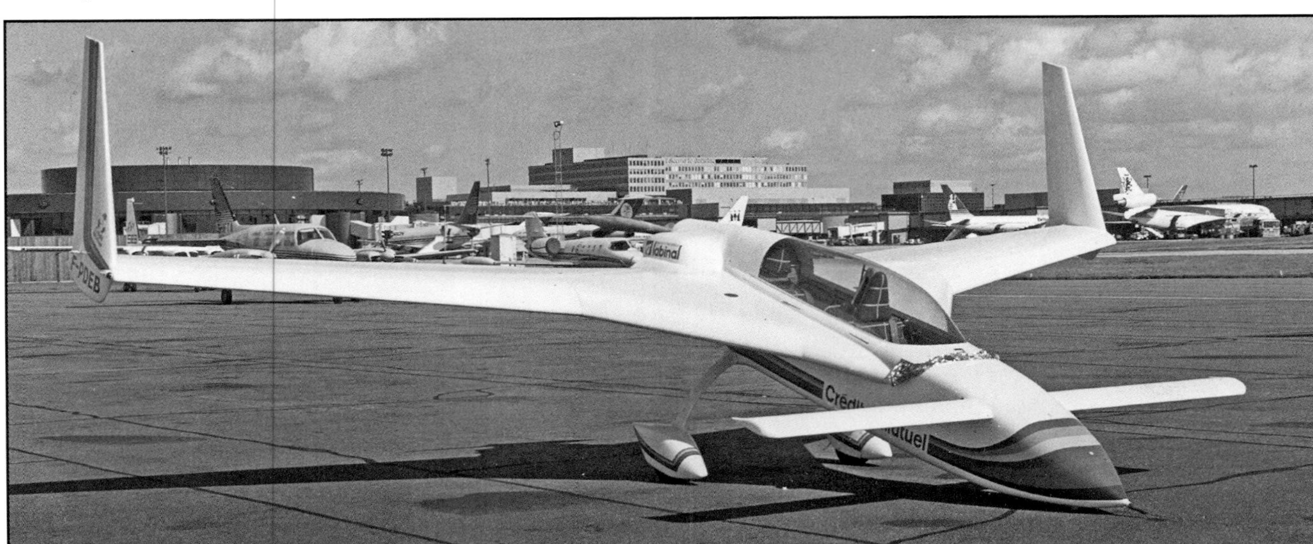

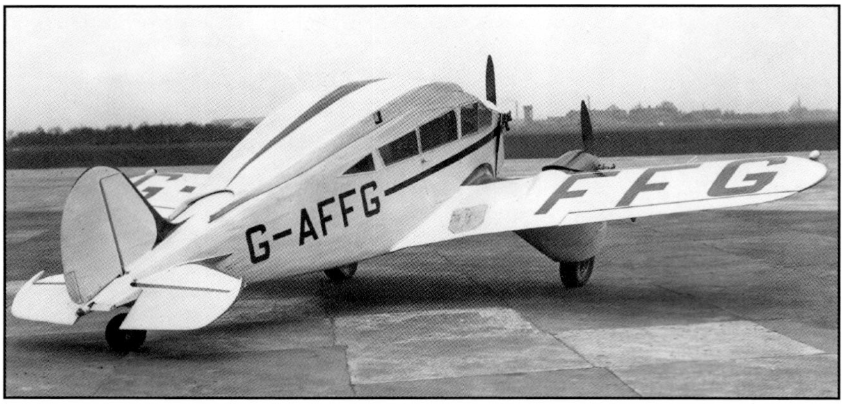

Flt.Lt Saleh Helmy was a talented engineer of Egyptian origin and, like many others such as Autogiro inventor Juan de la Cierva, devoted time and effort to eliminating the danger of the stall. Inspired by Handley Page's automatic slot, he came up with a curious 'sky-hook' in the form of a high-lift airfoil section fitted to the cabin roof of a light aircraft which could be raised at a high angle of attack at the moment of stall to provide additional lift. Helmy designed and hand-built an aircraft to prove his concept. The three-seat Aerogypt, G-AFFG, was powered by three 22 hp Douglas Sprite two-cylinder motors. He joined the

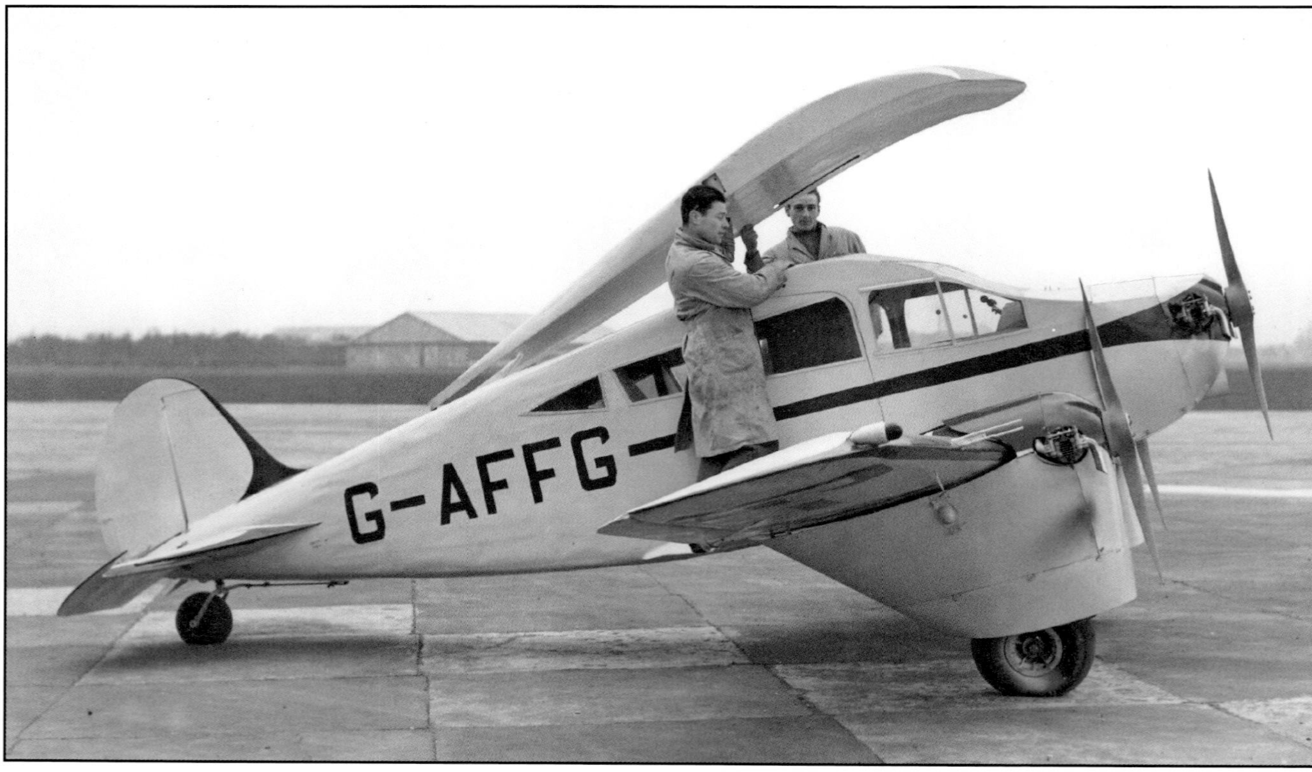

RAF in 1940 as Technical Officer. This allowed him unique status for he was allowed to continue development work including even test flights all through time of war. Over the years from its first flight at Heston early in 1938, the Aerogypt went through four stages of progressive development. The sky-hook, understandably, was scrapped in 1940 and after an extensive rebuild at White Waltham in 1943, it emerged with two Continental A-65 engines as the Mk.IV. Helmy's scheme was to make a range of Aerogypts in various sizes for use in Egypt after the war. On September 26th, 1947, Helmy and his wife set off for Cairo in the Aerogypt, landing first at Northolt to clear Customs. On final approach, G-AFFG snagged a perimeter telephone wire and stalled over the road smashing into the hedge. Later an airfield crane lifted the damaged aircraft clear but the cable slipped. This second crash finished off both the Aerogypt and Helmy's hoped-for plans.

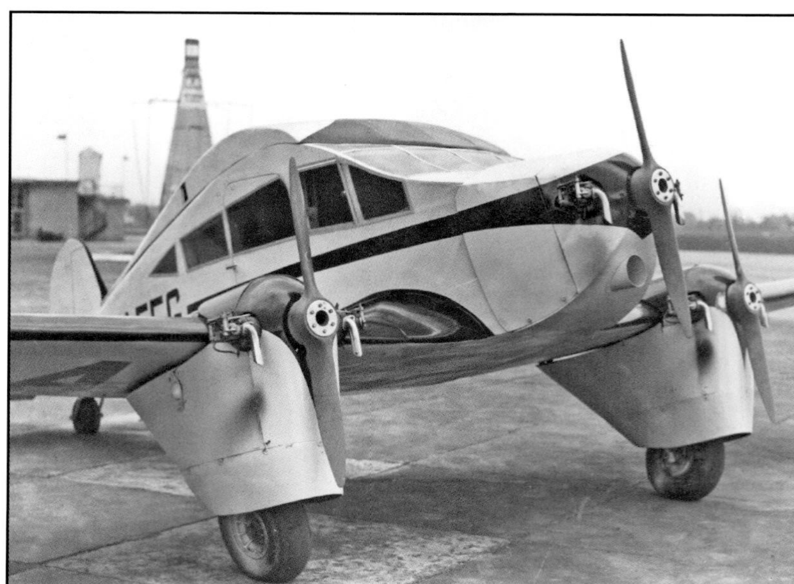

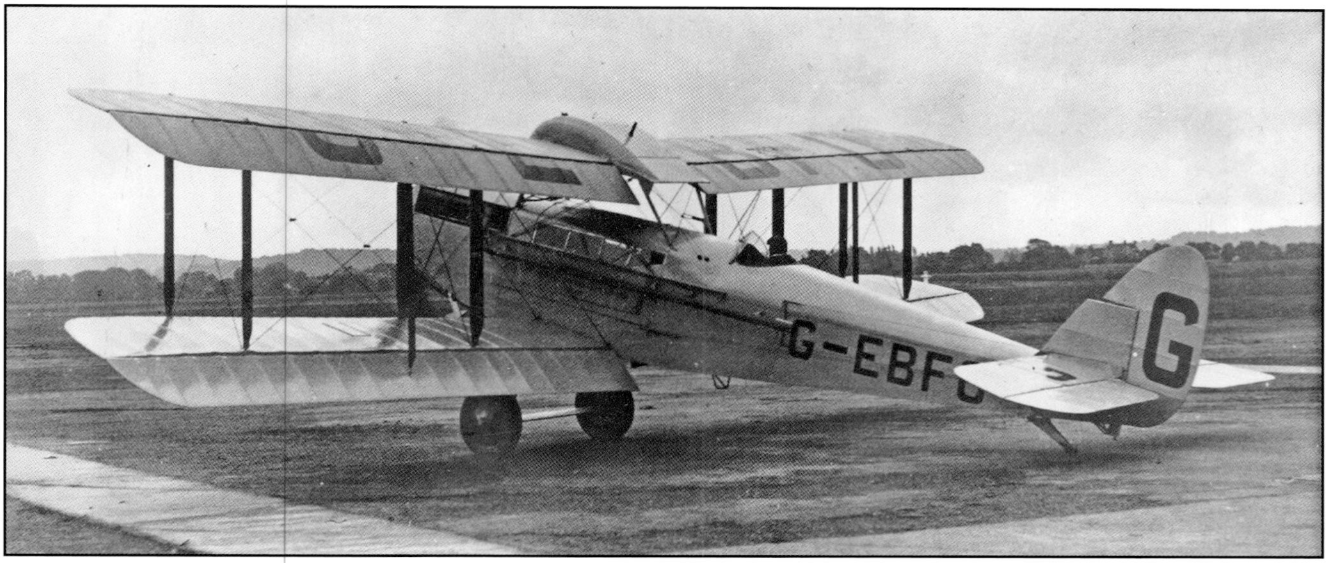

The benefits of altering the shape of a wing became a recurring mantra of aircraft designers throughout the ages. The Wrights warped their wings to a different shape, but the real excitement came with the discovery of the effects of slots, slats, flaps and spoilers. Geoffrey de Havilland's Stag Lane works were not to escape one of these periodic waves of enthusiasm and so, in May, 1924, a DH.50, G-EBFO, was fitted experimentally with full-span automatic camber-changing flaps on all four wings. As the speed declined and the air resistance on these flaps diminished, elastic cord pulled them down further and further. While the flaps remained operable as normally-controlled ailerons, the result seemed impressive – a 6 mph drop in the stalling speed. On May 30th that year, G-EBFO with its quad-flaps was flown by H S Broad with AVM Sir Sefton Brancker, Lord Thompson (Christopher Birdwood Thompson, Secretary of State for Air, who, along with Brancker, would be killed in the R101 disaster) and Mr. Frank Hughes to the Prague Aero Exhibition. However, the trials did not convince de Havilland to follow up the development. When Alan Cobham flew Sir Sefton to Rangoon that November, G-EBFO had been re-fitted with ordinary wings with conventional ailerons. Camber-changing flaps, for the moment at least, were out.

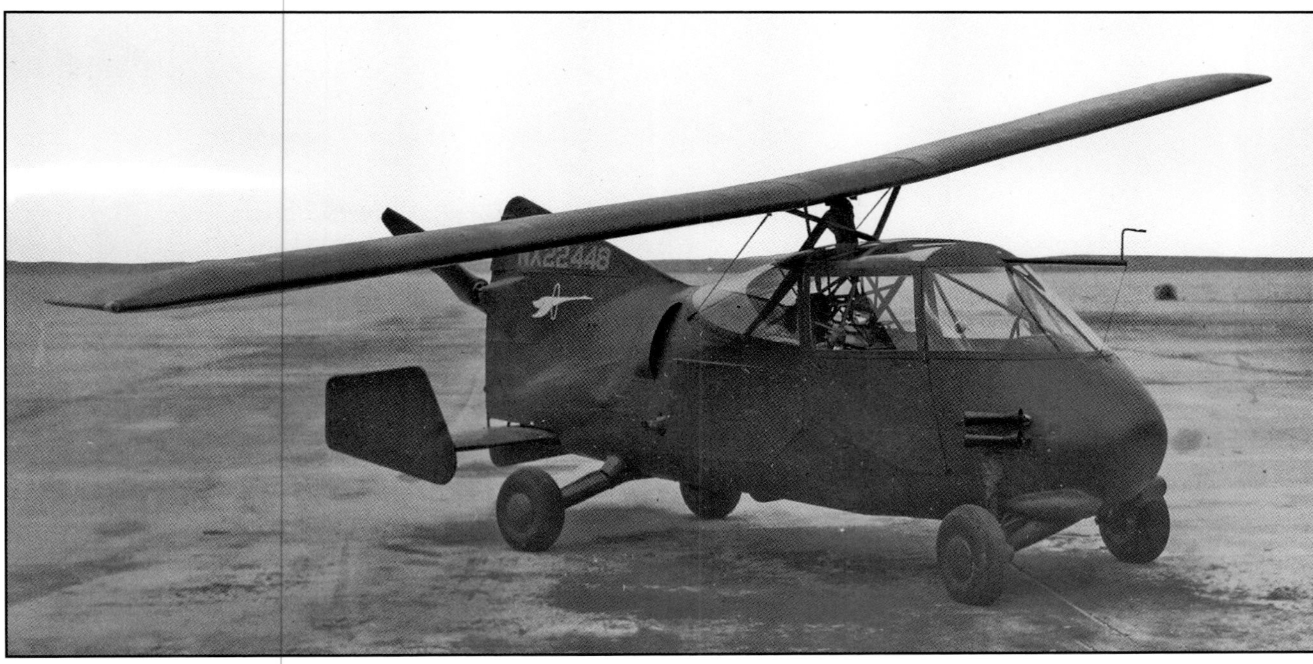

No, it's not a gyroplane but a pusher aircraft with a tiltable wing like that fitted to J B Gurney Grice's Mosquito built at Dunstable in 1935. One of the Wright Brothers' helpers was a man called George A Spratt who was firmly of the opinion that they (the Wrights) had the wrong idea about controls and that the solution was to rock the wing. The brothers and Spratt parted company. However, his son, George G Spratt was determined to prove his father had been 'wright' all along, so to speak, and so in 1945 he designed a single-control aircraft that would steer 'like an automobile'. This latter-day Henri Mignet got Consolidated Vultee and Chance-Vought interested, both companies at that time building curious prototypes. Brought to Elizabeth City, North Carolina, from Dearborn on January 1st, 1945, the first flight of NX22448 took place on January 25th by test pilots R D Suchner and R F Townsend who expressed their satisfaction. Vultee's works manager, K F Leaman, said that steps were being taken to put it into production. You can probably guess what followed – but it certainly wasn't a tilt-wing flying car.

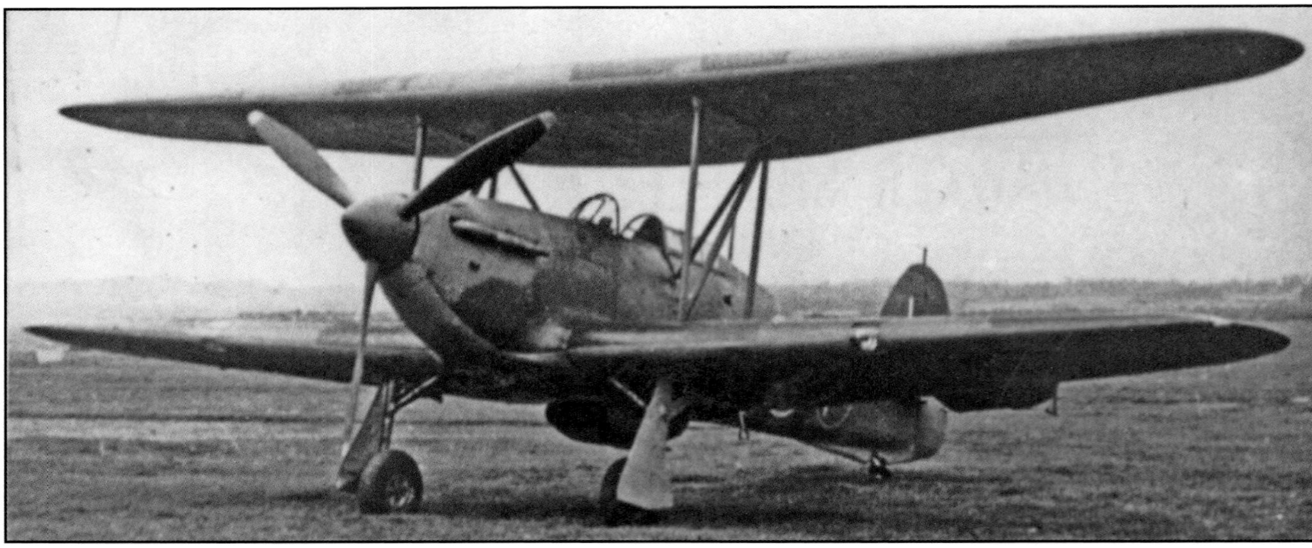

Amongst the many curious ideas experimented with during the 1939-45 war was the so-called Slip-Wing Hurricane, a project developed by F Hills & Son of Trafford Park, Manchester. Known as the Hillson FH.40, this was the culmination of trials with a very small experimental aircraft built and flown during 1941-3. The reasoning was that the extra wing would provide greater lift enabling the aircraft to take off with a much higher fuel load. As an aid to long-distance operation, once the upper wing had done its duty and its fuel tank was exhausted, the pilot could jettison the appendage and revert to monoplane status. Successful trials were undertaken but the ever-present fear was that the release mechanism would either fail or, even worse, partially fail, leaving an attached but flailing spare wing. Explosive bolts were yet to be perfected and so, with the need for long-range operation diminished by the arrival of better fighters (such as the long-range Mustang), trials with the sole example, L1884, were concluded in January 1944.

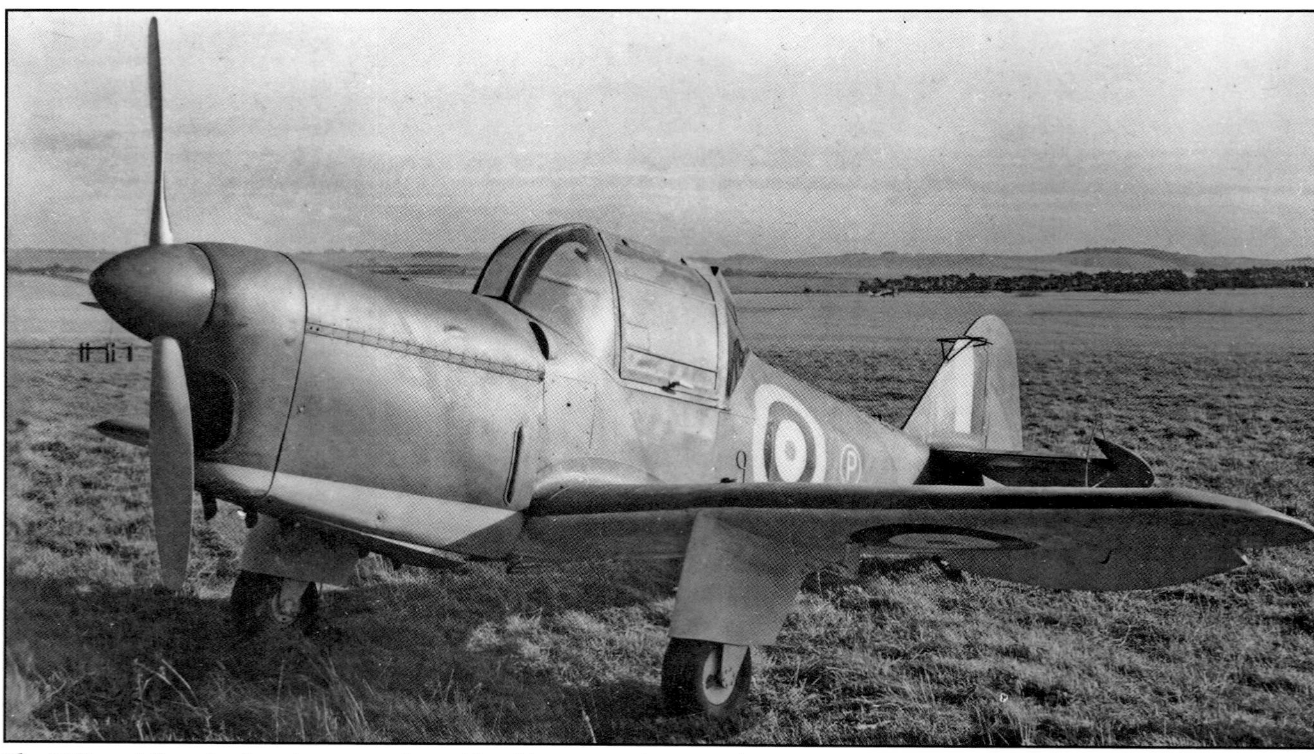

The Hillson 'slip wing' project was of considerable interest because the reason for its development changed. First proposed by the outspoken Noel Pemberton Billing (the man who founded what became Supermarine), the idea was to increase wing area and lift to enable short-field take-off of a fully-loaded aircraft and hence potential operation from very small airstrips. As the project advanced, besides added lift it was realised that the upper wing might also be used as a fuel-tank to extend the range. Hills' test vehicle was a delightful little machine designed on the lines of a racer. Powered by a 200 hp Gipsy Six (like the high-speed Percival Mew Gull) the wing-span was only 20 feet. Overall length was 19 feet 9 inches and the wing area was 66 square feet just three-quarters of the Mew Gull's wing area. Although not designed as a speed-chaser, it is reputed that the cruising speed was in excess of 210 mph.

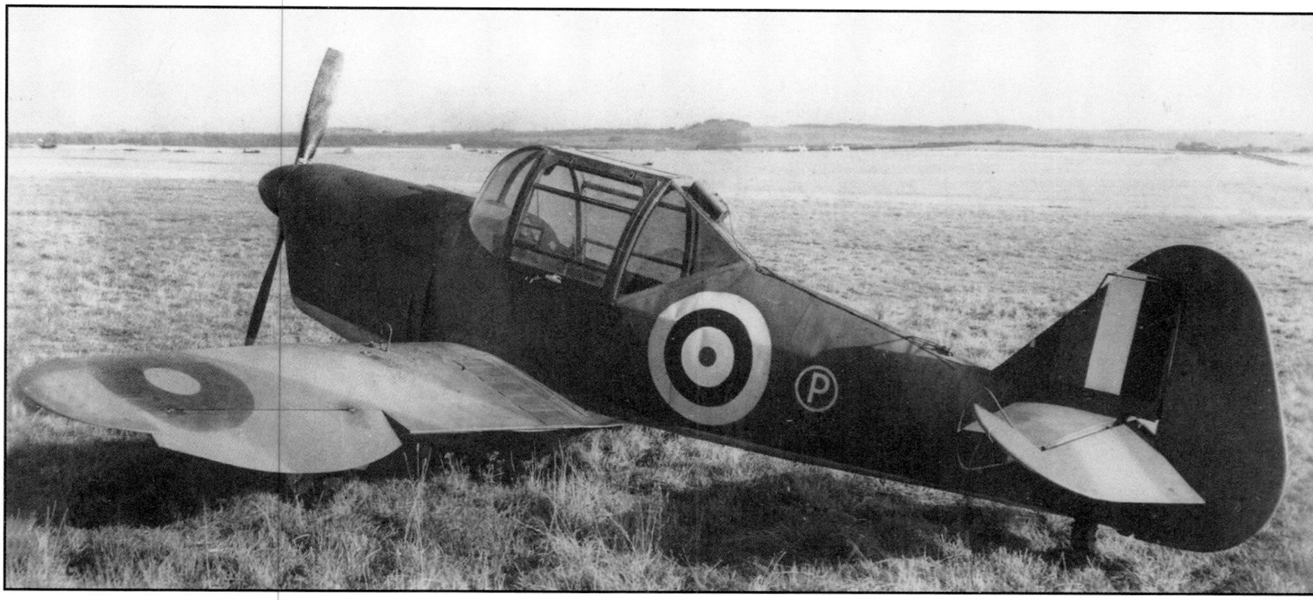

F Hills & Son's experiments with the slip-wing idea called for the construction of a small test vehicle, seen here in monoplane format. Mounted just behind the single-seat cockpit canopy was an emergency parachute just in case things went wrong and to avoid risk of the parachute shrouds fouling the tail, both the elevator and rudder horns carried protective quadrant brackets.

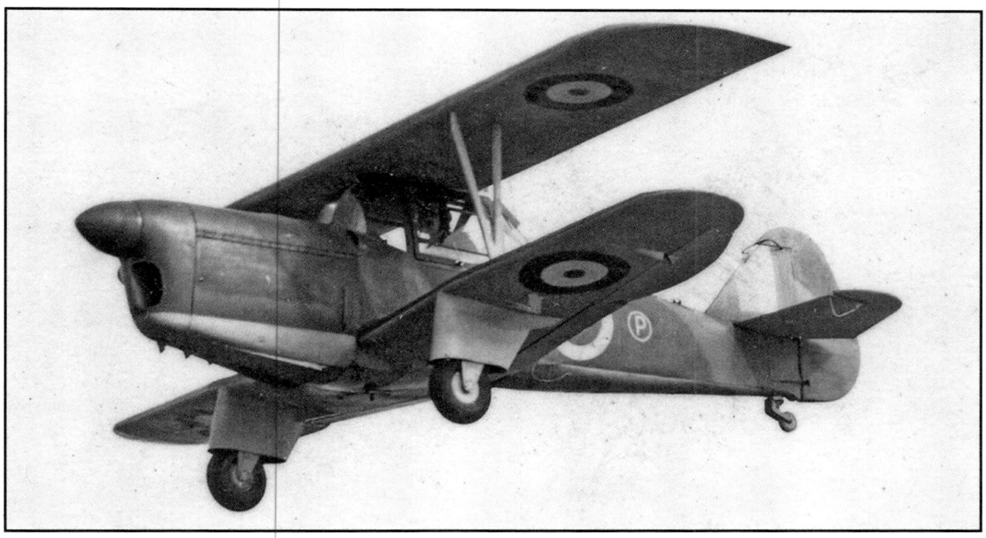

With the slip-wing in place, the wing area more than doubled to 146 square feet and the all-up weight of 1,940 lbs gave a mean wing-loading of 13.3 lbs/sq.ft – around half that of the Percival Mew Gull. The combination was flown extensively during 1941 both as a monoplane and as a biplane as pictured here. On July 16th, 1941, while flying at 4,500 feet over the sea off Blackpool, the first successful 'slip' was made: the wing floated down into the sea and was actually retrieved although not flown again.

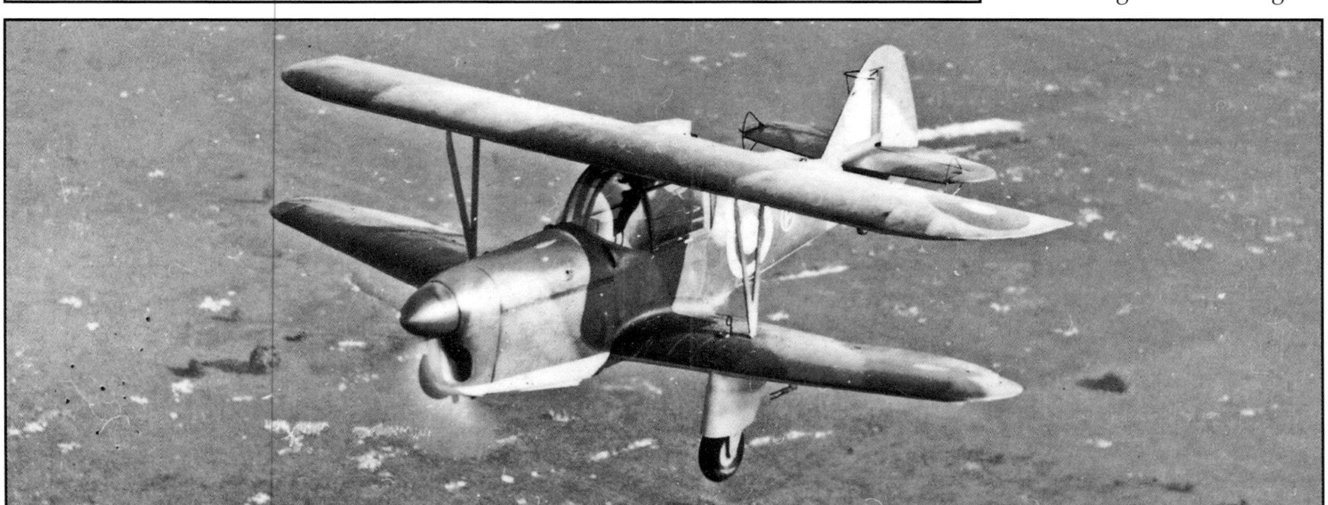

Here the Hillson Slip Wing test vehicle is seen in flight as a biplane with the quick-release wing in position.

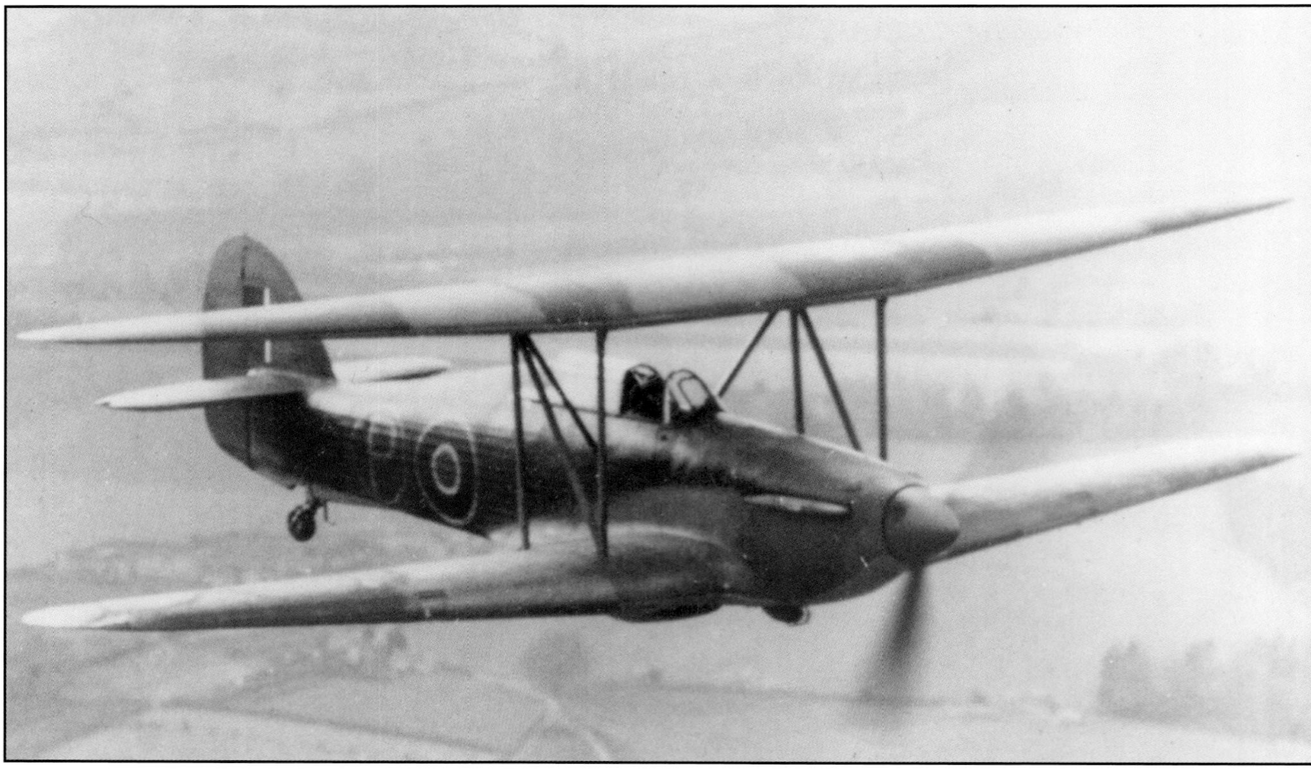

Hillson trials now led to the installation of a Slip Wing onto a special test Hurricane. Unlike the trials aircraft, the larger wing on the faster aircraft required more extensive strut bracing which increased concern that in the jettisoning process one or more of the attachments might not release instantaneously as demanded.

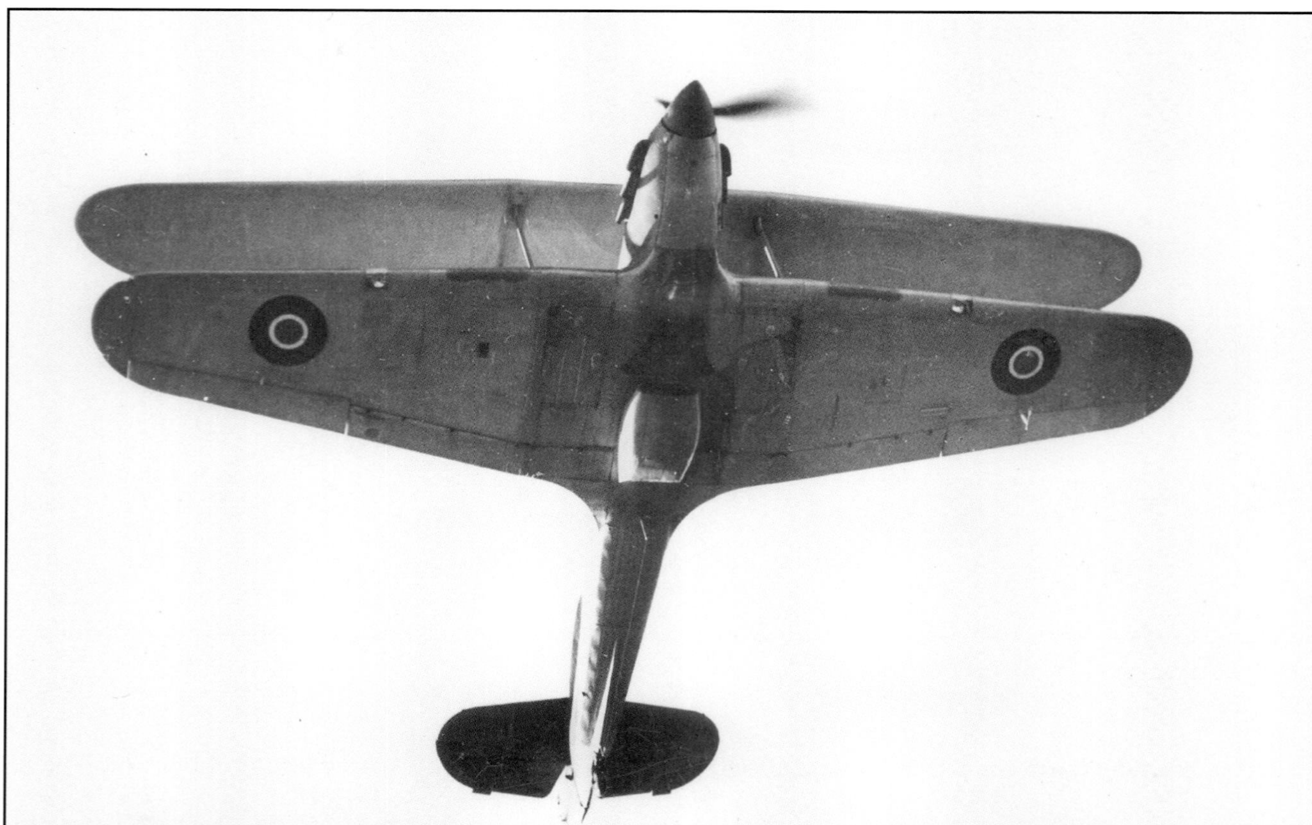

The Hurricane's slip-wing was built to the same design as the aircraft's main wing but without any ailerons or flaps since it was intended merely as a lifting surface-cum-fuel tank offering an additional source of lift.

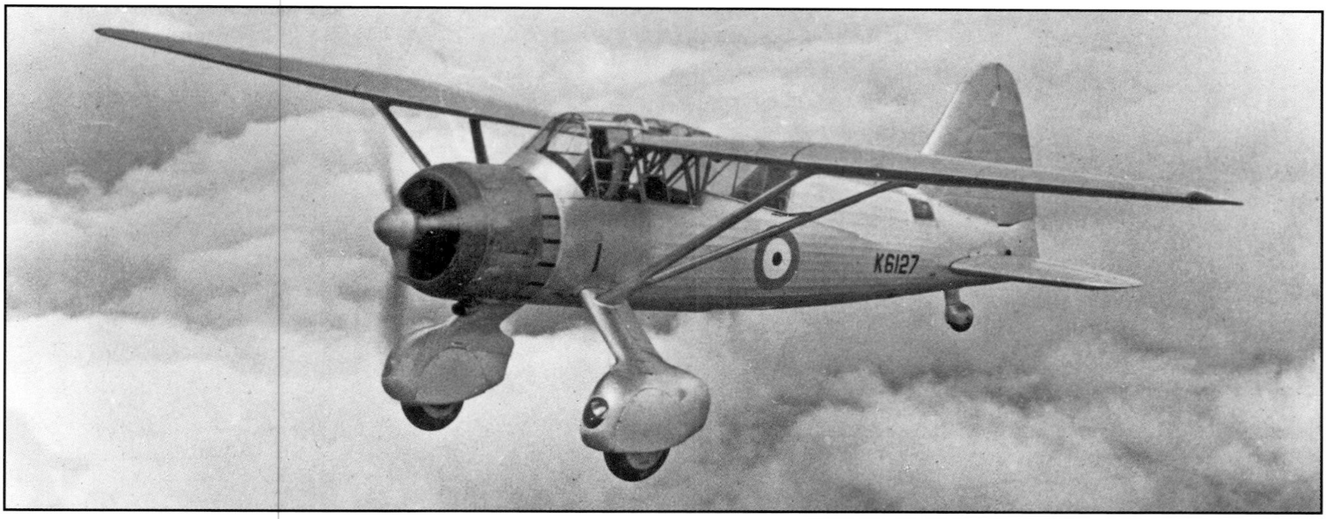

A great deal has been written about the Westland Lysander that was experimentally fitted with the Delanne tailplane. Popular journalists have associated the work of the French experimental aerodynamicist Maurice Henri Delanne with that of Henri Mignet and the Flying Flea, seeing a visual similarity in an aircraft with a large tail wing and the Pou-du-Ciel. Unfortunately this simile, however attractive, merely demonstrates those writers' lack of understanding of Delanne's work. Here is a photograph of the prototype Westland Lysander, K6127, which would earn a place in history, even if that history was invariably wrong! Powered by a 905 hp Bristol Perseus engine, the first flight was at Boscombe Down on June 15th, 1936. The rectangular window under the fin leading edge allowed a pre-flight visual check of ballast weights.

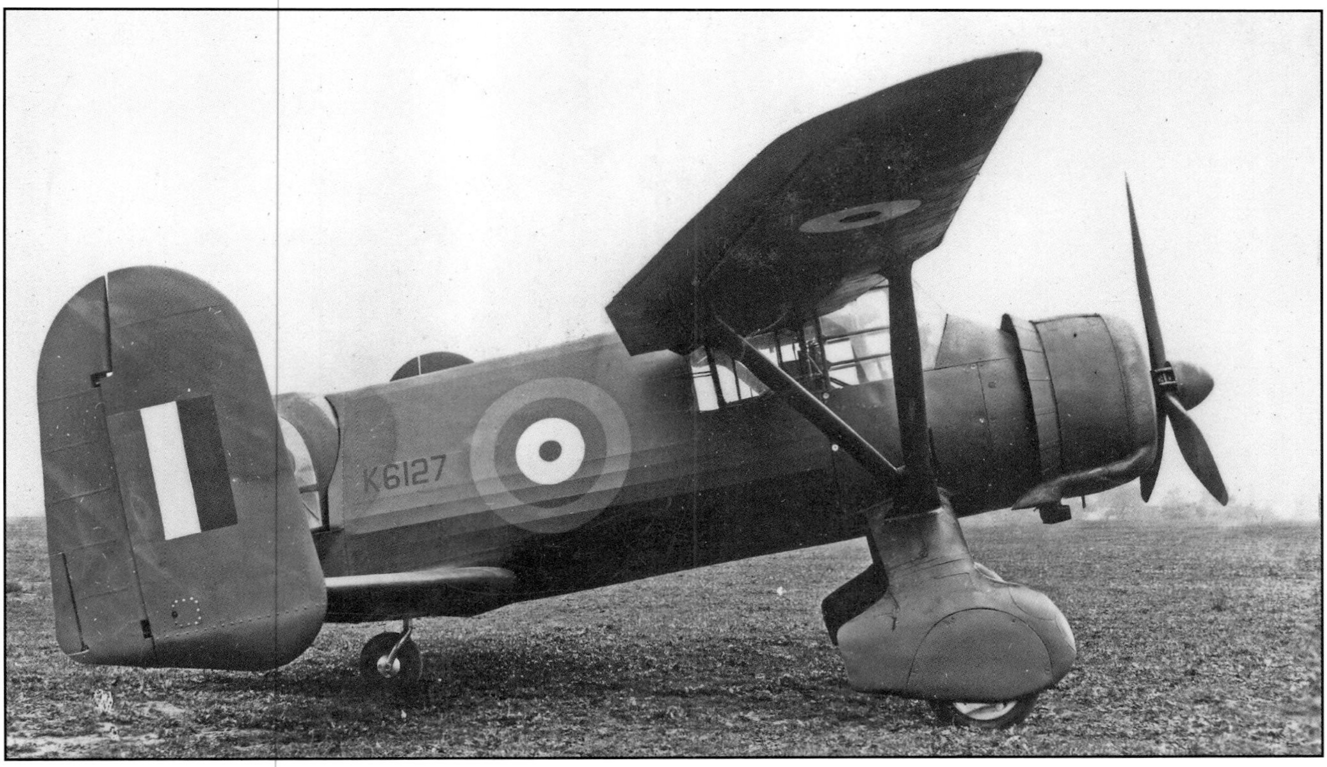

Arming the Lysander was seen as a probable need so experiments were carried out with dorsal and ventral gun positions. The problem was that the weight of crew, gun and ammunition moved the position of the centre of gravity too far aft. During the 1930s, Delanne had addressed just such a problem, evolving a principle using tandem wings of unequal span. His first aircraft, the Arsenal-Delanne 10-C2 had performed extremely well and now the new 20-T inspired Westland to visit and inspect the machine. Unlike Mignet's Flying Flea with which it was later compared, the tandem wing was provided to exploit a forgotten characteristic of many of the pioneering aircraft such as those of A V Roe, namely the lifting tailplane which spread the load between a front wing and a usually smaller rear wing. So long as the airflow was constant over each wing, the centre of gravity did not have to be anywhere within the chord of the main wing (typically at 30 percent chord) and could be somewhere between the two. The aerodynamic advantages of this, to Delanne, seemed worth re-evaluating. Westland designer William Petter redesigned the prototype aircraft with a short, stubby fuselage to take a Frazer-Nash or Boulton Paul rear turret and a Delanne-type rear wing.

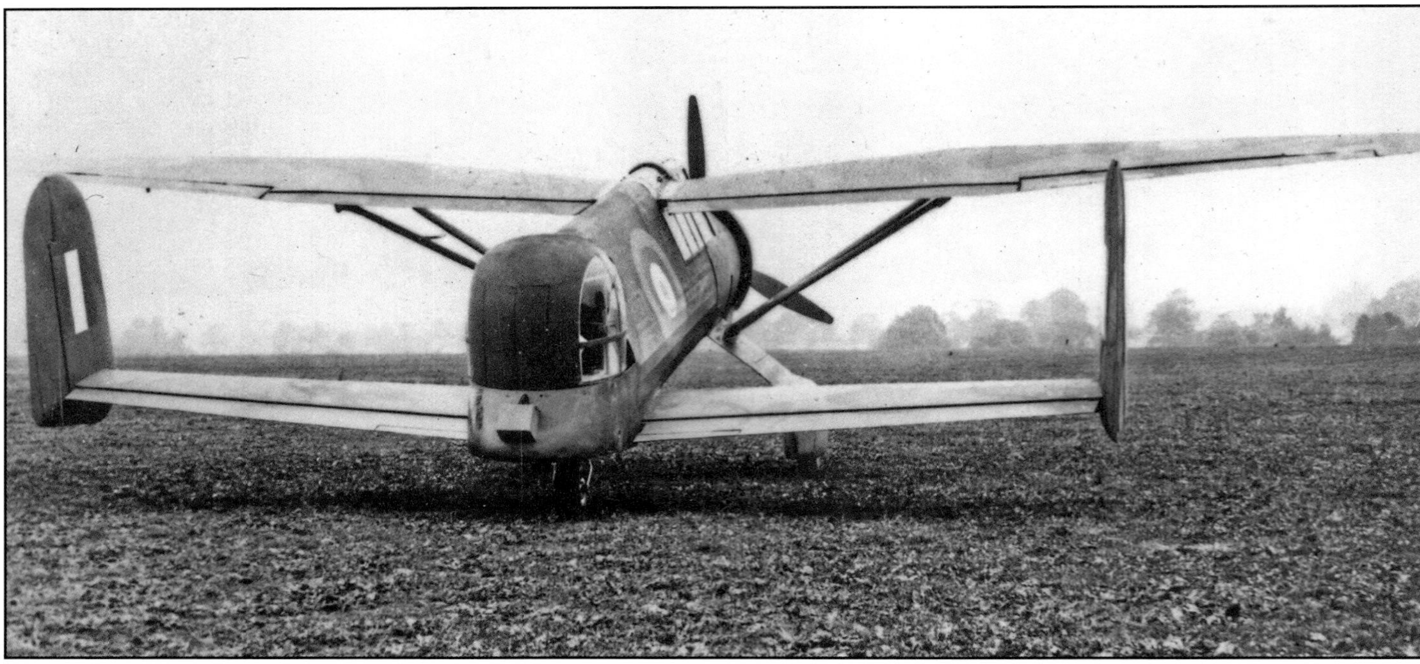

The tail turret was a mock-up and no real gun turret was actually installed. K6127 went to A&AEE for handling trials and to explore the extended centre of gravity range which the format could accommodate.

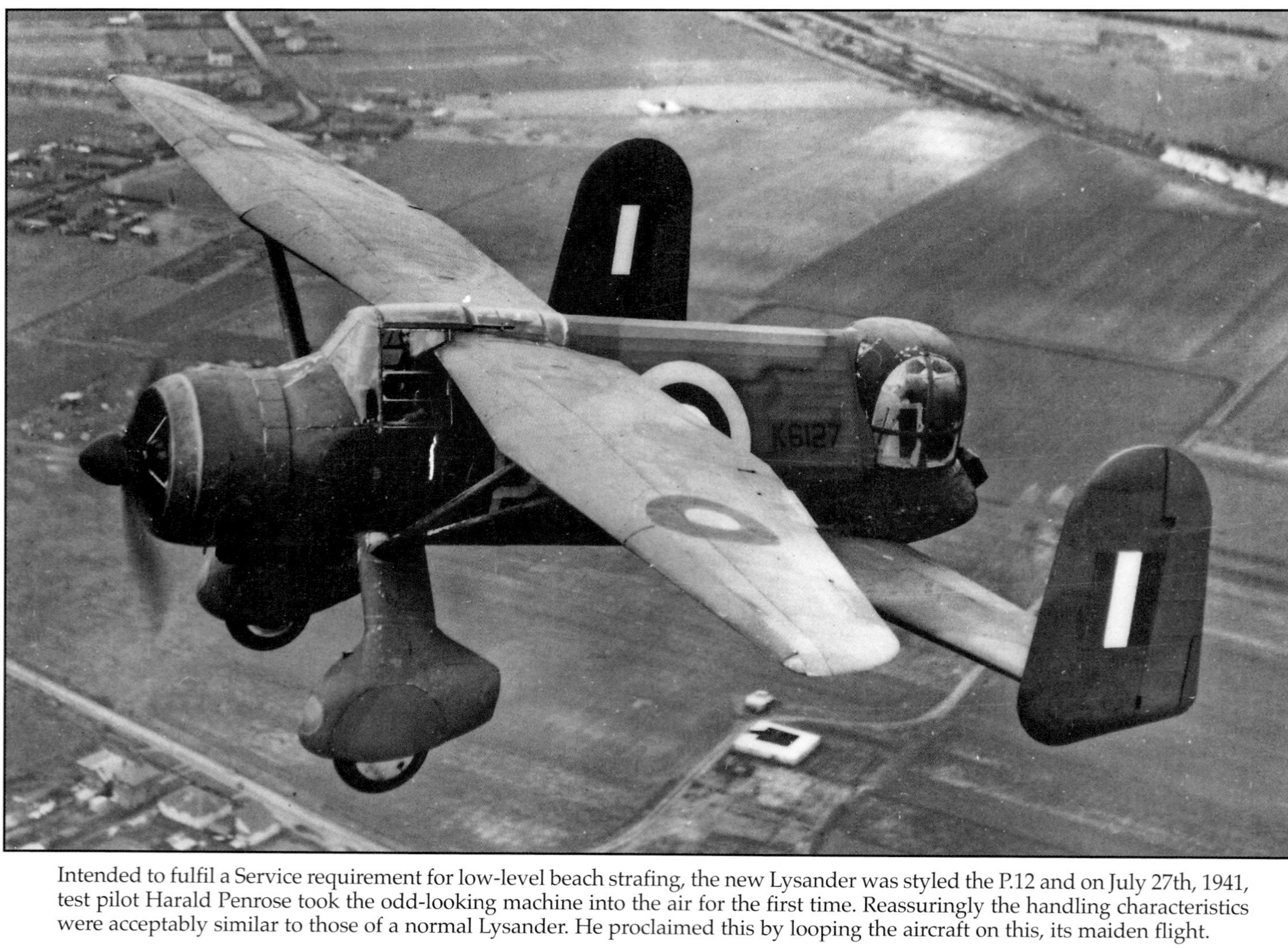

Intended to fulfil a Service requirement for low-level beach strafing, the new Lysander was styled the P.12 and on July 27th, 1941, test pilot Harald Penrose took the odd-looking machine into the air for the first time. Reassuringly the handling characteristics were acceptably similar to those of a normal Lysander. He proclaimed this by looping the aircraft on this, its maiden flight.

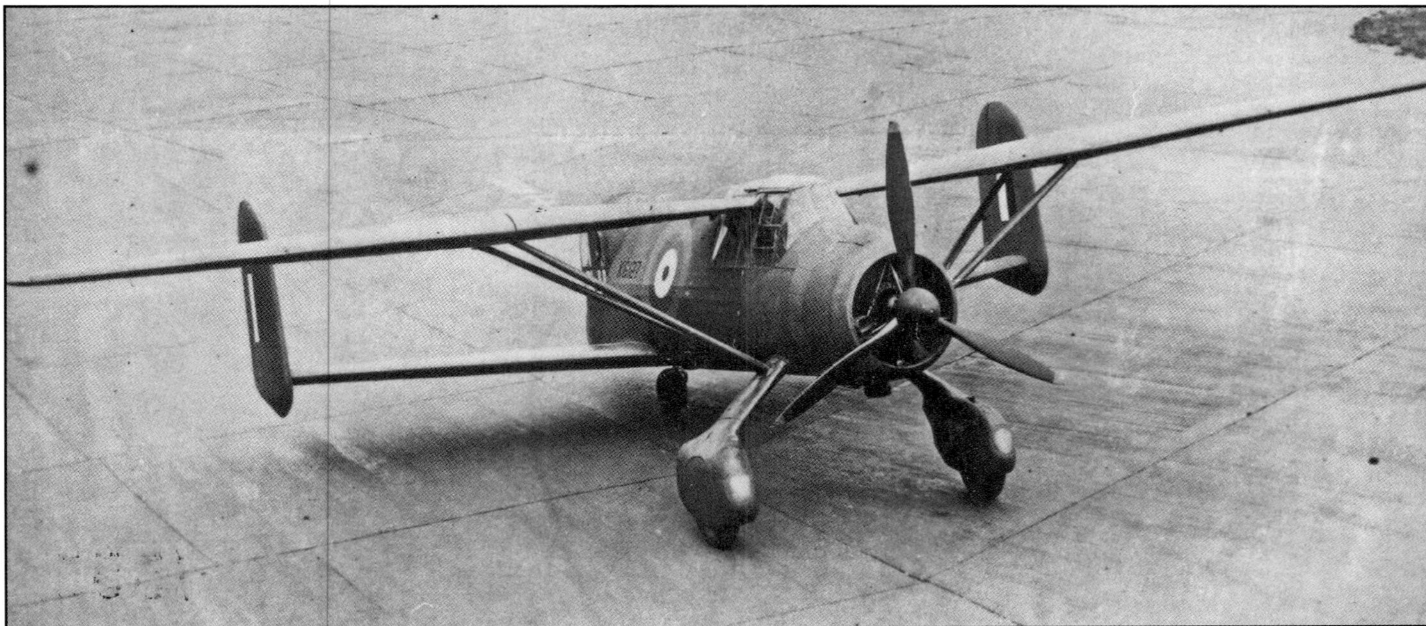

In keeping with so many experimental aircraft built during time of war, no hard data were published on the Delanne-tailed Lysander. What is known is that the aircraft was able to operate within an 'extensive' Centre of Gravity range considerably in excess of that of a normal Lysander. Its appearance was remarkably similar to the original Arsenal-Delanne 10.C2.

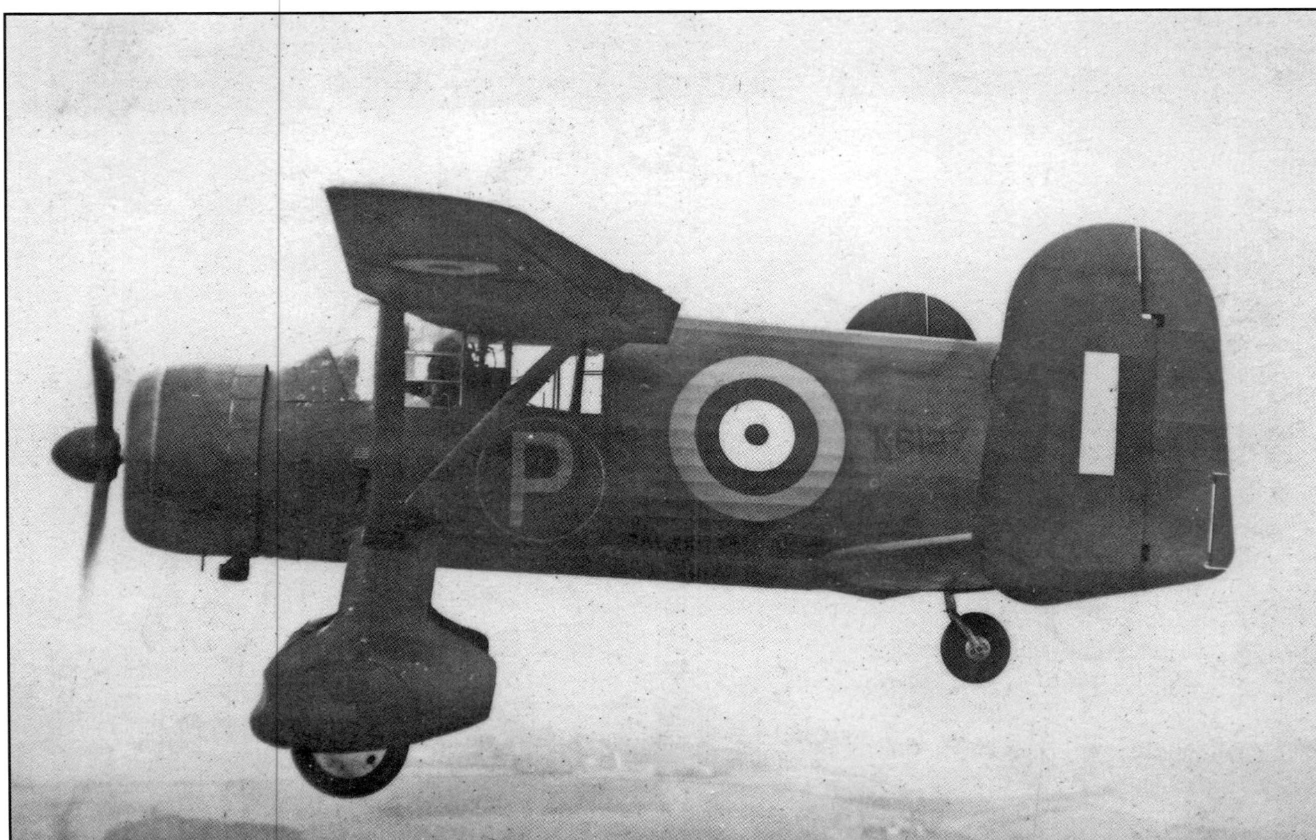

By the time the flight test programme had been completed, the needs of the Services had moved on and low-level beach-strafing was no longer on the agenda. K6127 had served its purpose and on June 13th, 1941, the aircraft was struck off charge and, in the official jargon of the Maintenance Units, 'reduced to produce'. In post-war years, Delanne went on to make several more aircraft in France using his principles. For Thomas Harrington & Sons, a firm of Hove, Sussex, coachbuilders which operated from 1897 to 1966, it had been just another job. Already in war-production with the Lysander, it was this trusted firm that built the unique Delanne tail for Westland.

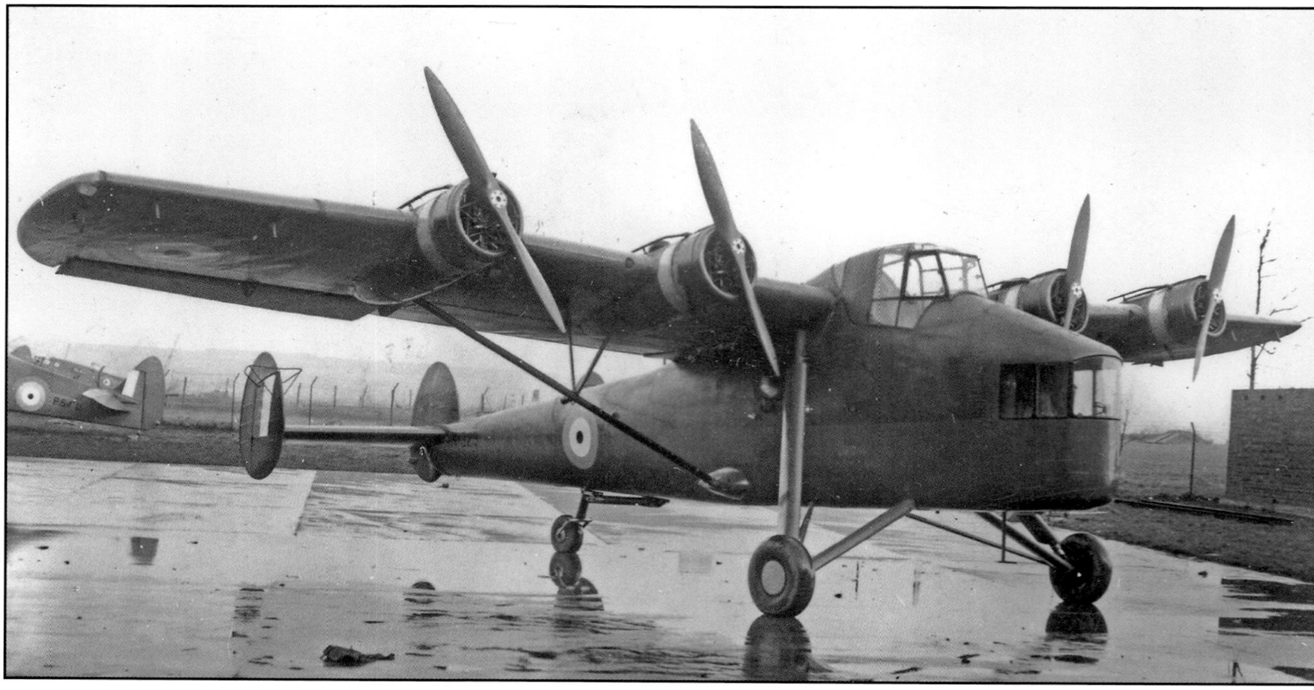

Rarely do aircraft designed by different companies to the same specification actually look alike. An exception were the two aircraft built to Air Ministry Spec S.23/37, one by General Aircraft Ltd at Hanworth and the other by Airspeed (1934) Ltd at Portsmouth Airport. In the end neither was a success, in the main because the Air Ministry kept 'refining' its requirements until the point was reached where neither submission was practical. N1323 was the Airspeed AS.39 Fleet Shadower powered by four 140 hp Pobjoy Niagara V radial engines.

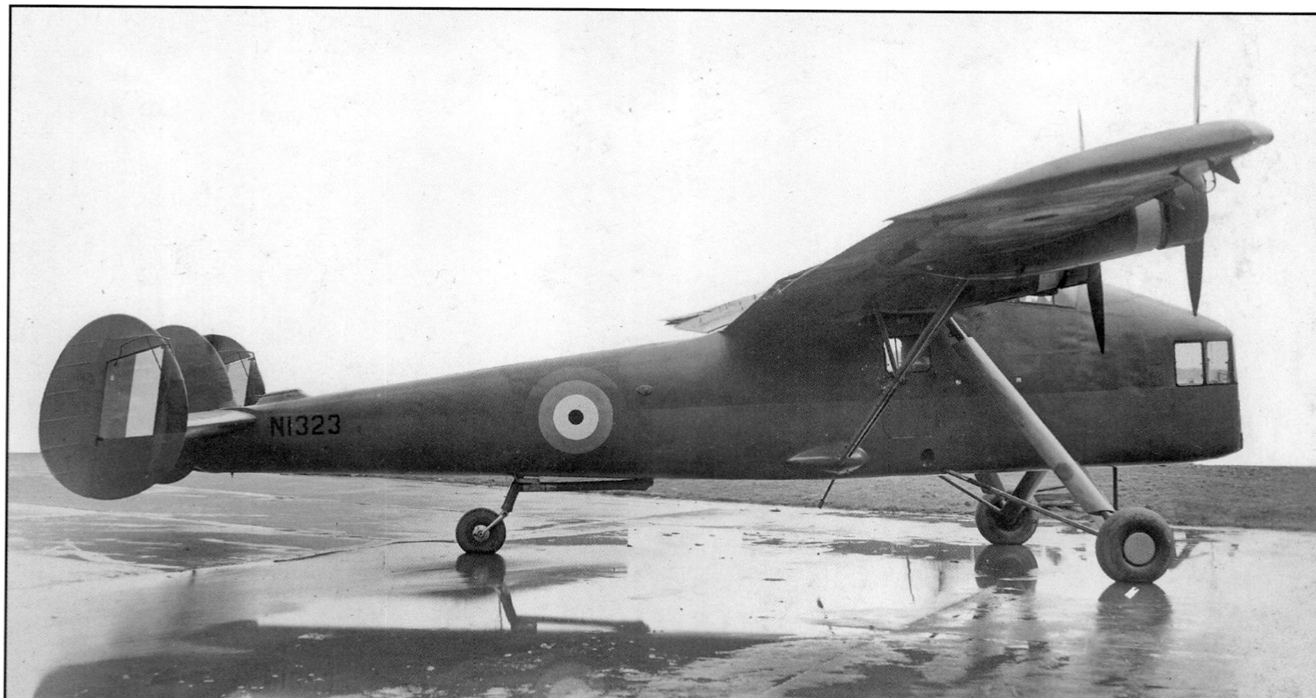

The requirement was for a carrier-based aircraft suitable for shadowing an enemy fleet at night. The special requirements called for the ability to remain in the air for up to six hours while flying at exceptionally low speed. Because of the carrier requirement, the wings had to be foldable. The Airspeed machine could cruise at less than 40 knots thanks to the Crouch-Bolas effect using full-span slotted flaps and ailerons. Because of the need for exceptional vision, the Fleet Shadower reverted to pre-war French airliner layout with a 'front-of-a-Parisian-tram' nose layout, the observer being provided with clear-vision side and front panels. A high-velocity undercarriage was fitted to absorb landings on a pitching deck. The only example was serialled N1323 and was first flown by Airspeed's chief test pilot, George Bertram Sainsbury Errington (1904-1966) on October 18th, 1940. It was not a good flyer being the product of a Whitehall committee's whims.

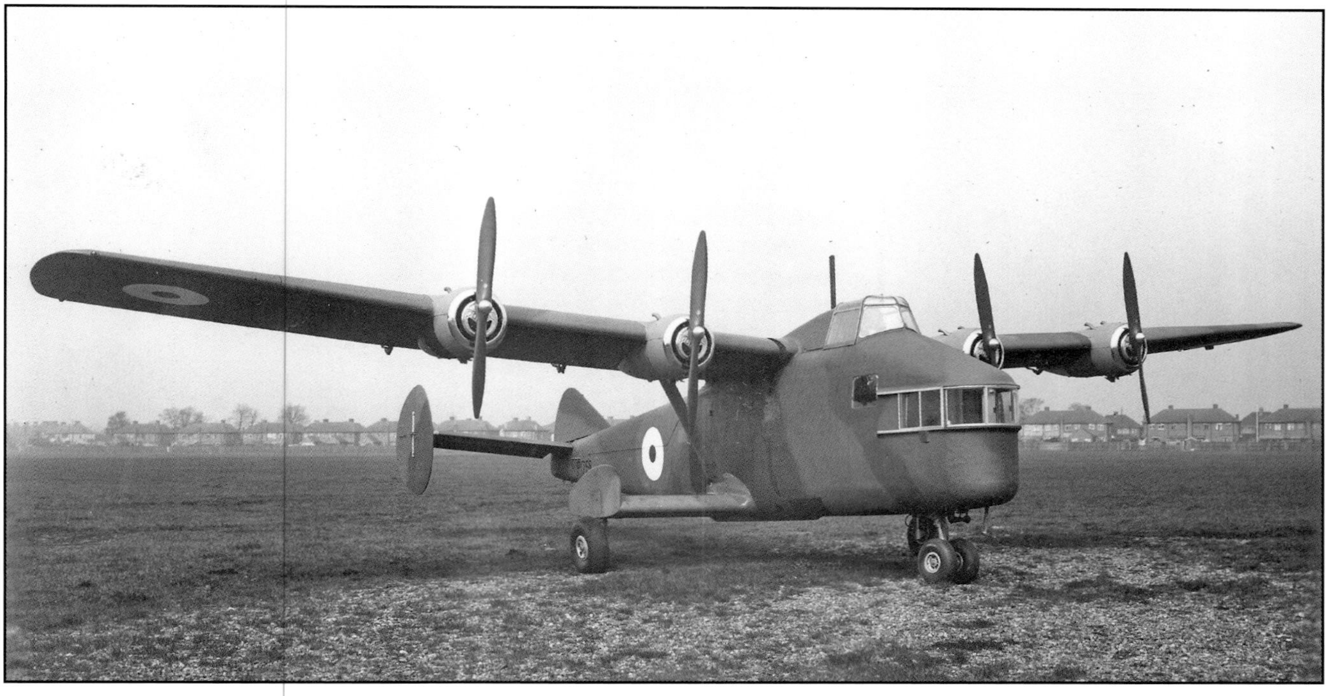

Bearing an uncanny similarity in size and appearance was General Aircraft's GAL.38. As with the Airspeed machine, it was built to a contract issued on November 15th 1938. Different only in detail from the AS.39, the GAL.38 had a tricycle undercarriage and main wheels on sponsons. Power came from four 130 hp Pobjoy Niagara III engines and the first flight was made on May 13th, 1940.

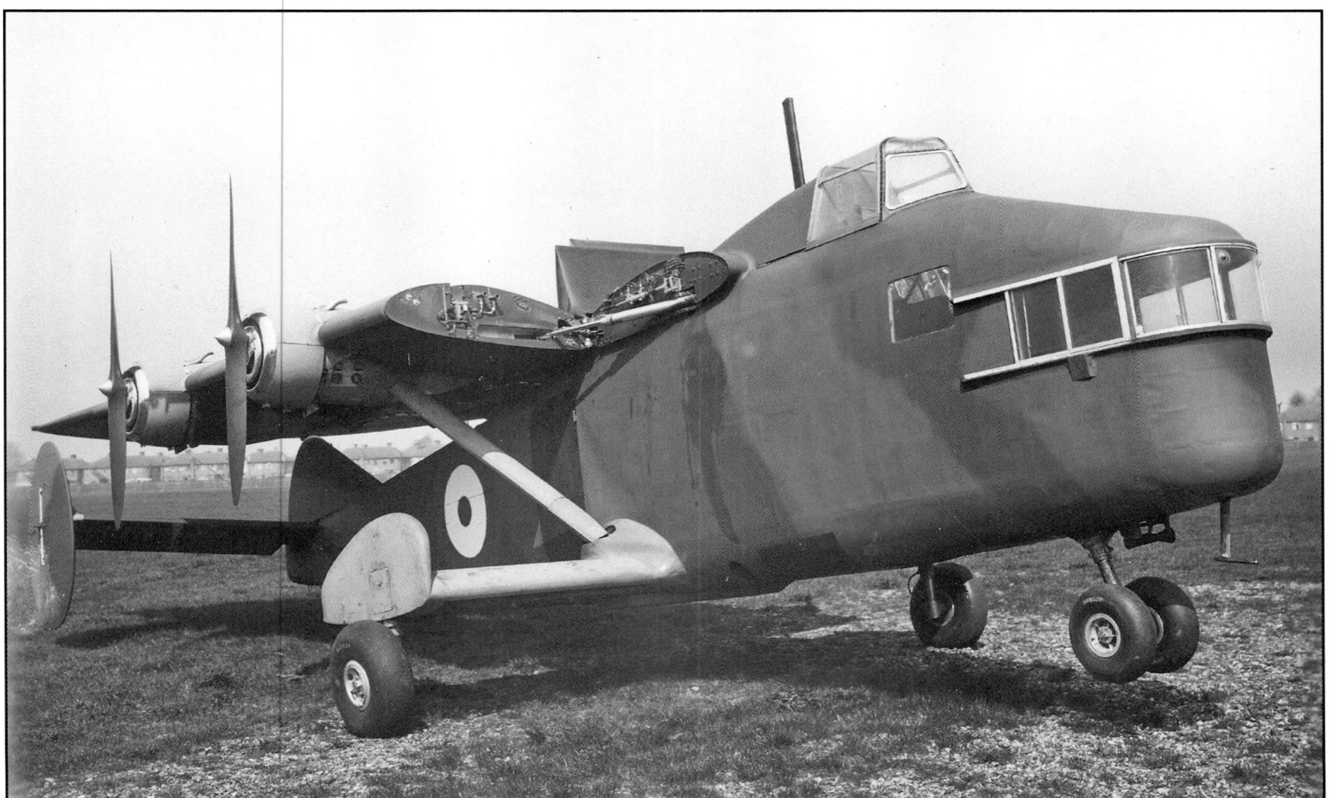

Wing-folding in both the Airspeed and General Aircraft machines was a major engineering feat for, besides the sheer weight, there were wing-mounted fuel tanks and, of course, all engine and flying controls had to unite through the hinge. These two machines earn the distinction of being the world's only four-engined folding-wing aircraft – unless anybody knows anything different! The GAL.38 recorded a maximum speed of 115 mph and a stalling speed of just 39 mph. Its duration was an impressive 11 hours.

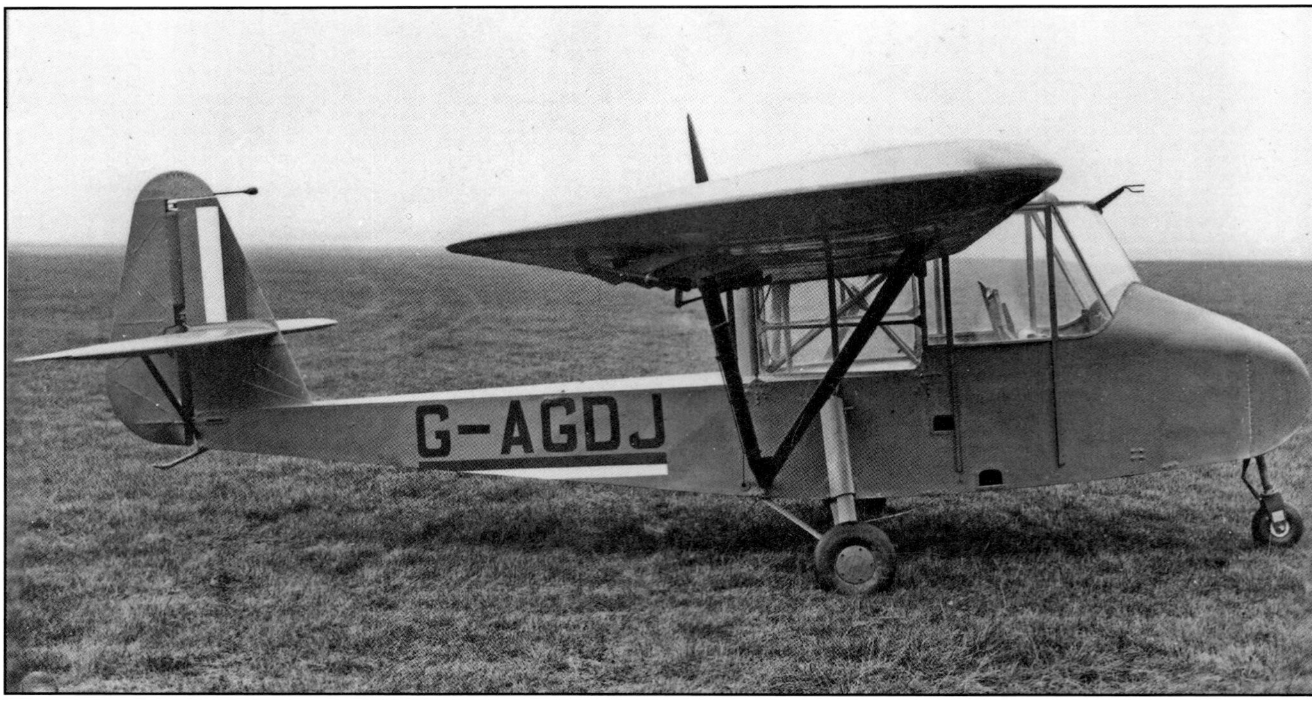

A mystery aircraft is the Fane F.1/40 Air Observation Post, a two-seater powered by an 80 hp Continental A-80 engine. Captain Gerard William Reginald Fane (1898-1979) was a friend of Nick Comper and owned and flew a Swift. Comper, ousted from his own company which had become Heston Aircraft Ltd, went on to develop two small pusher aircraft at Brooklands, the first being the Fly and the second the Scamp. After Nick Comper's unfortunate death in June 1939, Fane took the unfinished Scamp to his home at Norbury and, on August 9th, 1939, registered a business called Comper Fane Aircraft Ltd – surely the last aeroplane-maker to be listed before the outbreak of war less than a month later. In 1941, Fane offered his AOP aircraft to the Air Ministry. Scamp by another name? Nobody quite knows.

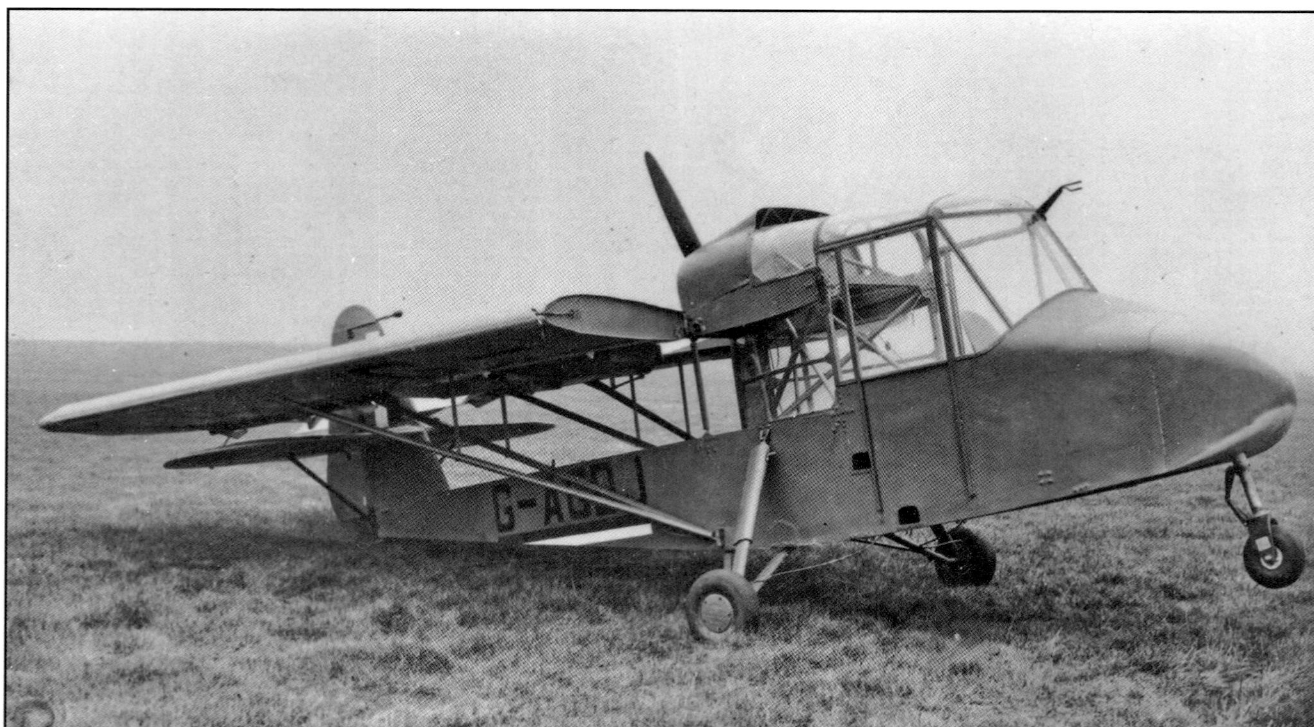

With a tricycle undercarriage, the two-seat Fane G-AGDJ, also known as T1788, had folding wings and the necessary tail-skid. It was not an unattractive aircraft and may well have been far more Nick Comper than Gerard Fane. But the Taylorcraft was already in production and, under the military name 'Auster', was distinguishing itself in the AOP arena. Fane's product was last flown in the autumn of 1941 after which it disappeared, scrapped during the war.

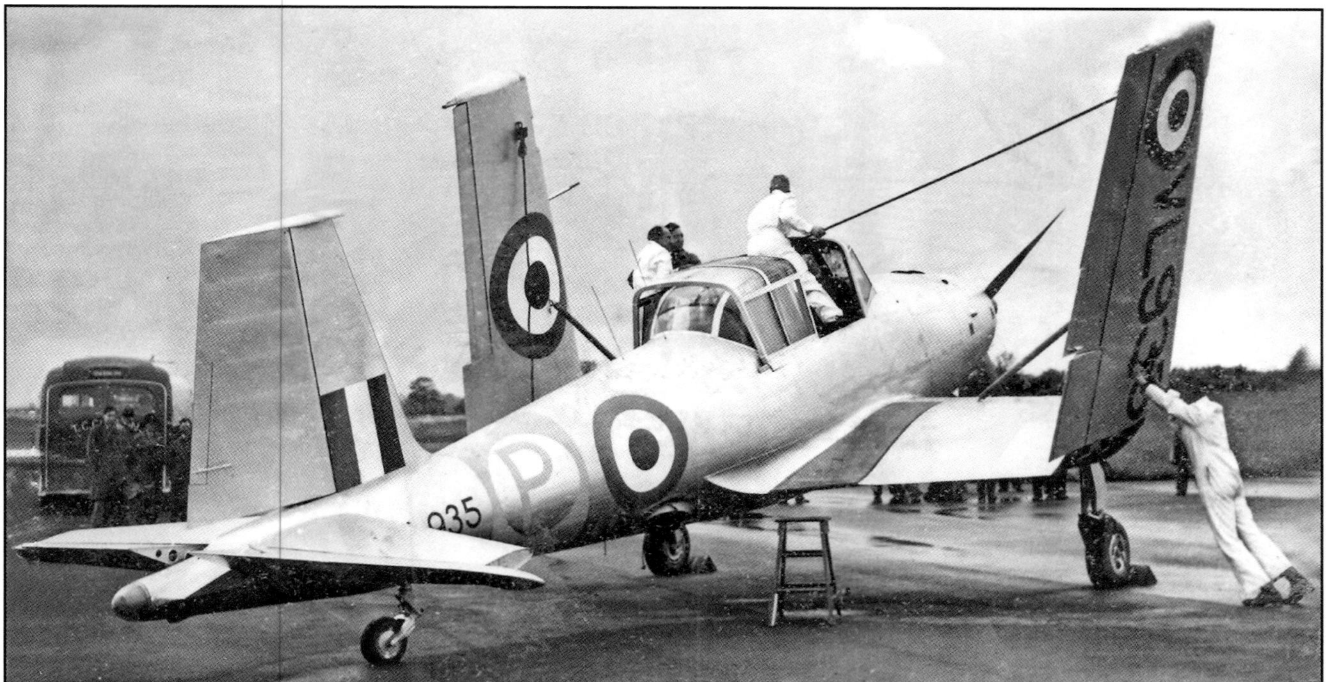

Naval aircraft with folding wings were commonplace in the mid-20th century. Initially, however, wing-folding was neither hydraulic nor electric but a manual operation achieved by ropes and long poles. Here is the Boulton Paul Balliol T.1, promoted as the first jet-powered trainer aircraft. Powered by an Armstrong Siddeley Mamba propeller turbine, the 300 mph Balliol was said to be the first aircraft in its category to fly by this type of power plant. Here the third prototype, VL935, is seen being demonstrated at Bitteswell Aerodrome on June 28th, 1948. An energetic ground-crew was required to fold the wings for stowage.

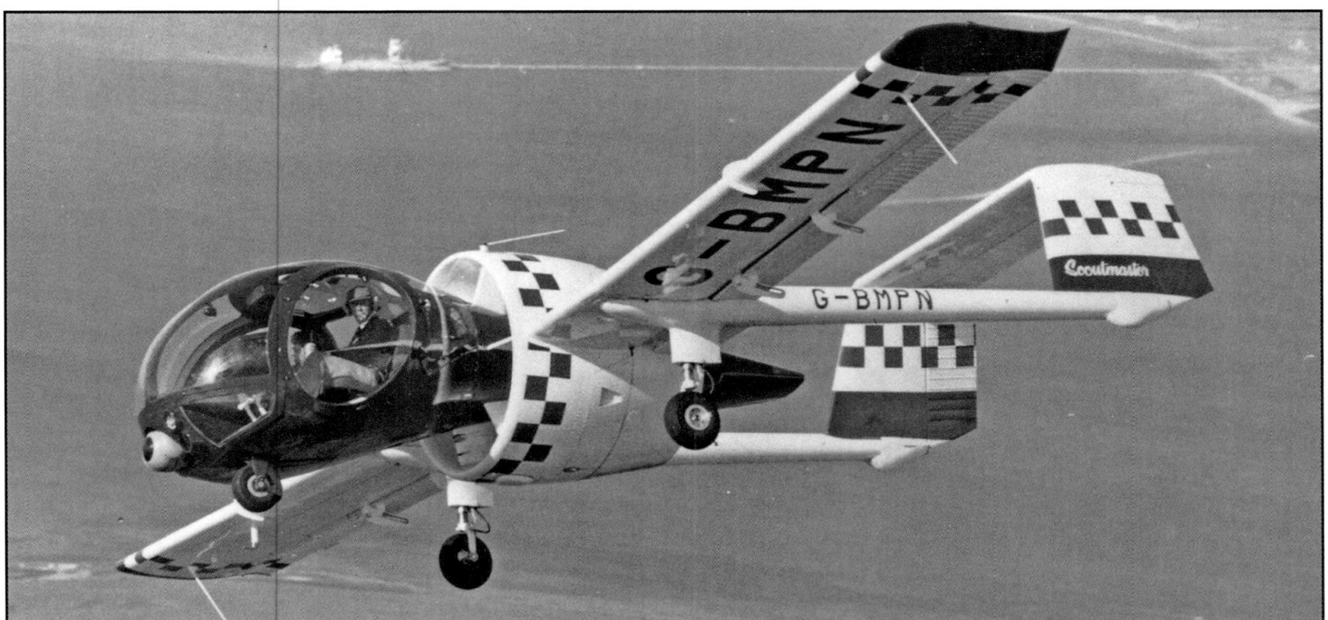

Quite the most novel new light aircraft to appear in the British skies after the war was the Edgley Optica designed by a former schoolmaster, John Edgley. Intended as a slow-sped spotter/surveillance/photographic platform as a cheaper alternative to the increasing use of expensive helicopters, the Optica was powered by a 150 hp Lycoming engine driving a six-bladed ducted fan: later this was replaced by a 200 hp model. The crew of three were seated in line abreast in a bubble cockpit which extended from the duct. A cleverly-engineered concept, a potential drawback was the almost total invisibility of any other of the airframe structure from the cockpit: a potential for in-flight disorientation existed. After the first flight in December 1979, some 14 examples were built and several were tried out by police forces, in particular Hampshire and Wiltshire. The former G-BLFD was re-registered G-KATY on April 2nd 1985. On May 15th that year, while being operated by Wiltshire Police surveying traffic at Ringwood, it was seen to lose height and crash, the crew of two being killed in the ensuing fire. The Optica suffered again when, in October 1985, an arson attack on its factory destroyed a large number of finished and semi-complete machines. A reconstructed company called Brooklands Aircraft went bankrupt in March 1990. Looking like a 43 Sqdn tribute flyer, the picture shows a police model, G-BMPN, later VH-BMC.

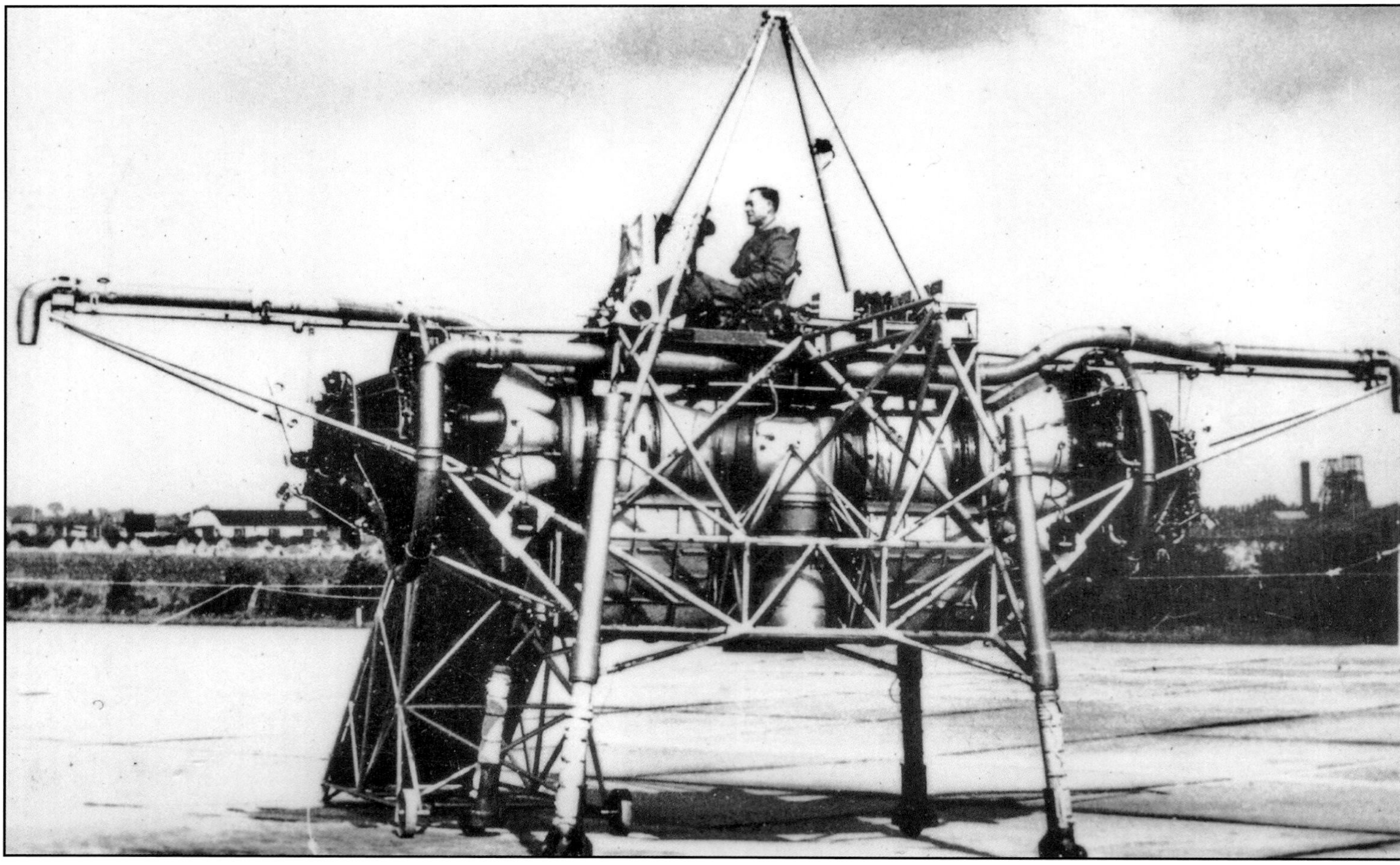

The Rolls-Royce Thrust Measuring Rig (TMR) was dubbed 'the Flying Bedstead' and a memorable press release said 'The Flying Bedstead is actually a Flying Test-Bed' – which created many a news-desk groan. The thing was conceived by Rolls-Royce's Dr Alan Arnold Griffith (1893-1963) who was one of the first to identify metal-fatigue and was also a pioneer of the jet as far back as 1926 at the RAE. He joined Rolls-Royce in 1939 and suggested the TMR as a means of testing the practicality of controlling a jet-lift vertical take-off aircraft in hovering and low-speed flight. With two Rolls-Royce Nene jet engines, the Bedstead was built at Hucknall while the autostabiliser was designed and built by RAE Farnborough. A four-leg undercarriage was designed to absorb touch-down at up to 34 feet/second while the failure of one engine at up to 50 feet altitude could also be accommodated safely. The all-up weight was 7,600 lbs and the flight duration of eleven minutes was met by a fuel capacity of 190 gallons. Constrained in a massive gantry, the first flight took place on August 19th, 1953 but it was almost a year later (on August 3rd) before the first free flight was attempted. In March 1955 it was transferred to Farnborough for further tests before going to Bedford in June 1956. Here it was severely damaged on November 28th, 1957, in a mishap that took the life of test pilot Air Commodore Henry Gordon Francis Larsen. He forgot to check his tank before lifting off and simply ran out of fuel. Two examples were built: the first, pictured here, being preserved in the Science Museum Collection.

Opposite top: The immediate post-war decades were redolent with curious and sometimes frightening flying machines. While Rolls-Royce was flying its thoroughly non-aviation-looking Bedstead, Bell in America undertook a private-venture programme to seek similar results. The Bell Experimental VTOL was built by the Niagara Division of the Bell Aircraft Corporation but, unlike Rolls-Royce, their approach used the same engines for both lift and forward thrust. A pair of Fairchild J44 turbojets, each rated at 1,000 lb static thrust, were pivoted either side of a small fuselage. In the centre was a Continental-Turboméca Palouste as a gas generator. A pair of roll-jets exhausted at the wing-tips while pitch and jaw was controllable by little jets acting as tail controls. The wing had an area of 130 square feet and was probably sufficient to allow a safe descent in the event of engine failure. It spanned 26 feet and the overall length was 21 feet. The all-up weight was in the order of 2,000 lbs. The first free vertical flight was made on November 16th, 1954, but the project lost impetus in the face of military helicopter work and the dustbin-powered ski plane was consigned to scrap.

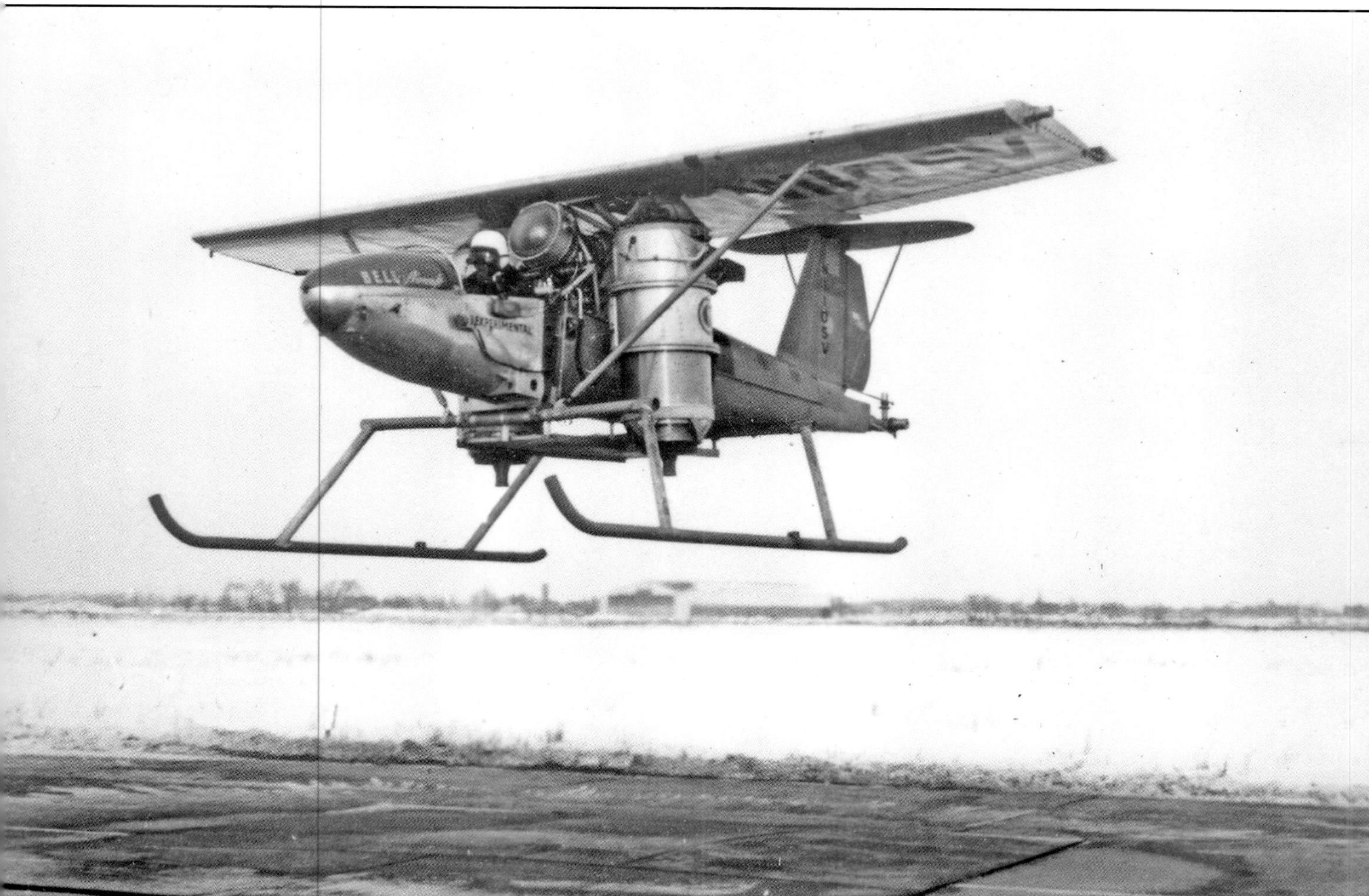

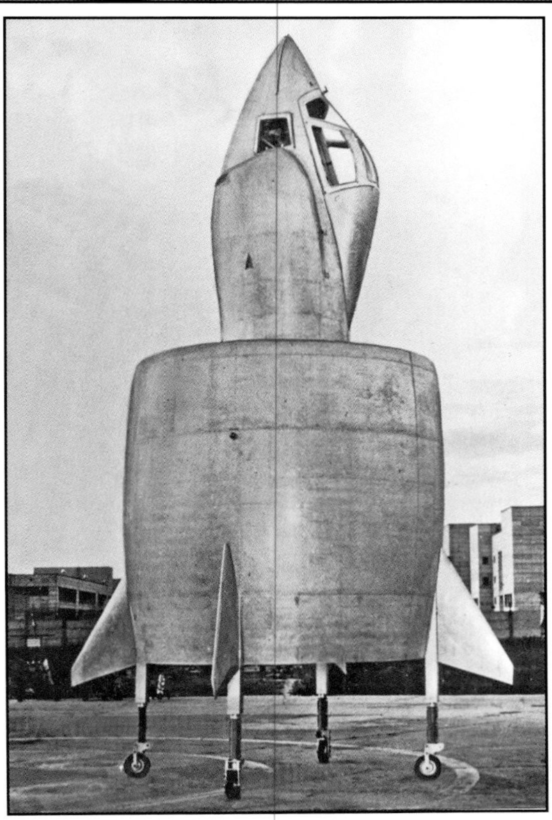

Occasionally one has to introduce into conversation a subject which is not really understood by most people and creates a nervous silence while feet shuffle and eyes frantically scan high ceilings in the hope of finding a Heaven-sent escape route. Talking about ghosts in a tennis match green-room is one example. Ring wing aircraft are assuredly a similar subject. The aerodynamics of the annular duct are curious and require a clear head and higher maths to get around. It began with the annular drum-like 'wing systems' of Claude Givaudan's tandem aeroplane of 1909 (also known as the Vermorel triplane) and proceeded to Henri Coanda's ducted fan-propelled aeroplane of 1911. The curious Custer Channel Wing in America was a late 'thirties variation on the theme. By the 1950s we were in the realms not merely of pioneer aviation but of supersonic possibilities, rocket science and top secret work in Germany. At the end of the war, Dornier and Heinkel, among others, were experimenting with 'flying barrels' and Helmut Philip von Zborowski (one-time BMW rocket motor engineer who had worked on the V1 and V2 weapons with von Braun during the war) coined the new name for the genre – coléoptère, so named after the sheath-winged beetle. His design seemed to offer extraordinary prospects. Besides climbing like a homesick angel, it was reckoned that it could fly at 800 kph although its maximum endurance was just 25 minutes. The initial rate of climb was likely to be 'radical' with 7,800 metres/minute being quoted as 'feasible'. The French conglomerate SNECMA designed and built the prototype for military development. It made its first vertical flight on May 6th 1959 at Melun-Villaroche and the plan was for it to translate from vertical into horizontal flight but on its first attempt on July 25th pilot Auguste Morel lost control and was forced to eject. The Beetle (left) was no more.

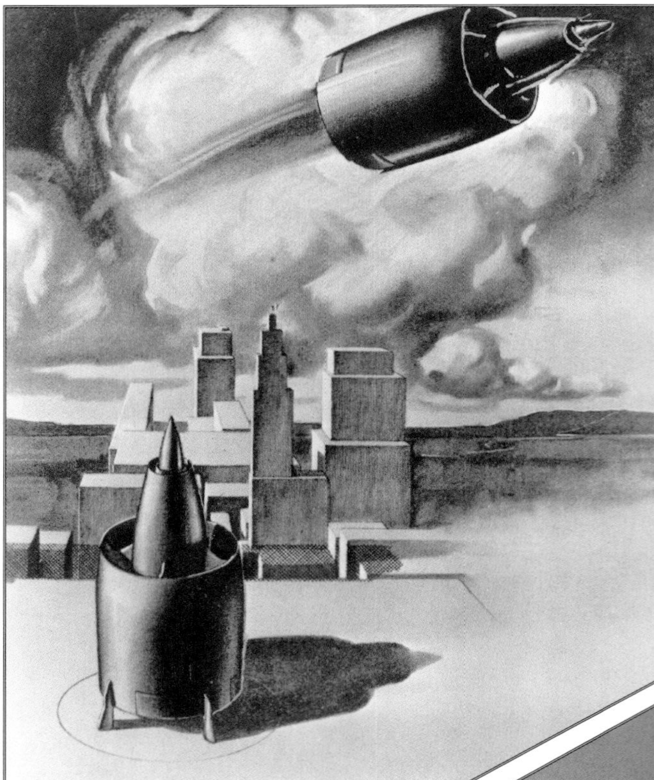

SNECMA's Coléoptère, first announced in about 1955, instantly inspired others and in next to no time it had netted a small handful of transatlantic band-wagon-jumpers, among them a scheme launched by the US Office of Naval Research which promptly devised its own look-alike. The name, though, was too hard for American aeronautical tastes to which any accents other than Brooklyn and Texan were unthinkable, let alone Coléoptère's assorted treatments of the letter 'e'. The 'when in doubt, go to page one' approach coined the name 'ring wing aircraft'. America at this time was riding the crest of a wave of success when flying never seemed simpler as Time and Technology advanced, so when news that the Kaman Aircraft Corporation of Bloomfield, Connecticut, had secured a research contract, the Press eagerly published this 'hand-out' artists' impression and the news that 'the wing is the barrel-shaped outside ring open at both ends. The smaller body of the plane is mounted inside and in flight air passes over both inside and outside surfaces of wing [sic]. Engineers say it is supposed to rise vertically like a helicopter or fly horizontally like a conventional plane using either jets or propellers'. The US public was suitably in awe and mouthed 'Gee!' It was January 10th, 1956. It is uncertain if Kaman actually did anything on this contract for other reasons. And after the loss of the French machine in 1959 it seems quietly to have been forgotten.

America has produced more than its fair share of curious flying machines and many have appeared in its quest for the ideal VTOL aircraft. Ryan in California built a naval fighter called the FR-1 Fireball which had a thrust-to-weight ratio of one. This inspired the Navy's Bureau of Aeronautics to ponder the question whether the grimly named Fireball could be made to land and take-off vertically, meaning pointing straight up and not the way our Harriers used to fly. Given the soubriquet Verti-Jet, Ryan's single-seat Model 69 stood on its tail against a vertical launch platform while its pilot sat in a rotatable seat no doubt hoping for the best. But the Verti-Jet began by making conventional rolling take-offs before effecting in-flight transition. First flown on December 10th, 1955, the Verti-Jet was eventually able to stand on its tail and, like a model rocket in a milk-bottle, go straight up. Inspiring a fresh take on the term 'fly on the wall', having been trialled for a year the machine was still in one piece (as were its two test pilots) and is now a museum piece. Ryan went on experimenting in the STOL world and in 1960 made its less-confrontational Model 92 deflected slipstream VZ-3RY Vertiplane. That proved fairly remarkable but, after 21 flights, its British-made Martin-Baker ejection seat saved its pilot's life when something terminal broke.

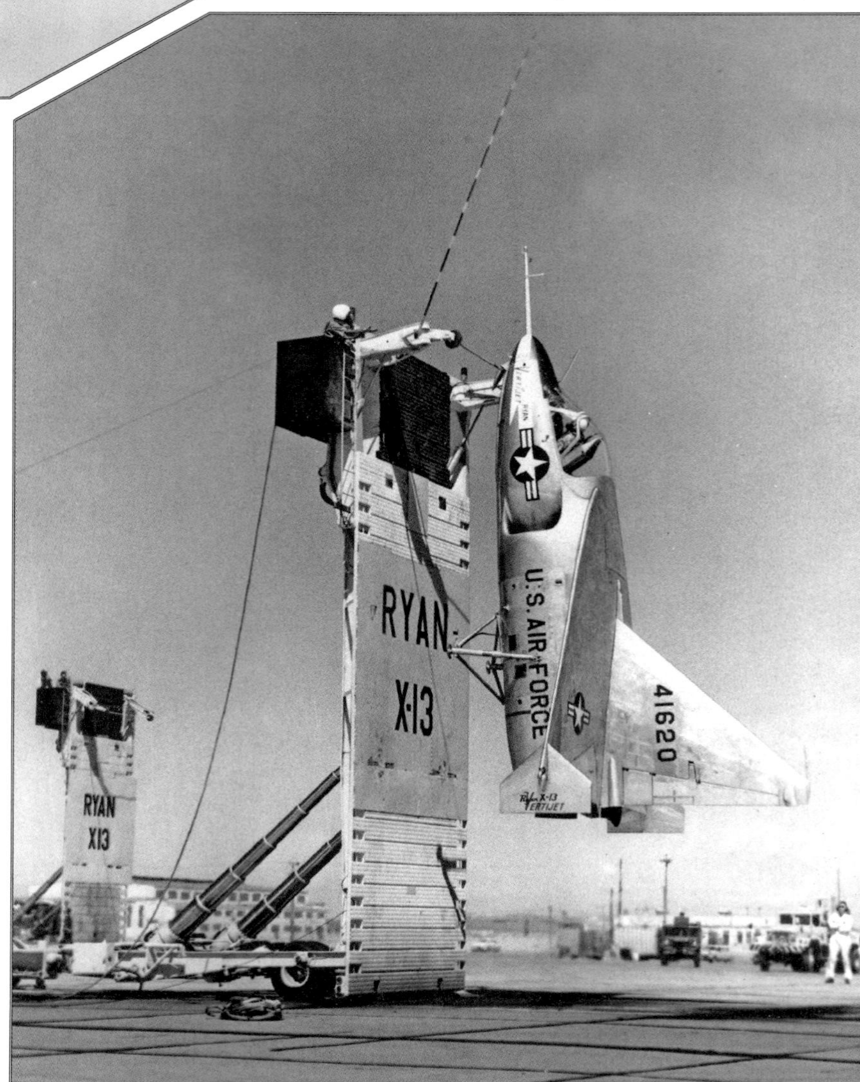

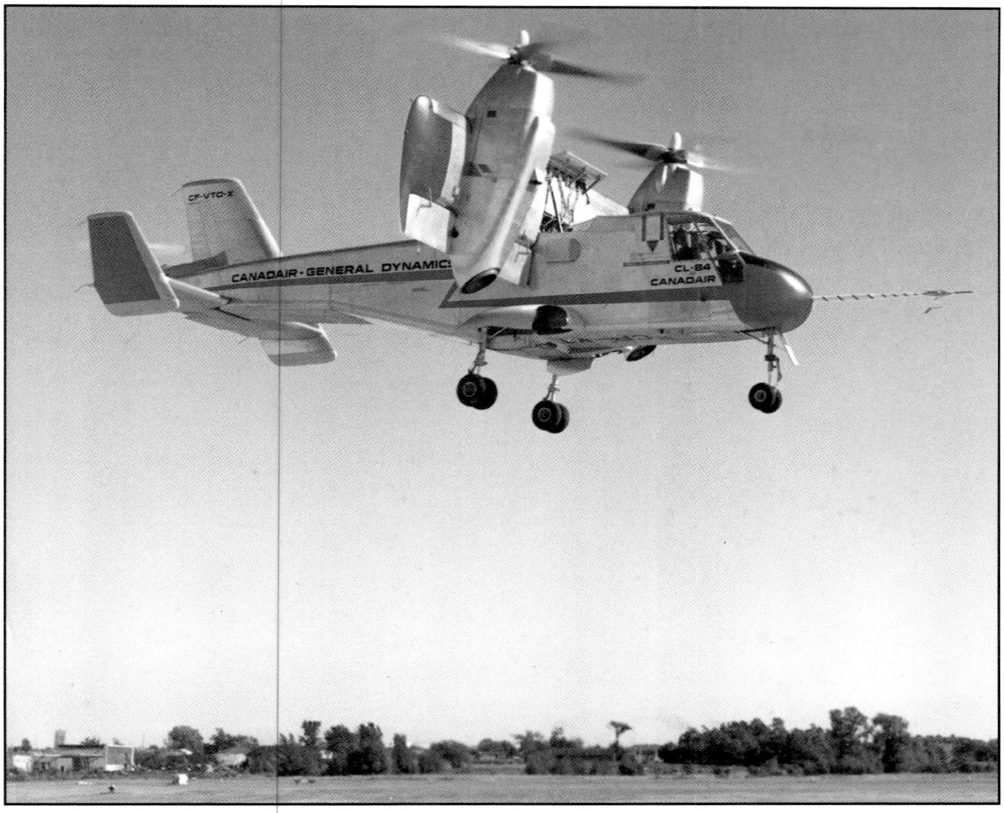

One of Canada's great aircraft manufacturers was Canadair and between 1957 and 1963 the company carried out considerable research into VTOL aircraft in conjunction with the National Research Board (NRB) and the Defense Research Board (DRB). The option being explored was the tilt-wing and designer Fred Phillips came up with the CL-84, a vertical take-off machine which could hover and also translate into fast forward flight. Power came from a pair of 1,500 hp Lycoming T.53 shaft turbines driving 14 feet diameter airscrews. A complex tilting mechanism rotated the wings and engines through 100 degrees of incidence. The prototype, seen here, was CF-VTO-X first flown on May 7th, 1965, by test pilot Bill Longhurst. Four examples were built and widely demonstrated as 14-seat capacity transports. Everybody liked them, including the pilots. CF-VTO-X was loaned to the US for evaluation: it was carelessly crashed in an unofficial attempt to exceed an altitude record when excessive loading caused a gear-box failure and the crew had to eject. The CL-84 offered great potential but in the end nobody was prepared to order it, least of all the Americans who broke the original one.

Canadair was based at Montreal's Cartierville Airport and in 1956 embarked on the design of its own twin-engined tilt-wing STOL 12-passenger transport aircraft as a project financed by the company, the Canadian Government and the Canadian Defence Research Board. A $10-million programme was embarked upon to design and build two prototypes. Chief of design was Fred Phillips. With a pair of 1,400 shp [shaft horsepower] Lycoming T53 turboprop engines driving interconnected handed Curtiss-Wright glass-fibre reinforced 14 feet diameter lightweight propeller blades and, additionally, a horizontally-mounted pair of contra-rotating twin-bladed tail rotors 7 feet in diameter, the Canadair CL-84 was not an attractive-looking aircraft but it was a spectacular aircraft to see in flight. In this early photo, a very long tripod-like tail skid is fitted.

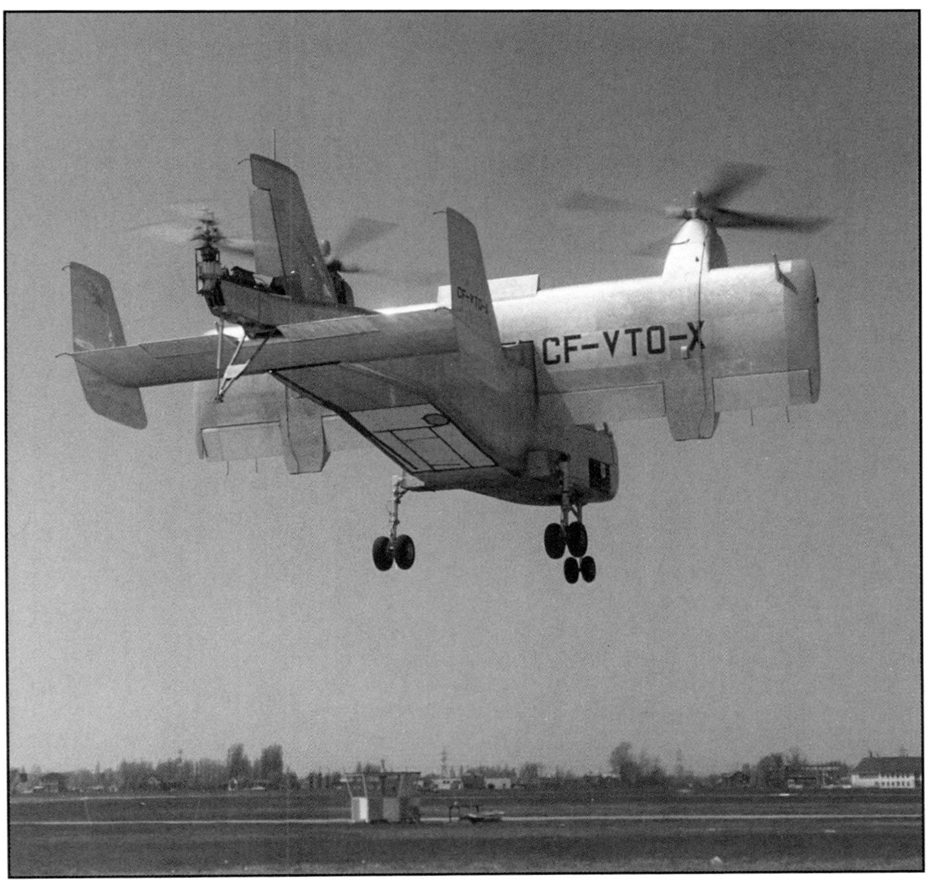

Development work was well in hand by 1964 by which time the decision had been taken to increase the number of prototypes to four. In the end, three would be air-tested of which two, including this, the very first (CF-VTO-X) would be lost in accidents without loss of life. With a wing-span of 33 feet 4 inches and a length of 45 feet 6 inches, the all-up weight was 10,600 lbs for a vertical take-off or 12,700 lbs for STOL. Maximum level speed was 330 mph. CF-VTO-X first flew in the hover on May 7th 1965 under the command of company chief test pilot Bill Longhurst. On September 12th, 1967, after no fewer than 305 more or less incident-free flights, Longhurst and his observer were returning from a flight when, at 3,000 feet, a bearing failure occurred: both men safely parachuted to earth.

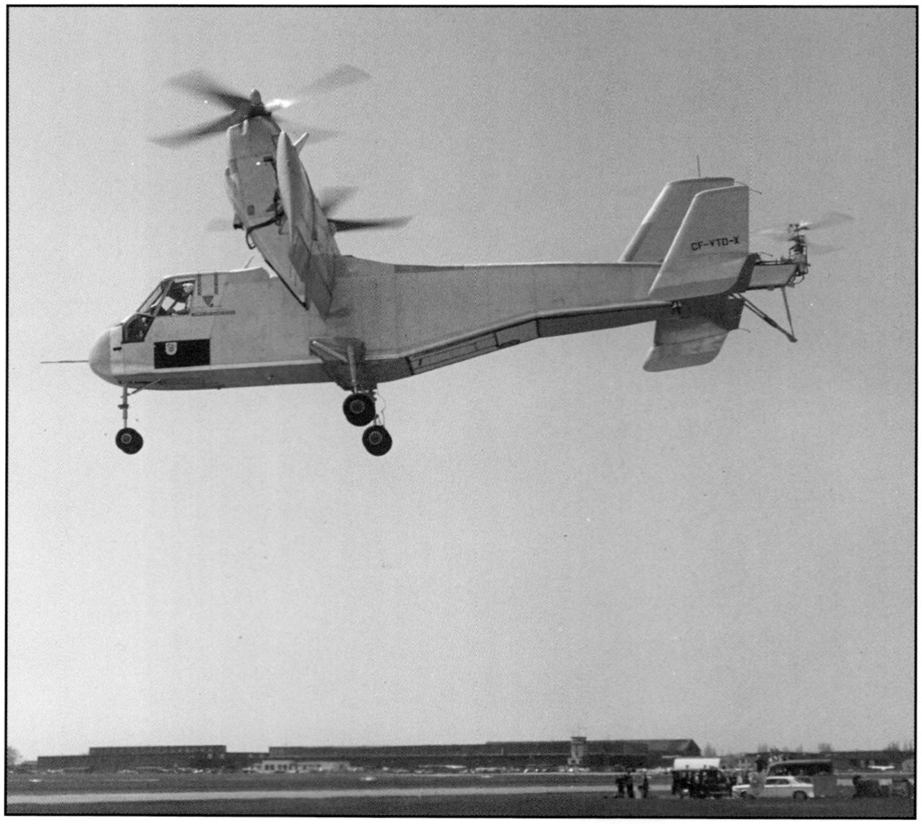

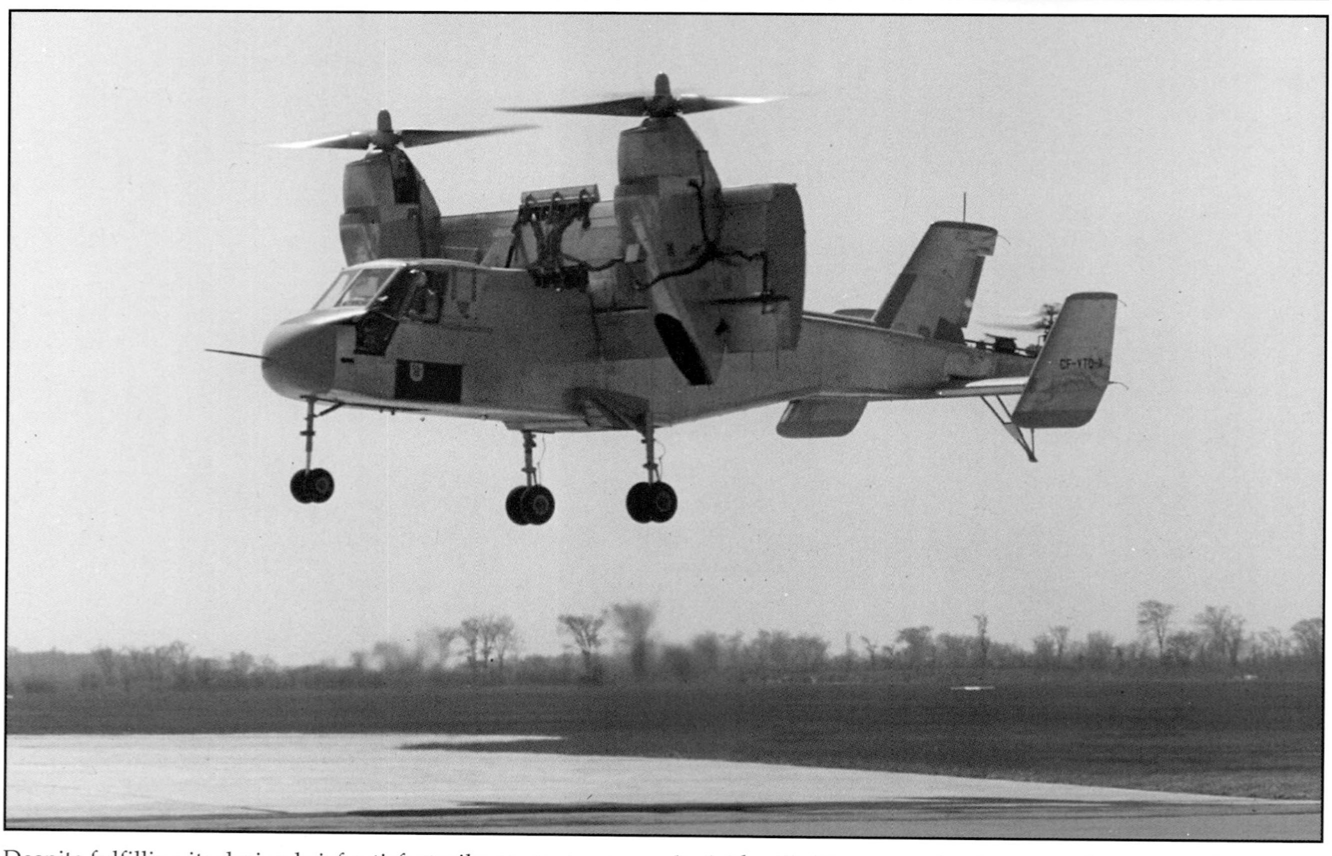

Despite fulfilling its design brief satisfactorily, no contracts resulted. The CL-84 was another instance of a concept ahead of its time when other paths to similar technology were being exploited. The ordinary helicopter was a cheaper option. No complete CL-84 survives and, as with Britain's aircraft industry, Canadair became a casualty of Canada's industry realignment. It is all part of a rich era of invention and skill that has long gone.

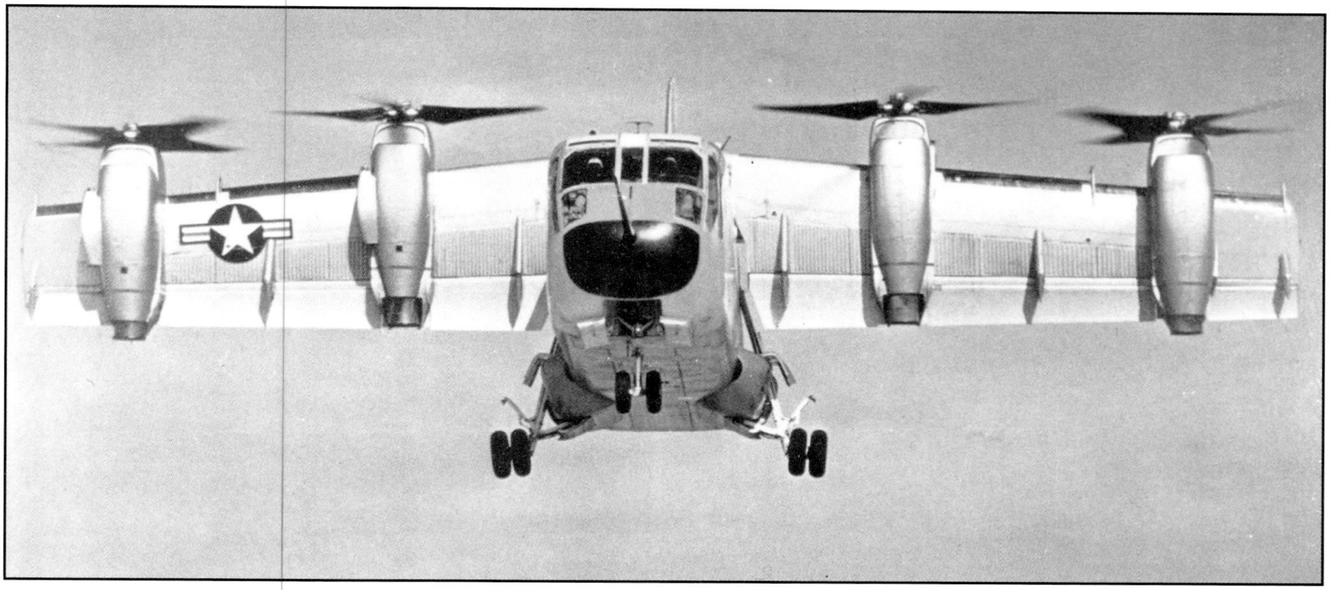

There are some ideas that appear absolutely brilliant. One is the vertical take-off and landing aircraft. Build a heavy transport that can take off from a village green and you've surely got a winner! So felt America's Vought company when, initially in partnership with Ryan and Hiller, they devised this amazing tilt-wing transport called the XC-142. After all, the Canadians had done it so the Yanks must go one bigger! When Vought was absorbed into the Ling-Temco group becoming LTV, the project continued but without the superior helicopter experience of its former partners. To remove the fear of engine failure, the aircraft was over-powered so that it could comfortably lift off with one motor out. This did, though, create a problem – downwash. The 67-foot wingspan aircraft had an all-up weight of 45,000 lb and was powered by four 3,080 shp engines. By comparison, the C.130 Hercules with an all-up weight of 125,000 lbs had four engines each of 3,750 hp. In the fully-tilted condition, people got blown over on the ground beneath and bricks and small cars became missiles. Not quite the thing for convivial operation. This picture shows the aircraft in the hover over Vought's runway.

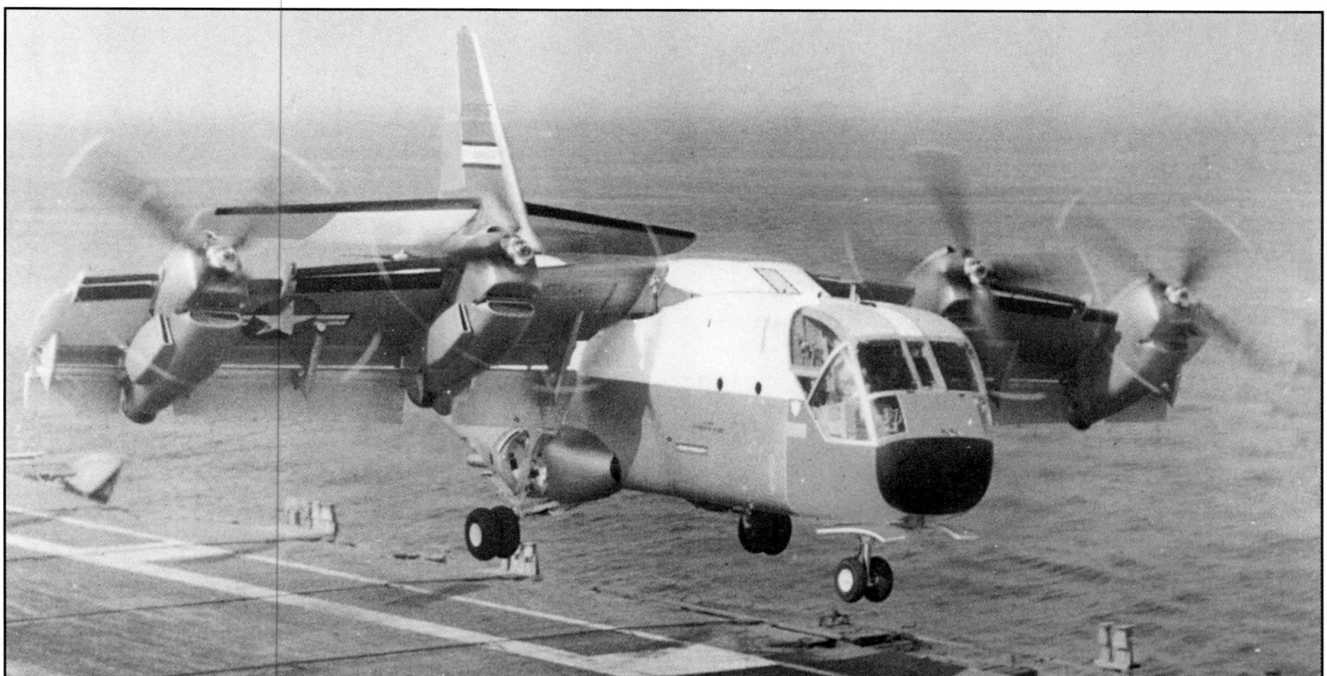

The first flight in 'conventional' mode took place on September 29th 1964. On January 11th the following year came the first successful transitional flight. Five of these XC-142A aircraft were built and here one of them is seen making a STOL take-off from the USS 'Bennington' in 1966. There were plans to make a fully civilian 40-seater version called the 'Downtowner' but the risk of injury and collateral damage from flying debris militated against it. Furthermore the trials were anything but incident-free and heavy landings and excessive vibration from the cross-linked drive shafts did not go down well with the Air Force observers. Failure of a tail-rotor led to one fatal crash. With hopes for a military order gone, the project was abandoned and NASA took over test and evaluation work from May 1966 until May 1970 but after that work stopped. One example survives as a museum curio.

The helicopter has fascinated many since Leonardo da Vinci first drew his ideas for a flying machine with rotating wings. Many of the experimenters that followed met with failure and, significantly, Leonardo avoided this sort of embarrassment by not bothering to even try, leaving his design for others to apply time and money to. One man who deserves some recognition was a Danish-born watchmaker, Jacon Christian Hansen Ellehammer (1871-1946). A competent engineer, he also built a motorcycle and, bitten by the aviation bug, claimed to be the first European to fly, ascending on a flying-machine at Lindholm on September 12th, 1906. He designed and built the three-cylinder 6 hp engine which powered it. In 1910 he turned to rotary-winged aircraft, builing a scale model in 1911. The following year he made the machine pictured here. His 6 hp engine drove both rotor and tractor propeller so making it a compound helicopter. The rotor was unusual, comprising two 19 feet diameter contra-rotating rings, the lower one being covered in waterproof cloth. Around the periphery of each were six equi-spaced slightly tapered vanes each five feet long by about two feet wide. These were of variable incidence, being pivotally attached to the rings. The incidence of these could be controlled by the pilot – a masterful application of the principles of collective pitch control with the possibilities also of cyclic pitch control. A number of tethered indoor flights were undertaken as seen here where two assistants are actually holding the machine down. Shortly afterwards Ellehammer began proper tests and in 1912 completed an ascent in the presence of Denmark's Prince Axel. Late that September, however, disaster struck and what was probably ground resonance tipped the machine over and destroyed the rotors. The designer later proposed a revolutionary compressed-air rotorcraft which was not built.

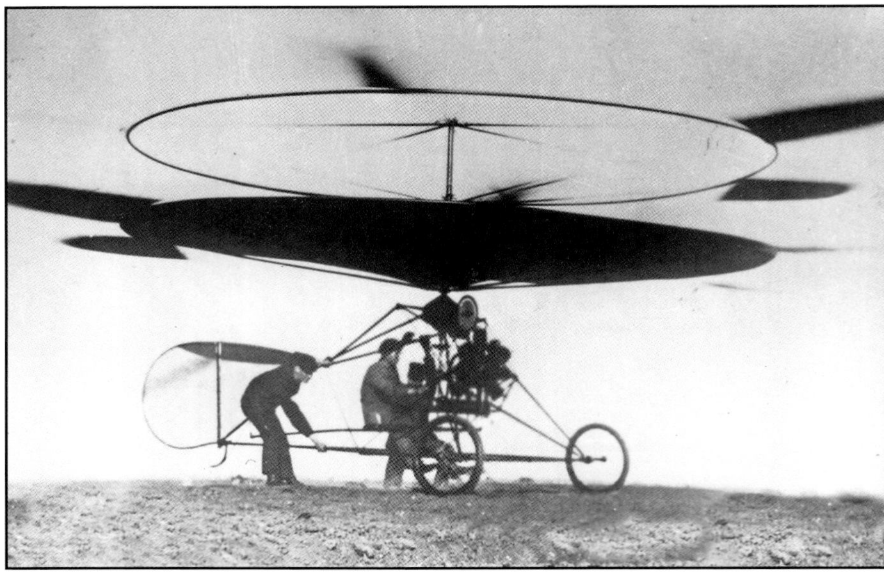

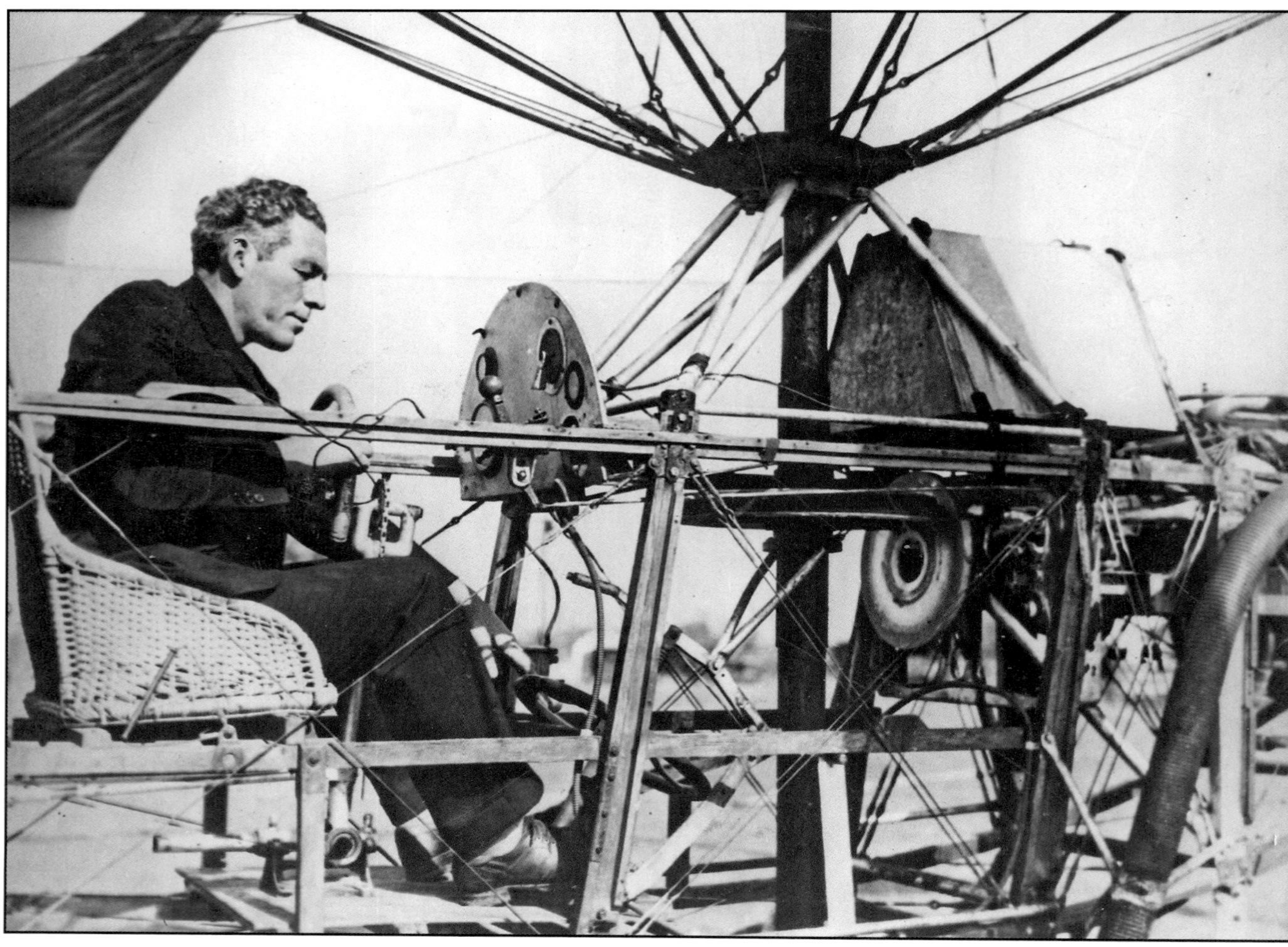

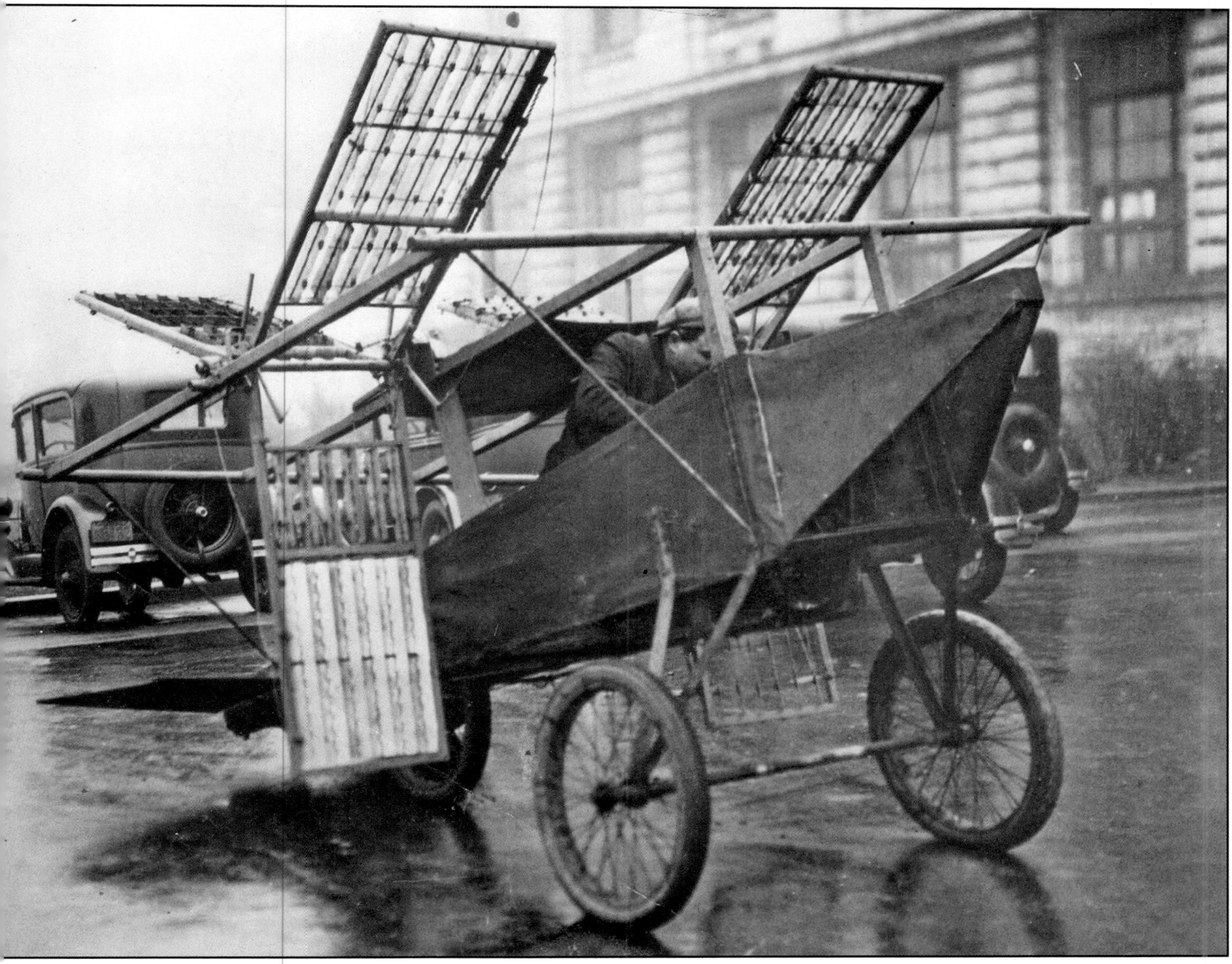

Once news of Adolf Rohrbach's perfectly feasible (if ultimately impractical) paddle-plane broke around the world, it was inevitable that it would inspire the 'wheelbarrow artisans' to come up with their own earth-shaking projects. One, pictured here, was the talk of a patent convention staged in Philadelphia, Pennsylvania, in the 1930s. News was released of the 1,500 mph paddle plane invented by John Sabas of Grand Rapids, Michigan. The story was taken up by some newspapers, in particular one for which the news reporter eagerly wrote: 'This strange-looking craft… is the centre of much attention. It is propelled by means of paddles on each side, the vanes on blades opening and closing as the paddles rotate. The inventor expects to attain a speed of 1,500 miles per hour with a completed craft of the same model but larger dimensions'. Perhaps it was the sight of the wheels, but most ignored what even the more inexperienced of news hawks felt was suspect. But just think! Faster than Concorde, not to be created for around another half century! With fears of a supersonic gyroplane, Mr Sabas had his day of glory and both he and his creation quietly disappeared before too much damage could be done to the progress of aviation.

Opposite: A fascination for rotary wings is easy to understand because of its sheer (apparent) simplicity: you simply twist a rotor round very fast and up you go! Reality kicks in many thousands of pounds/dollars and bruises later. In 1928, Jesse E Langdon of Bell, a small city in Los Angeles County, California, decided he had thought of something new when he applied for US Patent No. 1,684,880. It was for 'a combination of a helicopter, gyroscope and an airplane' and the inventor added that 'after the helicopter has gained altitude it may be flown like an ordinary plane'. Technically this was what is known as a compound, but you and I would call this a whole step too far. Mr Langdon started out by taking a leaf out of Cierva's book, planning his machine round an existing airframe. He chose a Curtiss JN-4D (the famous 'Jenny') fuselage, heavily modified to take a 26 feet diameter rotor with helical van arrangement supported by a large number of bracing wires. The rotor was driven by friction disc which provided speed control (said the inventor). A single-seater powered by a 140 hp Hisso A, the contraption was 'rolled-out' in 1929. It seems that the designer spent the following three or four years trying to coax flight out of his creation for it was still being described as a 'new idea in flight' as late as 1934. Flight, however, successfully eluded this machine.

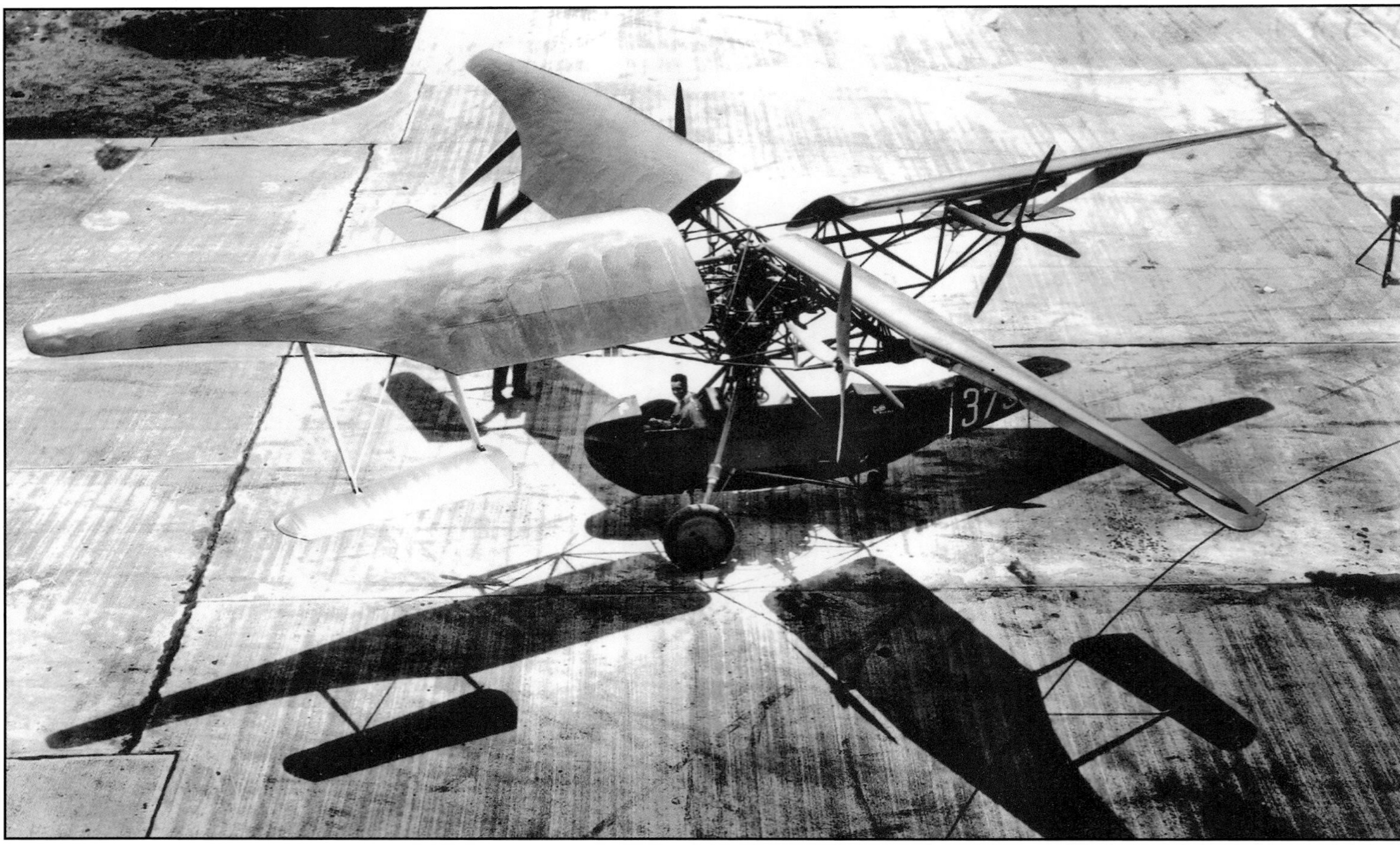

For inventors, the notion of the helicopter was just too simple to miss out on! It seems everybody had a go at creating one. Some were allowed to tinker in private, failure being ameliorated by obscurity, while others were allowed the encouragement of 'official' backing and, when it all went pear-shaped, their failure was written into history. One noble attempt which made an indelible mark in this latter category was the creation of Michigan University graduate Maitland Barkelew Bleecker. Born in 1903, descendent of New Amsterdam settlers from 1658, Bleecker's student days were spent in the company of several men who would become aviation legends including Fred Weick, the light aircraft designer. In his graduation year, 1924, Bleecker devised a unique torqueless rotary-winged craft which, two years later, he talked the Curtiss Company of Valley Stream, Long Island, into building. It featured four wing-like rotors, each impelled by its own four-bladed propeller which was shaft-driven using universal joints from a central, vertically-mounted 420 hp Pratt & Whitney Wasp engine. Trailing behind each rotor blade was an independent control surface on outrigger arms. He called these 'stabovators' and claimed that they regulated the angle of each rotor. Four years in development at a cost of $250,000, the Curtiss-Bleecker helicopter began trials in 1930. The rotors turned at 60 rpm (and up to 100 rpm 'for cruising') but, apart from some fifteen hesitant indoor hovers, the machine was deemed by its backers to be a failure. Disappointed, Bleecker went on to other things taking out many patents throughout an active life. He died aged 99 on October 19th 2002, leaving a valuable archive of aviation papers to the National Air & Space Museum Archives. The picture shows the two-seater on a rare, but firmly grounded, outing in June 1930.

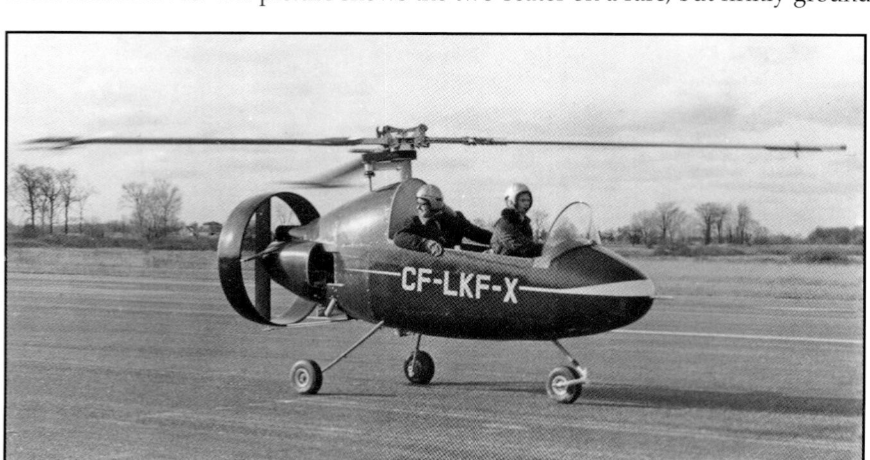

Canadian company Avian Industries was founded in 1959 to develop an experimental 2-seat autogyro having a 3-blade rotor with compressed air nozzles at the blade tips to provide a jump-start facility to 200 feet. The machine had a pusher-mounted 180 hp Lycoming and unusual features including a yaw vane inside the propeller duct, and steel-tube rotor blades with flapping hinges but no drag ones. Inadequate directional stability led to fixed fins being fitted outside the duct. The prototype was later destroyed in an accident, a second model was abandoned and rising costs led to the cancellation of the project.

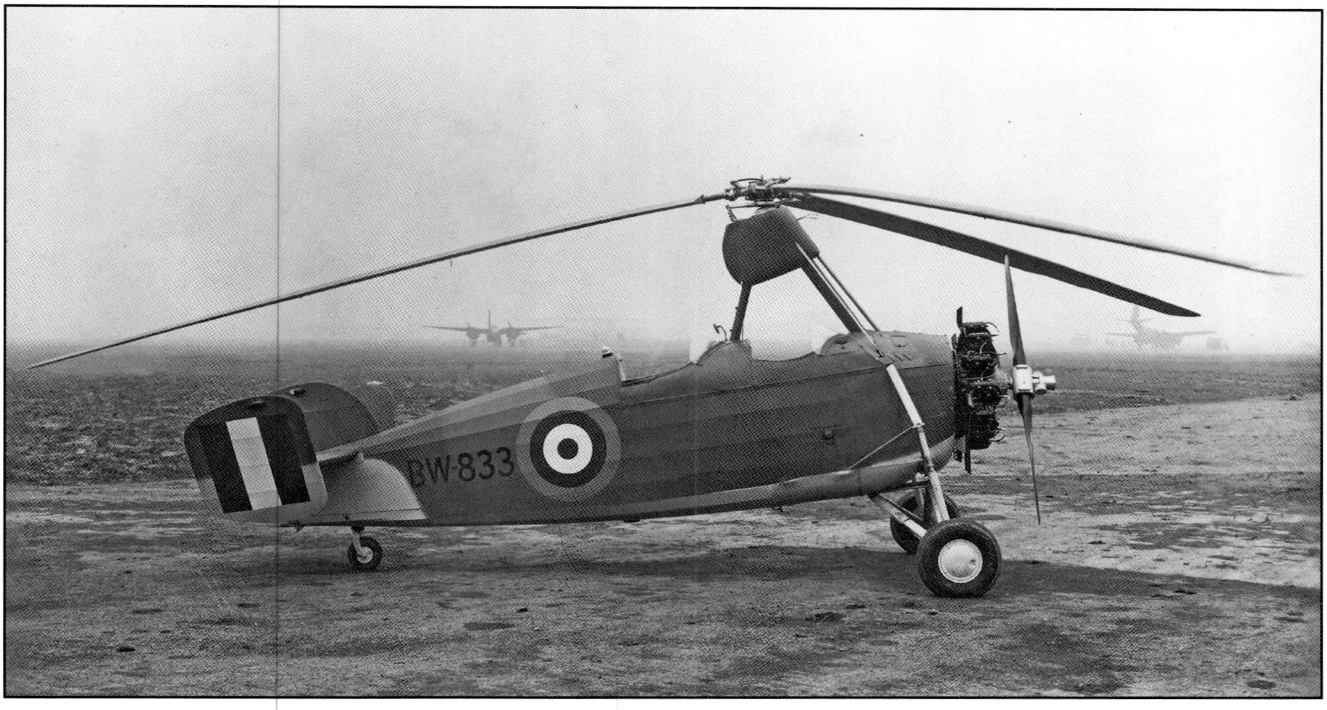

The one that got away – or should it be one of the few that survived! After Cierva's untimely death in 1936, the man who progressed the Autogiro was his American disciple, Harold Pitcairn, who battled the Depression and associated negative marketing forces to promote Cierva's work. In 1941, the Royal Air Force ordered from Pitcairn a quantity of his PA.39 Autogiros. Revised from his established PA-18, these wingless two-seaters had a direct-control rotor and a Warner Super Scarab. Seven machines together with an adequate inventory of spares comprising rotor blades, undercarriages and spare engines, were despatched at the height of the German U-Boat blockade. The consignment was split between two ships; one was sunk taking three Autogiros and all the spares to the bottom of the sea. The four surviving Autogiros, devoid of replacement parts, survived but could not be put into service. This is a rare Air Ministry photograph of BW833 undergoing trials at A&AEE Boscombe Down in December 1941.

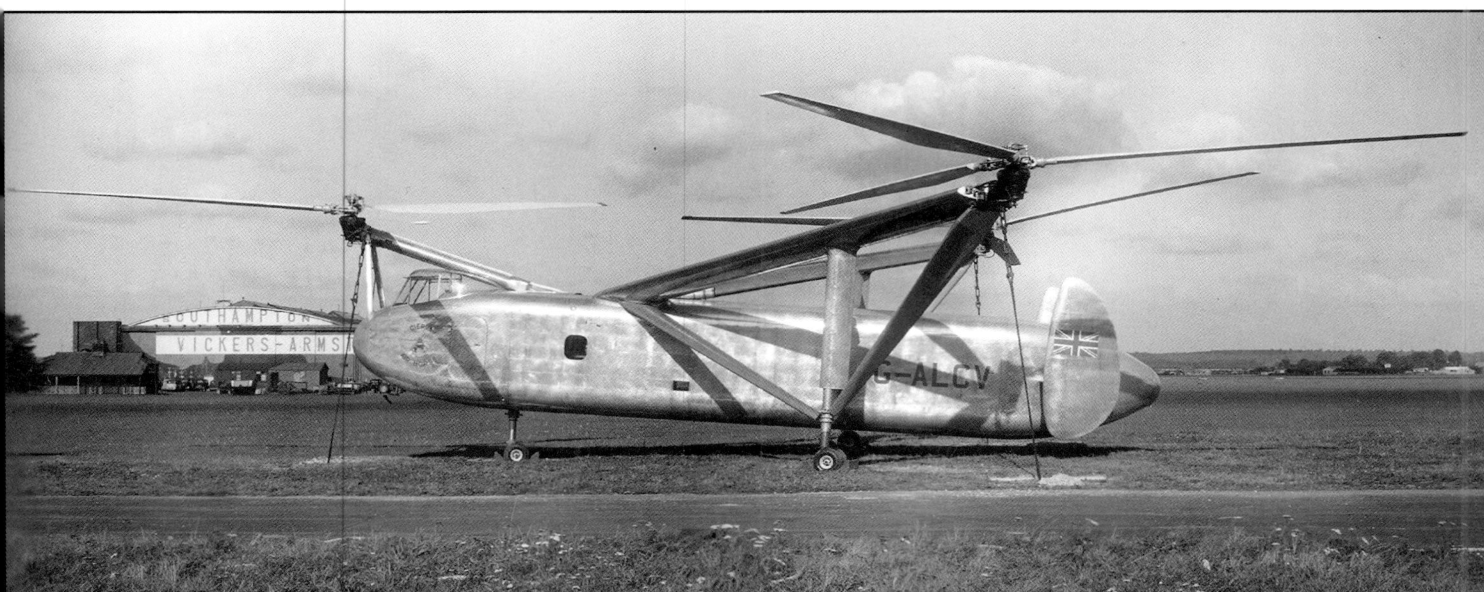

A curiosity of the post-war aviation scene was G-ALCV, the Cierva W.11 Air Horse. Initially promoted as a pest-control vehicle, the sheer size of this helicopter rendered such a proposition impractical. Powered by a single 1,620 hp Rolls-Royce Merlin 24, the Air Horse was built at Eastleigh by the Cierva Autogiro Company Ltd. It was first flown there by Henry Alan Marsh on December 7th 1948 as VZ724 and soon after took the world record for the greatest lift achieved to that time by a helicopter – 14,000 lbs. But the complexity of the machine with all its gearboxes and shafting became its downfall: on June 13th 1950 fatigue failure of a rotor hub shed one of the three sets of rotor blades and Marsh and his crew were killed in the crash. Wind turbines didn't exist in those days: today its resemblance to a horizontal wind farm is uncanny.

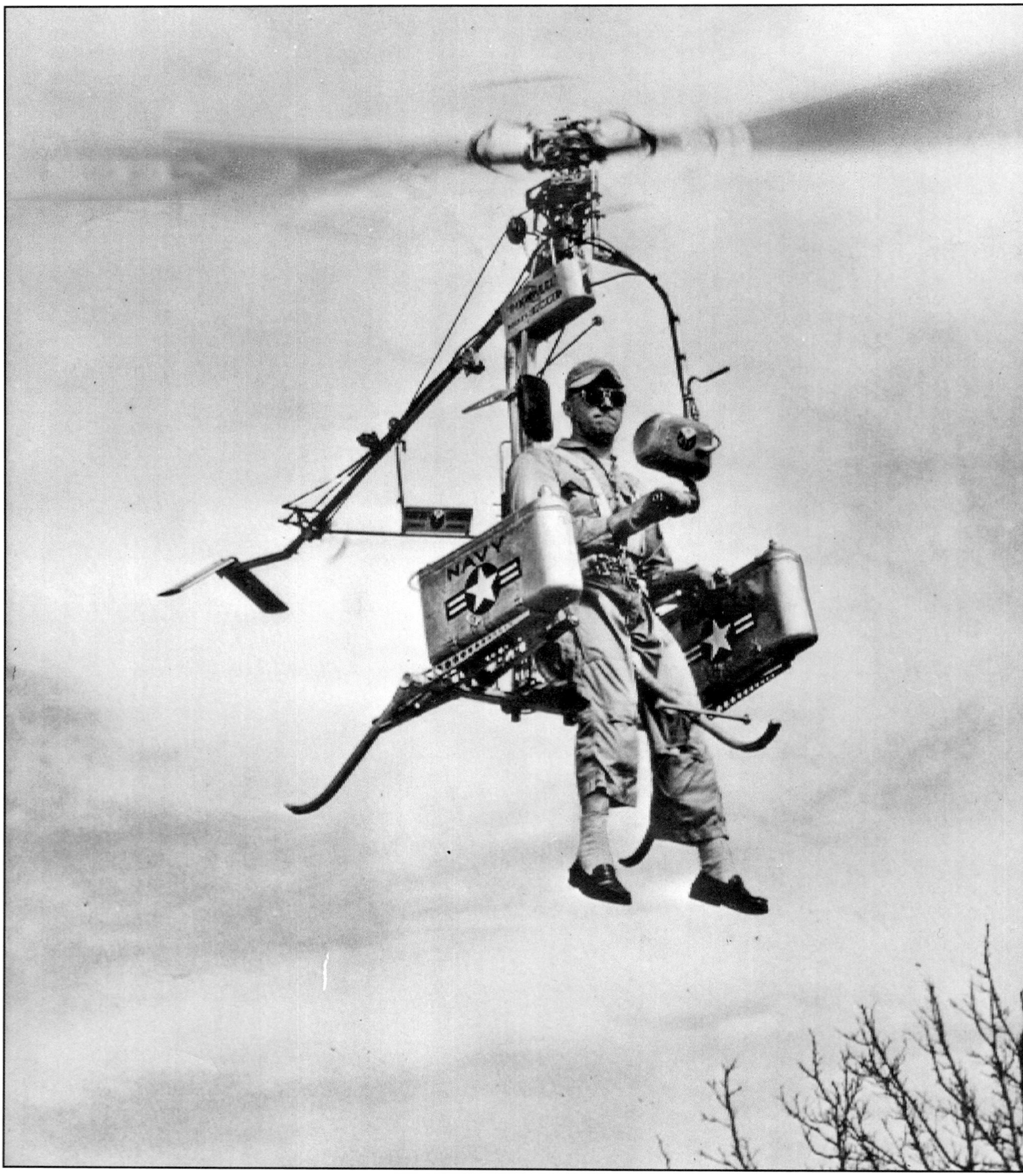

Rotary wings have always made headlines in the curious flying-machine category but in the 1950s there was a spate of machines that required the pilot to provide his own landing-gear. The Rotor-Craft RH-1 Pinwheel was one of these. Designed and built to a US Navy contract, this was a rocket-driven two-blade rotor with a belt-driven tail rotor, the pitch of which was controllable using a chain-operated lever worked by twisting the horizontal cyclic handle on the dangling control stick. This control stick also mounted a basic instrument panel, the most important feature of which was an indicator as to how much fuel remained. The mono-propellant fuel was liquid 90 percent hydrogen-peroxide provided in two rectangular tanks either side of the pilot's saddle. The complete machine weighed less than the average pilot and was said to be capable of lifting twice its own weight. It was foldable, could be dropped by parachute, stowed aboard a submarine and a pair of them could be transported in a station wagon. It made its first free flight in 1954 at Glendale, California, site of its makers. Here test pilot Dick Whitehead is seen on his epic first flight while wearing what looks very much like bedroom slippers.

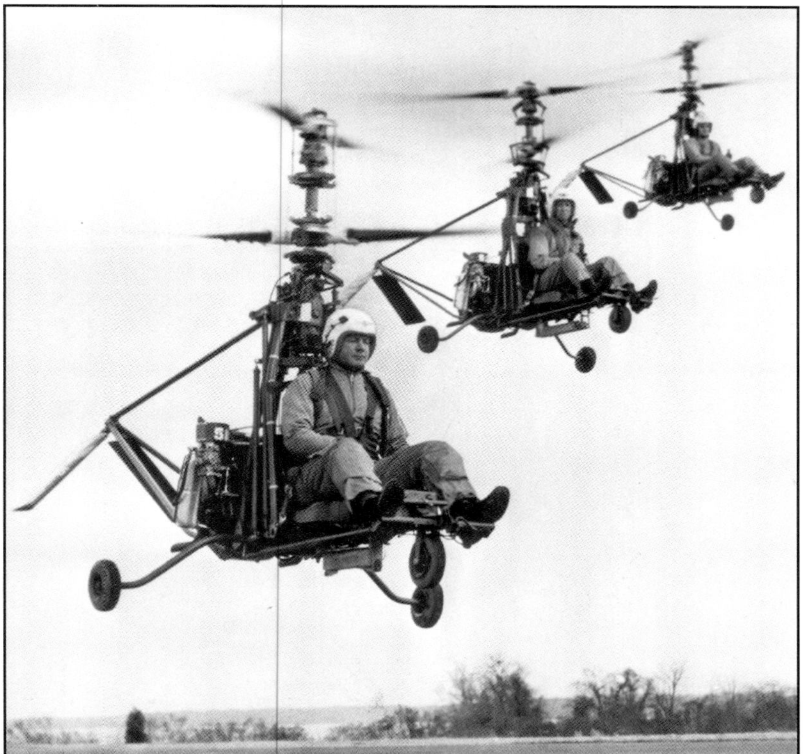

Somebody in a high place in America had a brainwave one day. Why not train the Marines as helicopter pilots and let them fly themselves into combat zones! The idea of the portable military helicopter – a powered version of the foldable military autogiro gliders the RAF experimented with in the early days of war – soon captured the US popular imagination and in next to no time two companies had offered models for trials. Both were experienced rotorcraft-makers. The first was Gyrodyne of Long Island, New York. Its GCA-41 was designed and built in less than a year, becoming the US Navy's XRON-1 Rotorcycle. A portable single-seater with two contra-rotating two-blade rotors, the original engine was the 44 hp Nelson, later replaced by the 62 hp Porsche. The length was 11 feet 6 inches, height 8 feet and rotor diameter 17 feet. With an empty weight of 425 lbs and an all-up of 650 lbs, the Rotorcycle first flew in the autumn of 1956. The initial rate of climb was 600 feet/min, the cruising speed 45 knots and the range 51 nautical miles. Here three flyers from the Marine Corps Schools at Quantico, Virginia, show how it could be done.

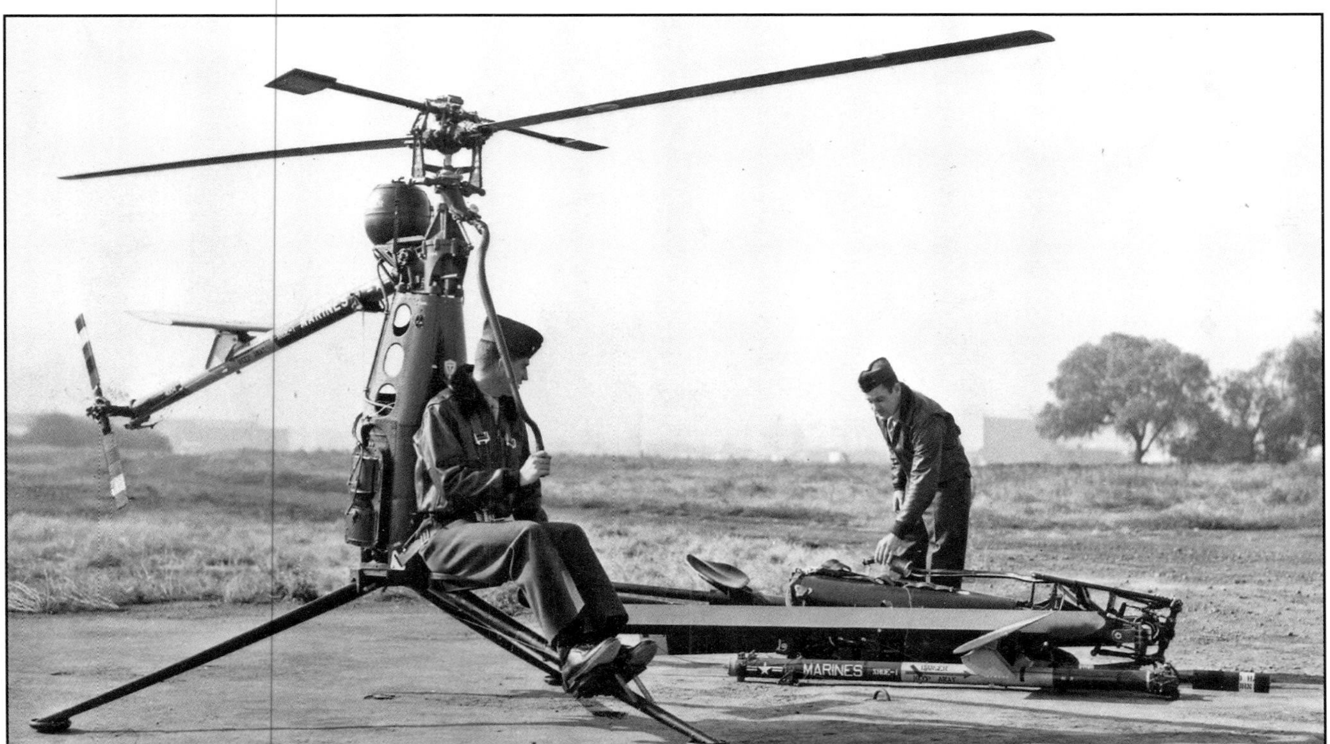

The second maker was Hiller and its design became the XROE-1 Rotorcycle also developed to the order of the US Navy. With a single two-blade rotor controlled by the Hiller patent 'paddle control' servo system, this Rotorcycle required a small tail rotor. Instead of a wheeled undercarriage, the pilot sat on a motorcycle-type seat on top of a tripod landing gear. Designed for observation duties in conjunction with the US Marines, the Hiller was first flown in January 1957 powered by a 45 hp Nelson. With a width of 8 feet 4 inches and a height of 6 feet 10 inches, the rotor diameter was 18 feet 6 inches. Empty weight was 300 lbs, all-up 496 lbs and the machine would cruise at 52 mph with a top speed of 70 mph. The initial rate of climb was 920 feet/min and the range 40 miles. The picture shows the fold-up helicopter in flat-pack form and assembled. Saunders-Roe at Eastleigh built ten as the Saro-Hiller 1033 Rotorcycle, the first flying there on October 19th 1959 at the hands of Hiller test pilot Philip Johnston. One became G-APYF (formerly G-46-1). There was no military future in Rotorcycles and they quietly died away.

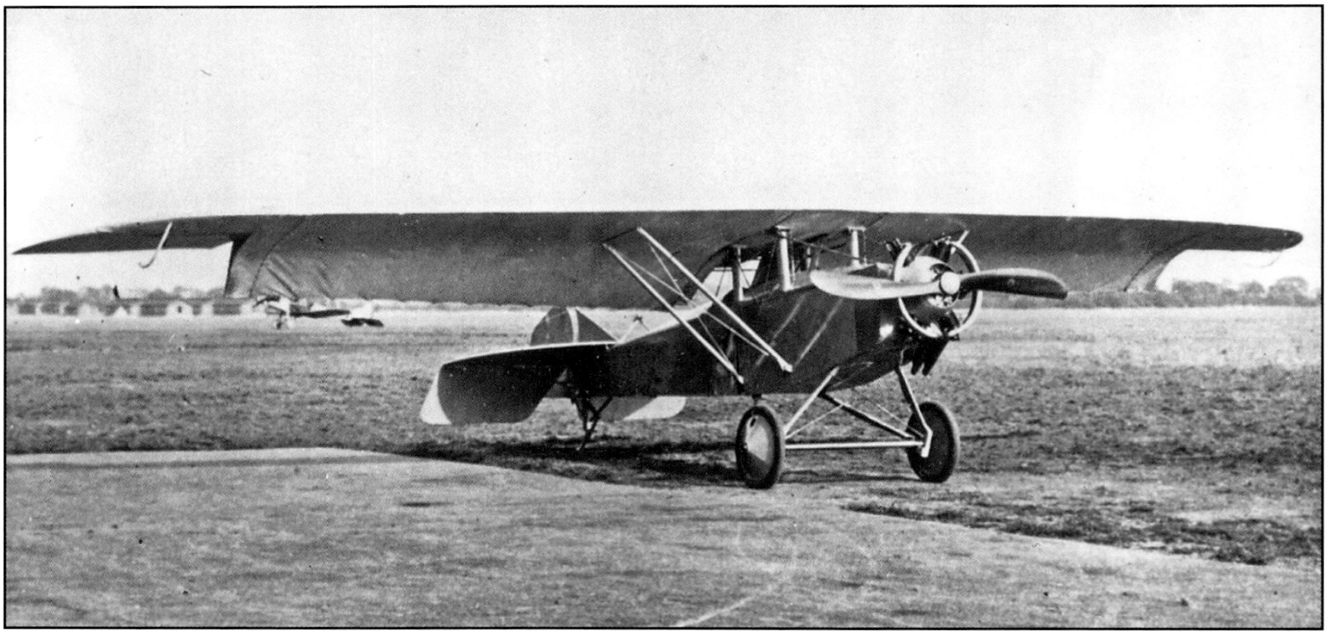

Turning from rotary wings to high-lift fixed wing, the Holle Varioplane, built and flown in 1917, was a very advanced idea for its time. The idea of Dutch-born Alexander Herbert Holle, it was the subject of British Patent No.103,400 of April 1916. Backed by the famous coach-builders H J Mulliner Ltd and with co-patentee Arthur William Judge, Holle's idea was to make the entire rear half of the wing fully-articulated so that it became a perfectly smooth camber-changing surface. In 1919, Robert Blackburn formed the Commercial Aeroplane Wing Syndicate Ltd with £30,000 capital 'to acquire from A A Holle and the Varioplane Co Ltd of 19 Half Moon Street, Piccadilly, an invention for improvements in aero-foils for aeroplanes and the like'. The Varioplane Company was to appoint three directors and Blackburn Aeroplane & Motor Company two. The post-war slump in aviation led Blackburn to investigate any way of expanding his business and this wing seemed an answer. The venture eventually lapsed.

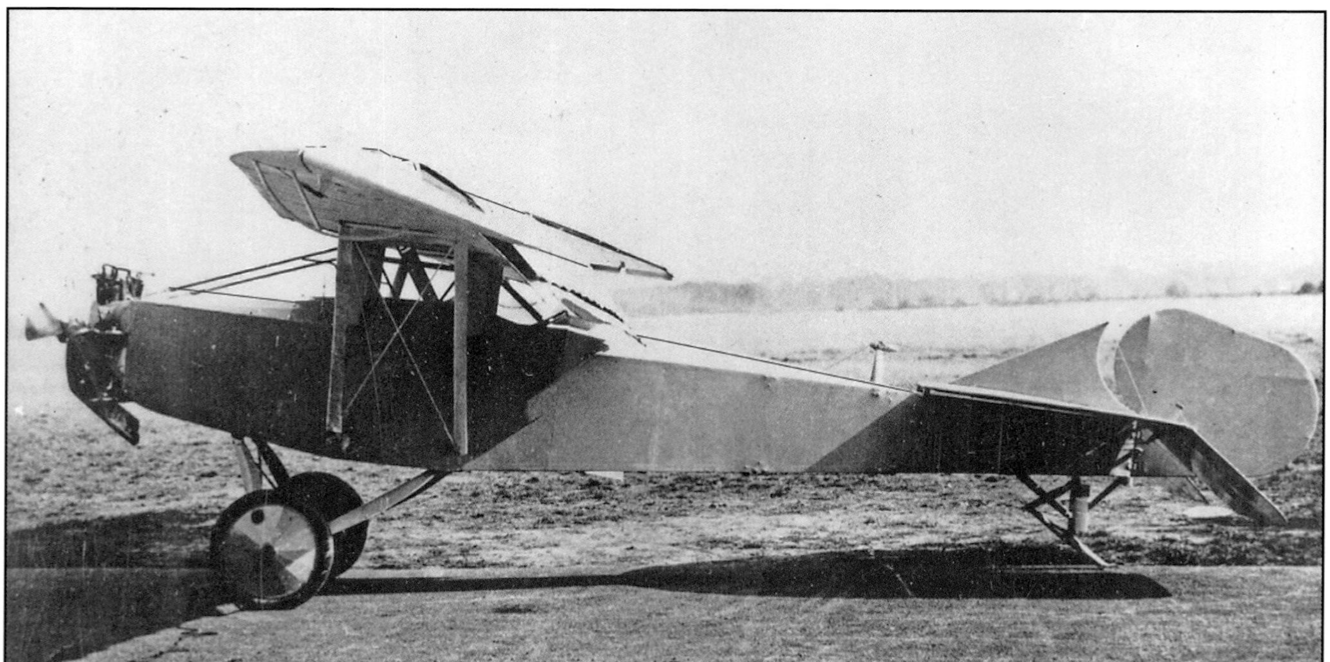

The complexity of the Holle wing militated against its adoption and the 60 hp Anzani-powered sole example was soon forgotten. However, the inventor went on to devise the curious Alula wing made of mahogany and fitted to a Martinsyde Semiquaver, G-EAPX, and flown at Northolt in 1921 by Blackburn's test pilot R W Kenworthy. With the later development work by Fairey on improvements to the Sopwith Baby, a new and simpler form of camber-changing flap was evolved on the Fairey Baby better known as the Hamble Baby and test-flown by Maurice Wright, RN. Holle's original invention was too perfect to combine ease of manufacture and lightness of weight with aerodynamic efficiency. Holle believed the surface integrity was vital: today we know that holes, slots and slits in a wing surface actually improve performance.

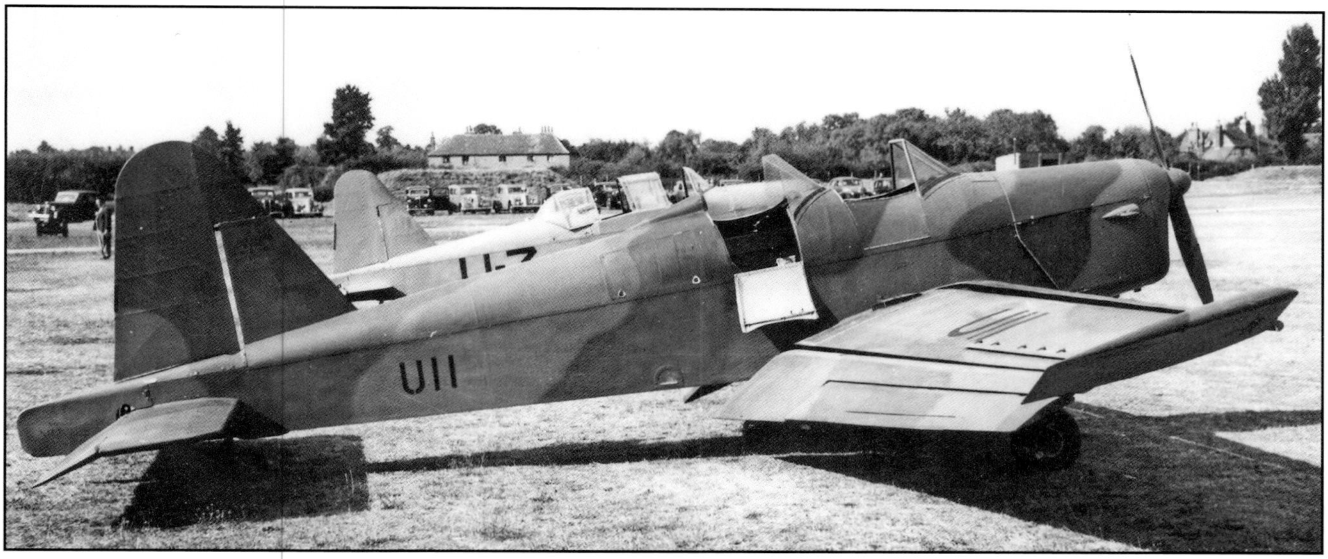

As soon as experimenters discovered that curious things happened to the lift characteristics of an airfoil section the moment you started to mess about with the trailing edge, aeroplanes began to appear with metamorphic wings. After Holle probably the best-remembered is the Youngmann-Baynes High Lift Monoplane built in 1947 by Heston Aircraft Ltd. But there were several other very advanced experimental machines, one being the Miles M.18 High Lift of 1942. This was the fourth of the small series of M.18 aircraft made at Woodley by Phillips & Powis Ltd and was used by the Royal Aircraft Establishment to obtain data on the characteristics of high-lift devices intended for the Supermarine S.12/40 ship-borne aircraft. These included full-span fully-adjustable leading edge slots, and full-span slotted flaps with inset ailerons. Initial trials revealed greater than expected transitional or spanwise flow which created lateral instability at low speeds. Upturned wing-tips were fitted, as pictured here, to attempt to remedy the problem. The M.18, offered as an improved version of the Magister, never caught on and of the three original aircraft built – G-AFRO, G-AHKY and G-AHOA – only 'HKY survives. And the high-lift test vehicle pictured here? It disappeared during the war.

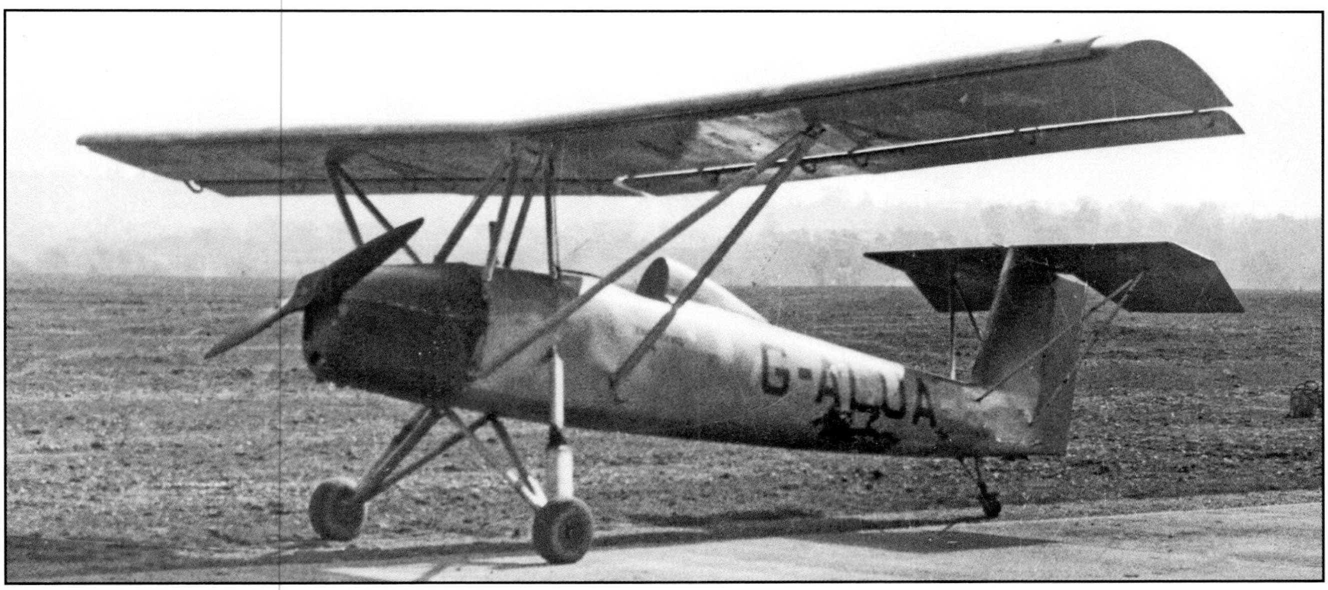

The theory behind the floating-wing aircraft was to make a fuselage that would remain horizontal at all times, regardless of whether the aircraft was in an attitude of climb or descent. While the greater majority of aircraft employ the fuselage as an 'aiming tool' to increase or decrease the angle of attack of the wing, the floating wing allowed the attitude of the body to remain unchanged. The most renowned demonstration of this was unfortunately never taken to its ultimate conclusion. Students at the Brunswick Technical High School built this delightful aircraft, the Zaunkönig (Wren). A single-seater powered by a 50 hp four-cylinder inline inverted Zundapp, it was an exercise in controllable slow-speed flight and was flown in April 1945 as D-YBAR. A small number was built by the students during the war but the increasing pressures of the war in Europe brought the project to a halt before research could be undertaken. What was doubly interesting was that the Zaunkönig was intended to have a floating tail as well. At the end of the war, the Allies discovered this example hidden at Hartzberg and brought it to Farnborough as VX190. Deemed of little interest to the authorities it was sold to the Ultra Light Aircraft Association, becoming G-ALUA. As a conventional aircraft with full leading-edge slots and trailing-edge flaps, this delightful aeroplane could fly easily at 31 mph and was enormous fun. The only drawback was that it was a mistake to be in a hurry…

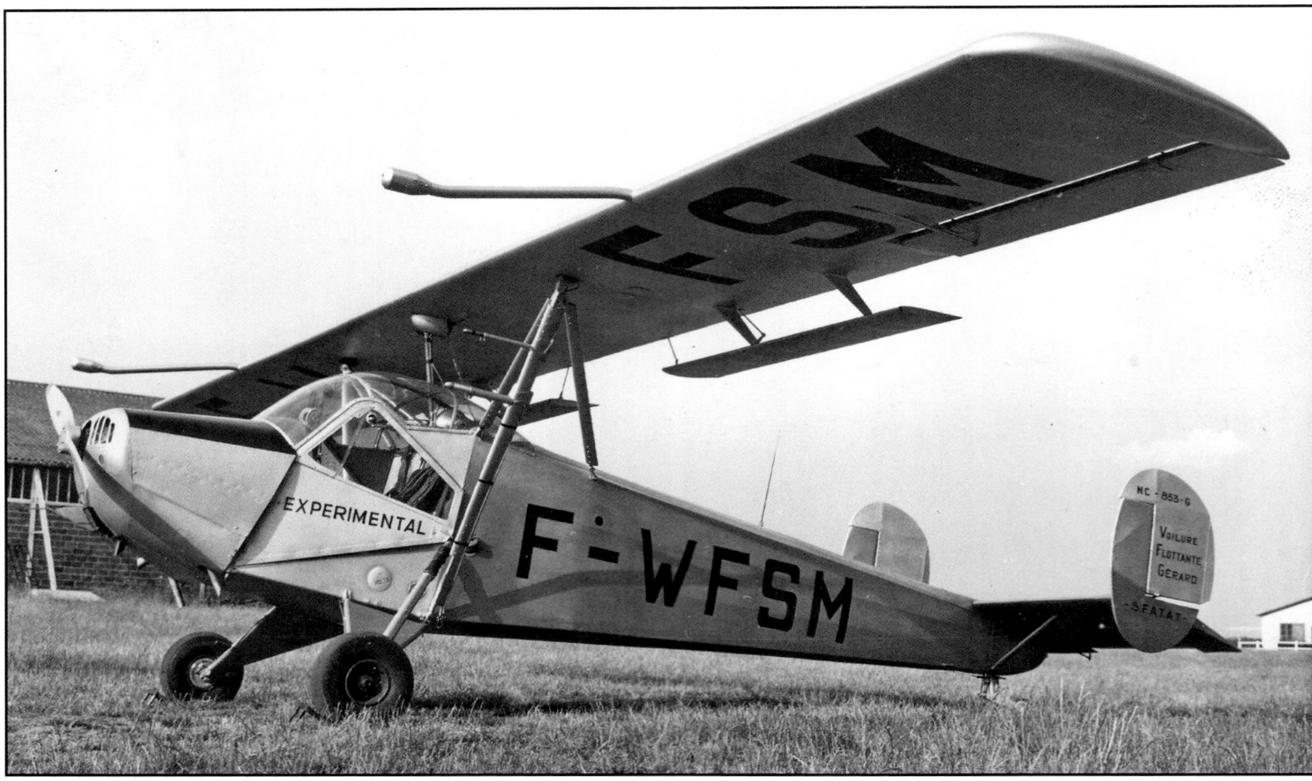

The 'floating wing' goes back to experiments in the 1930s and, besides being exploited (in derivative form) by Henri Mignet in his Flying Flea, was one of the original aspects of the Brunswick Zaunkönig. It was revived in 1950 by the French experimenter André Gérard who took a standard Nord NC.850 and modified it. First built by SNCAN (Société Nationale de Constructions Aéronautiques du Nord) as a cantilever shoulder-wing light aircraft for the use of French flying clubs, the NC.850 was originally produced as the Aérocentre NC.840, the name changed after the coalescence of France's aircraft industry. The design revised from the 1940s original, F-BFSM was converted to NC.854S by replacing the original 80 hp Minie 4-DC.30 engine with a 65 hp Continental A-65 in August 1956. This was further upgraded in May of 1958 with a 90 hp Continental, now becoming a model NC.858S. It underwent various other upgrades until delivery, in 1964, to SIPA (Société Industrielle pour l'Aéronautique) where it was experimentally fitted with Gérard's *voilure flottante* or floating wing. This was a one-piece assembly mounted above the fuselage on a single-point pylon at each side. The wing was static-balanced by two forward-protruding lead weights which also damped out any tendency to flutter. Behind and beneath the trailing edge of the wings inboard of the ailerons were fitted large Flettner flaps which operated like Dornier-type 'park-bench' controllable trim surfaces. The idea was that whatever the pitch of the wing, the datum line of the fuselage was always horizontal. With the French Class 'B' registration F-WFSM, the first flight of this took place on June 15th, 1965. It became apparent early on that the added weight and drag of the modification cancelled out any major advantage of the system and, after numerous, if desultory, trials, it was withdrawn from use in November 1968, the aircraft going into store at St Cyr.

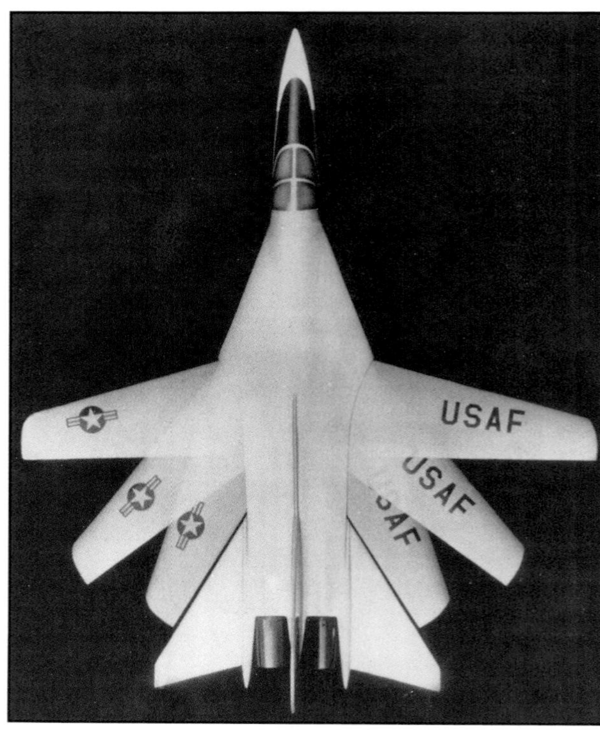

Variable-geometry aircraft are nothing new and from the Holle Varioplane to the recent American and Russian jet fighters, means of adjusting the characteristics of flight are almost as old as flight itself. Our own Barnes Wallis, working for Vickers at Weybridge and Brooklands, experimented with swing-wings and swept wings in projects such as the Swallow. Swept back wings for very high speed; extended wings for slow landing speeds: it was a challenging engineering task, but one worth exploring. The principle migrated to America and Russia and gave rise to a raft of curious aircraft from the MiG 27 to the Bell X-5, French Dassault Mirage and American F-111. Looking like something from a David Attenborough nature documentary, this impressive multiple-exposure picture of the F-14 Tomcat illustrates the system quite well. And not a spanner in sight!

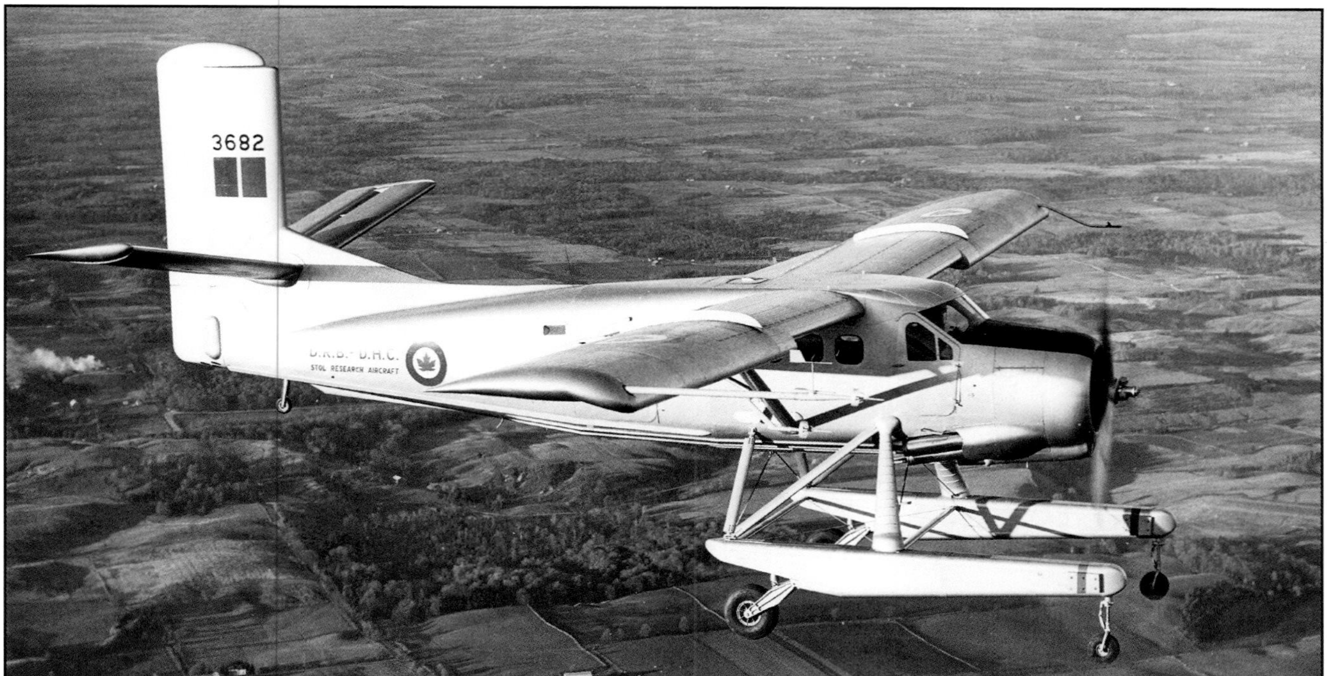

During the summer of 1956 and in conjunction with the Canadian Defense Research Board, De Havilland Canada of Downsview, Ontario, undertook a programme of experiments associated with a STOL version of the successful Otter. Two RCAF machines were modified and provided with a metamorphic inboard wing comprising a three-section telescoping trailing-edge flap system which could be drooped to 60 degree. There was also a drooping leading edge, slotted elevators on a high-dihedral tailplane and boundary layer control on the wings. Note the discontinuity of the leading edge as well as the upper surface fences. The lower fuselage was strengthened with the fitting of long external strakes visible in this view.

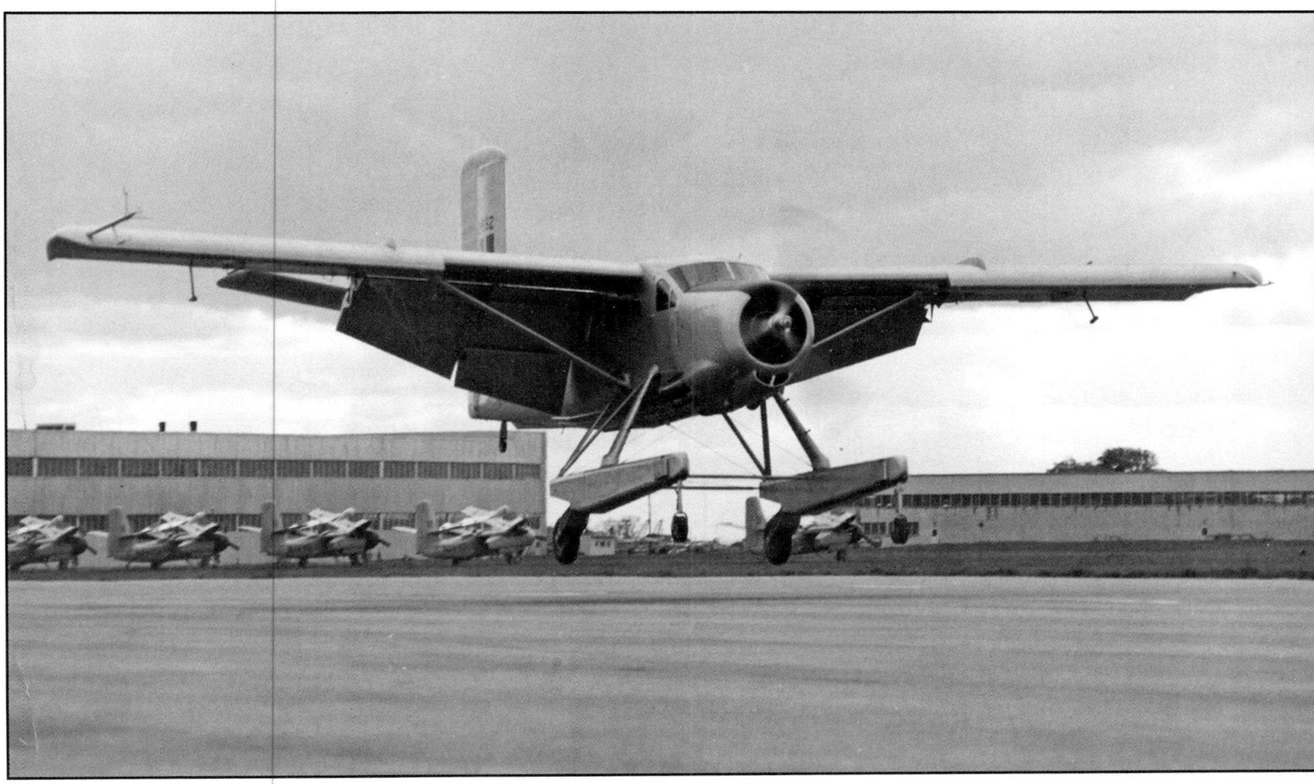

Trials showed that at the fully-extended position of the flaps, the STOL Otter could maintain altitude at an airspeed of 40 mph at which speed the lift coefficient of the wing was actually four. Here the aircraft approaches at almost 90 degree flap. Lower speeds could be achieved at increased angle. To simulate a tricycle landing gear installation, a novel four-wheeled undercarriage was made using wheels attached to beams that resembled small floats. Landing at 7,500 lb in zero wind conditions produced a run of less than 200 feet while the landing run needed to clear a 50 feet high obstacle was less than 500 feet.

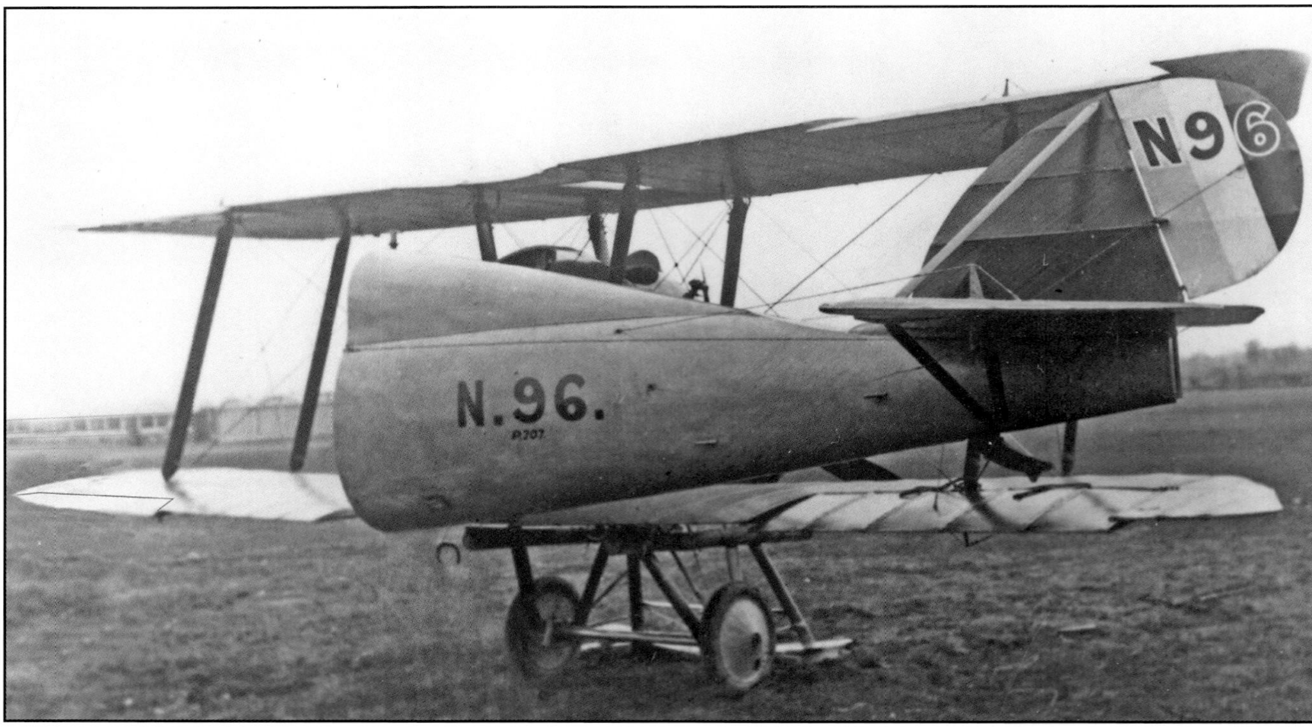

Folding wings are an invention of some aeronautical antiquity. Less common were folding fuselages. When the Admiralty issued a specification in 1917 for a two-seat reconnaissance and spotting aeroplane capable of being operated by the Royal Naval Air Service (RNAS) from what then passed as an aircraft carrier, one submission came from Parnall Aircraft. The work of Harold Bolas, the Parnall N.2A, the fuselage was a plywood monocoque made in two halves which could either be separated completely to allow the aircraft to be carried, fully-rigged, on a lorry, or hinged so it could be stored in a minimal space. Another novelty was the use of air bags inside the fuselage to aid buoyancy in the event of a ditching. Six prototypes were built, the type name Panther being allocated to the last, followed by a production batch of about 150 between 1919 and 1920. Some remained in service as late as 1926. At that time, carrier decks were provided not with arrester wires across the direction of landing, but longitudinal wires stretching the length of the deck, the idea being to serve as guide lines to safe braking. There were frequent mishaps with this system.

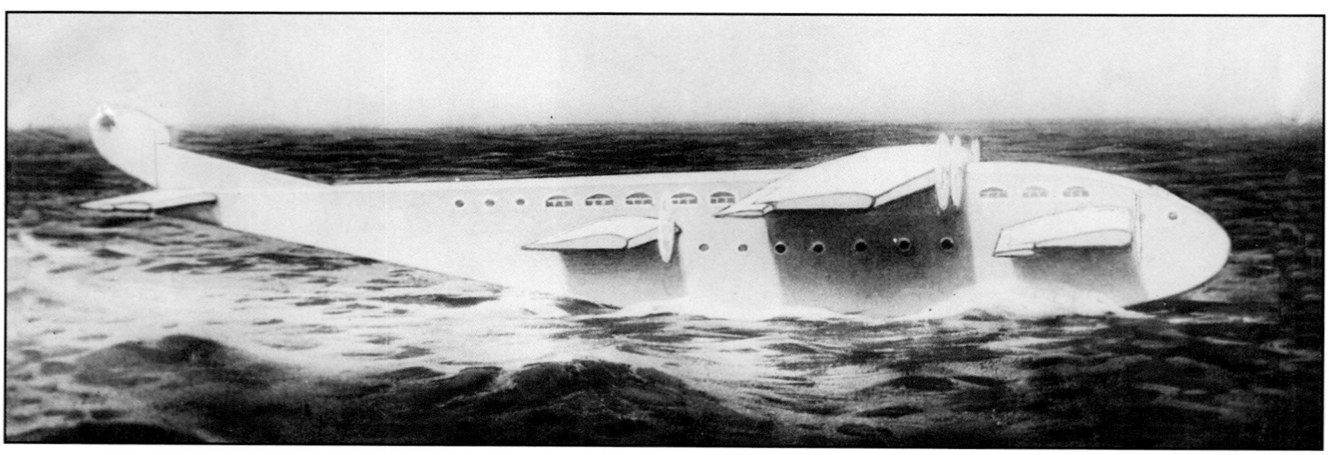

Back in the 1920s, the idea of being able to fly the Atlantic with passengers was so far-fetched that to the majority of people it verged on the 'not in my lifetime' category. The crossing by Alcock and Brown in the Vickers Vimy in June 1919 aroused the interest of entrepreneurs and aeronautical visionaries at a time when nobody had any really firm data to go on. And so the formation of a company in New York called the Trans-Oceanic Airport Company of America during 1925 attracted curiosity. Its flamboyant head was a man called Armin DeMuth who proposed a series of giant flying boats to carry up to 200 passengers between New York and Europe. His vision for this enormous 'boat was interesting for what it foretold. An eight-engined flying boat with a four-engined main wing and two subsidiary wings, the forward and rear of which would each carry two engines was projected, the two-deck passenger cabin having a large-windowed lounge area upstairs was at least a decade ahead of the Short long-distance flying boats of the late 1930s and even by the end of 1939 transatlantic crossings with passengers were only just feasible.

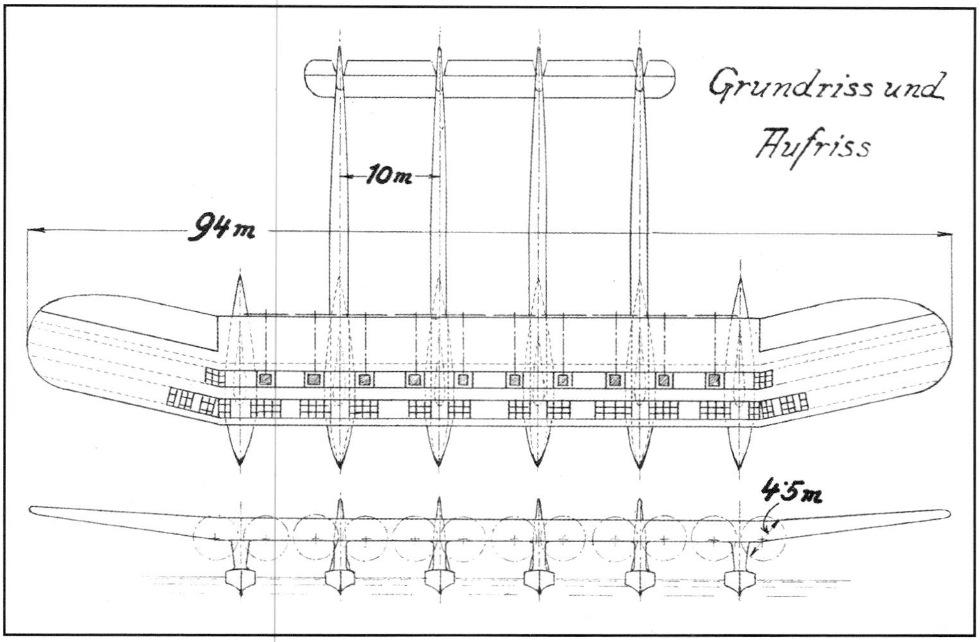

The Germans were also interested in transatlantic flight and, like the Americans, they proposed flying boats as the idea option. The Rumpler company produced a number of designs for multi-hulled vessels culminating in this project of October 1927. Designed to fly from Hamburg to New York in a mere 37 hours, the scheme showed a machine with a dozen engines and six hulls and the passengers apparently seated in a cabin running along the leading edge of the wing. Rumpler took out many patents for similar aircraft: perhaps it is fortunate that they were never built: an average sea swell would have imposed enormous bending loads on such a structure.

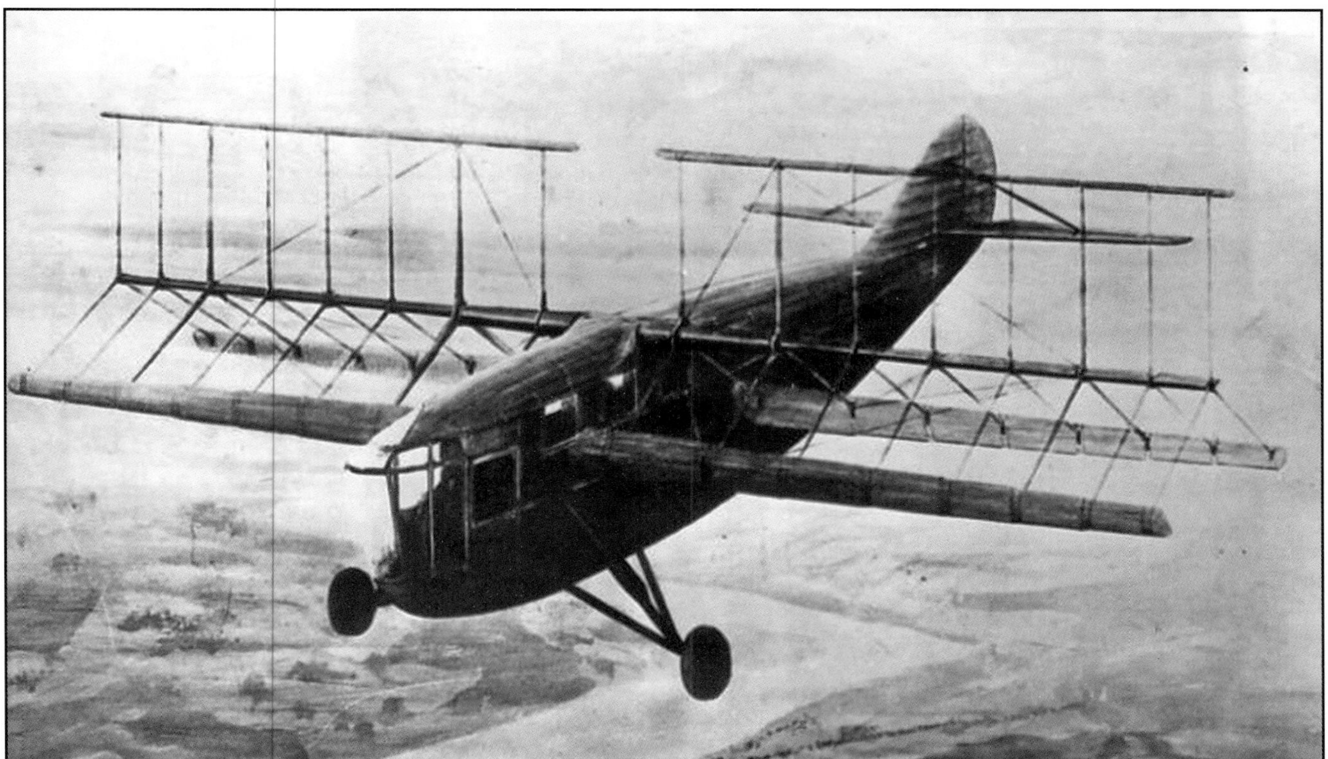

One of the most brilliant of German inventors in the 1930s was Dr Adolf Rohrbach (1889-1939). In January 1933 he announced to an incredulous world his scheme for a new type of aircraft, dubbed the paddle-wheel plane by the popular press. However wild it looked, the theory was satisfactory and even Autogiro inventor Juan de la Cierva had not discounted this approach to rotary lift. Each 'wing' comprised three blades which were revolved about an axis by a motor in the fuselage. In this artist's impression approved by the designer, there is no apparent provision for the necessary adjustment of the pitch of the rotors as they revolve. However, Rohrbach calculated that the aircraft could rise and descend vertically and even fly backwards if necessary. The prototype aircraft, to be built in the designer's Berlin factory, would have a wingspan of 43 feet, a length of 46 feet and have two Argus engines each developing 120 hp. The 'paddles' would revolve at about 100 rpm. Thus built, this aerial side-wheeler was expected to attain a forward speed of 90 mph – and be capable of 20 mph in reverse. This story was taken up by the world press and almost to a man it invoked considerable criticism. Unfortunately for Rohrbach, this negative response killed off the project's finance and the device was never built. In Philadelphia, meanwhile, autogiro experimenter Havilland H Platt (later to work with Pitcairn and others) had experimented with his own paddle-planes: they hadn't worked. Adolf Rohrbach died of overwork at the tender age of 50 just two months before the start of the war that he had dreaded.

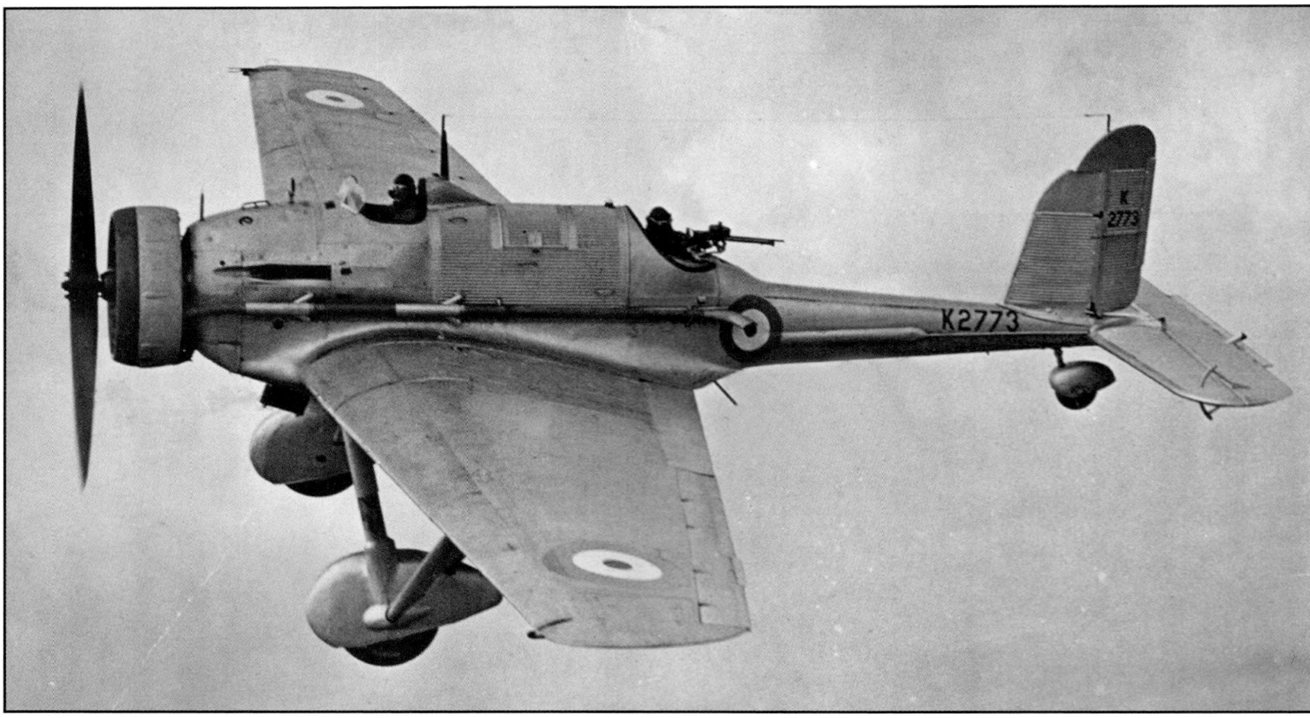

It takes an opportunist to turn a mistake into something else. In 1928 Handley Page was invited to tender for a high-speed Mailplane. Designer Gustav Victor Lachmann went for a single-engined design only too find out too late that the Air Ministry wanted a twin-engined machine. Not one to let a good idea go to waste, the design was quickly revamped to meet a later specification, G.4/31, for a single-engined general-purpose military aircraft. The outcome was the HP.47. Owing more than just a little to Junkers (the wide-chord, tapered wing and the use of corrugated skin) this peculiar-looking aircraft first flew at the end of 1932. It was powered by a 775 hp Bristol Pegasus III and had a 58-foot wingspan. Flight trials and modifications went on for four years but no orders were forthcoming. Marked K2773, it was relegated to slow-flight and engine-development work until scrapped in May of 1937. This picture shows the wide-chord leading-edge slots (which were independently controllable in two sections) in their tightly-closed position while the rear gunner, seated in his hip-bath, appears to take aim for a potentially terminal burst of fire into the fin and rudder.

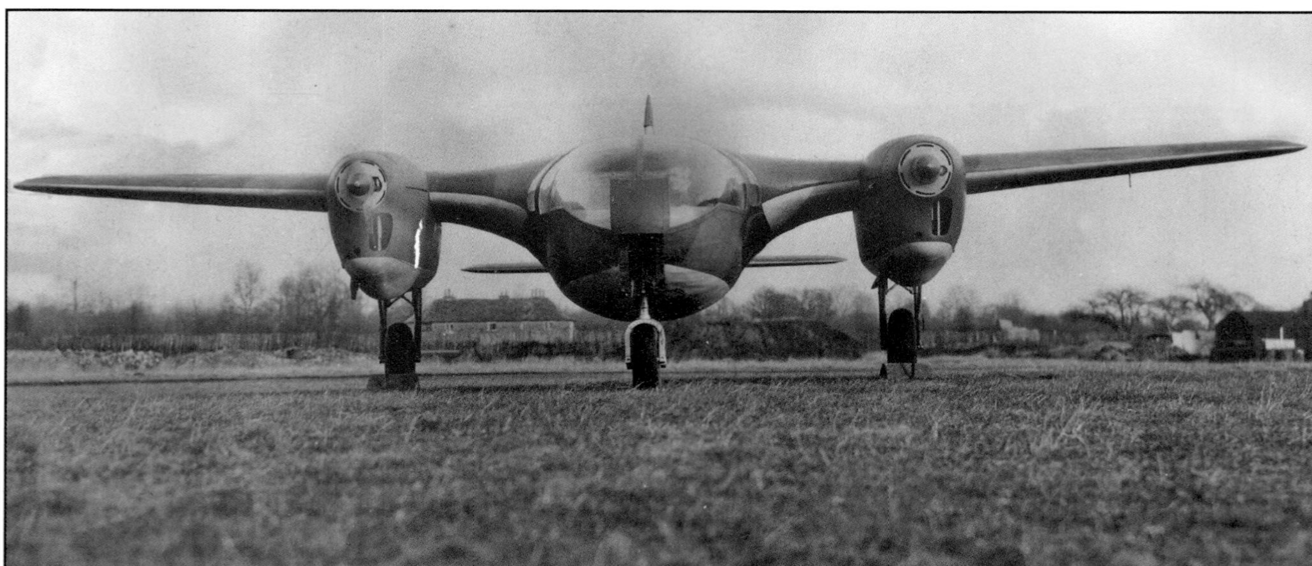

Among the strange shapes were some rather sexy ones and one of the sleekest came from the highly talented brain of Frederick George Miles (1903-1976) when, in 1936, he thought up how the large transport projects then being discussed in the press and industry might best be built. His answer was based on the flying wing but, unlike people such as Burnelli and the Russian Voevodskii as well as other 'big wing' theorists, his answer was a blended fuselage and wing. Known as the X project, it would have a broad but shallow fuselage of airfoil section which merged seamlessly into the wing aided by extremely large wing-root fillets. To test his theory, Miles would build a flying scale model to carry a crew of two. Powered by a pair of 130 hp Gipsy Major engines, the first flight was made in February 1942 by Tommy Rose.

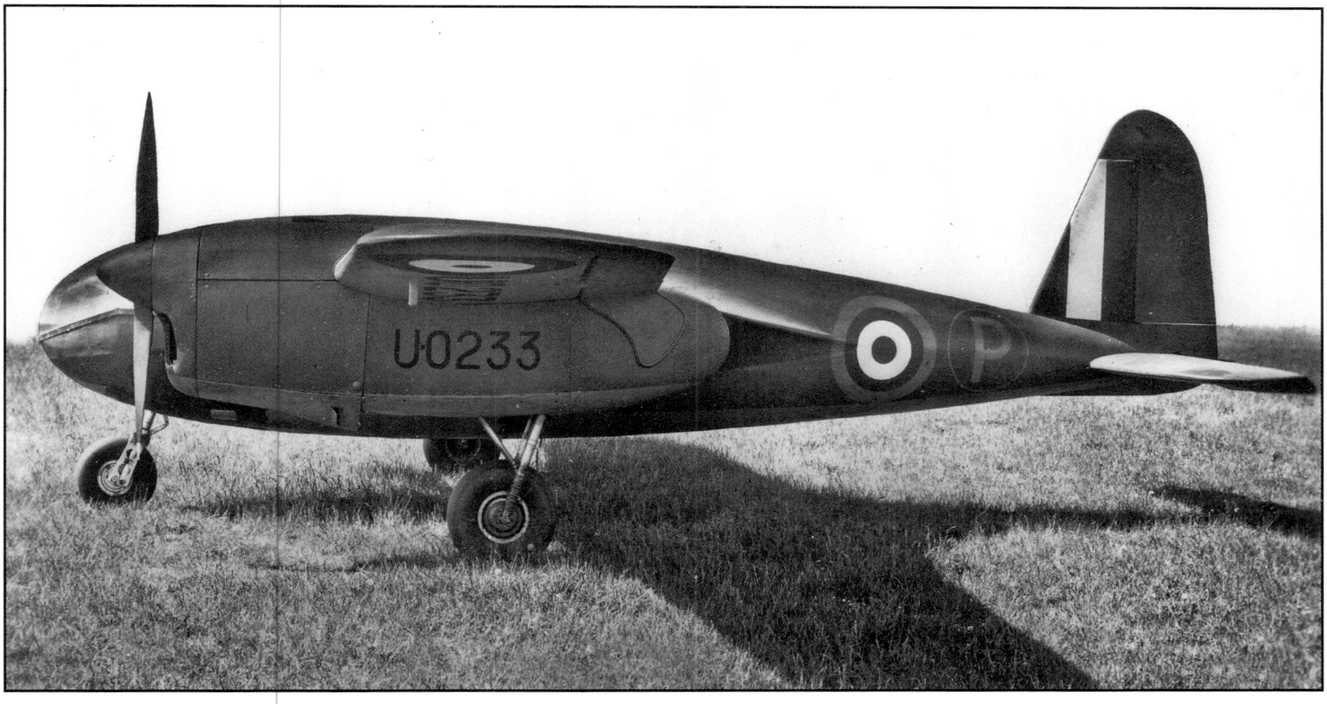

Carrying the marks U0233, the Miles M.30 X Minor had a wingspan of 33 feet (later increased to 38 feet 6 inches) and a length of 26 feet 3 inches, Wing area was 200 square feet and the aspect ratio remarkable low at 5.4. The empty weight was 2,710 lbs, fully loaded being 4,240 lbs. After many trials the scheme was shelved mainly because Miles was not in the same league as the established airliner-makers such as de Havilland and Handley-Page.

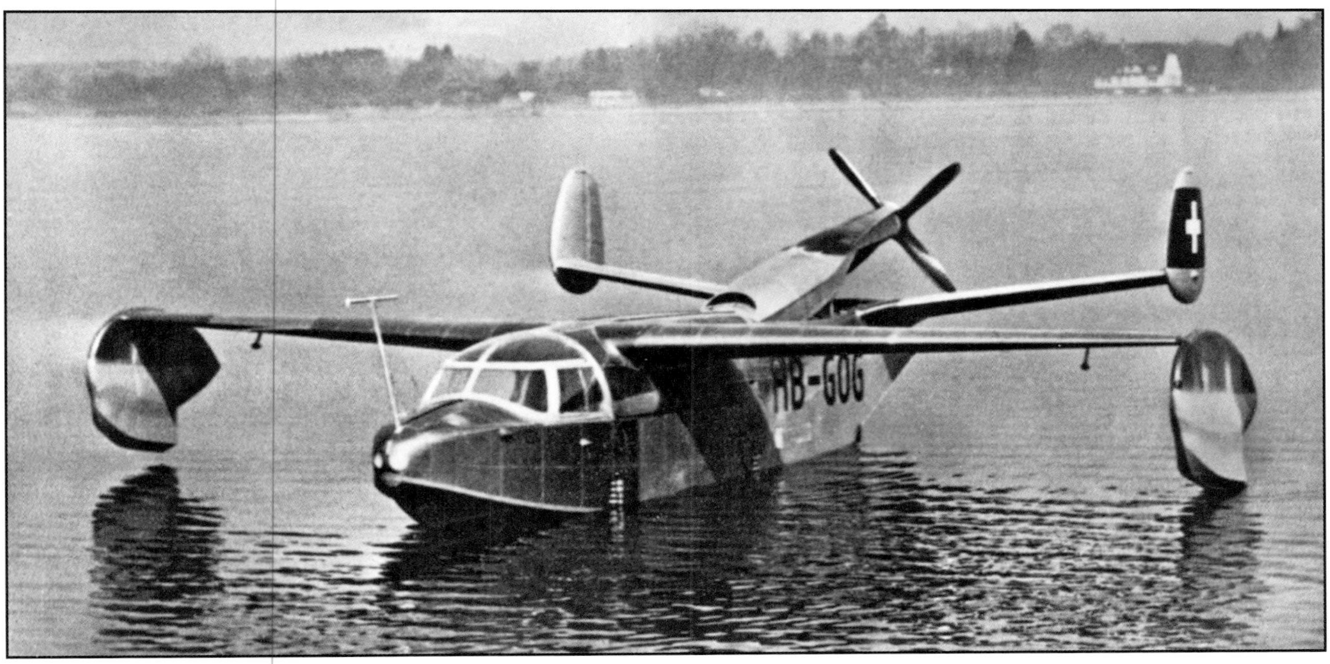

The Dornier Do.212 was an interesting aircraft that so nearly could have been a success. This four-seat all-metal amphibian with four-bladed pusher propeller was designed and built at Altenrhein, the Swiss works of the German company situated by the Bodensee (Lake Constance). Design work began in 1938 but the aircraft was not completed until 1942. Power came from a 460 hp Hirth 12-cylinder air-cooled engine installed behind the cabin. Its most novel feature was that in order to protect the airscrew from accidental contact with the water during landing and take-off, it was mounted on a 2.9 metre long shaft which could be raised through 12 degrees as seen in this picture. Entered on the Swiss civil register as HB-GOG, the Do.212 began sea trials in the hands of Dornier's chief pilot Egon Fath on August 3rd 1942. The aircraft would not unstick. A short hop was eventually achieved but the lack of control forced Fath to put it down immediately. Larger wing-tip floats were fitted (pictured here) but there was no improvement. It is not known if land trials were attempted but this unique prototype was scrapped the following year. It is difficult to pinpoint the cause of failure here, but the raised thrust-line would have countered any attempt to raise the hull onto its step and even with a wide-span tailplane, lack of slipstream effect could have restricted controllability at low speeds.

As the 1939-45 war progressed and the Brabazon Commission called for submissions for post-war civil airliners, Handley Page schemed out this as a four-engined passenger jet which would have the range to fly non-stop from England to Australia with 120 passengers. Futuristic in the extreme given the then-available engines and materials – the war was still on – it nevertheless showed that the Cricklewood-based design office was not afraid of a challenge. The first generation of passenger jets to emanate from America (Boeing 707, Convair 880 and Douglas DC-8) bore more than a passing resemblance to this pioneering project which was destined to be stillborn.

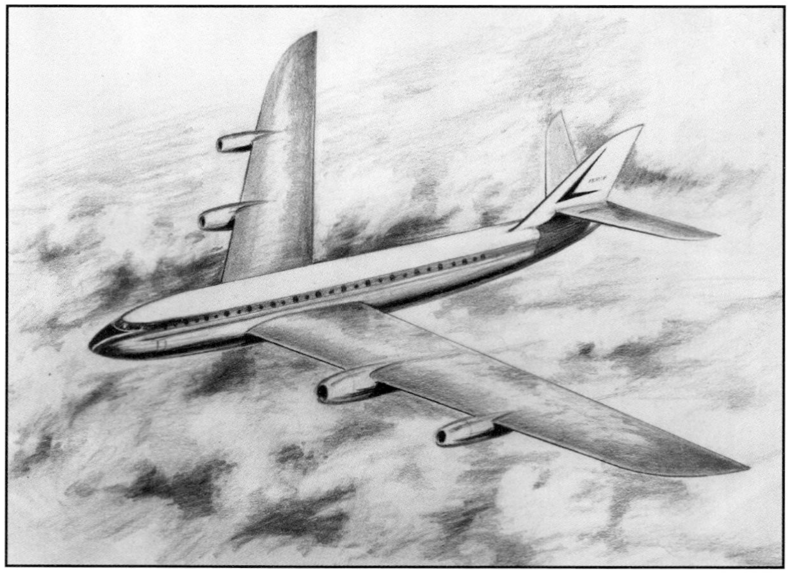

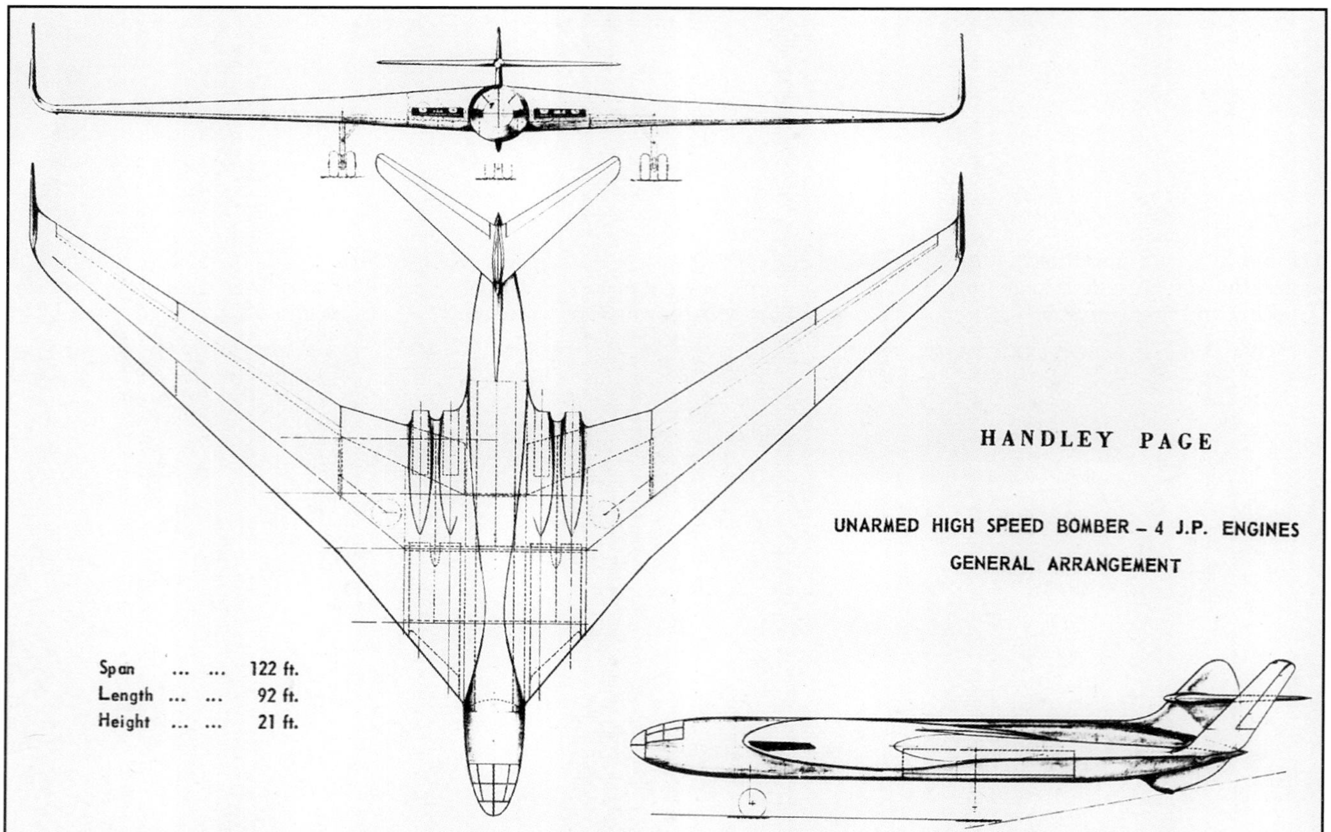

It is strange how some things, proclaimed as new developments today, turn out to be quite old. Take turned-up wing-tips. No self-respecting jet aircraft of today flies without pointing its wing-tips in upwards-cranked 'thumbs-up' salute. Yet if we were asked who had been the first, I am sure many would have said Boeing – or Airbus – in the late 1990s. Wrong, I fear, for it was a British idea, the result of research by Godfrey Henry Lee, a young aerodynamicist working under Handley Page's scientific research director, Gustav Victor Lachmann, and specialising on tailless aircraft. Later to become deputy chief designer for the company, Lee put forward a design for what he called an 'unarmed high-speed bomber' on February 25th 1946. Here 'unarmed' really meant defenceless, for its purpose was to transport a 10,000 lb bomb-load over 5,000 miles. Lee's aircraft possessed a tiny tail which was, in effect, a trim-tab to adjust for slow-speed flight in a flaps-down condition. Key to the aircraft's success was the virtual elimination of wing-tip vortices and Lee estimated that he could gain eight percent on speed and five percent on range by upturning the tips to which he also fitted rudders. Here is the original 1946 design. With a span of 122 feet and length of 92 feet, the key aspects of the HP.80 as it was designated were evaluated on the HP.88 (except the upturned tips) and this led to the HP.104 Victor V-bomber. Lee's tips, though, were omitted and it would be almost half a century before they would be reinvented as the very latest in tip vortex control.

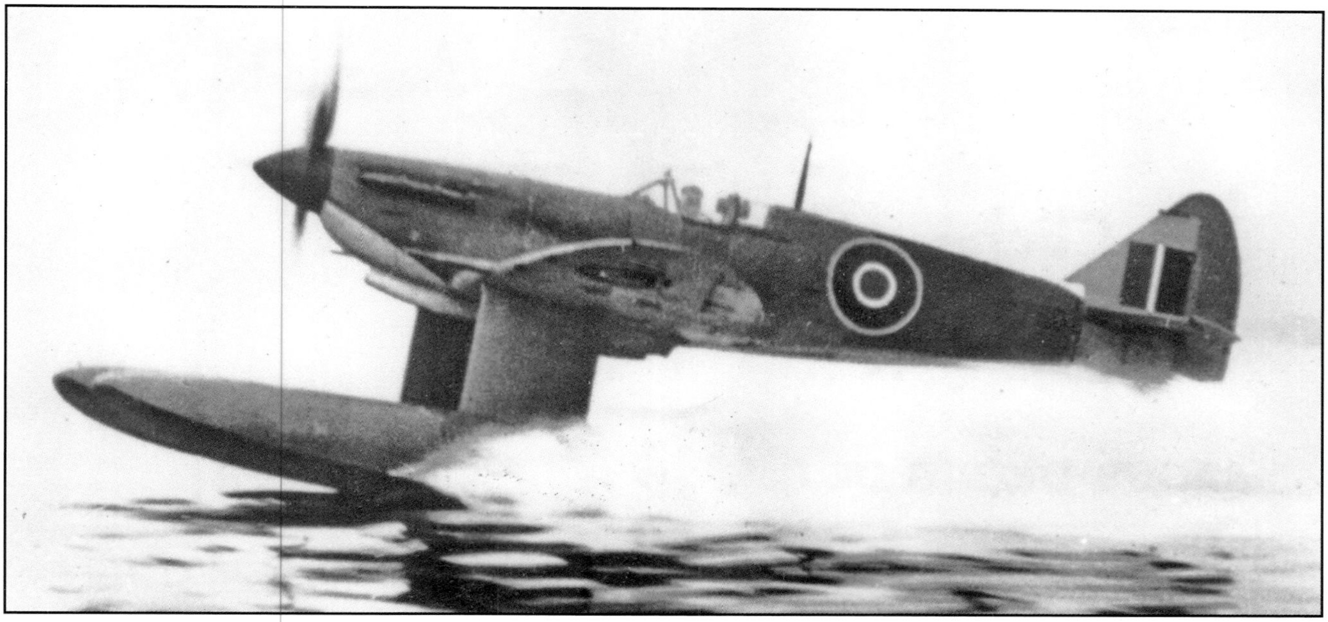

The existence of the Spitfire owes a great deal to the high-speed seaplanes Supermarine developed for the Schneider Trophy competitions. The S Series pushed the boundaries of both engine technology and airframe engineering and, in 1936, R J Mitchell's prototype Spitfire made its first flight. Some years later, the Spitfire would return to its S Series roots and acquire floats of its own, initially with those already in use by Blackburn's Roc fighter. Four of Blackburn's rather slow Rocs were equipped with floats already used on the even earlier Shark. When in 1940 the Norwegians needed a fighter floatplane for fjord operation, a Mk.I Spitfire R6722 was modified with the floats but trials were not all that successful and ceased with the end of Norway's war plans. In 1942 the idea was revived for operation from Middle Eastern waters and Spitfire VB W3760, pictured here, was modified with Supermarine-designed floats mounted on single cantilever struts. A revised rudder and ventral fin were installed. In all nine floatplane conversions were made, six for the Middle East and three used at Alexandria. Handling and manoeuvrability were, of course, seriously compromised by the added side area and drag.

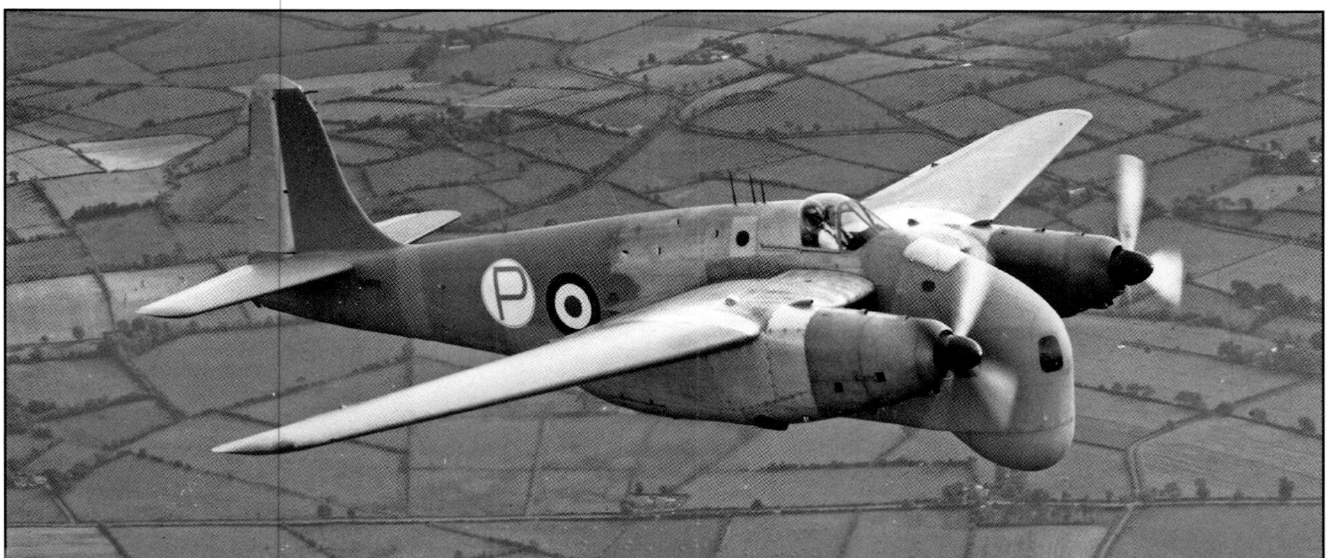

The Sturgeon was never one of Short Brothers' most attractive aircraft. Designed by Claude Percival Thomas Lipscomb after Arthur Gouge had left the company to join Saunders-Roe, the aircraft was intended as a high performance naval torpedo-bomber and reconnaissance monoplane expressly for use on aircraft carriers. Although to meet a 1943 Specification, the folding-wing'd twin's first flight did not take place until 1948. It was a good flyer and popular with its pilots despite some models requiring coal-miner's crawl-ways between flight stations and a strange folding nose on the Mk.II (to allow the aircraft to fit on aircraft carrier lifts). But then things became interesting! Revised specifications included one for anti-submarine search and patrol. The familiar and homely Sturgeon had a makeover. More powerful Armstrong Siddeley Mamba turbine engines each of 1,475 hp and driving four-bladed airscrews were fitted and provision made for carrying a 2,620 lb weapon load comprising bombs, mines, depth charges and sonobouys. But it was the large search radar scanner in a nose radome that converted the poor Sturgeon Mk.III from mere ugly to the grotesque. WF632 was shown at the SBAC exhibition at Farnborough in 1950. Early the following year it was scrapped.

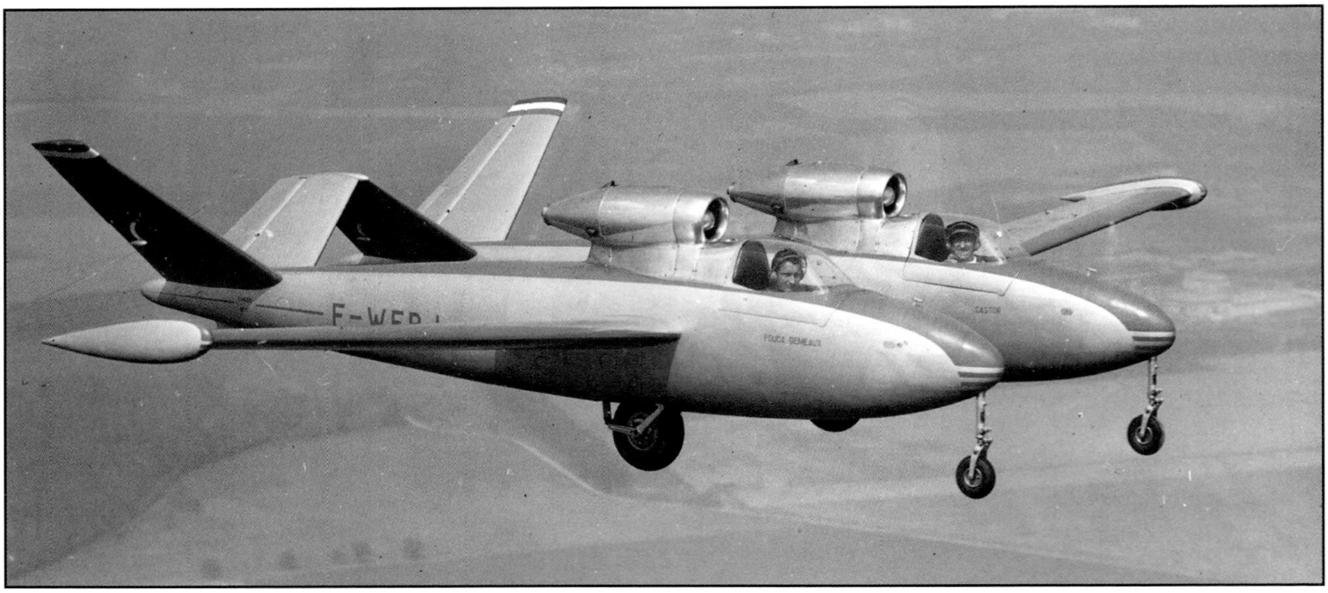

In the immediate post-war years there was a spate of twin aircraft. Probably inspired by the US P-51 Lightning and its twin tail booms, joining two aircraft together for the fun of it gave rise to such aeronautical anomalies as the Twin Mustang and, at the other end of the scale, the Twin Piper Cub. In France, Établissements Fouga at Aire-sur-Adour joined the club with the 88-R Gemeaux (Gemini). It all began with an advanced glider called the Sylphe. Fitted with a Turboméca Palas turbojet, this became the Mk.III Sylphe single-seat aerobatic trainer. Chosen by the French Air Force's Patrouille d'Etampes, the little butterfly-tailed jet was a great success. Then somebody suggested joining two together and the Gemeaux was born. There were five varieties, each used to test various Turboméca jet engines such as the Marboré I and II, and the Aspin I and II. The first example, F-WEPJ, retained two engines – the little 220 lbs static thrust Piméné. Test pilot Léon Bourriau made the premier flight on March 6th 1951. The left-hand fuselage nose carries the name Castor. With one pilot in each cockpit the scope for potential disagreement regarding destination must have been quite high.

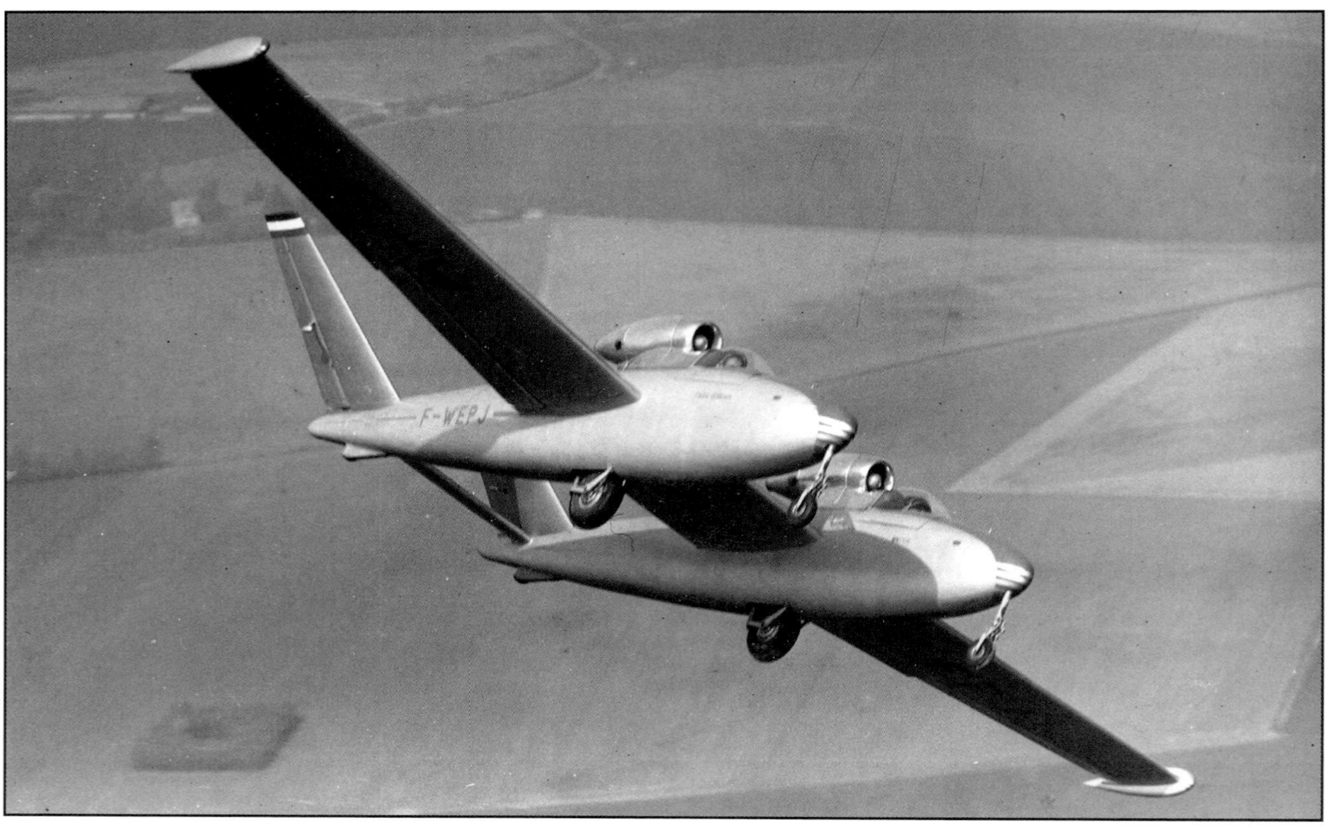

Clearly with both pilots in full agreement as to which way to go, the Fouga Gemeaux banks away from the camera revealing not just the wing centre-piece, but the heavy horizontal strut used to join the two rear fuselages together beneath the tailplane. The intakes for the Piméné engines are clearly seen above the cockpit canopies.

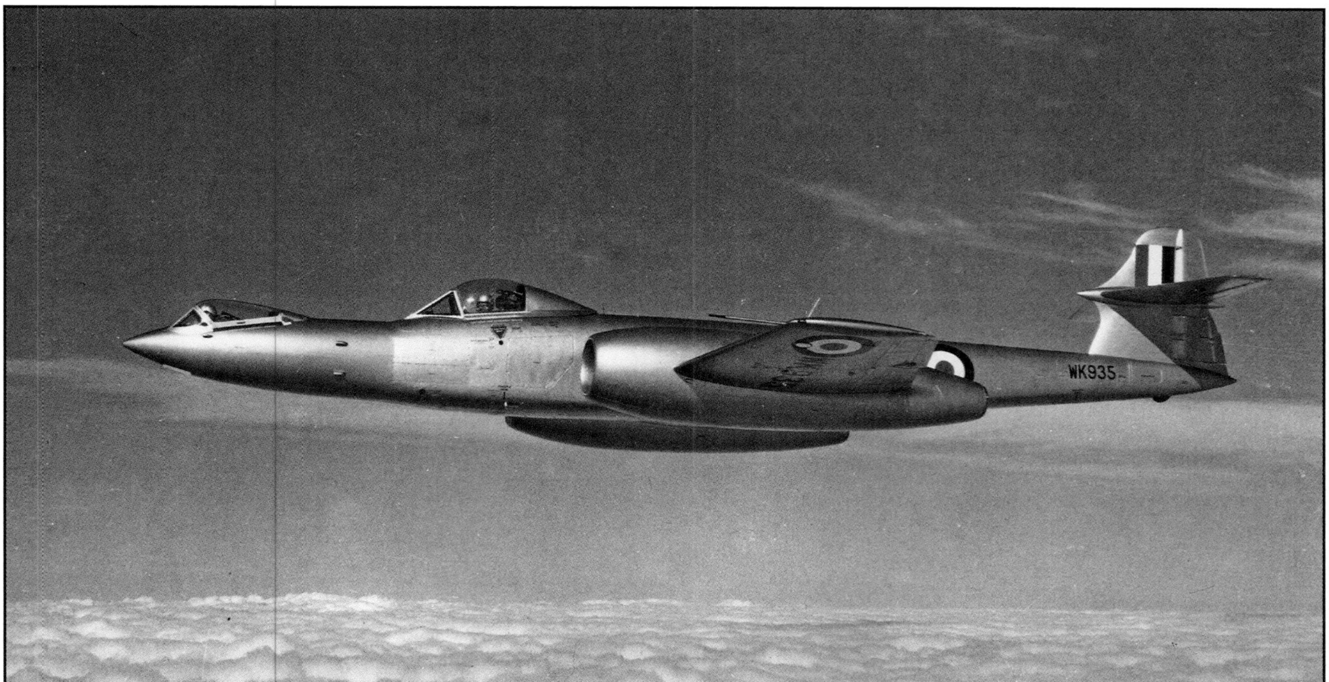

During the 1950s there was some considerable thought given to employing jet fighter pilots in the prone position since it was believed that greater 'g' forces could be experienced without blacking out. Armstrong Whitworth converted Meteor F.8 WK935 into an extended-nose model with a prone-pilot cockpit. The extra 7 feet 9 inches to the aircraft produced the longest model of this excellent twin-engined jet at 52 feet 5 inches. To compensate for the longer nose, the tail was modified from a NF12 and the prone pilot lay in a custom-built couch with a suspended rudder bar, hand control column and greatly-modified other controls and instruments. The first flight was undertaken on February 10th, 1954, by chief test pilot Eric George Franklin and subsequently prone flying was conducted by Bill Else. At all times, though, a 'normal' pilot was carried. After some 55 hours of extensive test-flying, the trials were abandoned on July 31st, 1955. It was found that there were insufficient advantages to prone-pilot flight. Among the disadvantages was the complexity of emergency exit. A further factor in scrapping the project was the arrival of the first pressurised 'g' flying-suits. WK935 went to the RAF Museum at Cosford where it is preserved.

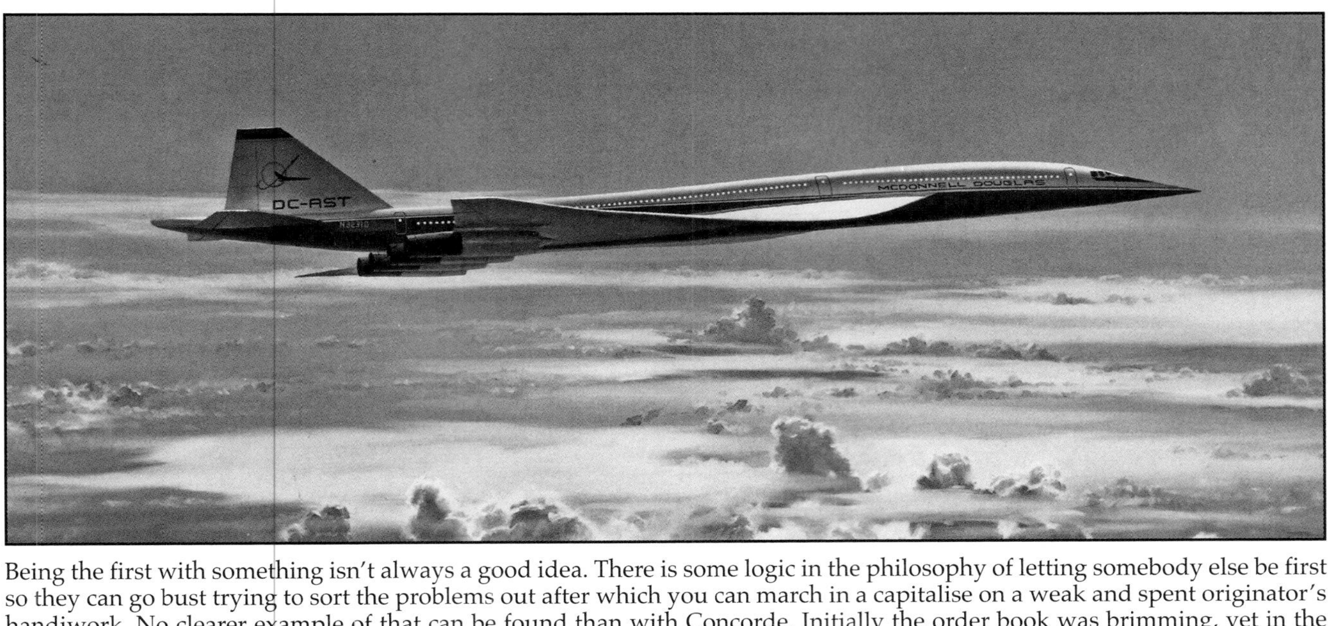

Being the first with something isn't always a good idea. There is some logic in the philosophy of letting somebody else be first so they can go bust trying to sort the problems out after which you can march in a capitalise on a weak and spent originator's handiwork. No clearer example of that can be found than with Concorde. Initially the order book was brimming, yet in the end Concorde failed to find a single user outside British Airways and Air France. Why? Because of objectors and rabble-rousers who campaigned and successfully got it barred from all but a small handful of airports. However this did not deter the then American giants from announcing that whatever we did in 'Yerp' they could do better! 'Yurpean' enterprise was worth following, at least that's what McDonnell Douglas Aircraft believed when it launched its AST (Advanced Supersonic Transport) 'which could be built for service in the 1990s. Announced in the summer of 1979 (some three months after the last Concorde had limped off the production line), the strangely familiar shape was for an aircraft to seat 275 passengers, fly non-stop for 5,000 miles and attain a speed of Mach 2.2.

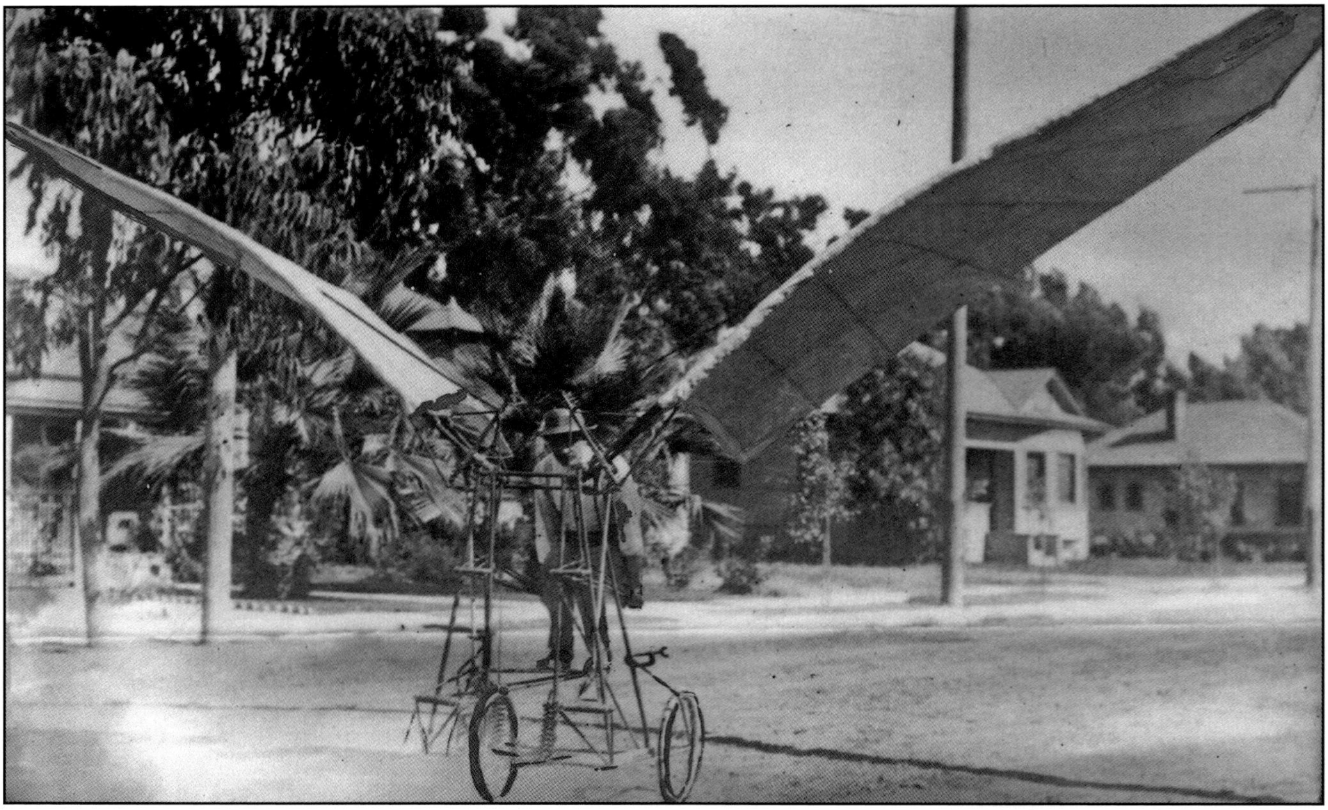

In the summer of 1909, Professor Harry La Verne Twining of the Polytechnic High School in Los Angeles unveiled to the world his Ornithopter which had wings that spanned 27 feet and were 'carefully modelled after those of an eagle'. They were attached to a frame of bicycle tubing and flapped up and down through a tip distance of 15 feet. Operation was by alternately pushing down on levers with the feet while pulling up on hand levers, and then reversing the process although he never quite explained how you pulled levers up with your feet. He calculated that it was possible to exert a combined force of 50 lbs on each stroke. The problem seemed to be that his machine, with him on board, weighed 240 lbs. After some futile trials he went away to re-adjust the leverage so that he could apply more force. Twining was an example of a brilliant man who was challenged in a field he didn't fully comprehend, for he was also the author of a ground-breaking and pioneering American handbook on wireless which has been reprinted many times – and is still in print!

Opposite: Enea Bossi (1888-1963) was the first to make a human-powered aeroplane that actually worked. Born in Milan, after education at the Instituto Technico at Lodi where he read mathematics and physics, he emigrated to the United States of America in the summer of 1918 and became a US citizen. In 1928 he founded a company to manufacture Savoia-Marchetti seaplanes under licence but the Depresion following the Wall Street Crash hampered sales. In 1932 he learned of an aircraft that had successfully flown with a one-horsepower engine and this prompted him to calculate how much power would be needed to fly a man-powered aircraft. The answer (0.94 hp) suggested that man-powered flight might just be attainable. After many experiments, including some conducted in Paris using a propeller-driven bicycle, he concluded that the gyroscopic effect of a propeller created instablity at speed. The answer was a pair of contra-rotating airscrews. Impetus to his work was gained when, during 1933, the Frankfurt Polytechnische Gesellschaft offered a cash prize to promote man-powered flight. At this time, whatever Germany did, Italy duplicated in a rather childish game of one-upmanship. The Italian Government now offered a prize of 100,000 lira for a human-powered flight of 0.61 mile made by an Italian citizen. Bossi was aware that he could not receive the prize due to his American citizenship, but he nevertheless opted to attempt to win it. Bossi's design for the contest utilized conventional glider configuration and construction hence its name Pedaliante (Pedal Glider). Built in 1936-7 by sailplane manufacturer Vittorio Bonomi, a top cyclist called Emilio Casco was brought in to fly the 17.7-m span machine. After trials in early 1936, Casco took off in the 213-lb Pedaliante and flew approximately 300 feet under his own power, the first time an aircraft had been flown under control in sustained flight entirely by the muscle-power of one man. While later calculations verified that his flight was physically possible, most agree that it was Casco's considerable physical strength and endurance which secured the accomplishment. Later flights employed a catapult launch and September 13th, 1936, the Pedaliante made a flight of several hundred metres at a height of about 30 feet. On March 18th, 1937, at Milan's Cinisello Airport the plane was launched at a height of 29.5 feet and Casco successfully pedalled the craft for its full 0.61 miles or one kilometre.. This set a world record for human-powered flight, but as the rules prohibited a catapult launch, the Pedaliante did not win. It was retired the following year having made a total 80 flights of which 43 were without a catapult launch.

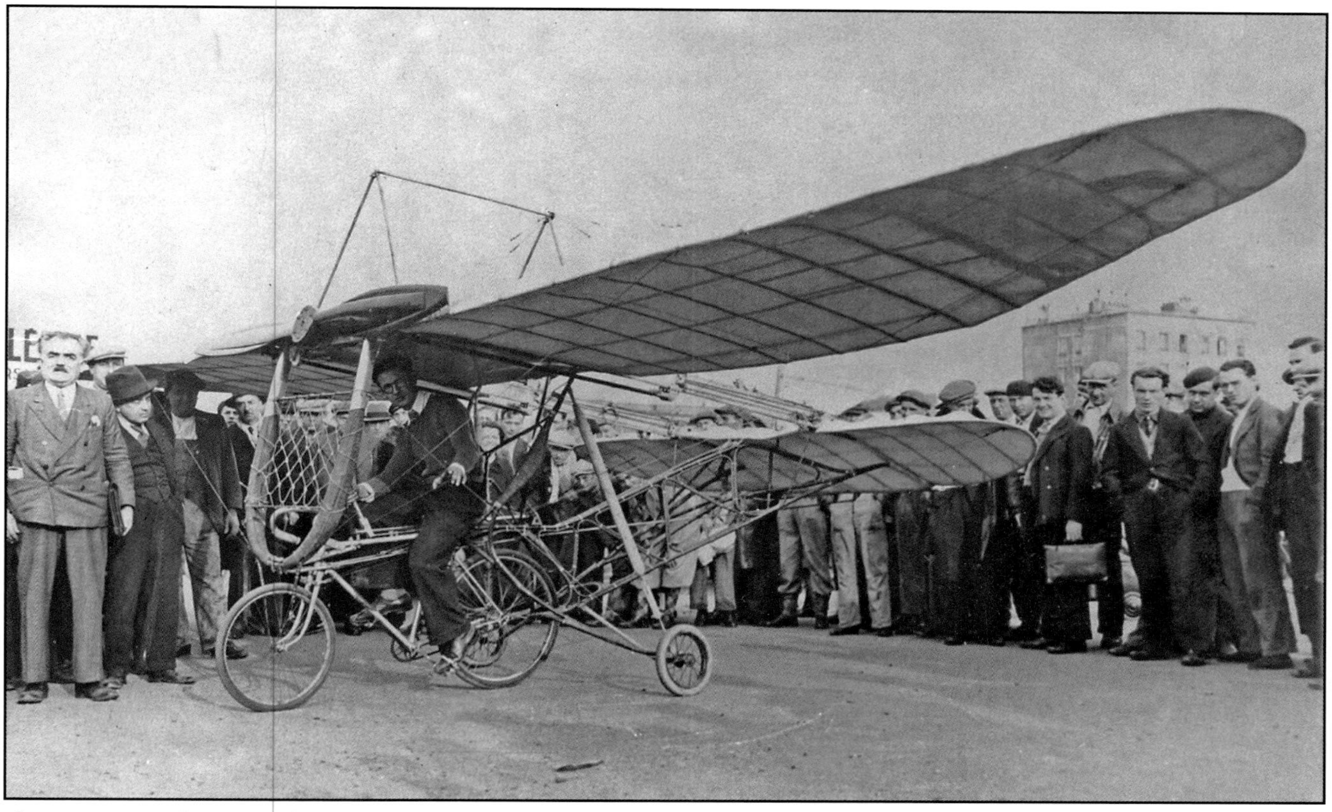

The inventor of the bicycle has a lot to answer for! In the past, presenting an inventor with the availability of a bike suddenly stirred in him the urge to convert it into a flying machine. So it was with François Baudot, the former chief engineer of the Blériot aircraft factory outside Paris who, in 1936, contrived this flying safety-bicycle. Here it is pictured at Issy-les-Moulineaux being prepared for first trials. Baudot calculated that once the cyclist attained a forward speed of 35 miles an hour, the machine would lift off, accelerating through the air under the influence of the coarse-pitch propeller. To prevent the unintentional decapitation of the pilot should the thing come to a sudden stop, a net supported by a stout hoop would restrain him. Built out of cycle-tubing frames joined in place by tape rather than welding, the fuselage extension supported a curious tailplane, the outer extremities of which were pivoted for use as elevators. There is no reason to suspect that this would not have flown since the wing area suggests a loading of less than two pounds per square foot. The problem was that it could not attain flying speed under pedal-power and after a month of trials and tweaking, Baudot's Flying Bike disappeared from the scene. Note that some sources say this event occurred in 1915 which is wrong.

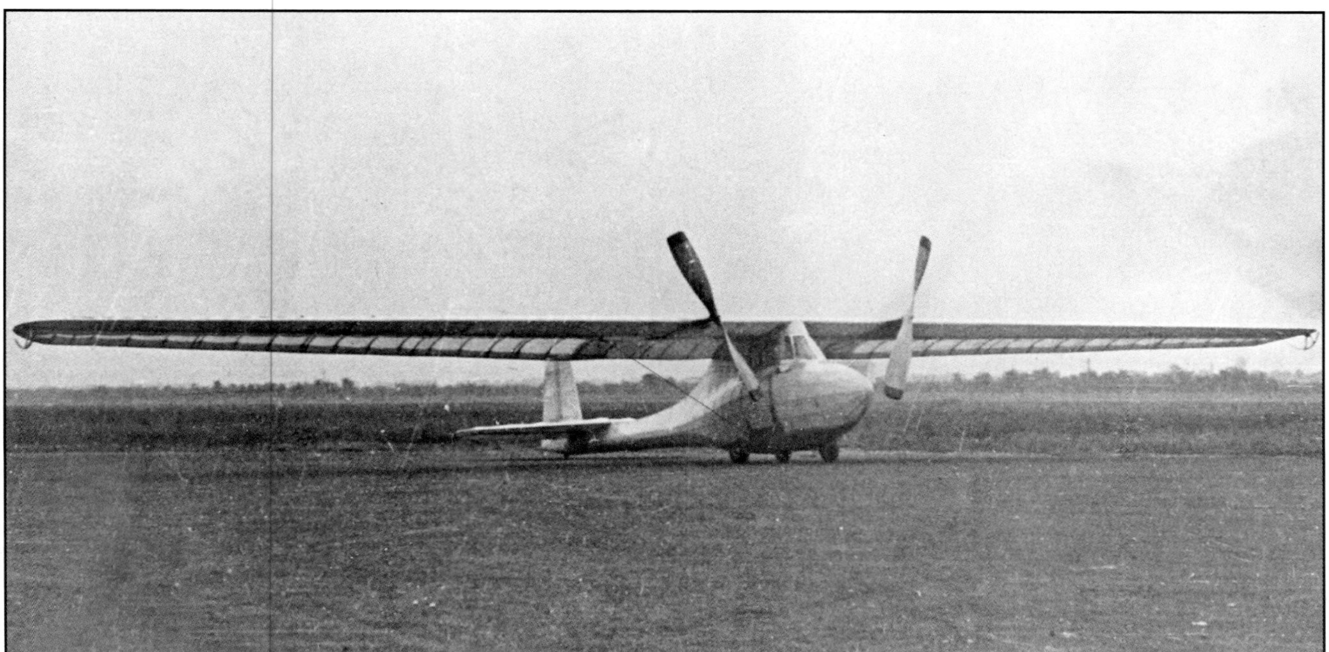

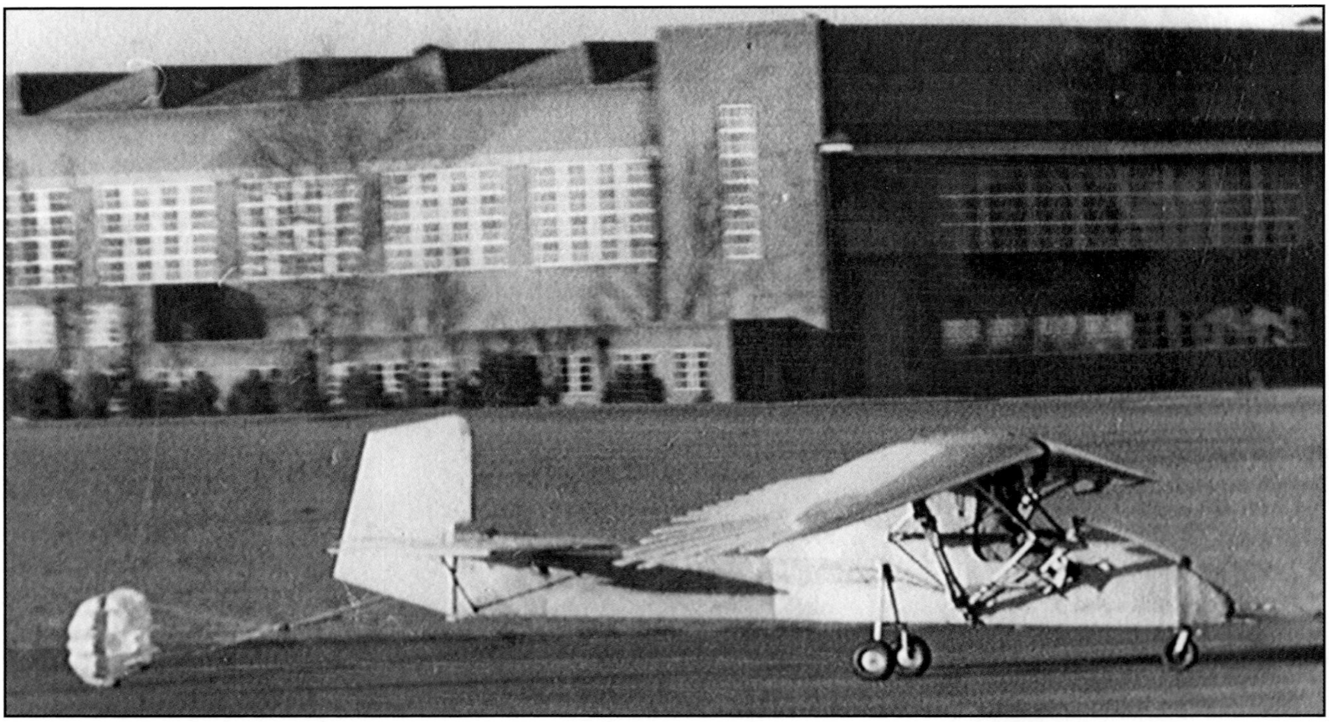

Man-powered flight has bubbled up at intervals since the beginning of aviation but the announcement of the Kremer Prize created a more intense interest in the 1950s. This culminated in the Royal Aeronautical Society forming a special Manpowered Aircraft Group in October 1959. It was in that month at a London sculptor named Emiel Hartman unveiled his Ornithopter. Unlike many of an earlier time, the days of pure dabbling were long past and his design, begun in February 1958, was properly stressed by an independent organisation before being entrusted to Don Campbell, the then-renowned 'glider-doctor' of Hungerford, for construction – a process which extended from March to September 1959 and required the expenditure of 4,600 man hours. Tested at the College of Aeronautics, Cranfield, by Flt-Lt Angus McDonald, a rowing action by the pilot flapped the 36-foot span wings using a scissors-type lever system while rubber cord was used to counterbalance the 'return' stroke which would bear not just flying loads but the weight of the wings. All told it was well thought out and the idea was to tow the glider into the air whereupon the pilot would take over and attempt to propel his 282 lb aircraft though the air. The machine did fly quite well as a glider when towed by a car but proved unflappable. Sponsored by the Daily Mail newspaper, it had several minor mishaps before being abandoned. In this photograph, a brake parachute is deployed probably more in despair than hope.

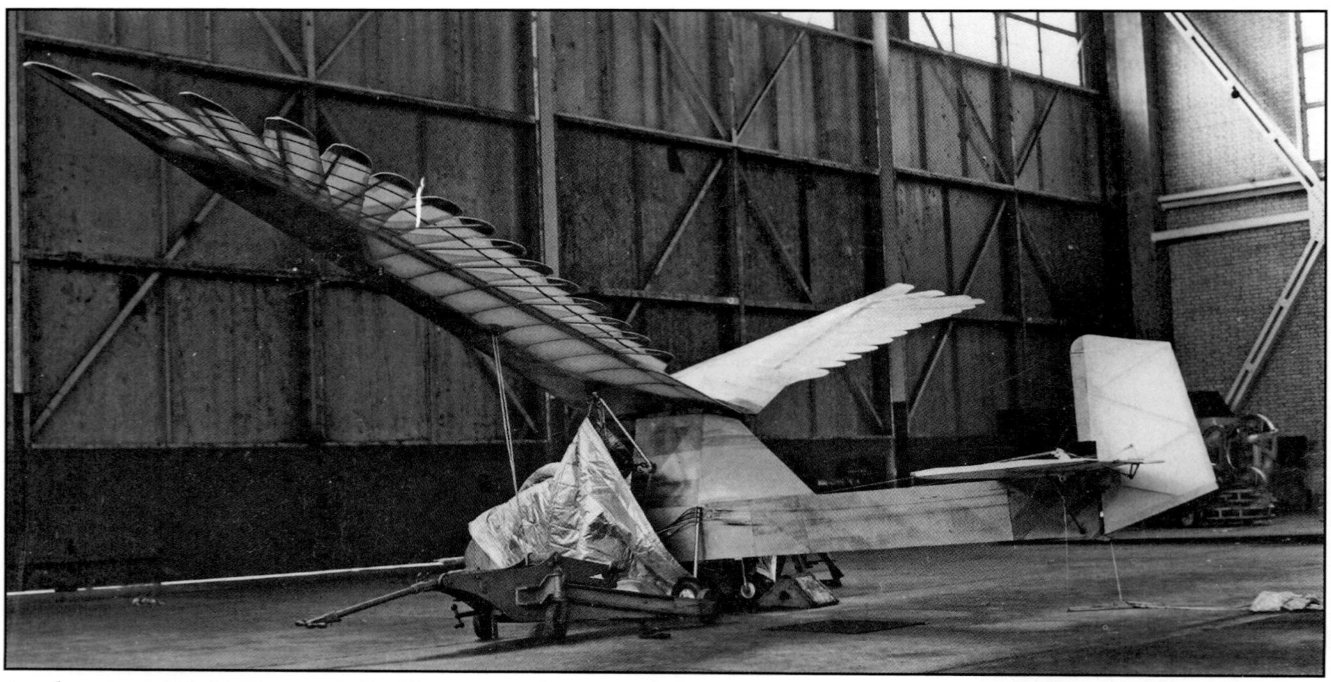

Another view of Emiel Hartman's Ornithopter in its hangar with the cockpit carefully covered to conceal the controls from prying eyes. What this picture does show is the superb construction of the aircraft with its controllable bird-like wing-tip 'feathers'.

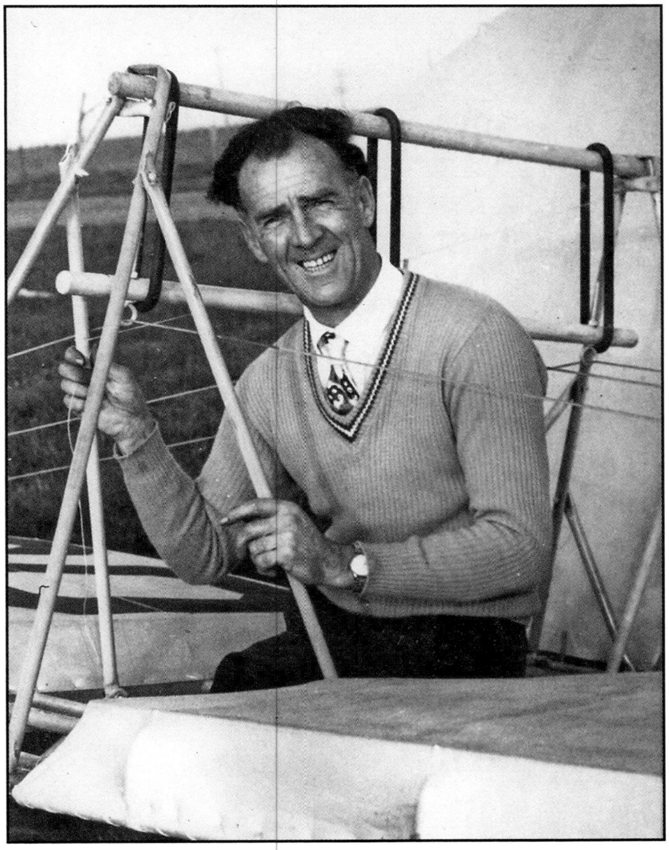

One admires a man for trying, even if he admits he doesn't know if it will work. Here's 46-year-old Ron Costello described as a groundsman employed by Australia's Civil Aviation Authority of West Sale, Victoria. He built his Ornithopter in 1963 only to receive a curiously-phrased letter of warning from his employers telling him that 'history records some occasions where experiments have been attended by disastrous consequences'. They should have reassured him that these 'disastrous consequences' only usually occurred once the aircraft had got into the air. In this regard, Mr Costello was not even at risk and his machine remained aeronautically-challenged. See inside back cover for another view of this odd machine.

The subject of man-powered flight has risen to the surface many times over the past hundreds of years. The flapping-wing approach has intrigued many an inventor and as recently as 1963 Alan Stewart of Greenhill, Sheffield, tackled the challenge of the Royal Aeronautical Society's £5,000 prize with an ornithopter that he proposed to pedal through the skies for the stipulated one mile distance. The 32-year old made several unsuccessful attempts between 1959 and 1979. Here he is pictured in the garden of his home on May 22nd 1963. He was destined to fail. Curiously, very recent scientific research by designers of robotic aircraft to be used for surveillance and defence have come out in favour of tiny flapping-winged aircraft so maybe the ornithopterologists were not so misguided after all.

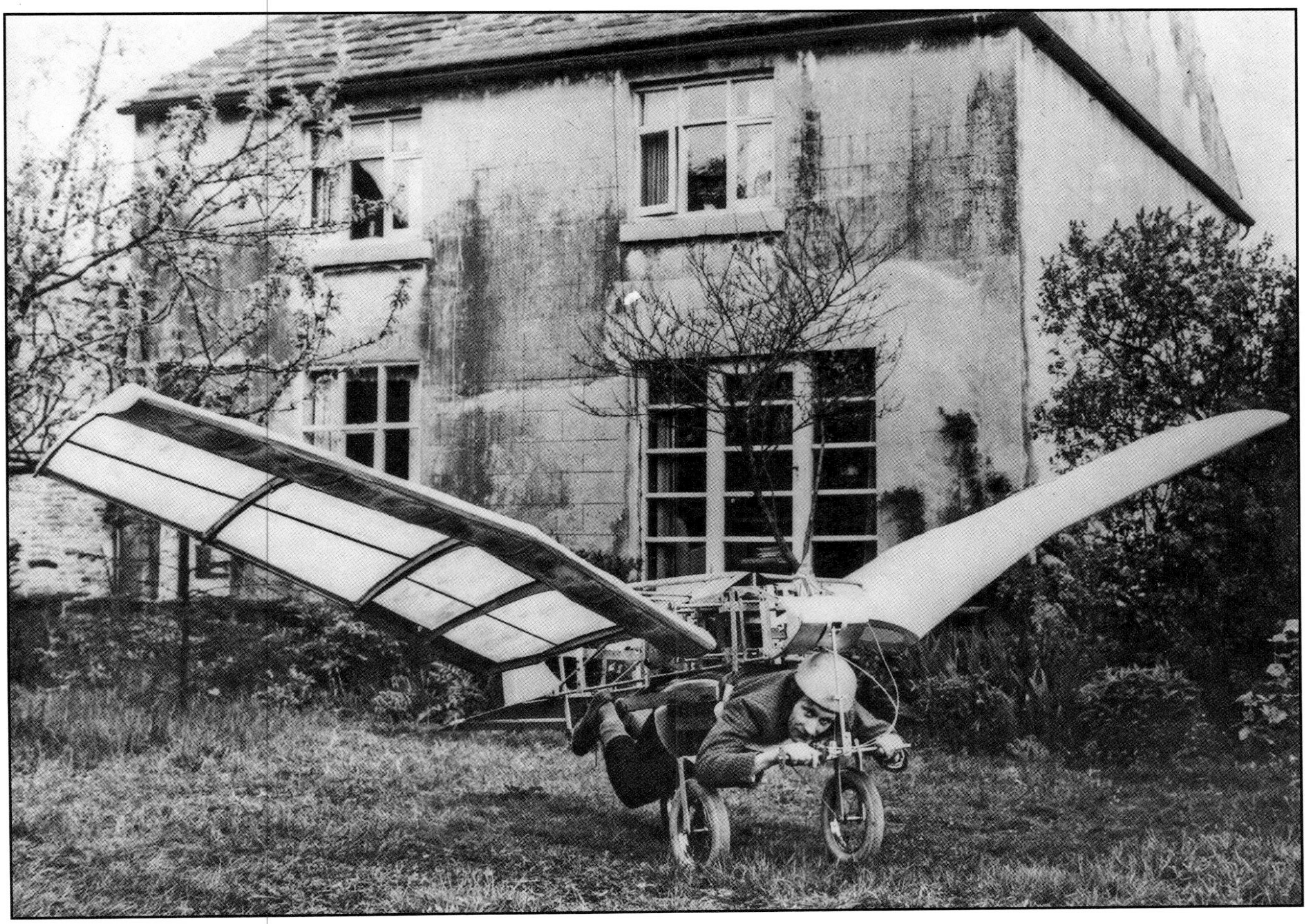

Graham Rouse, an engineer from Locks Heath, Titchfield, Hampshire, is pictured here in his pedal-powered helicopter at Southampton. Clearly pictured at a high security secret test site, cost the chap £100 to make and marked his attempt at the Kremer prize. This picture, taken on July 17th, 1966, shows the hopeful designer who revealed that he was training a young racing cyclist to be its first pilot. This was one of a depressingly large number of pedal-powered planes designed by would-be Kremer contestants. And, of course, its maiden voyage never came.

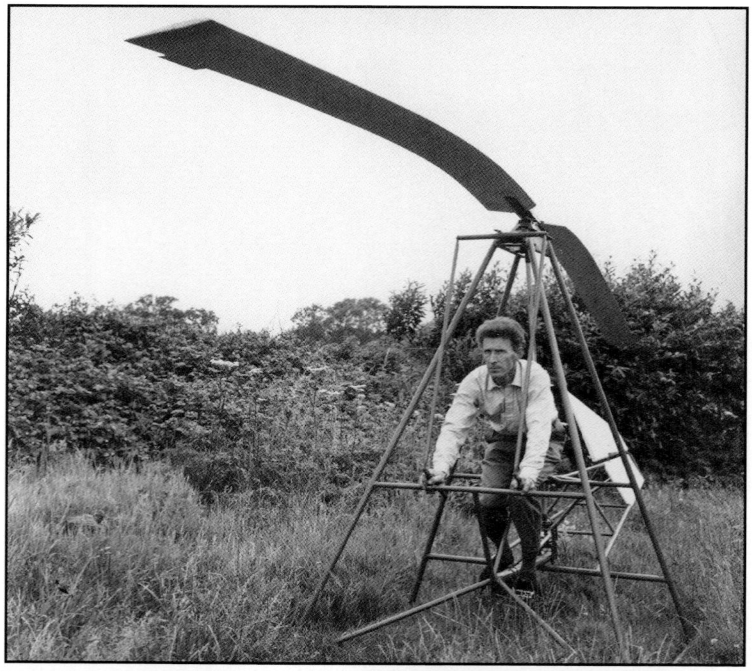

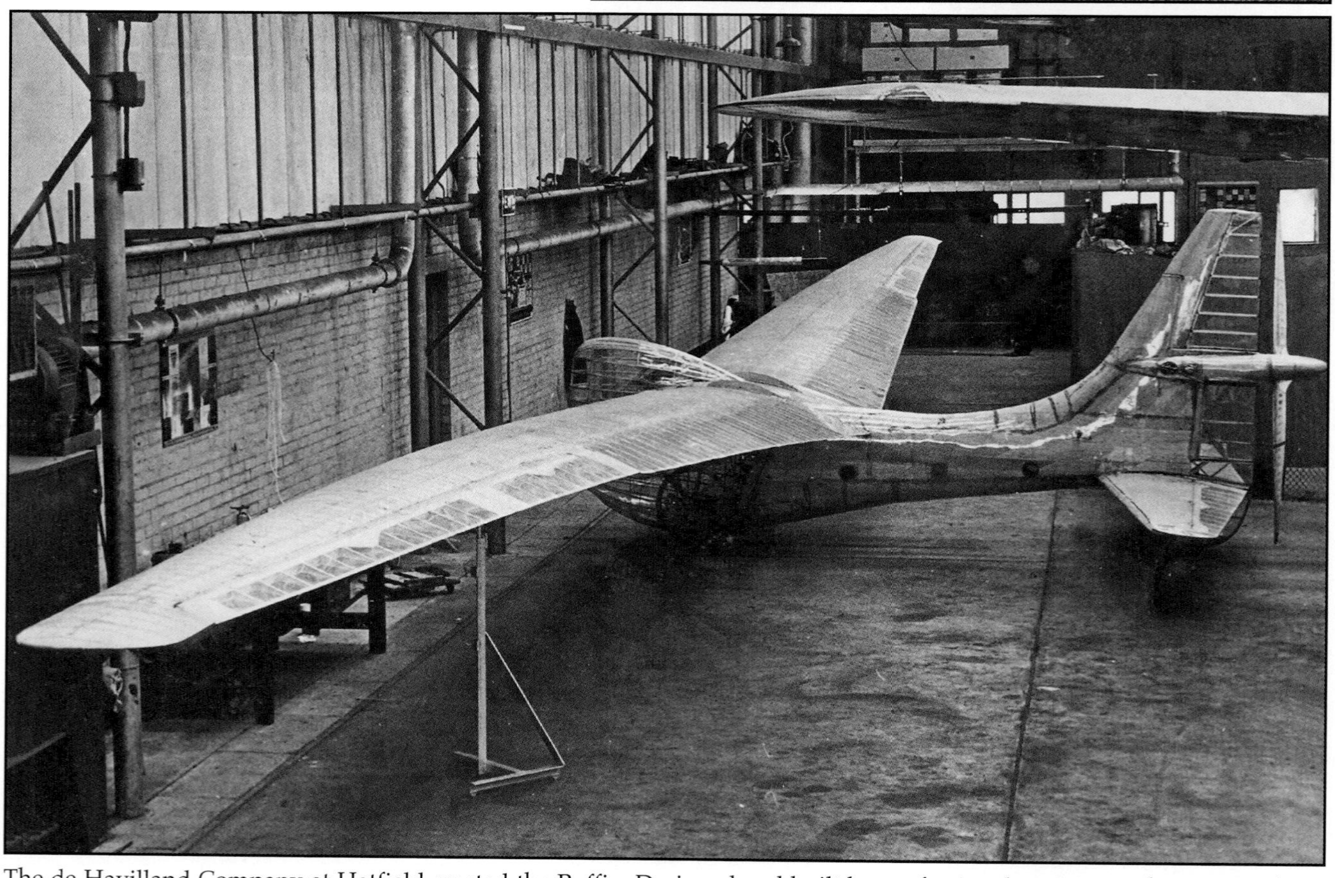

The de Havilland Company at Hatfield created the Puffin. Designed and built by professional engineers who were perhaps more accustomed to larger aircraft such as the Trident airliner, Puffin was a triumph of technology and the result of considerable brainpower. Leading the team was John Wimpenny and among the problems encountered was the key one of roll and yaw control. At slow speed, ailerons are poor controls but little else is available as an alternative. Consequently Puffin was given huge ailerons. The roll out of this microlight pusher on November 15th 1961 was followed by the first flight the following day, the pilot being J H 'Jimmy' Philips, a DH test pilot. Puffin undertook numerous flights – more than fifty in all – with distances approaching 1,000 metres, but there were several incidents culminating in a serious crash when the pilot, in poor visibility, could not assess his attitude and crashed hard, breaking both wings and the fuselage. Although repairable the decision was taken to build from scratch and so appeared Puffin II with a slightly revised airfoil section.

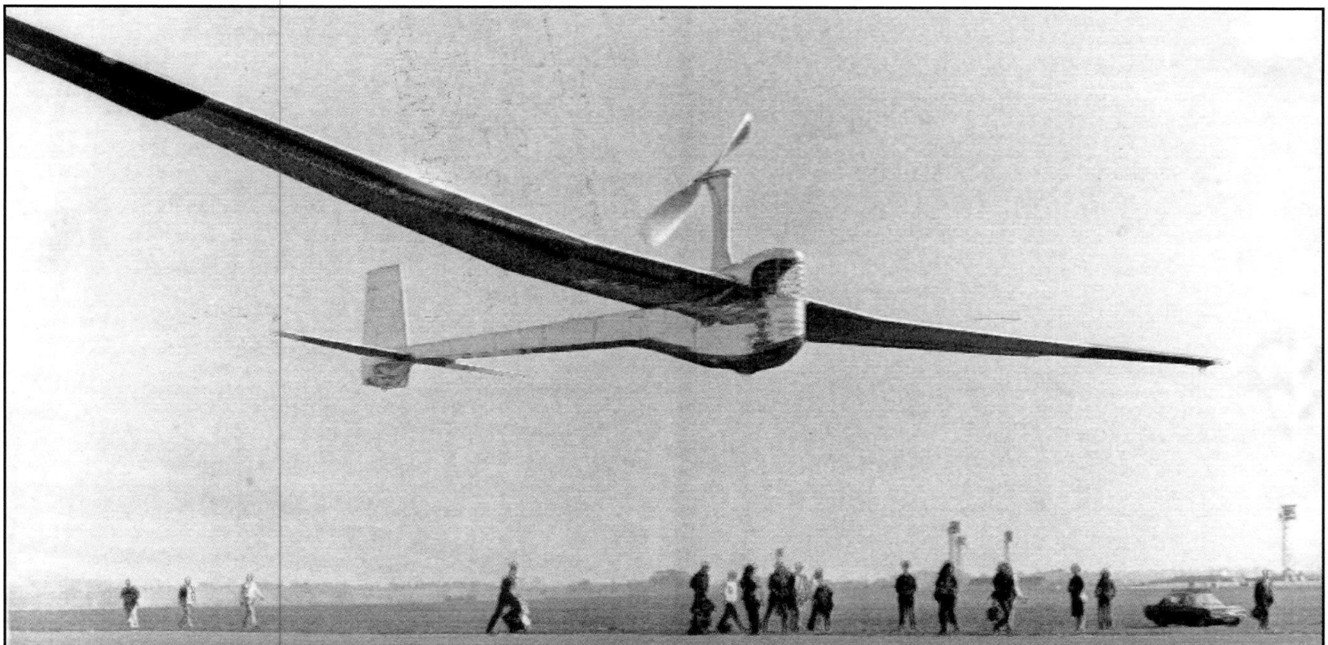

Staying with manpowered flight, the early success of its Jupiter craft made the sceptics sit up and think. Built at Halton RAF College in about 4,000 man-hours, Jupiter spanned 80 feet and had an all-up weight of 300 lbs. Using the principle of the bicycle, the ultra-light Jupiter proved an early triumph. It is pictured here in flight at Benson Airfield in the hands of 28-year-old Flt-Lt John Potter. Unfortunately this 500-yard flight ended in a damaging crash but the machine was quickly repaired. On June 29th 1972 it achieved a then-record flight of 1.07 km. When Latvian-born industrialist and benefactor Henry Kremer (1907-1992) announced his competition in February 1960, the prize offered was £5,000, later increased to £10,000. By the mid-1970s, and with the increasing professional interest in the contest, Mr Kremer accepted that entrants were now incurring far larger expenses than originally anticipated: very sportingly, he increased the first prize to £50,000. The first prize would not be won for eight more years.

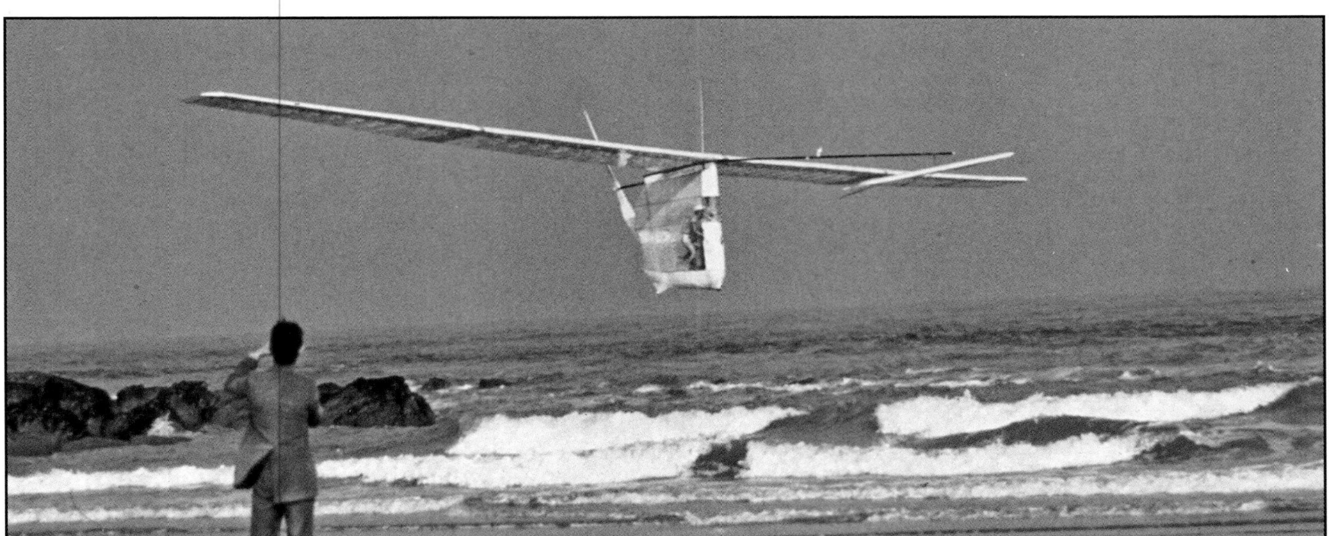

The pedal-powered Gossamer Albatross created a sensation when, on June 12th, 1979, it flew the English Channel to win the second Kremer prize. Designed by Paul B MacCready, an American aeronautical engineer, it was the successor to the earlier Gossamer Condor which won the first Kremer award on August 23rd, 1977, by negotiation of a one-mile-long figure-of-eight course. The 97 feet 8 inches span aircraft was made of high-tech materials, a carbon-fibre framework with extra rigidity provided by expanded polystyrene foam, the whole covered with extremely thin transparent Mylar film. This created a complete airframe 34 feet in length that weighed just 71 lbs, the all-up weight with pilot being 220 lb. A canard with the tail extended on a boom at the front, the elevator acting more as a Hook predictor. The extremely high aspect ratio of the 488 square feet wings allowed a minimum flying speed of 18 mph for an expenditure of under half of one horsepower. The athletic pilot Bryan Allen succeeded in maintaining an average of 0.4 hp for the two hours and forty-nine minute crossing of the water, average altitude being between no more than five feet and highest speed being 29 mph. The pedals drove a large two-blade pusher airscrew. The team went on to build an Albatross II and, in 1980, a solar-powered model called the Penguin. The aircraft survive in the Smithsonian Institution's museum (Albatross I) and Seattle's Museum of Flight (Albatross II).

In the early 1980s, the American government embarked on a top secret programme to develop a high-altitude, long-endurance surveillance aircraft to be powered by batteries. A group called AeroVironment, Inc, of Monrovia, California, built a prototype but the scheme was cancelled and the aircraft stored for a decade until the autumn of 1993 when it was revived under NASA'a Dryden Flight Research Center. Solar cells were added until they covered the whole upper wing surface and on September 11th, 1995, Pathfinder reached an altitude of 50,500 feet, setting a new record for a solar-powered aircraft driven by six electric motors. Taken to a testing-base in Hawaii in April 1997, Pathfinder undertook more high-altitude flights, one setting a fresh record for a propeller-driven solar-powered aircraft of 71,530 feet. Pictured here, the 98.4 feet span carbon fibre and plastic foam/sheet aircraft cruised at between 17 and 20 mph with a weight of 560 lbs With a gross wing area of 787.2 square feet this gave a wing loading of an astonishing 0.71 lbs/sq.ft. Later, this aircraft was revised with an increased span of 121 feet and two more electric motors giving an endurance of about 15 hours daylight with two to five hours extra on back-up batteries. The maximum power output rose from 7,500 watts to almost 12,500 watts.

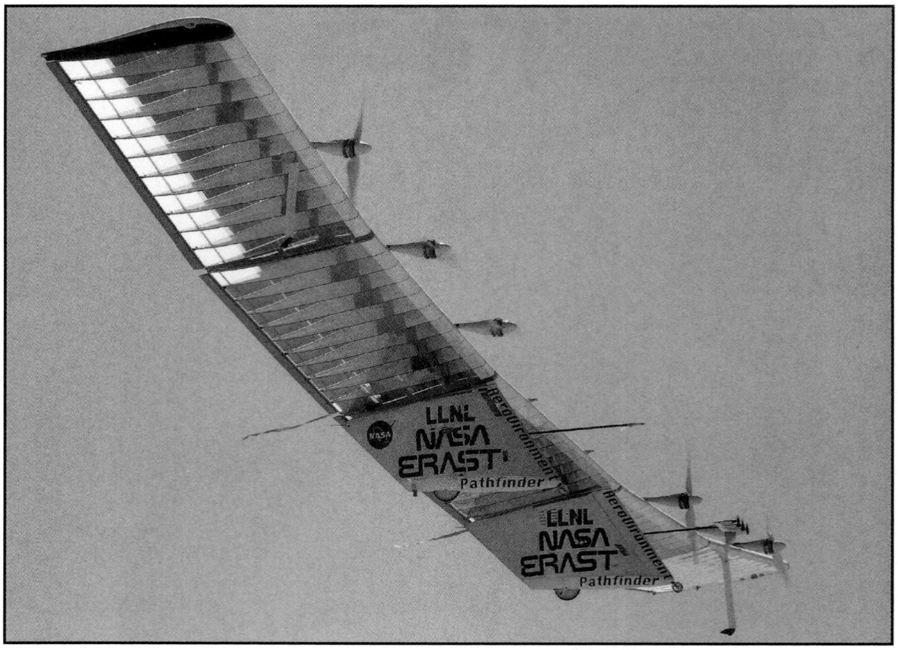

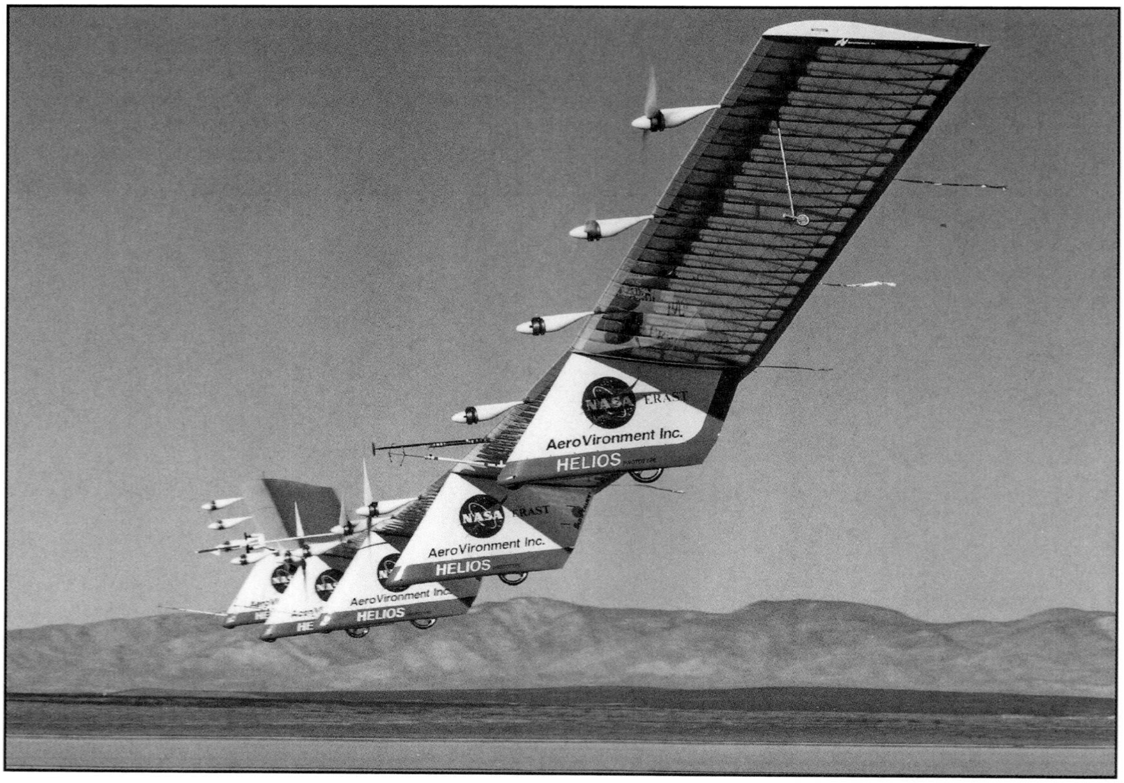

After the success of Pathfinder, AeroVironments went several steps better with its 247 feet span Helios. With 1,976 square feet of wing area and a gross weight of 2,048 lbs, power came from 14 brushless DC electric motors each rated at 2 hp and driving 79 inch diameter laminar-flow propellers designed for high altitude efficiency. With its solar cells and battery back-up, estimated time aloft went from several days to a number of months and in August, 2001, it achieved a world record altitude for non-rocket-powered aircraft of 96,863 feet. Developed from Pathfinder, Helios was prone to extreme flexing of the carbon-fibre single-sparred wing and eventually, on test on the Hawaiian island of Kauai on June 26th, 2003, turbulent air caused what the accident report called 'abnormally high wing dihedral (upward bowing of both wingtips)' resulting in structural failure, the aircraft crashing into the Pacific Ocean where it was lost as the remains sank to the bottom.

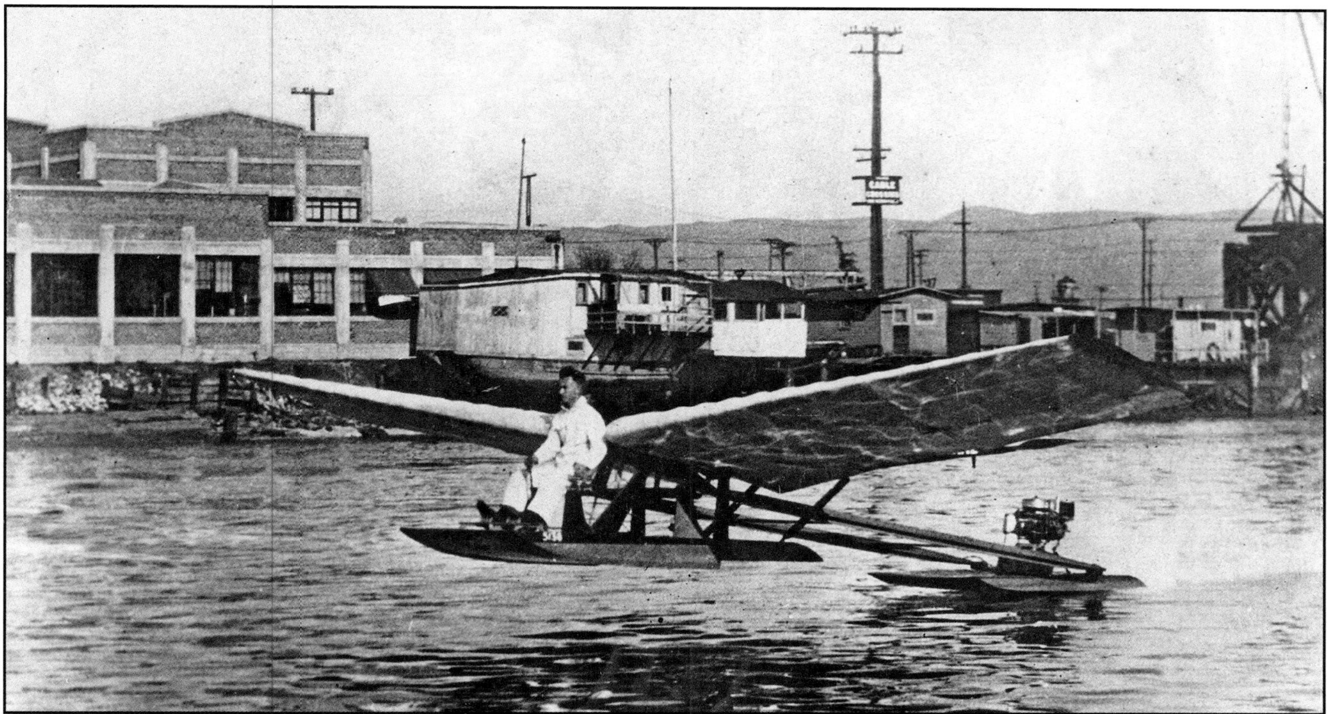

One of the most curious devices ever to be used to get a man into the air was tested out on the river at Almeda, California, in 1930. Designed by Milton and Russell Robertson, it was intended as a really cheap way of experiencing flight in relative safety under the power of a 32 hp Evinrude outboard motor. The 32 feet span shoulder wing was strut-braced to a pontoon-like float which also carried the pilot and his controls. A horizontal pivoted frame extended aft to a second pontoon upon which was mounted the outboard motor and its submerged water propeller. Attached to the wing was a secondary pivotally-mounted frame connected to the first by a scissor-like pair of links. This carried a horizontal stabiliser and elevator. With the outboard motor running, the whole machine ran along the water in a seafaring manner. As the speed increased, at about 30 mph the front pontoon lifted off, the tail boom outstretched behind it and now responding to the elevator control. The aft pontoon remained in the water at all times and the front could be flown to a height of about ten feet, freely pivoting in pitch under the control of the elevator. A novel extension of the tethered-flight principle, an unfortunate by-product was the ear-shattering noise of an unsilenced outboard motor running at full throttle. This picture was taken on March 21st, 1930.

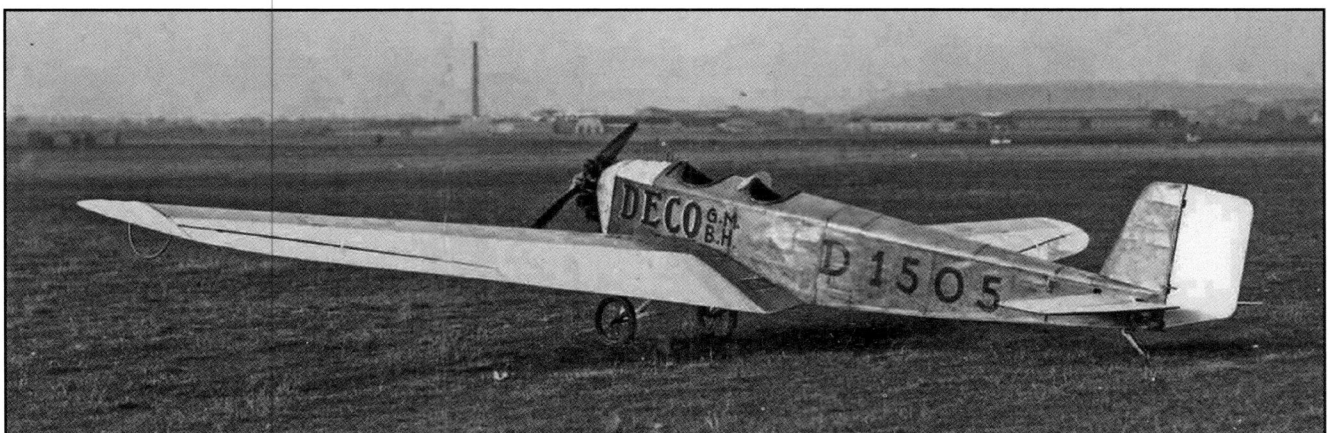

There are a few aircraft which earn a place in history for being nothing more but simply very good flyers. The aircraft division of Germany makers Daimler-Benz employed a man who would emerge as that nation's genius of lightplane design – Hanns Klemm. While Britain was still immersed in the era of the strut-and-wire-braced biplane, Klemm was already well advanced into cantilever-winged monoplanes. In 1926 he formed his own business as Klemm Leichtflugzeugbau GmbH at Böblingen, Baden-Württemberg, in south-western Germany. The dynasty of high-performing lightplanes that followed was to influence the world of light aviation. We in Britain were biplane-besotted and eyed them as curiosities, adding 'they'll never catch on!' Here is a Klemm L.25, works no 109 which was registered to a man in close-by Stuttgart in September 1928 (it was destroyed in May 1931). More than 600 of these were built with licence-manufacture in many places, not the least British Aircraft at Hanworth as the Swallow. The aircraft could be powered by no fewer than fourteen different types of engine. The original finish was usually varnished plywood and clear (transparent) dope as here. Germany's second noted woman pilot Elly Beinhorn (the first was Melli Beese) flew from Europe to Australia, winning the Hindenburg Cup in 1931: she was the second woman to undertake such an epic journey and her Klemm (an L.26) was fitted with an Argus inline motor.

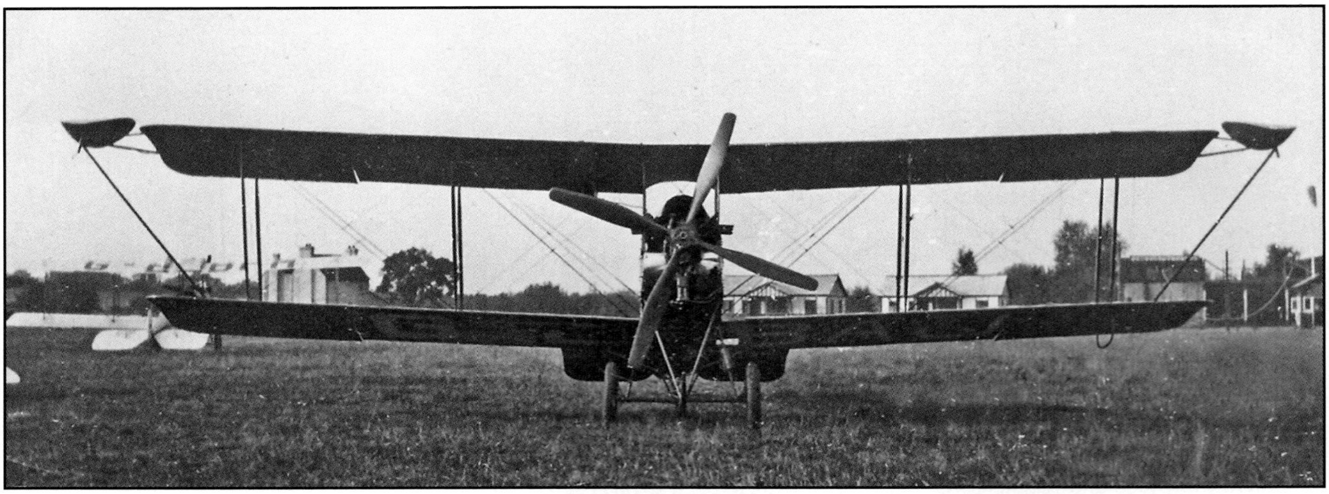

A First World War RFC pilot, Kenneth Noble Pearson, tackled the perennial problem of trying to make the ideal aileron. Geoffrey de Havilland had considerably reduced drag with his differential gear but Pearson pondered whether the aileron was the right shape and form. He came up with his so-called 'rotary aileron' which he patented in 1929. It was shield or heart-shaped, steeply-cambered and turned on an inclined pivot. In normal position both retained a small positive angle of about 4 degree. At full movement of the pilot's control column, one increased to about plus 6 degree and the other to about minus 40 degree causing great drag on the inner aileron and aiding the turn. The prototype installation was on one of Colonel G L P Henderson's Avro 548 aircraft, G-EBAJ. In an act of supreme faith, for air-testing, the normal ailerons were disconnected. The snapshot was taken at Brooklands.

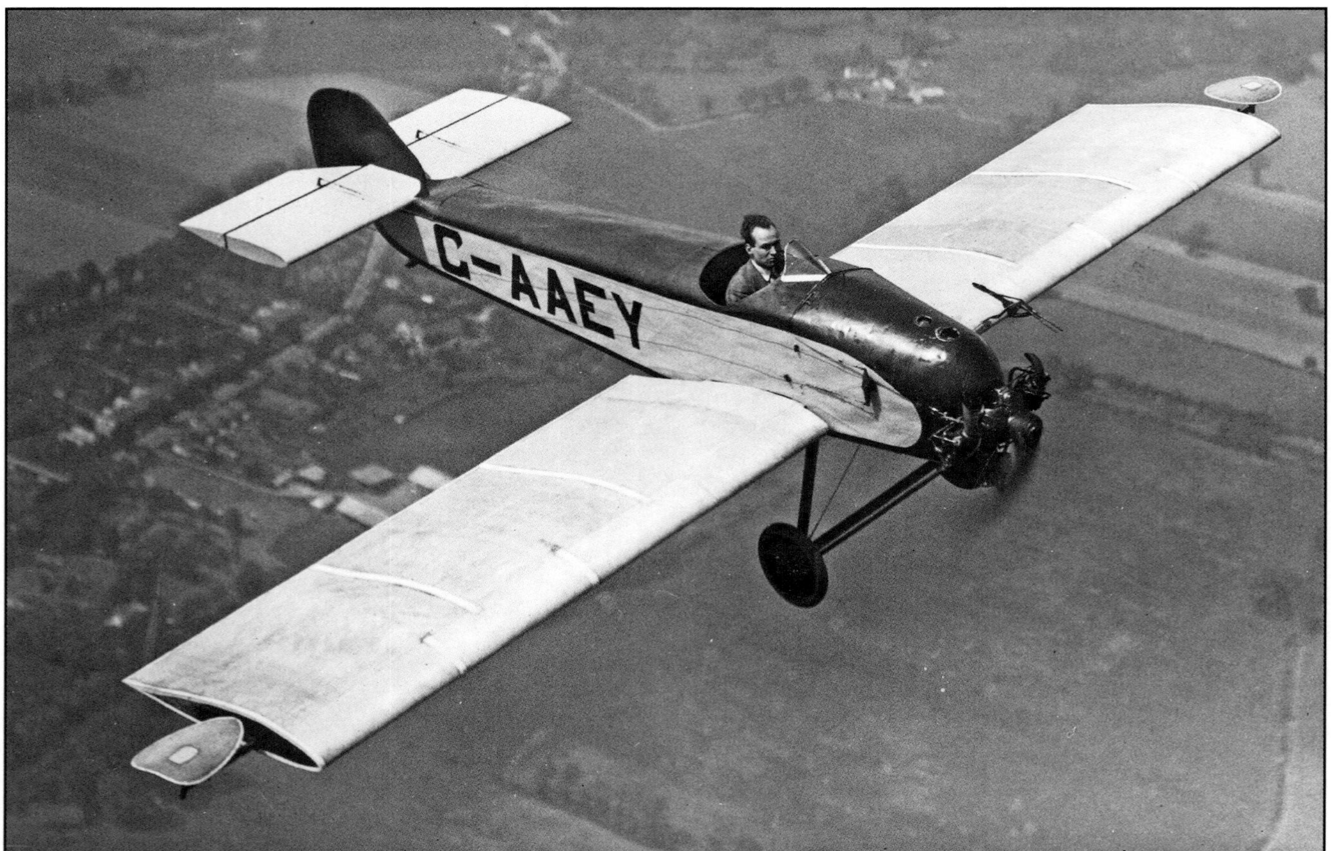

Deciding that the Pearson Rotary Aileron was a suitable alternative to the time-proven hinged flap, the moment was right to try it out on a purpose-built aeroplane. The Glenny and Henderson Gadfly was the candidate for its use. Keith Pearson designed the single-seater ultra-light. Three were made for the UK register, two Mk.I and Mk.II fitted with 35 hp ABC Scorpion II flat-twin engines, and one Mk.III with the 40 hp Salmson AD.9 radial. The first was G-AAEY first flown at Brooklands in April 1929. It achieved the world's altitude record in the 200 kg class with a height of 3,021 on May 16th at the hands of Col George Lockhart Piercy Henderson (1888-1930). Pictured here in June 1929, A P Glenny flies the prototype prior to its exhibition at the Olympia Air Show.

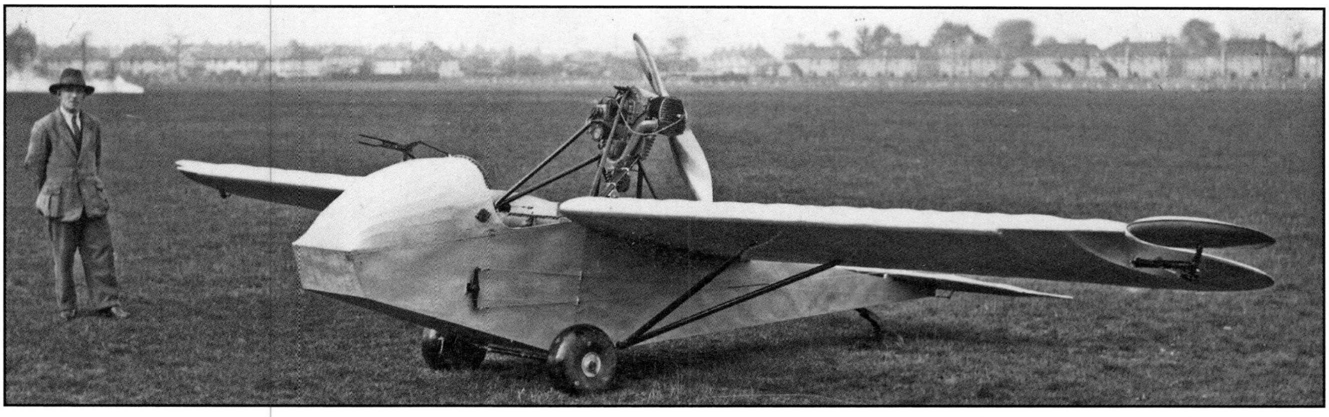

After flying his rotary ailerons on the Avro 548 at Brooklands and then on the Glenny and Henderson Gadfly, Kenneth Noble Pearson decided to build a special aircraft to show off the latest refinement of his brainchild. The Pickering-Pearson KP.2 monoplane was built at Hanworth in 1933 and registered G-ACMR. A 26 hp Aeronca E-107A single-ignition flat twin engine – a precursor of the E.117 motor fitted to the Aeronca C.3 which was licence-built in Britain by J A Prestwick as the Aeronca J.99 JAP for the British-built Aeronca 100 – was installed on a pylon as a pusher. The special tip 'ailerons' were of revised form and section. For some reason, the aircraft had neither fin nor rudder, the designer's confidence in his ailerons extending to their potential for provision of steering and directional control. In September 1933 the aircraft began its trials but quickly proved to be uncontrollable on the ground. Sometime later it appeared with a fin and rudder but it seems that even thus equipped it never flew and the machine disappeared.

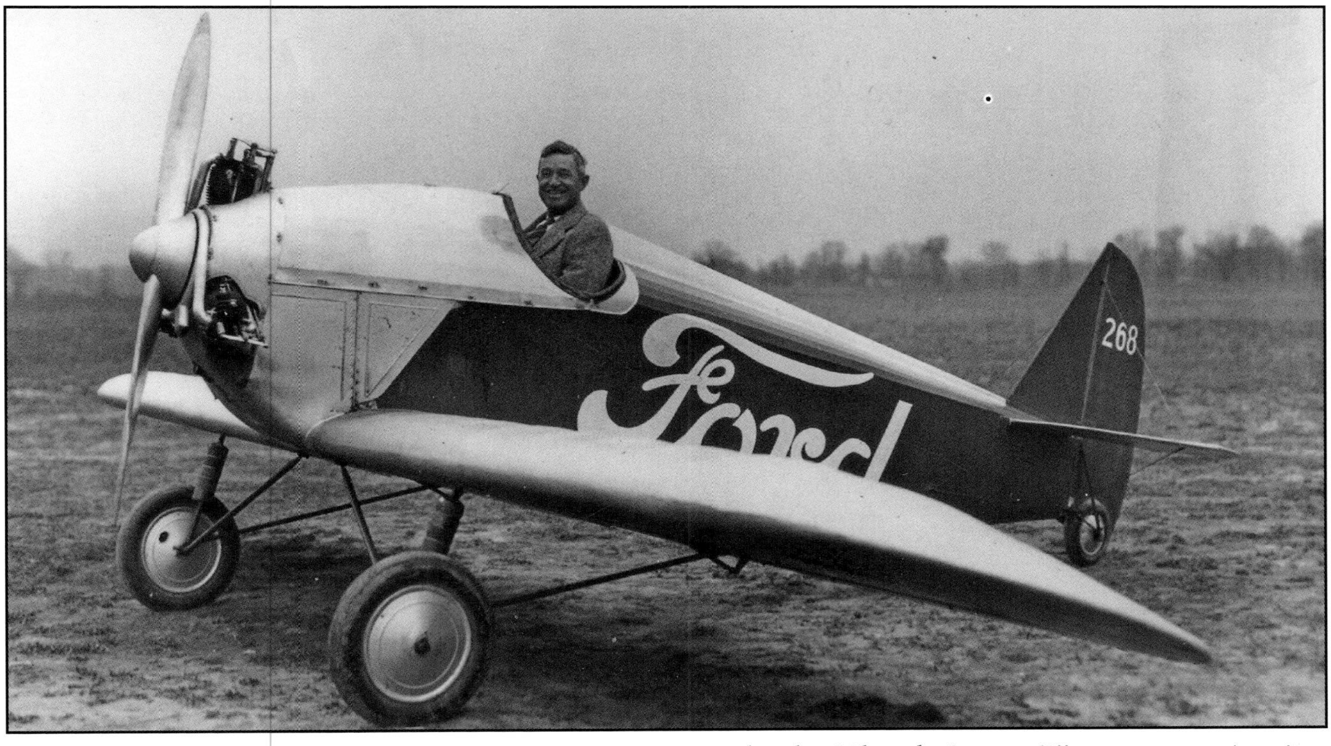

This is not so much a curiosity of flight as a misguided moment in time that should have had a very different outcome. American motoring guru Henry Ford (1863-1947), aware that the US had established almost 5,000 nationwide landing sites, decided he would like to do for aviation what he had done for motoring by offering a small, cheap aircraft. He hired Otto C Koppen (the man who later designed the Helio Courier) and told him to contrive an 'airplane' that would weigh no more than 500 lbs and fit into his office. The outcome was a true utility flyer with welded steel-tube fuselage and straight, dihedral-less wing. Span was 21 feet 9 inches, length 15 feet 6 inches. The airfoil selected was Göttingen 387 – an unusual choice for an aircraft with a wing area of 100 square feet and such a low aspect-ratio. The prototype was powered by 36 hp three-cylinder Anzani and bore the number '268'. Maximum speed was a useful 90 mph and the stall came at 30 mph. Ford's chief pilot, Harry J Brooks, used to commute between his home and work in this machine. When Charles Lindbergh visited Ford on August 11th, 1927, he was invited to fly what was now named the Ford Flivver: he later described it as 'one of the worst aircraft I have ever flown'. Here in this publicity picture American comedian Will Rogers (who did not fly) poses for the camera. In all six Flivvers were built, each a slight improvement on the previous, and briefly the machine held the World Endurance Record, then standing at 986 miles, in the 440 lb to 880 lb class. But on February 21st, 1928, Brooks was killed when he crashed the second prototype into the sea off Florida. His body was never found. Ford, deeply moved at the loss, promptly scrapped the whole project. The Flivver, however, deserves a small place in history as if not the first, then a very early attempt at making a 'people's plane'.

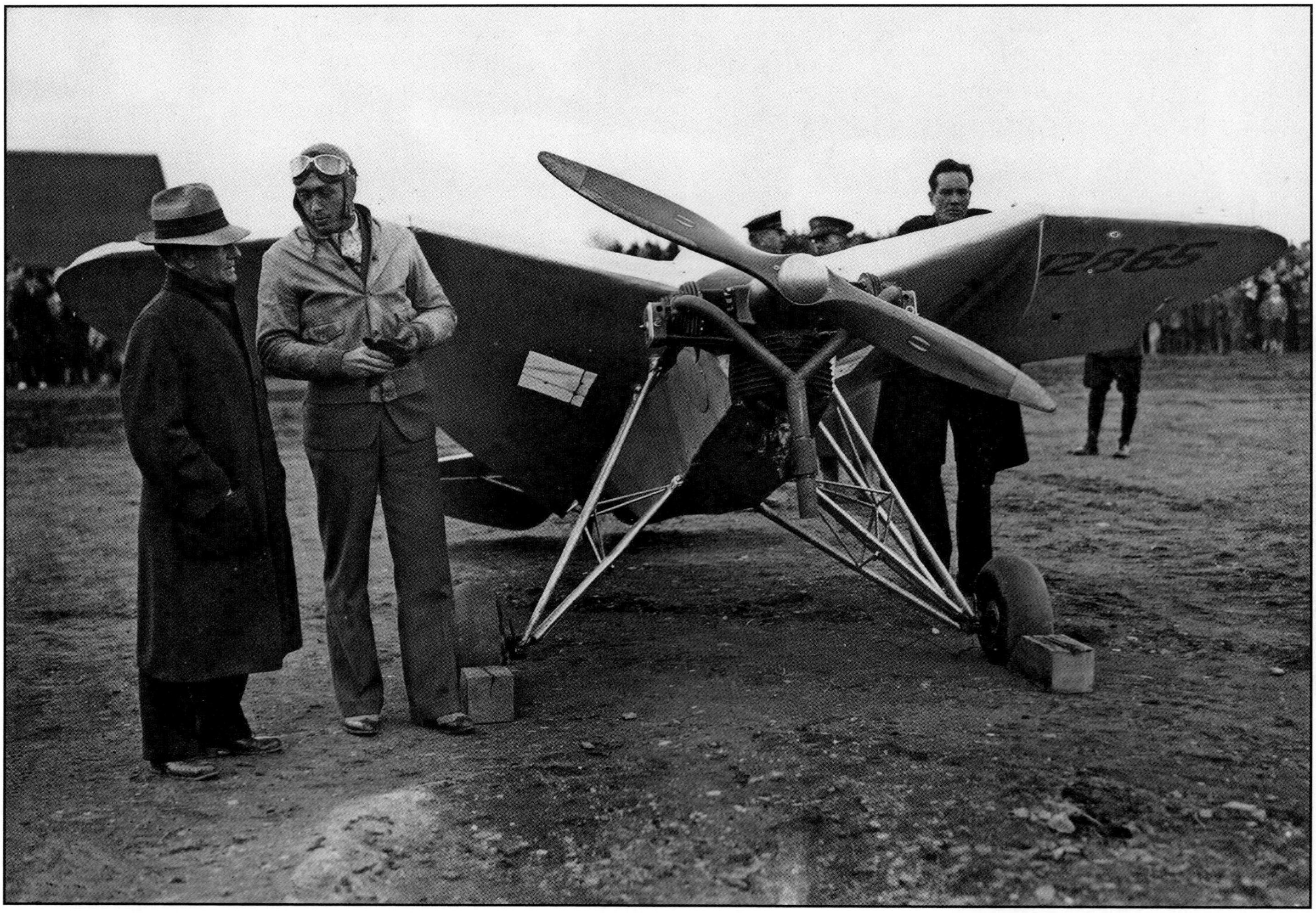

Make something that's a different shape from the norm and people dub you crazy. Certainly Cincinnati-born Edward H Lanier's Vacuplane was derided and its designer branded short on the marbles. Part of this was due to Lanier's confessed account as to his inspiration for his curious flying machine. His family business was in ice cream and his father was the inventor of the ice cream cone. Young Edward noticed that if you dropped an ice cream cone it always landed on its side and this, he thought, was a fundamental truth of flying. He made a series of aircraft, all of which managed to fly with varying degrees of success. But his XL-5, pictured here, proved to be an astounding flyer. Described at the time as 'one of the smallest airplanes ever built', the tiny aircraft with its huge wing spanned 14 feet and was just 16 feet in length. Powered by an Aeronca E.113C engine of 37 hp and with an all-up weight of 350 lbs, the aircraft had a range of 250 miles at a cost of eight US gallons of fuel. So impressive was the performance and handling that it was hired as a feature of the dedication and opening of New York's Troy Airport on October 27th 1934. In this picture the 23-year-old pilot Wendell T Fleming is seen talking to the designer, far left, prior to flight. The Vacuplane, X12865, had underwing fences at the point of dihedral change and the outer wings folded downwards for storage. The wide track undercarriage displays some comprehensive bracing indicating that the only suspension was the doughnut tyres. Troy Airport, Albany, was closed in 1964 and built over. See also the back cover.

Opposite: Throughout the history of aeroplanes there have been instances designed by artists. Just as bad are aircraft designed by scientists! For years master cabinet-makers have excelled in creating metamorphic furniture – tables with mechanisms to extend them in fascinating ways, chests of drawers that become library steps and so on. But metamorphic aircraft! In 1925 Armstrong Whitworth found itself in the unenviable position of building three aircraft to the specification of RAE aerodynamicists who wanted to play with what today we would call 'variable geometry'. Uncompromisingly named the Ape, A-W's unwilling creation was a monstrosity in the fullest sense. First was the undercarriage and tailskid – structures designed to absorb enormous vertical loads (known to you and me as heavy landings). Next was the fuselage which was built to accept 'plugs' – additional sections to push the nose out further and to extend the tail. The length ranged from 28 feet 3 inches to 39 feet 3 inches and the height from 13 to 15 feet. Weirdest of all was the hinged tail which, by the aid of a screw-jack, could be wound up and down through a wide range of incidence. The three Apes – J7753 (first flown on January 5th, 1926), J7754 (pictured here), and J7755 – carried a variety of engines from 180 hp to 215 hp Lynx. Used to experiment with low-speed flight, the Ape proved to be disappointing in performance, not really a surprise. In May 1929, the one seen here crashed and the four-aileroned biplane passed into history. The fate of the other two is unknown.

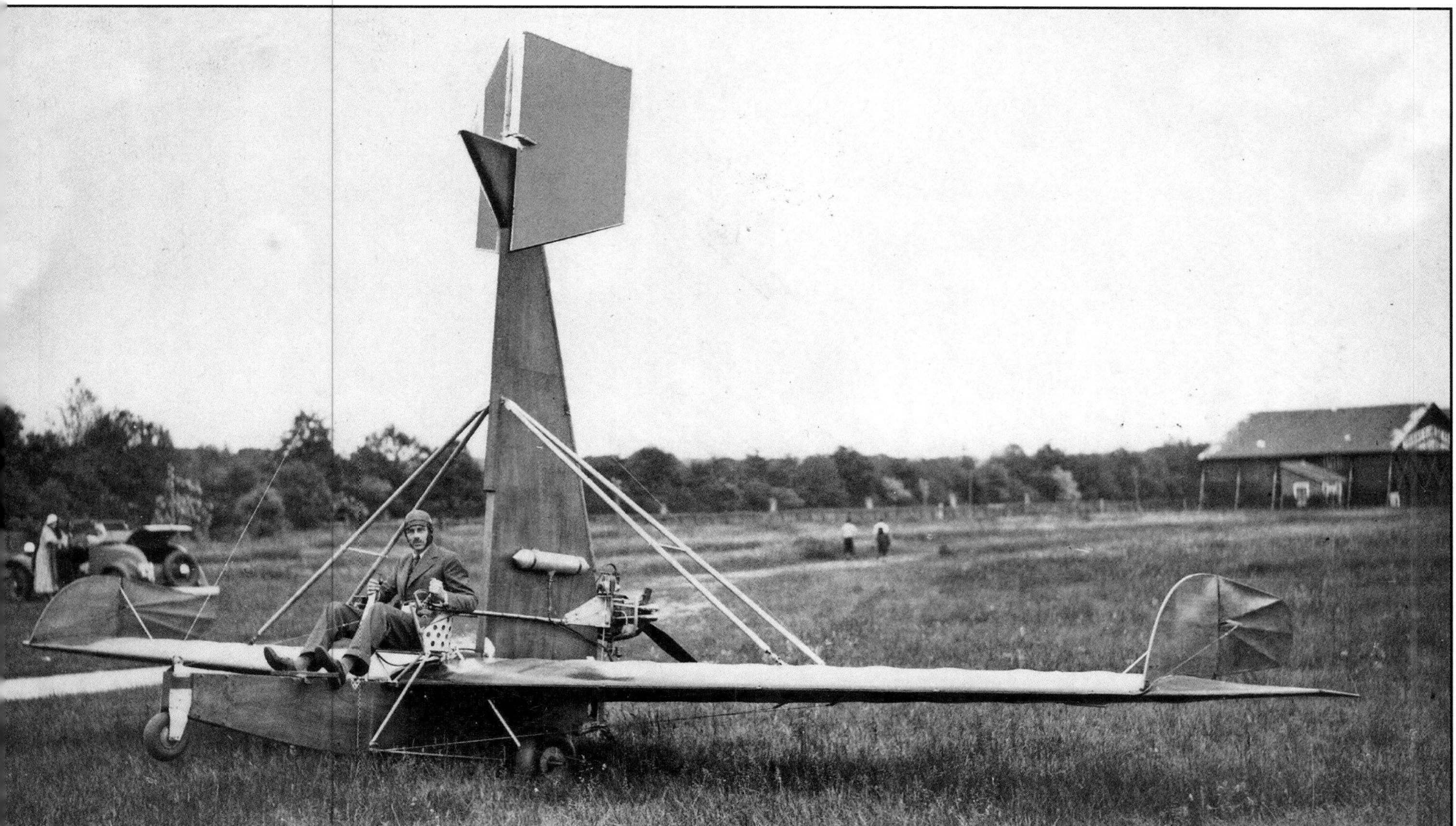

Certain inventors are imbued with unshakeable faith in their inventions in the same way that in another age perpetual motionists were denied the ability to see just why their scheme would not work. The Vicomte Charles de Rougé was one of these unfortunates and when, on June 12th, 1935, he unveiled his Helytrophan to the Parisian press corps, his scheme was so outrageous that just about everybody printed his picture! Either that or it was a 'slow news day' but his audacious self-stabilising plane was certainly eye-catching. Tailless and powered by a 20 hp JAP motorcycle engine, the wooden aircraft shared something with the primary glider but the dominant feature was a huge plywood-clad mast that towered over the centre-section. At the top were two trapezoidal-shaped pivoting surfaces which could be rotated like a pair of grotesque elevators, or folded flat to the sides of the mast by cable-operated controls in the hands of the pilot. The good Count had first revealed his 'vanes on mast keep glider level' claim in April 1934 when he tried it out on a glider with the assertion that these could be used 'to correct any tendency to pitch forward or side-slip in flight'. Nothing further is known of this *rara avis*.

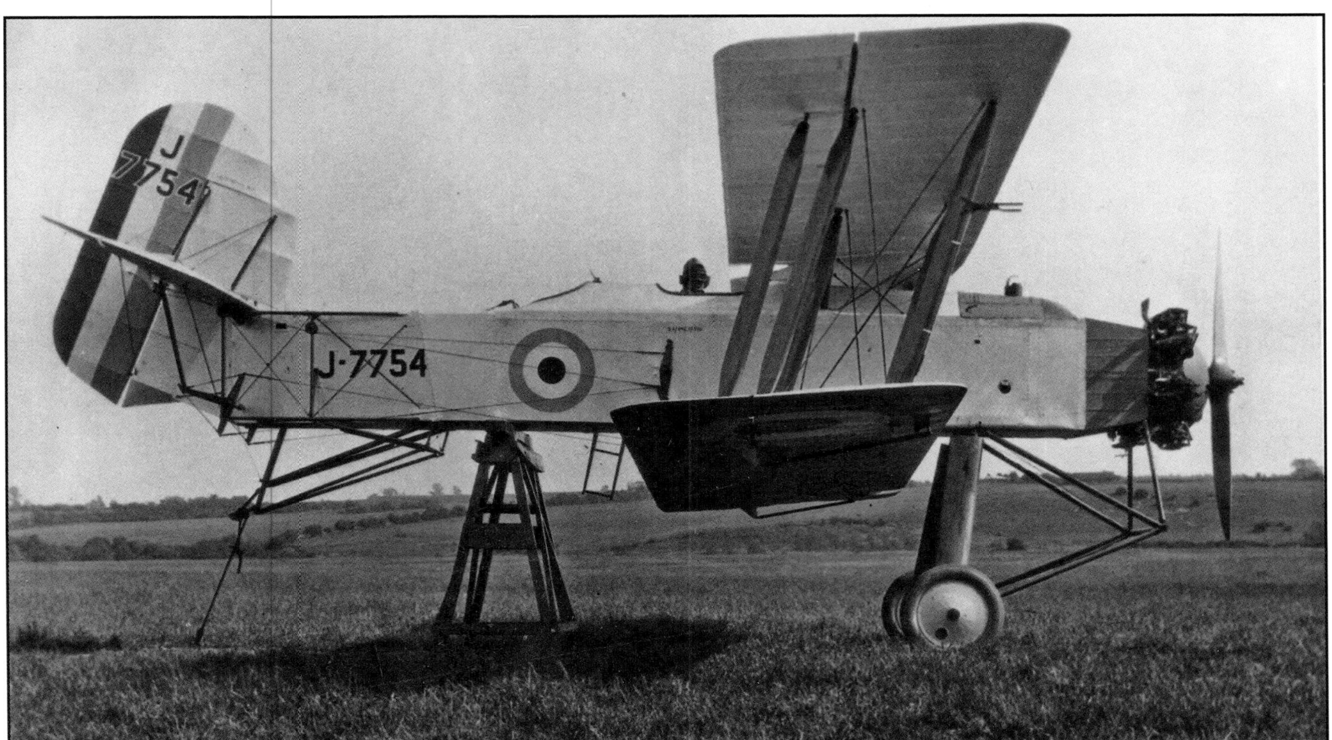

There were many American designers of light aircraft but one stands out and that was Fred Ernest Weick (1899-1993). Aviation engineering pioneer and a major designer, Weick worked at NACA (the National Advisory Committee for Aeronautics) where he invented the so-called NACA low-drag engine cowl, created the first full-size propeller wind-tunnel and wrote a book on airscrew design that became a worldwide text book. In 1934 he took on the challenge of making a safe, reliable 'family' aeroplane that would not stall or spin. He built his W-1 in his basement and, on March 1st, 1934, had it tunnel-tested at the NACA laboratories. His design exhibited the then-new tricycle landing gear while the wing mounted a full-span predictor-slat some way in front of the leading edge.

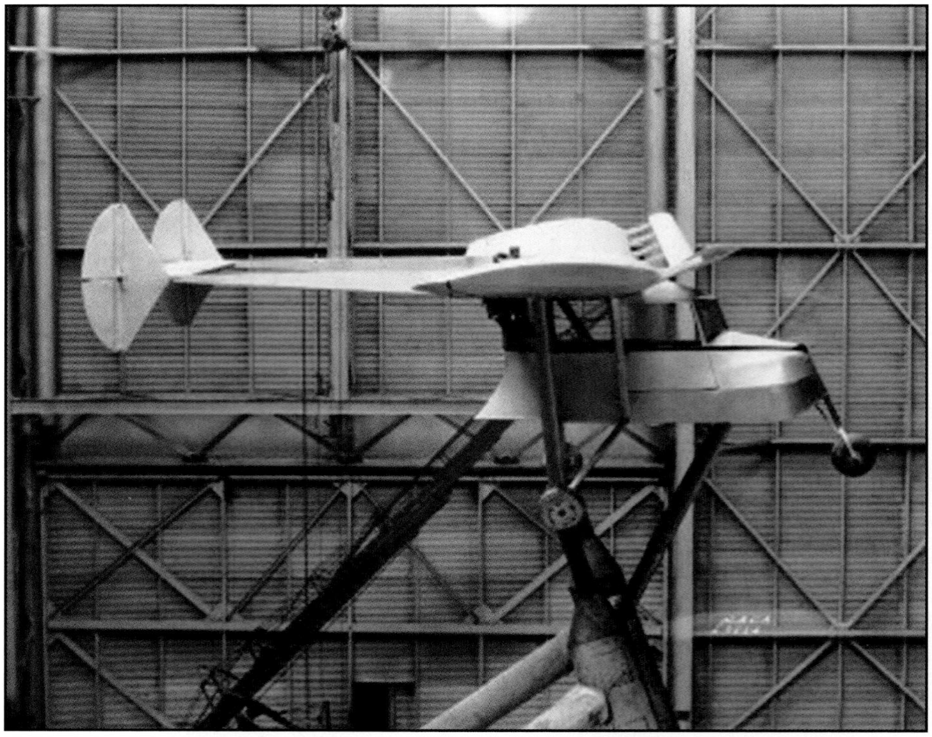

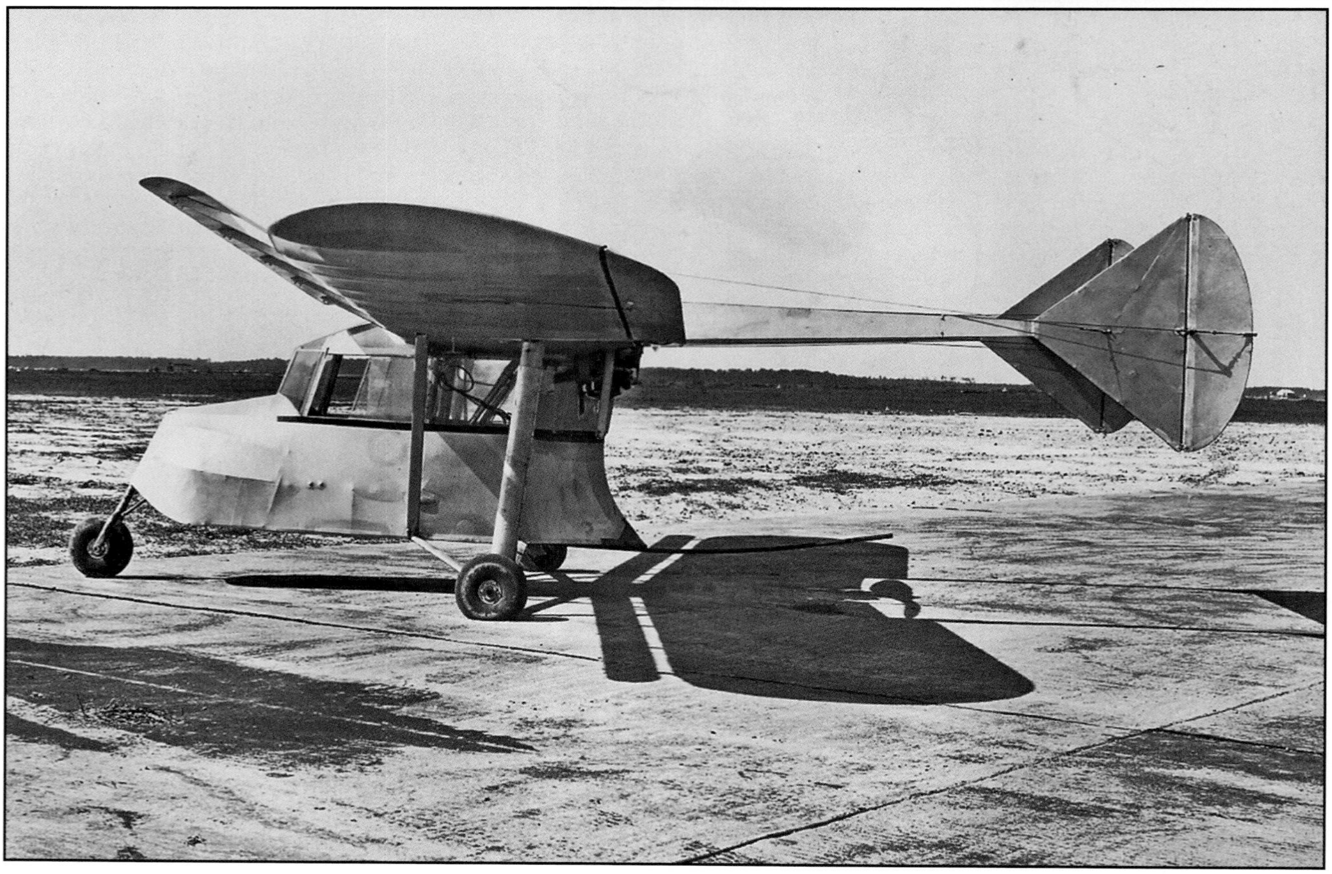

As a result of the wind-tunnel trials, the triangular fins of the W-1 were doubled in area. In this view of the revised model, the shadow on the ground in this picture reveals the detail of the wing slots. The engine was mounted as a pusher and the rear of the cockpit pod ended in a long, slender upturned skid to prevent the nose being raised too high for landing and take-off. The wingspan was 29 feet 11 inches and the length 21 feet 2 inches. It was found that the machine could not be held in a stalled condition nor would it spin unintentionally. Powered by a Pobjoy Niagara engine, the W-1 underwent many changes and refinements.

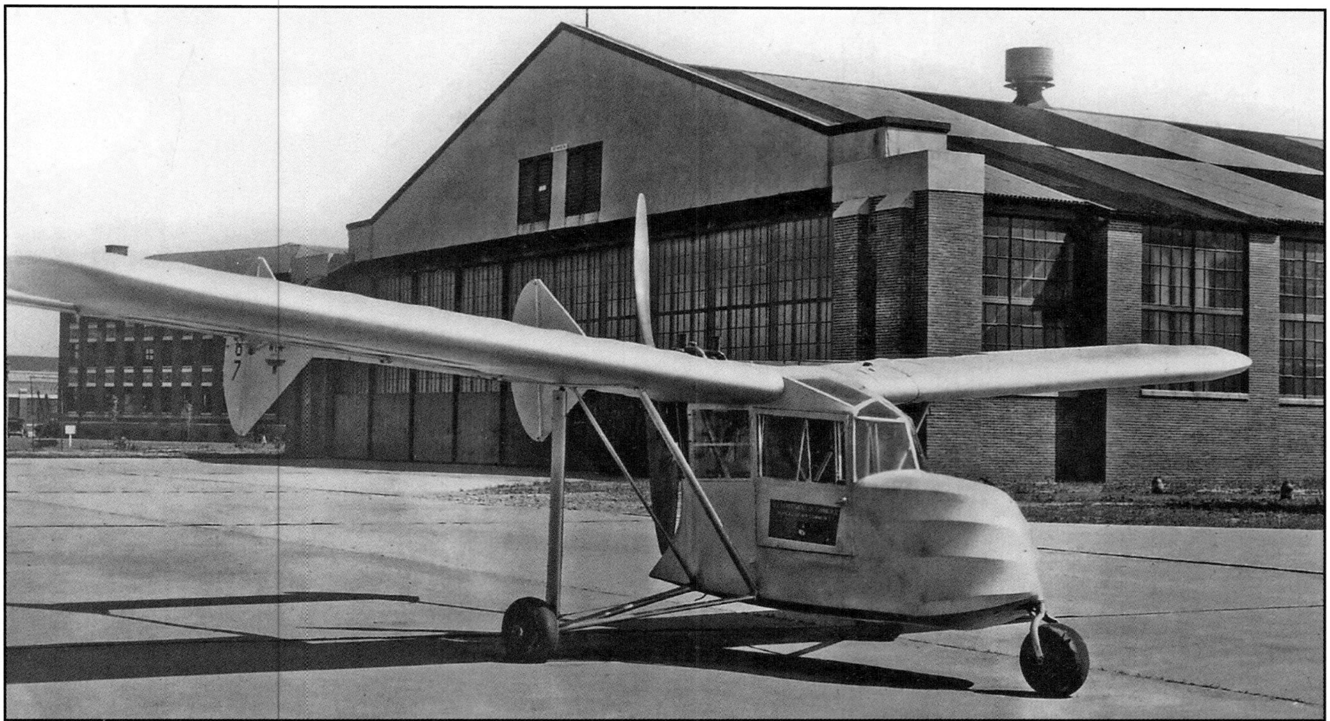

In its final form in 1935, the Weick W-1A lost both its rear fuselage tail-skid and the leading edge 'predictor' slots. Because the whole trailing edge of the wing was taken up by the extensive landing flaps, Weick now incorporated the newly-developed 'slat-lip' type of aileron which he had pioneered in the NACA wind-tunnel. This consisted of a wide-chord slot in the underside of the wing aft of the mainspar and more than five feet in span. The upper surface was closed by a flap or slat. With the slat closed the slot was ineffective: with it open slightly, air flowed through the slot and lifted that wing. Banking thus required the movement of just one wing mechanism which was both simple and low on drag. The huge propeller of the Pobjoy is visible in this picture of prototype NS67. Unfortunately the Weick was never put into production. Fred Weick went on to join the newly-formed Engineering & Research Corporation (ERCO) of Riverdale, Maryland, where he designed the Ercoupe – the ultimate safety aeroplane which, like the Mignet Flying Flea, had no rudder pedals. This hugely popular cabin aeroplane could easily cope with a 25 knot crosswind landing. He was later co-designer of the Piper Cherokee series of light aircraft.

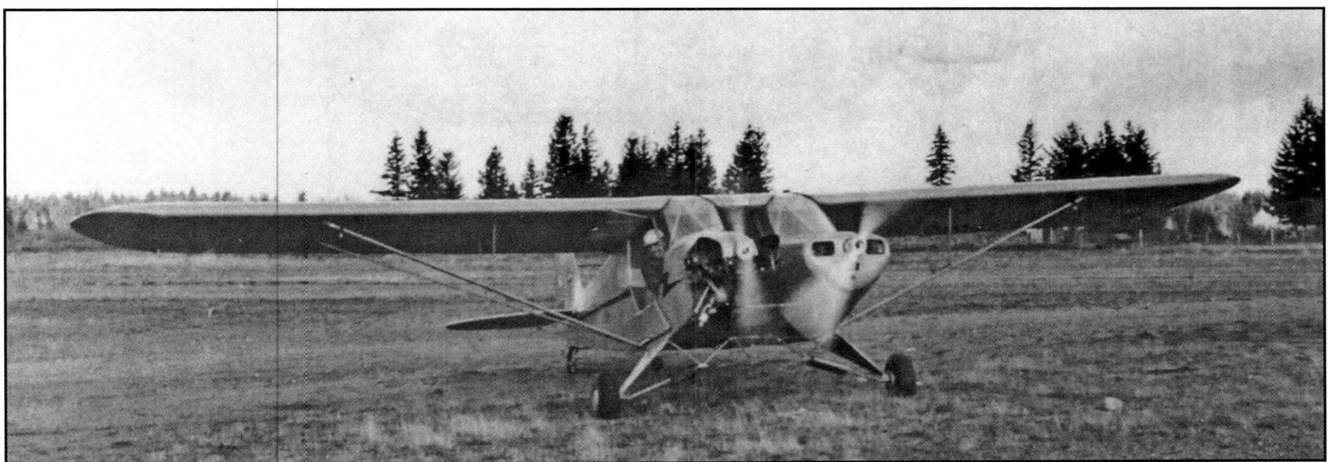

Sometimes one is moved to utter the word 'Why?' when seeing the brainchildren of some designers. In 1952, Harold Wagner of Times Skyport, Portland, Oregon, fancied he would like to make a low-cost sporting twin-engined aircraft and began by taking a Piper PA.18 Super Cub and fitting a second engine on top of the fuselage. This first flew on May 29th that year but suffered severely from tail flutter. He then took two Piper fuselages, one was a J-3 and the other a PA-11 Cub Coupe and mounted them side by side with a small centre-section wing and a 'middle' tailplane. The remaining parts were standard Cub components. There was only one problem: the Cub has access doors on only one side, so the closely-positioned fuselages meant that only the starboard one could be used by pilot and passenger. To prevent the propellers (which were unsynchronised) from striking each other, the port engine hub was provided with a distance piece. The twin Lycoming 85 hp engines gave the 38 feet 6 inches span aircraft a maximum speed of 120 mph, a cruise of 100 mph and a stalling speed of 38 mph. The 1,250-lb all-up weight aircraft had an initial rate of climb of 1,500 feet/minute. Having proved something or other, Mr Wagner dismantled his horror and restored a pair of single Cubs.

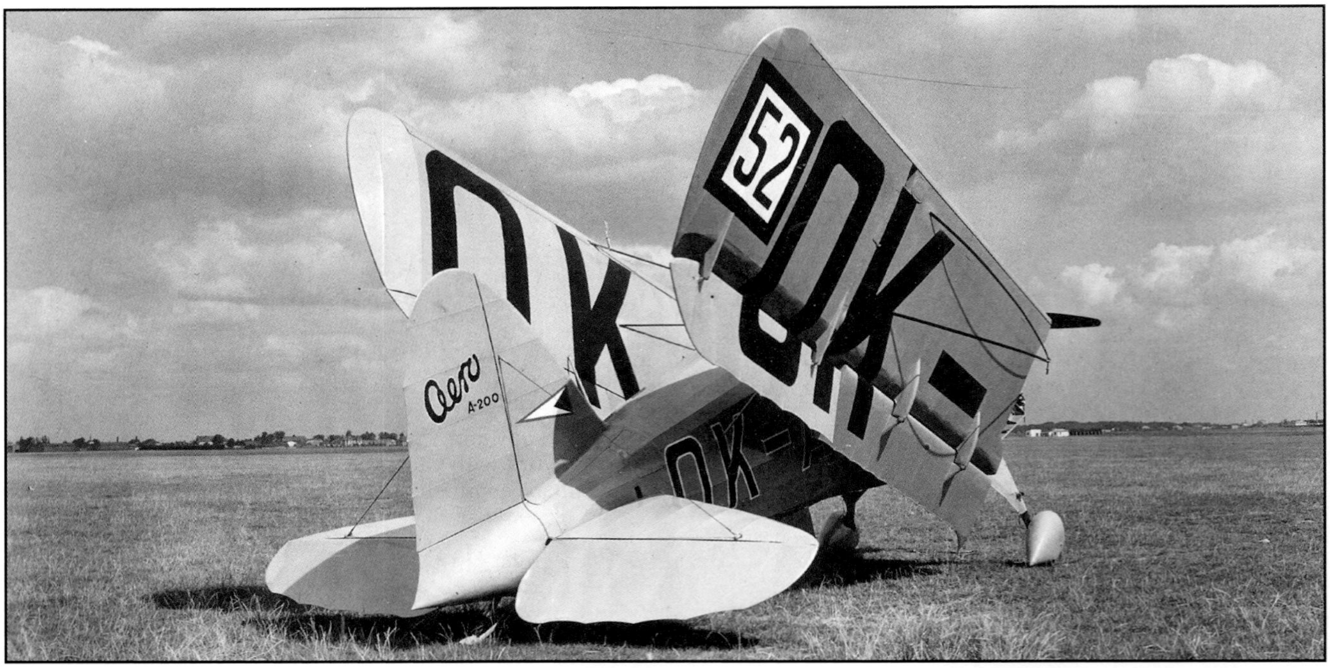

This picture is less of a curiosity but rather more of an amusing interlude. The Czechoslovakian Aero A.200 was designed and built by Aero Tovarna Letadel Dr Kabes at Vysochany. A business founded in 1919, for the sole purpose of competing in the 1934 Challenge de Tourisme Internationale. A four-seater wire-braced low-wing monoplane fitted with extensive leading-edge slots and high-lift flaps, the A-200 was powered by a 200 hp Walter Bora 9-cylinder radial. Two were built for the competition – OK-AMA and OK-AMB and both took part. On Monday, January 1st, 1934, the prototype made its first flight. Wingspan was 36 feet 5 inches (10 feet 7 inches when folded) and length was 25 feet 7 inches. With a high-lift wing of 178.6 square feet area, the A.200 could cruise at 136 mph for a range of 500 miles while the maximum speed was 160 mph. In the contest, the first aircraft was flown by Jan Ambro who finished in fourth aggregate position behind the outright winner (Poland's RWD-9 which gained first and second places), and a Fieseler Fi.19 which gave Germany third place. The second A.200 was flown by Vojtêch acek and this took overall 14th place out of the 34 competitors. The judges commented that the A.200 had the best short-take-off performance. This picture, showing OK-AMB with its wings folded, somehow reminds one of those 'Police Aware' stickers one sees on abandoned cars…

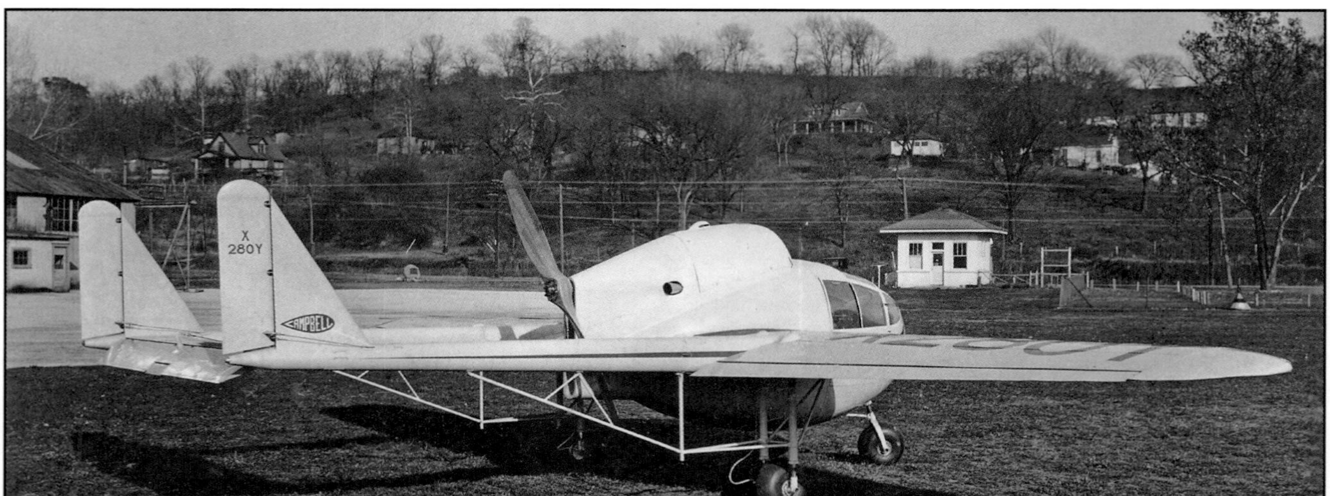

As America emerged from the early 1930s recession, a spate of 'feel-good' light aircraft designs appeared. Among these the genus 'aerial flivver' was the most numerous and in mid-'thirties a government-sponsored competition was announced for a safe, light and economical aircraft. Hayden S Campbell of St Joseph, Montana, as well as being vice-president of the Barling Aircraft Company, decided to enter and at the end of 1935 introduced his economical all-metal pusher. Built entirely out of magnesium and with a 30-foot wingspan, his design had an all-up weight of around 1,200 lbs. Uncharacteristically it had no name but the egg-like monocoque fuselage, straight, no dihedral wings and twin-boom tail gave this side-by-side two-seater a businesslike appearance. The motor was a Ford V-8 car engine with a modified car radiator grille atop the fuselage and the tricycle undercarriage had a steerable nosewheel. With the markings X280Y, the machine was evaluated at Bolling Field, Washington, DC, where it flew very well. Unfortunately it was damaged in an early demonstration flight and was never repaired. The external boom bracing is novel and suggests that the all-wood Arpin, flown at Hanworth before the war, was better designed.

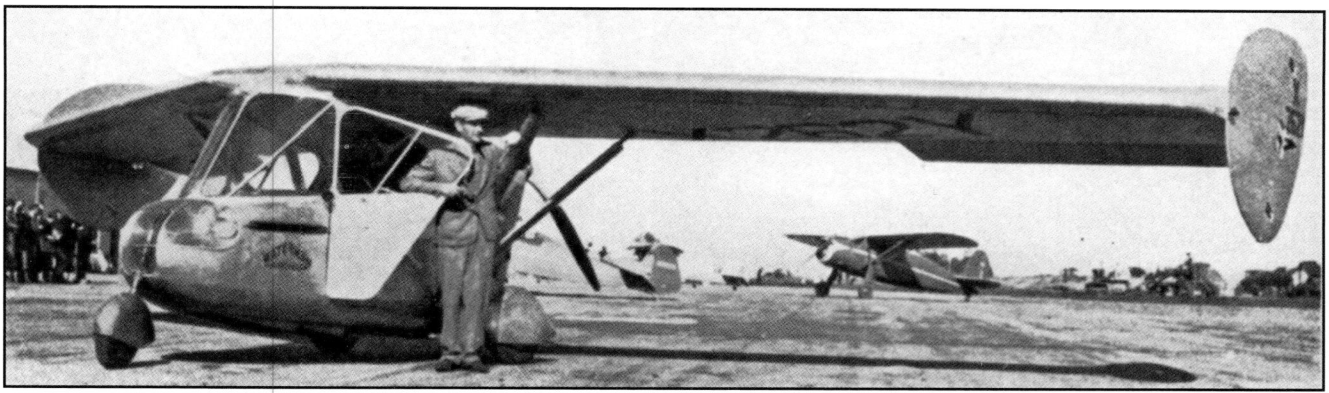

Flying cars were an American thing, pioneer aviator Glenn Curtiss contriving a cylindrical-bodied car with three wings as early as 1917. His 'Autoplane' never flew properly although it is said to have 'hopped about a bit' arising to unkind associations with a rabbit. It fell to a young engineer who had come to work with Curtiss to make the breakthrough. Waldo Dean Watermann (1894-1976) was a San Diego-born inventor and brilliant aeronautical engineer. With the outbreak of the First World War, he became head of the Theory of Flight Department, School of Military Aeronautics at the University, and later Chief Engineer at the US Aircraft Corporation. He remained to liquidate the company at the end of the war. With some assets purchased from this outfit, Waterman moved to Santa Monica where, by the late 1920s he had built and flown a successful all-wing aircraft with tricycle undercarriage which he called the Whatsit. As a low-cost, swept-wing tailless two-seat monoplane, he submitted the design to the US Bureau of Air Commerce in response to the Bureau's investigation into cheaper and simpler aircraft for the private owner. In August 1935, he founded the Waterman Arrowplane Corporation with Max B Harlow as his chief engineer. The first Arrowplane was built for the Bureau of Commerce. In the meanwhile he evolved his Arrowbile flying car which was powered by a 100 hp Studebaker engine both as a car and in the air. The pusher airscrew was driven by six Vee belts giving a 1.94:1 reduction. On March 21st, 1937, the first Aerobile X262Y flew with the designer as pilot/driver. The span was 38 feet and length 19 feet 4 inches and the road speed of 56 mph translated into a flying cruising speed of 102 mph. Empty weight was 1,941 lbs and maximum weight 2,500 lbs. With 50 gallon fuel, the duration was 350 miles. The wings were detachable. Five machines were made and successfully flown. These pictures show the designer with his Arrowbile in road and air conditions with the addition of a 'production' model, below, in flight.

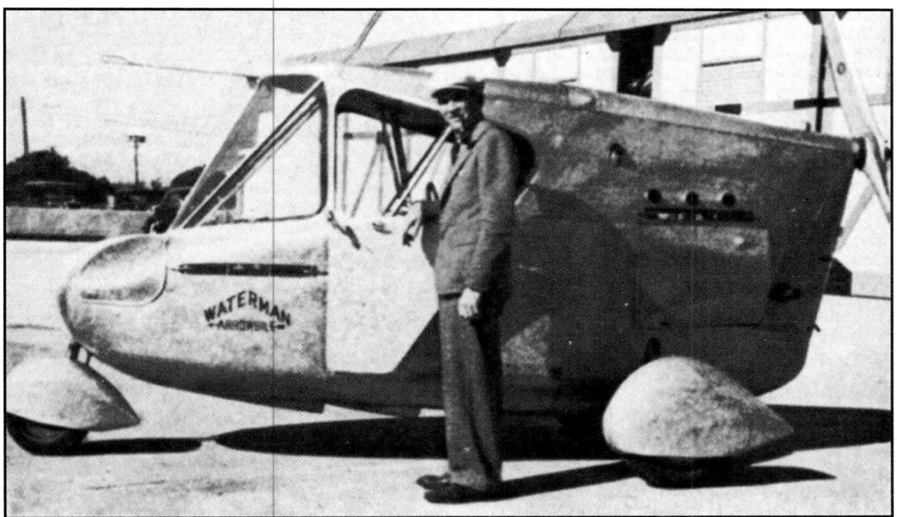

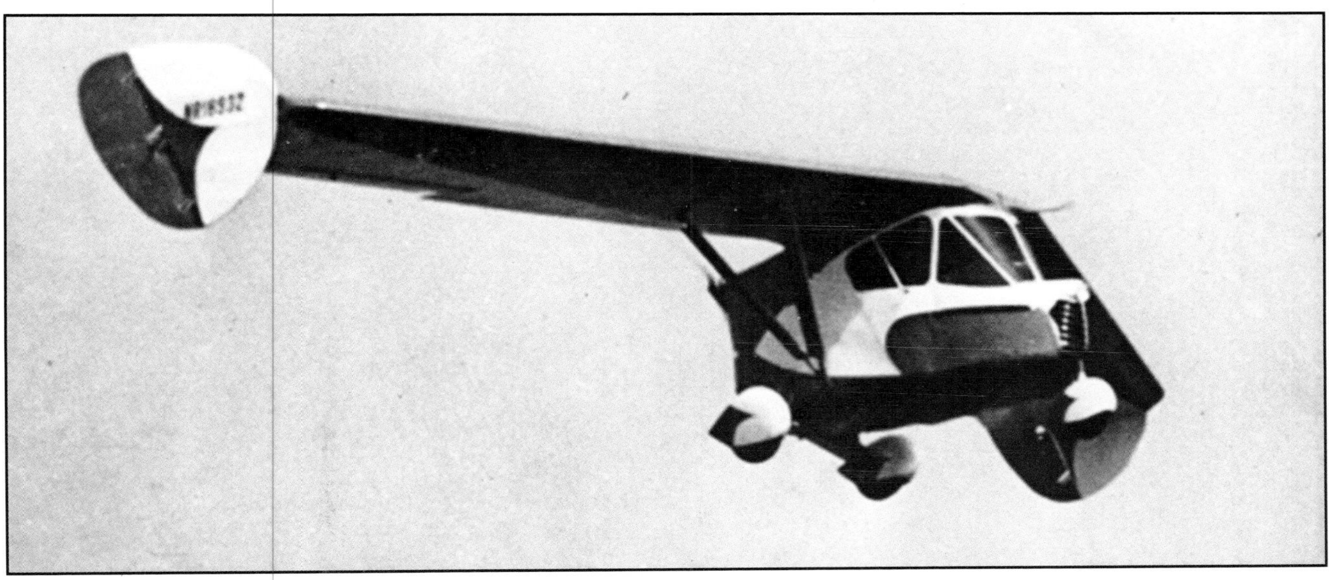

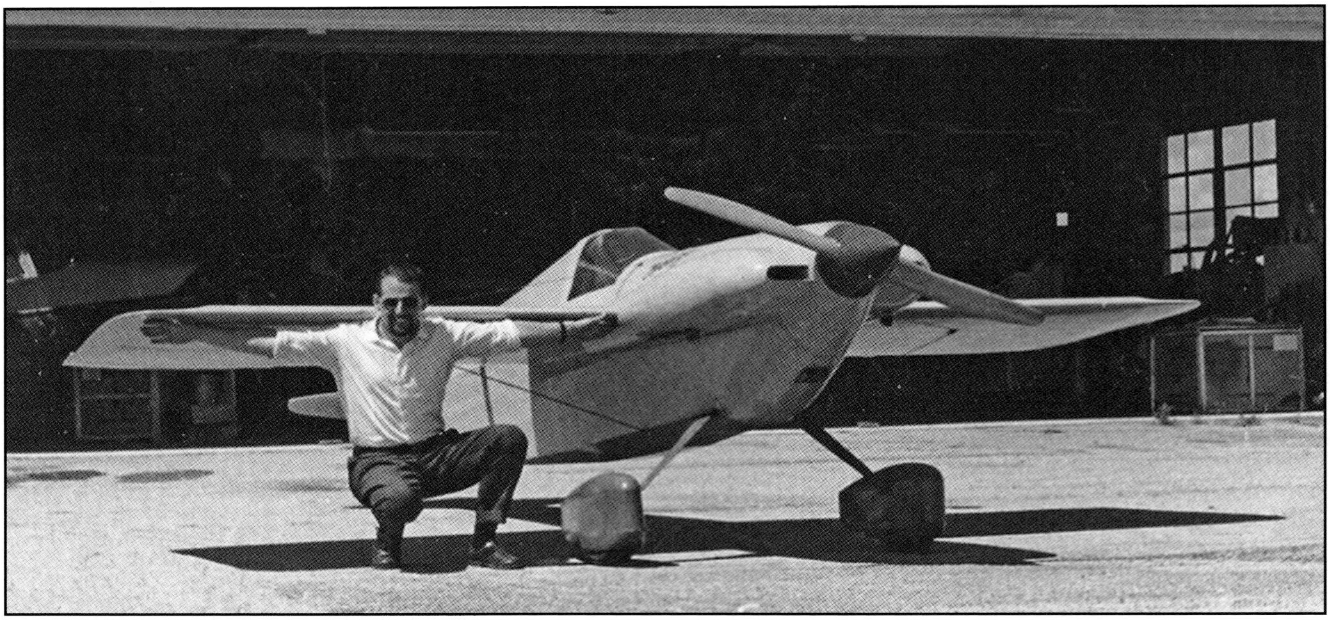

Aside from the huge aircraft built by some such as Howard Hughes' behemoth flying boat and Bristol's Brabazon, some aspire to make very small aircraft. In fact, it seems the quest is sometimes merely to find the smallest machine that will fly. Initially the quest was that of racing and in 1962 the present author had the delight of staying at the home of America's greatest designer-racer, Sylvester 'Steve' J Wittman (1904-1995) and his wife Dorothy. Steve's hangar at Oshkosh featured a raft of very small aircraft and this one, the Wittman Bonzo, had four sets of wings – each progressively shorter as his design refined. Here I am 'measuring' Bonzo's then-span of 15 feet 4 inches. The empty weight was 508 lbs and the top speed an astonishing 235 mph.

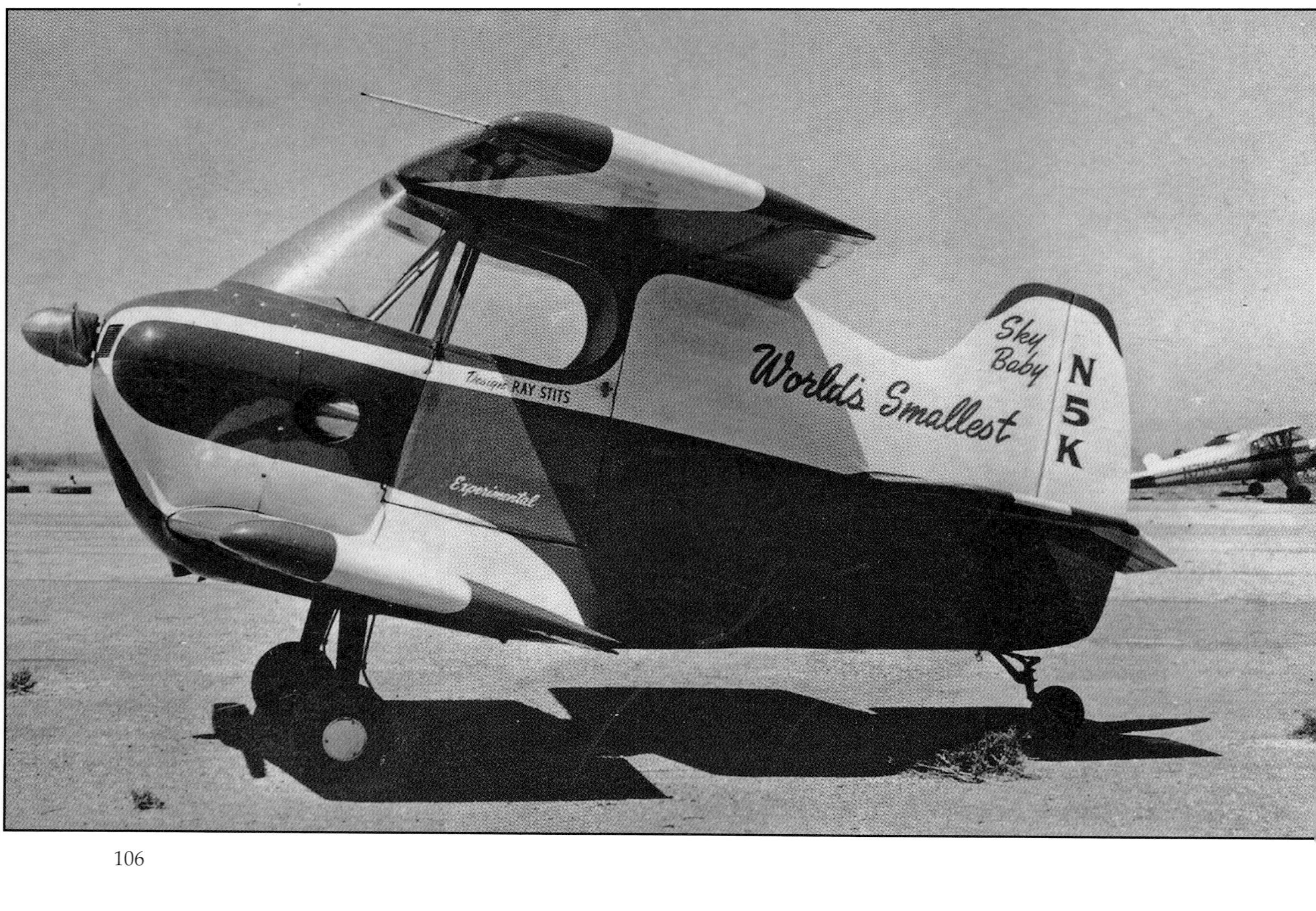

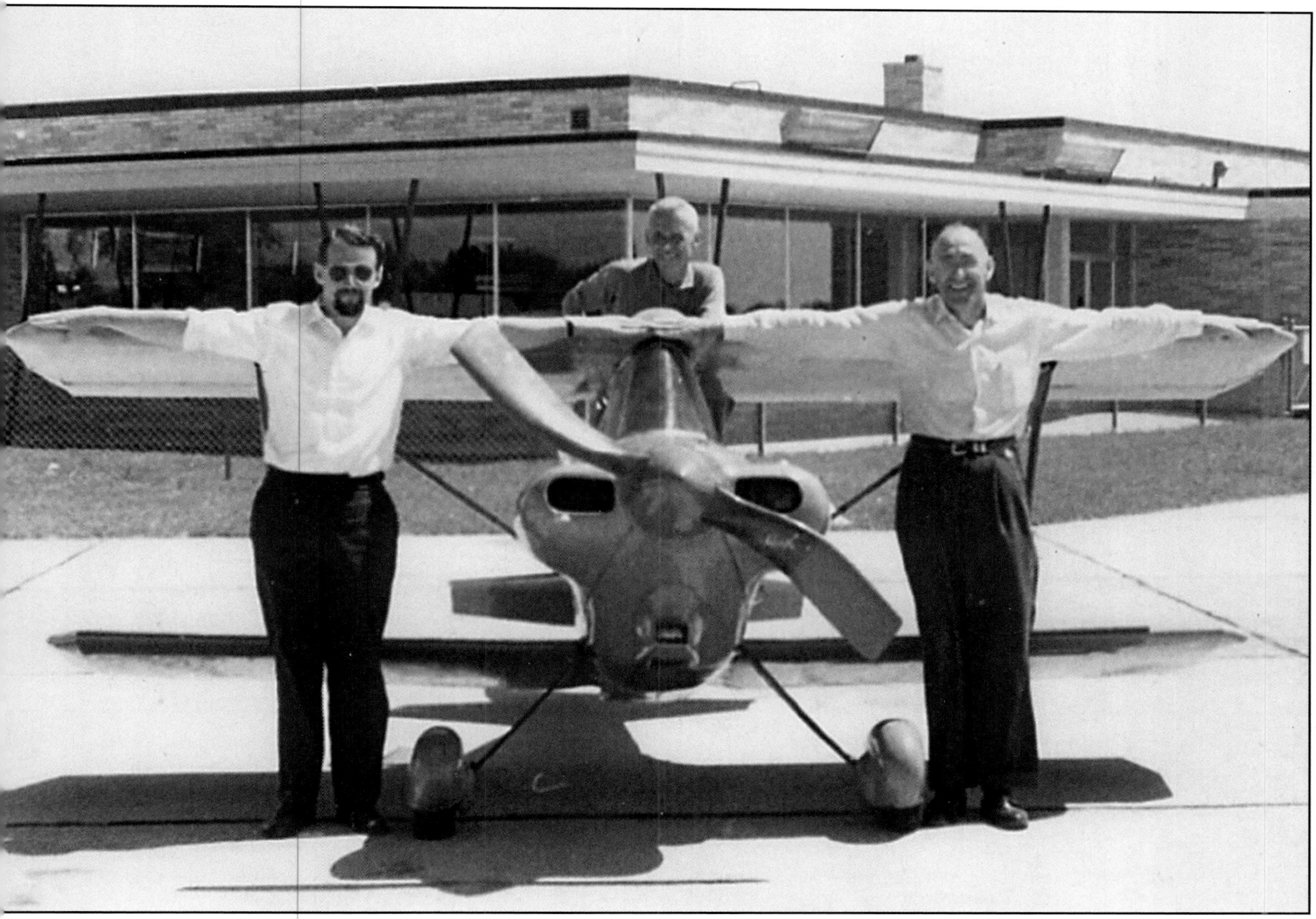

Ray Hegy was a furniture shop owner from Marfa in Texas and in 1948 decided to build an aeroplane that would fit him. A thin, wiry man with an abounding sense of humour, his design began merely as a chalk sketch on his workshop wall. The outcome, though, was one of the most famous miniature racers of its time, the scarlet A-65-powered El Chuparosa, Mexican for hummingbird. It took him nine years and $600 to build but the result was an amazing aircraft. The span was 12 feet 10 inches and the length 14 feet one inch. I had the pleasure of formation-flying with him at Oshkosh in 1962 and was permitted the rare opportunity to taxi the aircraft around the apron, an experience that proved how much smaller Ray was than me. In this snapshot, Ray stands in the cockpit with Steve Wittman (right) and myself 'measuring' the wings. Ray also excelled at propeller-making and his scimitar-shaped airscrews were greatly sought after by other racing pilots. Ray died in 2002.

Opposite: Another great American racing-plane builder-pilot was Ray Stits of Riverside, California. He cherished the desire to make the world's smallest aeroplane and, remarkably, did just that, entering the *Guinness Book of Records* on May 26th 1952 when his Sky Baby, N5K, actually took to the air for the first time. Nine feet ten inches long and with a wingspan of seven feet two inches, the 452-lb aircraft was propelled by a Continental C-85 engine. For the first flight, Bob Starr of Phoenix, Arizona, was the intrepid pilot. Although it flew at 200 mph, Starr said that he was unwilling to vary from level flight! The tiny cabin was so small that, invited to try it for size, it was the first time I have had to struggle to mount an aircraft – and the first time I have felt claustrophobic sitting in an aircraft in a hangar! It now lives in the EAA Museum at Rockford. Starr himself later made an even smaller aircraft flown in January 1984 but the contest to make the record books has, wisely, been closed on safety grounds.

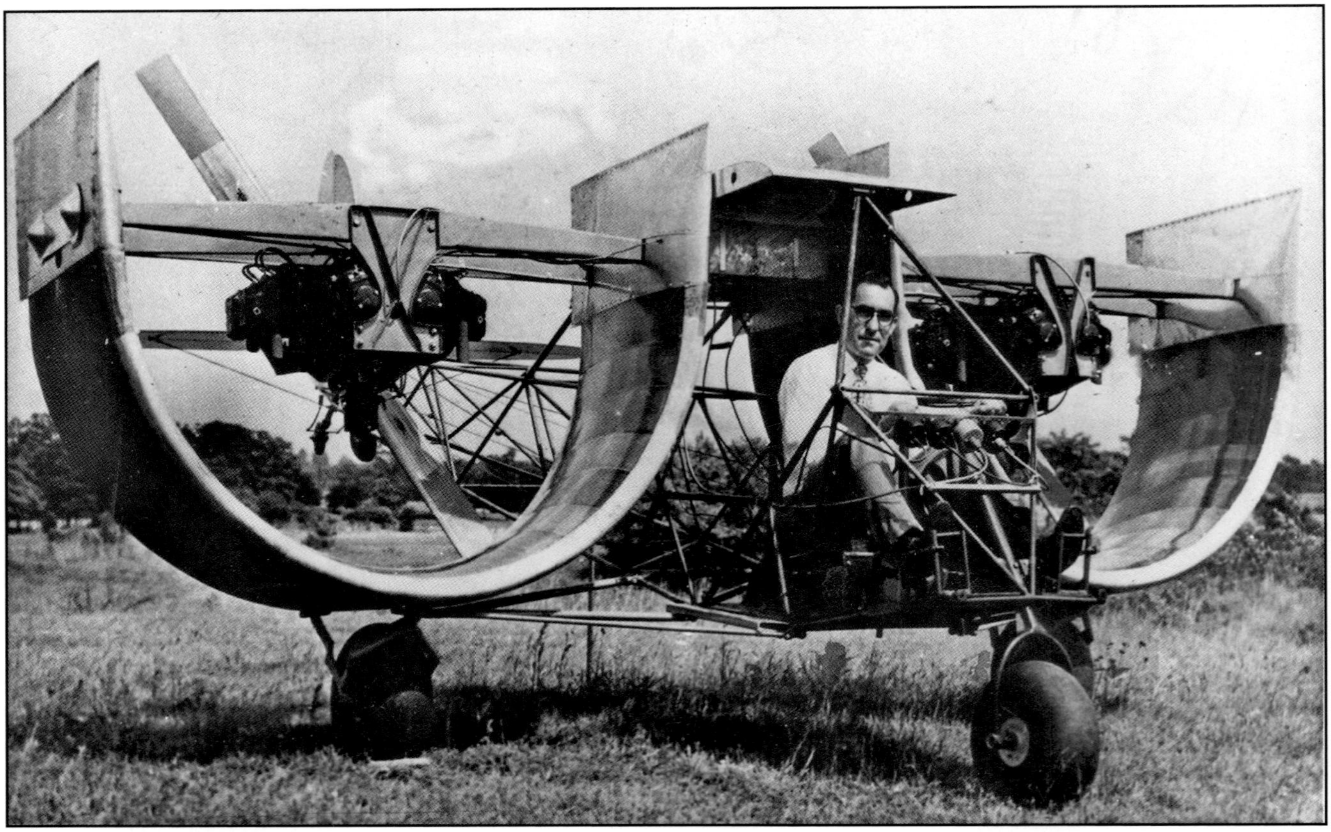

When he was in his mid-twenties, Pennsylvania-born Willard Ray Custer took shelter from a storm in an old barn and was astounded when the roof, hardly an aerodynamic shape, suddenly lifted off and flew into a near-by field. Custer (1899-1985) had hit on a curiosity (so he thought) of aerodynamics and the realisation of what he had witnessed created his personal mantra: 'it's the speed of the air, not the airspeed!' The answer to low-speed flight, he reckoned, was to be found in creating air at speed. The outcome of his experiments was the Custer Channel Wing concept, patented in 1929. It would be some time before he had a viable demonstration of his brainchild but this came in 1942 when, on November 1st, his CCW-1 made its first flight. Custer found that, thanks to Bernoulli's theorem, an engine and propeller enclosed in a half-cylinder of airfoil shape could produce 8 lbs of static lift per horsepower. In flight, he calculated, this rose to 13 lbs. His aeroplane was built and tested by the National Aircraft Corporation at Hagerstown, Maryland, the president of which, Frank D Kelly, is seen here seated in the machine. Later evaluated at Wright Field, the CCW-1 results were good enough to inspire the formation of the Custer Channel Wing Corporation of Hagerstown in 1954. The CCW-2 was a roadable version, outer wing panels folding down to give a total road width of 8 feet. There were five designs in all, the final one being the five-passenger CCW.5 powered by two 225 hp Continental engines with constant-speed propellers. This first flew at Oxnard, California, on July 13th 1953, and was controllable down to just 11 mph. Now production was planned, but almost inevitably nobody wanted – or needed – a new type of aircraft. The Channel Wing Corporation folded by 1957 and the design forgotten. The CCW-1, pictured here, survives in the Smithsonian National Aircraft & Space Museum, and the designer's son still hopes that one day…

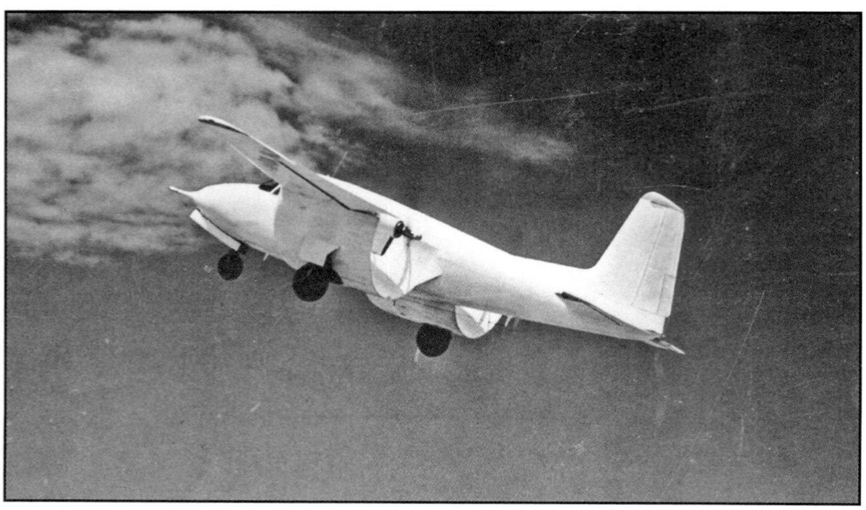

By 1954, Custer had secured backing to develop a new aircraft on the Custer Channel Wing principle. Here the CCW-5 demonstrates that it can fly and fly well. The semi-ducted propellers could generate lift at zero forward speed by drawing air over the airfoil-section of the duct. Custer was encouraged by Dennis Bushnell of NASA's Langley Research Centre, Virginia, who was convinced he was on to something great.

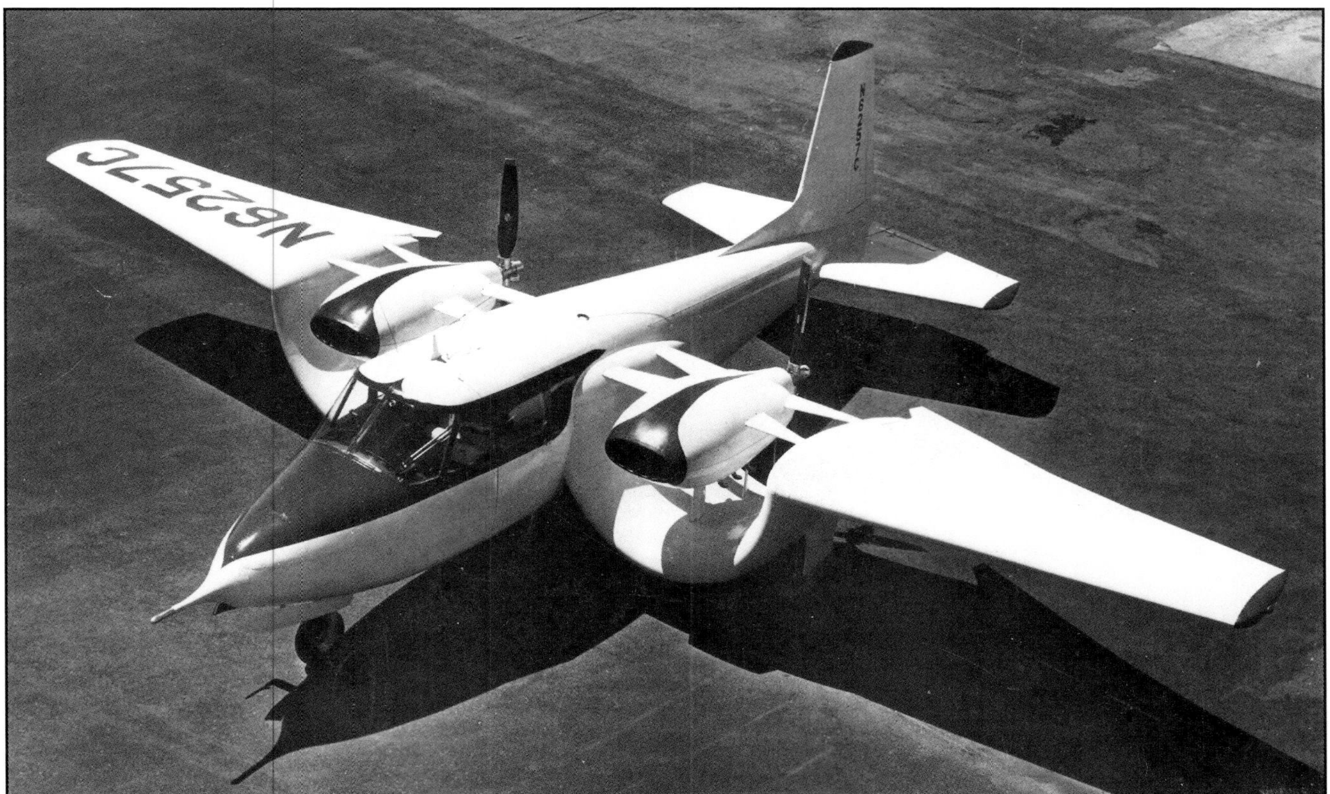

The Custer CCW-5 was certainly not short on good looks and appeared the ideal executive or business private transport. The death of Custer on Christmas Day, 1985, effectively ended the project although as with other, similar ground-breaking inventions, there have been at least two half-hearted attempts to revive the design.

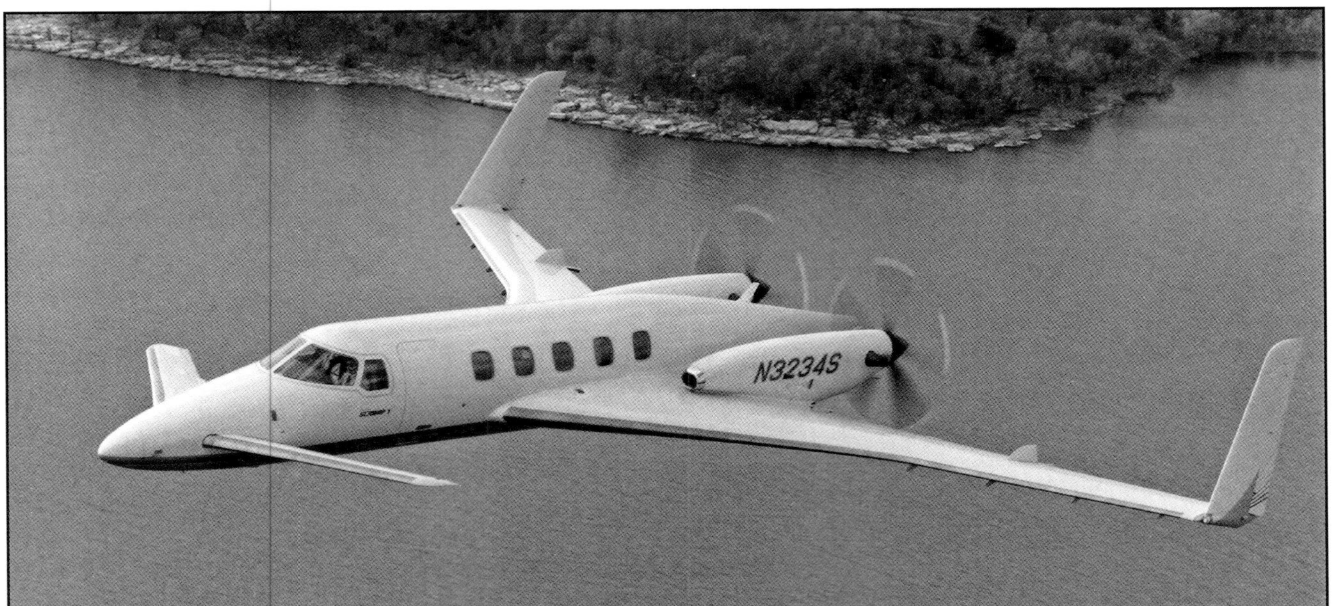

In 1979, Beech Aircraft Corporation wanted to replace its King-Air range of light twins with a new and eye-catching six/eight-passenger pressurised executive transport design and commissioned Burt Rutan, designer of some pretty smart lightplanes (see page 53), to come up with something special. The outcome was the Beech 2000 Starship, a variable-geometry canard foreplane being its distinctive 'back-to-front' signature. Powered by twin 1,200 shp Pratt & Whitney Canada PT6A-67A turboprops, the structure was entirely composite materials. The first flight on August 29th, 1983, was of an 85% scale model, pictured here. Work began on a production run in excess of 50 machines, each reckoned to cost more than $3.9m US. After certification, the company sold just eleven aircraft in the following three years. The last, built in 1995, marked *finis* to a fantastically far-fetched project. By 2003, Beech could no longer justify keeping lines open or maintaining these costly machines and most were bought-in on exchange and scrapped.

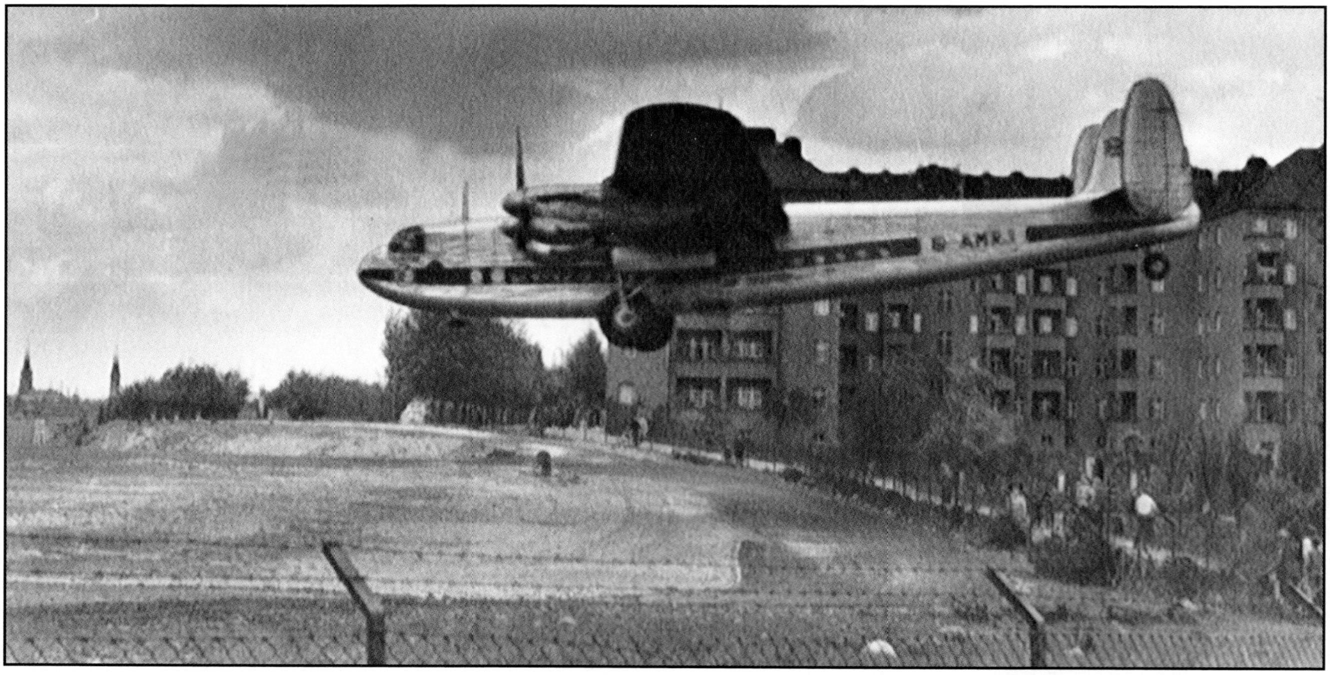

Not so much a curiosity of flight as of a particular aerodrome, in this instance Berlin's Tempelhof, combined with a lucky exposure captured by A J Whitlock in July 1953. Operated by Air Charter Ltd of Stansted, Avro 685 York G-AMRJ (MW326) drops in over the chain-link fence at Berlin's famous 'city centre' airport which was opened in 1923 and impressively remodelled by the Nazis in the mid-1930s. Famed as the pre-war airport where airliners taxied into a vast canopied arrival and departure area, it was already becoming too small after the war but became the vital hub of the Berlin Airlift from June 1948 to September 1949. Without it, Berlin would have starved. But the approach into the airport was best described as 'hairy'. Enormous tenement blocks obstructed one end while the other was a vast cemetery, neither inspiring confidence in the nervous pilot. Here the York's pilot has just negotiated the area of allotments between the high-rise flats and must get his wheels on the ground as quickly as possible. This approach was novel in that you had to let down between the flats and quite close to them, presenting startled passengers with albeit but fleeting sights of domestic life taking place around and above them. On one approach I spotted a couple – well, let's not talk about that... The York was sold to Lebanon in June 1955 becoming OD-ACE.

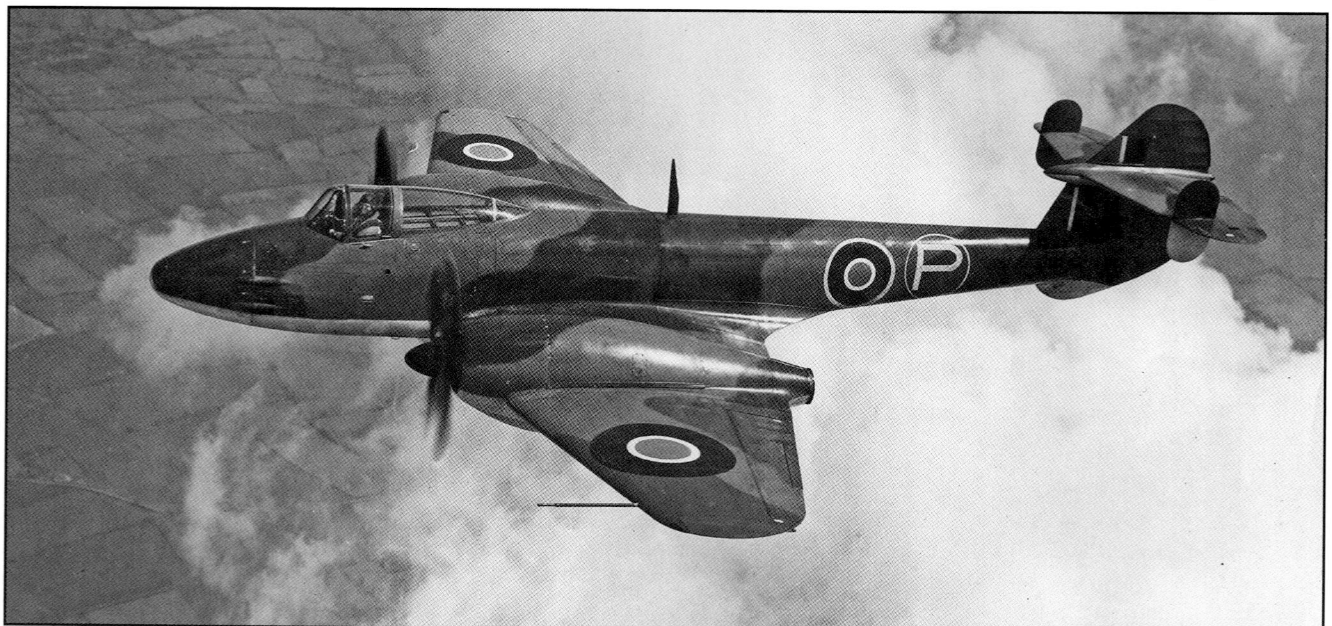

This book began with a photograph of a four-engined Gloster Meteor. Here's one of a turboprop Meteor, EE227. This was the 18th production Meteor F.1 which had undertaken directional stability tests at Farnborough with various modifications to the tail surfaces. In February 1945 it was restored to F.1 standard and despatched to Hucknall where Rolls-Royce installed a pair of RB.50 Trent propeller turbines driving five-bladed propellers. The first flight was made by Rolls-Royce test pilot Eric Greenwood at Church Broughton on September 20th, 1945. This Charles Brown picture shows this experimental aircraft in flight – the world's first flight by a propeller-turbine-powered aircraft.

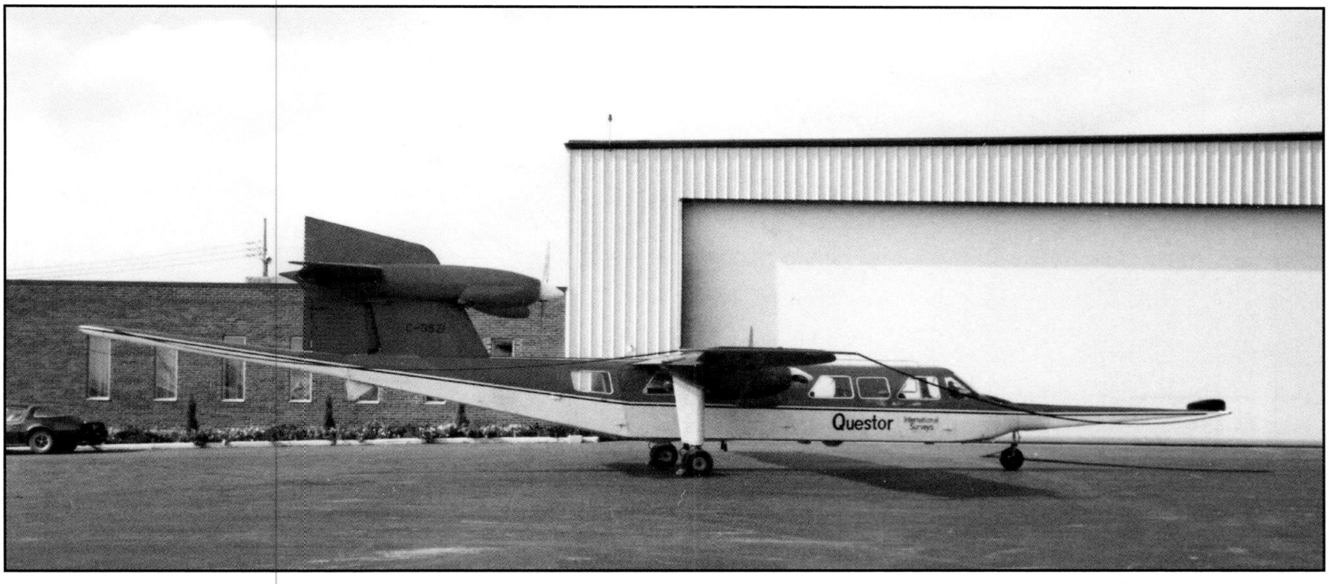

Sporting a Pinocchio nose and matching tail, this unusual Britten-Norman B-N2A Trislander Mk.III-1 had an interesting life. Built in 1974 and registered on January 14th as G-BBWO, it was sold to South Africa the following May. Now as ZS-JJC and modified by Barringer Surveys for aerial geophysical mineral survey work, the nose and tail were extended to carry a cable which extended around the entire aircraft from nose to wing-tip, tail, opposite wing-tip and back to nose. This allowed electromagnetic pulses to the ground from precise altitudes calibrated by radar altimeter. The received data was processed on board by a Geometrics G.803 Proton Precession Magnetometer. In July 1978 the aircraft changed hands again, this time to Questor Surveys based at Timmins, Ontario. From here it conducted an airborne electromagnetic survey of the Walker-Wilkie area of north-eastern Ontario for Esso Minerals. It went on to undertake various other mineral surveys until September 7th 1981 when there was a hijacking which resulted in the machine being damaged beyond repair, fortunately without loss of life.

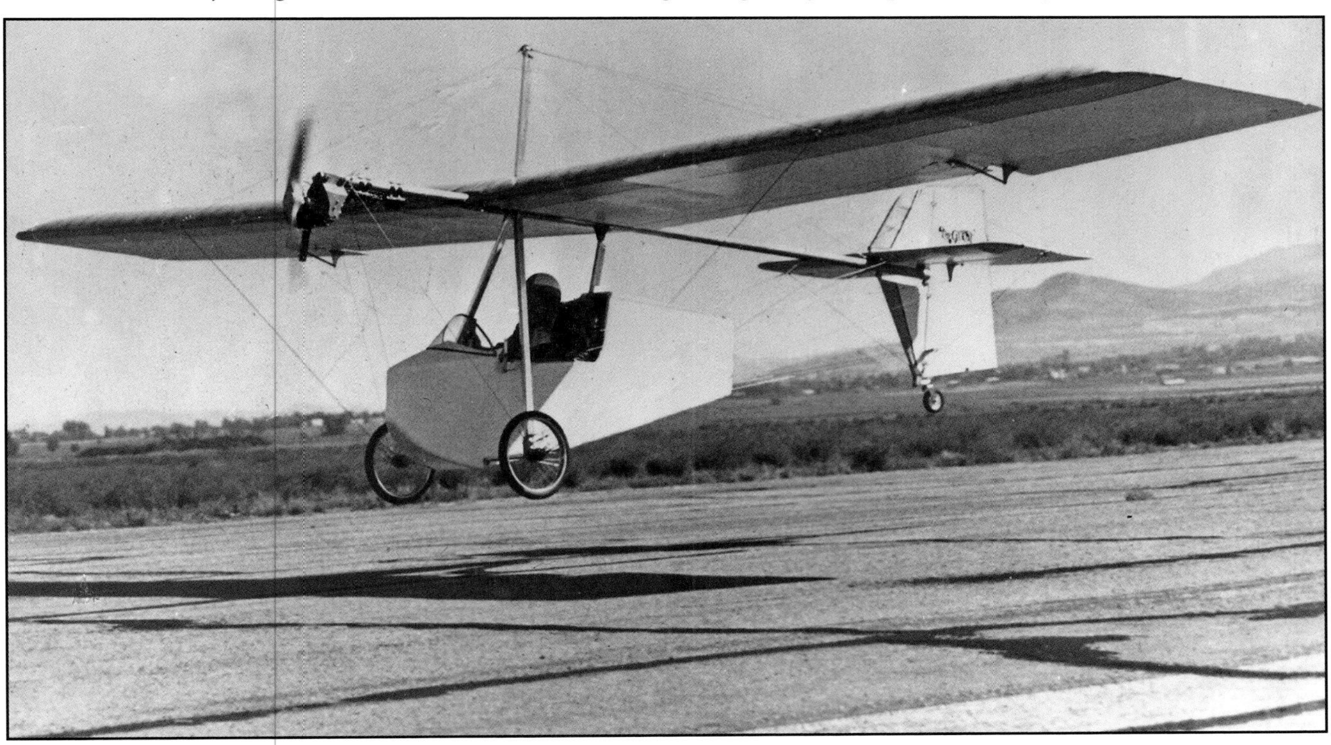

In the 1970s a curious family of microlights was started in America by a company called Weedhopper of Utah. The brainchild of John Frederick Chotia, these aircraft were an attempt to fulfil the then US microlight specification of 155 lb maximum. His Gypsy, pictured here, was available in kit form and many hundreds of this and an earlier model were built. Besides the wheels, a hole in the floor allowed the pilot to 'foot-launch' his aircraft. The engine, also designed by Chotia, was a single-cylinder two-stroke that developed 25 hp and gave the aircraft a top speed of 60 mph. Wingspan was 28 feet, length 18 feet 6 inches and the stalling speed 22 mph. Described as 'the absolutely simplest airplane', the covering for the undersurface of the wings was described as 'optional'. With shades of Henri Mignet's infamous words, he added 'build in 40 hours; fly without a license, No License Required!' John Chotia was killed testing one of his subsequent designs on October 26th 1981. He was just 35 years old.

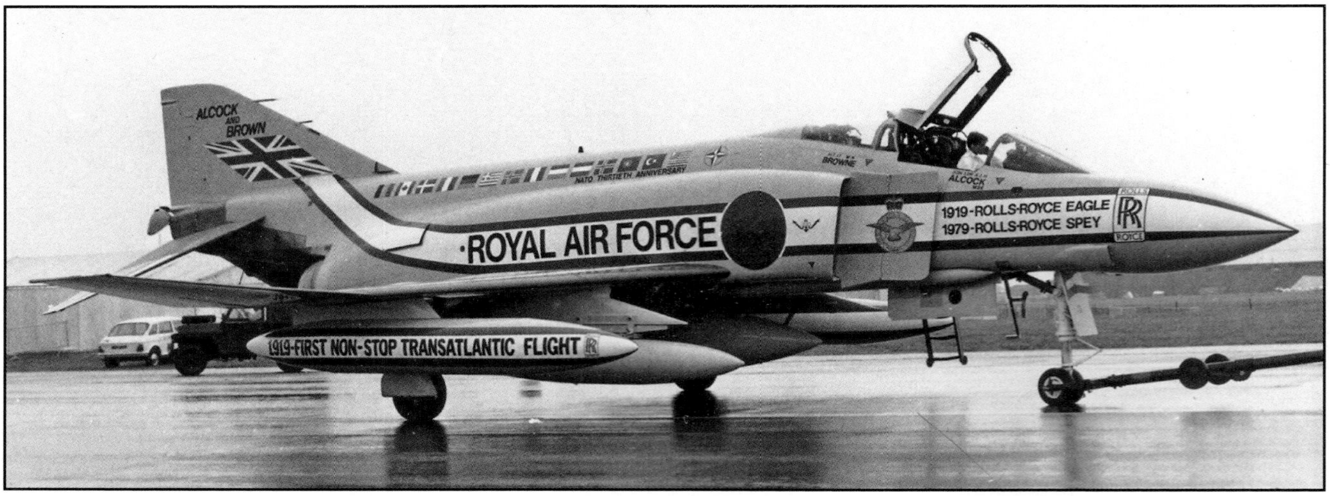

Sporting enough 'advertising sponsorship' to justify confusion with a rally car or the cover of a modern popular aviation magazine, this McDonnell-Douglas Phantom FGR.2, XV424 of 56 Sqdn, made history in June of 1979 when it completed a non-stop crossing of the Atlantic from Goose Bay in Labrador to RAF Greenham Common, Berkshire, for the Air Tattoo. Accompanied by a Victor fuel tanker, the subsonic flight was completed in five hours forty minutes, rather less than a third of the time Alcock and Brown took in their Vickers Vimy in 1919. The pilots for this event were named Alcock and Browne, Sqdn Ldr Tony Alcock being the nephew of the original Captain John Alcock, and Flt Lt Norman Browne just happening to have a similar-sounding name to Alcock's fellow flyer. Painted an overall sickly pale green with red, white and blue additions, the aircraft's flight marked 60 years of Rolls-Royce aero engines and 30 years of the North Atlantic Treaty organisation. It was not the first modern non-stop RAF crossing: on February 21st, 1951, a Canberra B Mk.II, WD932, flew from Aldergrove, Northern Ireland, to Gander, Newfoundland. It was not tarted up like an ice cream van though.

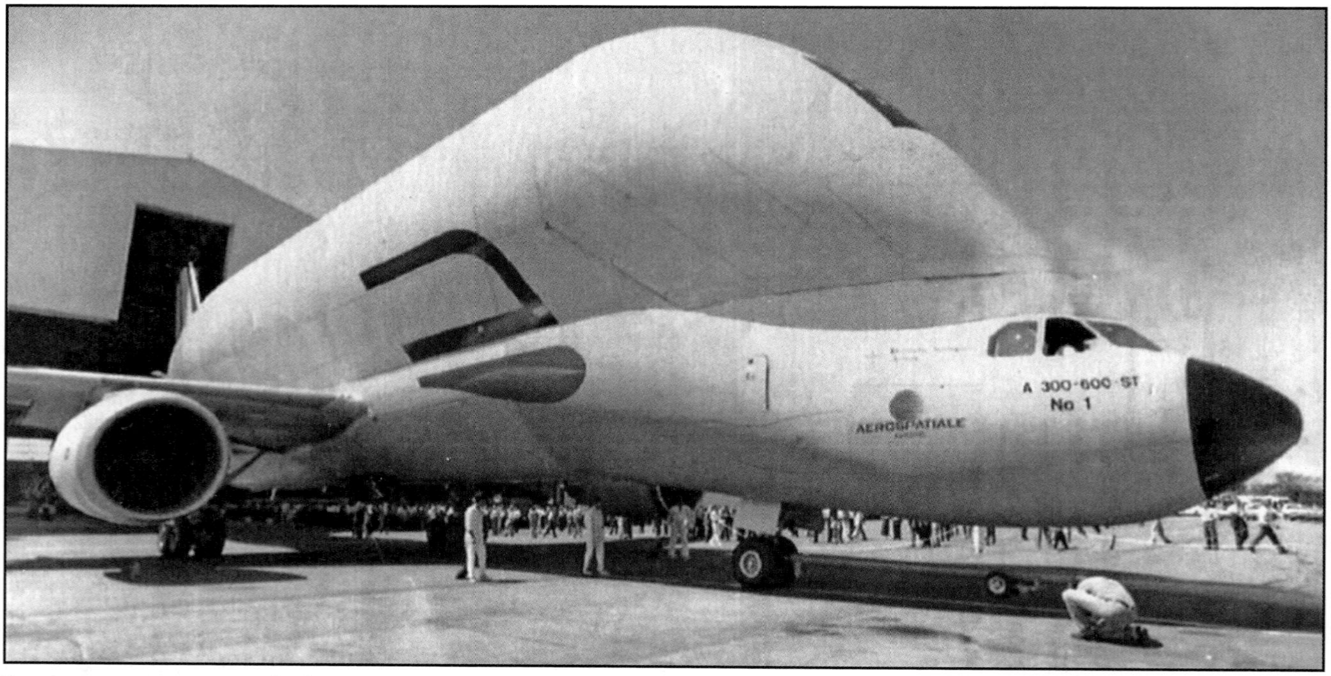

In an age concerned with the dangers of obesity, the oversize aeroplane still attracts interest rather than an entreaty to compliance with a diet of vegetables. The problem with ever-bigger aircraft is that they can no longer be built in one place but their construction has to be farmed out not just to close-by factories but to other countries. And that creates what, in modern parlance, is called 'a logistics problem'. Build a very big aeroplane – and you need an even bigger one to transport its components! When Airbus Industries realised it needed an aeroplane big enough to move Airbus bits, the only one big enough was another Airbus – and that had to be made bigger if the Chinese Doll principle was going to work. At one time Boeing in America used to make these giant transporters (the 747 Super-Guppy is remembered) but now Airbus does its own. With the intention of carrying complete Airbus sections to its assembly lines in Toulouse and Hamburg, the main cargo deck has a volume greater than that of the C5 Galaxy and even the vast Antonov 124 transporters. Taken at Toulouse on June 23rd 1994, this picture shows the Airbus A.300-600 'Super Goupil' or Beluga cargo plane as it leaves its hangar for the first time. The cockpit section has been dramatically lowered to allow space for giant cargo doors to access the upper fuselage blister. This monster made its first flight that September 13th.